ETHAN CONROY

pauline frommer's

WASHINGTON, D.C.

spend less see more

2ND Edition

by Pauline Frommer & Jim Yenckel

Series Editor: Pauline Frommer

W9-BGQ-014

WILEY
Wiley Publishing, Inc.

Published by:

Wiley Publishing, Inc.
111 River St.
Hoboken, NJ 07030-5774

ISBN 978-0-470-47359-7

Editor: Kathleen Warnock
Production Editor: Jonathan Scott
Cartographer: Elizabeth Puhl
Photo Editor: Richard Fox
Interior Design: Lissa Auciello-Brogan
Production by Wiley Indianapolis Composition Services

Front and back cover photo © Pictures Colour Library / Alamy Images
Cover photo of Pauline Frommer by Janette Beckmann
For information on our other products and services or to obtain technical support,
please contact our Customer Care Department within the U.S. at 877/762-2974,
outside the U.S. at 317/572-3993 or fax 317/572-4002.

Wiley also publishes its books in a variety of electronic formats. Some content that
appears in print may not be available in electronic formats.

Manufactured in the United States of America

5 4 3 2 1

Contents

List of Maps

About the Authors

Pauline Frommer is the creator of the *Pauline Frommer Guidebooks,* an award-winning new series aimed at adult budget travelers. There are now 13 titles in the series, with four more in the works. *Pauline Frommer's New York City* and *Pauline Frommer's London* were both named Guidebook of the Year (in 2006 and 2007, respectively) by the North American Travel Journalists Association. In addition, Pauline was awarded a Lowell Thomas Medal from the Society of American Travel Writers for her magazine work. She was the founding editor of Frommers.
com, and won a People's Voice Webby Award for her work there. Pauline's byline has appeared on hundreds of articles for such publications as *Budget Travel Magazine, Marie Claire, Nick Jr.,* MSN.com, MSNBC.com and the *Dallas Morning News.* She spent two years as the editor of the travel section for MSNBC.com, one of the largest news sites on the web. Her column, "The Vacation Doc," appears twice monthly on MSN.com. Currently, along with her writing work, Pauline co-hosts *The Travel Show* with her father, travel legend Arthur Frommer. The show is broadcast to over 100 radio stations nationwide. Every Wednesday, she appears on CNN Online to talk about the latest travel trends. She's also made appearances on *The Today Show, Good Morning America, Live with Regis and Kelly, The O'Reilly Factor, The Early Show, The CBS Evening News,* CNN, FOX, MSNBC, CNN Headline News, NPR's *Talk of the Nation* and just about every local news station you can name. Pauline is happily married to physical therapist Mahlon Stewart and the mother of two wonderfully well-traveled daughters, Beatrix (age 5) and Veronica (age 9). She's a graduate of Wesleyan University.

Jim Yenckel was a writer and editor for the *Washington Post* for 33 years. For 16 years, he was *The Post's* chief travel reporter, writing a weekly advice column distributed over the *Los Angeles Times/Washington Post News Service* wire. Subsequently, he has appeared in *Arthur Frommer's Budget Travel* magazine, *Newsweek, Preservation, Washingtonian Magazine,* and *NARFE,* a magazine for federal employees. He also has written for the *Los Angeles Times, Chicago Tribune, Newsday, Cleveland Plain Dealer, Denver Post, Hartford Courant,* and other newspapers. He
currently writes a weekly travel column for the *Washington Examiner* and the *Baltimore Examiner,* and he can be heard monthly on WAMU-FM, a National Public Radio outlet in Washington. He received the Traveler's Advocate Award of the American Society of Travel Agents and a Silver Lowell Thomas Award from the Society of American Travel Writers Foundation. His guidebook to the Mid-Atlantic Region earned him the Travel Writer of the Year Award from the State of Maryland. Born in Omaha, he attended school in Nebraska and California. He is a graduate in Spanish American history from the University of California at Berkeley, where he served a term as

editor-in-chief of the *Daily Californian,* the student newspaper. After college, he received a fellowship from the Inter-American Press Association for a year's study at the University of Chile in Santiago. While in Santiago, he served as managing editor of the *South Pacific Mail,* a weekly English-language newspaper. He has traveled in more than 80 countries and all 50 states. After an assignment as *The Post*'s night foreign editor, he obtained a year's leave of absence in 1972 and backpacked solo around the world mostly by bus and train, visiting 30 countries in Europe and Asia. Earlier in his career, he circled the United States on a 99-day/$99 Greyhound Bus pass. His most recent adventure, to celebrate the conclusion of this guide, was to hike the rigorous 21-mile rim-to-rim trail in Grand Canyon National Park. He lives in Washington with his wife, Sandy, who is also an avid traveler.

An Invitation to the Reader

In researching this book, we discovered many wonderful places—hotels, restaurants, shops, and more. We're sure you'll find others. Please tell us about them, so we can share the information with your fellow travelers in upcoming editions. If you were disappointed with a recommendation, we'd love to know that, too. Please write to:

Pauline Frommer's Washington, D.C., 2nd Edition
Wiley Publishing, Inc. • 111 River St. • Hoboken, NJ 07030-5774

An Additional Note

Please be advised that travel information is subject to change at any time—and this is especially true of prices. We therefore suggest that you write or call ahead for confirmation when making your travel plans. The authors, editors, and publisher cannot be held responsible for the experiences of readers while traveling. Your safety is important to us, however, so we encourage you to stay alert and be aware of your surroundings. Keep a close eye on cameras, purses, and wallets, all favorite targets of thieves and pickpockets.

Star Ratings, Icons & Abbreviations

Every restaurant, hotel, and attraction is rated with stars ★, indicating our opinion of that facility's desirability; this relates not to price, but to the value you receive for the price you pay. The stars mean:

No stars: Good
    ★ Very good
  ★★ Great
★★★ Outstanding! A must!

Accommodations within each neighborhood are listed in ascending order of cost, starting with the cheapest and increasing to the occasional "splurge." Each hotel review is preceded by one, two, three, or four dollar signs, indicating the price range per double room. Restaurants work on a similar system, with dollar signs indicating the price range per three-course meal.

Accommodations
  $ Up to $100/night
 $$ $101-$135
$$$ $136 to $175
$$$$ Over $176 per night

Dining
  $ Meals for $7 or less
 $$ $8-$12
$$$ $12-$17
$$$$ $18 and up

In addition, we've included a kids icon 🆙 to denote attractions, restaurants, and lodgings that are particularly child friendly.

Frommers.com

Now that you have this guidebook to help you plan a great trip, visit our website at **www.frommers.com** for additional travel information on more than 4,000 destinations. We update features regularly to give you instant access to the most current trip-planning information available. At Frommers.com, you'll find scoops on the best airfares, lodging rates, and car rental bargains. You can even book your travel online through our reliable travel booking partners. Other popular features include:

- Online updates of our most popular guidebooks
- Vacation sweepstakes and contest giveaways
- Newsletters highlighting the hottest travel trends
- Podcasts, interactive maps, and up-to-the-minute events listings
- Opinionated blog entries by Arthur Frommer himself
- Online travel message boards with featured travel discussions

I started traveling with my guidebook-writing parents, Arthur Frommer and Hope Arthur, when I was just 4 months old. To avoid lugging around a crib, they would simply swaddle me and stick me in an open drawer for the night. For half of my childhood, my home was a succession of hotels and B&Bs throughout Europe, as we dashed around every year to update *Europe on $5 a Day* (and then $10 a day, and then $20 . . .).

We always traveled on a budget, staying at the mom-and-pop joints Dad featured in the guide, getting around by public transportation, eating where the locals ate. And that's still the way I travel today, because I learned—from the master—that these types of vacations not only save money but also offer a richer, deeper experience of the culture. You spend time in local neighborhoods, meeting and talking with the people who live there. For me, making friends and having meaningful exchanges is always the highlight of my journeys—and the main reason I decided to become a travel writer and editor as well.

I've conceived these books as budget guides for a new generation. They have all the outspoken commentary and detailed pricing information of the Frommer's guides, but they take bargain hunting into the 21st century, with more information on using the Internet and air/hotel packages to save money. Most important, we stress "alternative accommodations"—apartment rentals, private B&Bs, religious retreat houses, and more—not simply to save you money, but to give you a more authentic experience in the places you visit.

A highlight of each guide is the chapter that deals with the "other" side of the destinations, the one visitors rarely see. These sections will actively immerse you in the life that residents enjoy. The result, I hope, is a valuable new addition to the world of guidebooks. Please let us know how we've done!

E-mail me at editor@frommers.com.

Happy traveling!

Pauline Frommer

1 Washington: Symbol and City

Sampling the Very Best D.C. Has to Offer:
An Introduction to the Guide

By Pauline Frommer

FOR MANY VISITORS A TRIP TO WASHINGTON, D.C., ISN'T JUST A VACATION. It's a pilgrimage of sorts. Schoolchildren are bussed in by the thousands and swarm the Mall in organized platoons, determined teachers feeding them facts about its importance. Veterans pay homage at memorials to fallen comrades. And ordinary citizens arrive in droves to be part of the most powerful city in the world, at least for a short time. Where else, after all, are decisions made that affect not only the lives of every American citizen, but also the lives of people all over the planet?

The city was designed, from its very inception, to be a worthy place of pilgrimage. The city's first planner, the great Pierre Charles L'Enfant, felt that every element of its design should have a meaning, one that glorified this new form of democracy. He insisted that it boast avenues as grand as those of Paris. These would be connected by a series of traffic circles, to symbolize the light of the sun, the streets heading off them "rays of wisdom." No building could be taller than the Capital dome to ensure its primacy on the cityscape. And the form the buildings took, with their porticos and columns, would echo those of the last great democracy in ancient Rome. If Washington, D.C., impresses, well that's what it's supposed to do.

But Washington, over the years, has become even more multifaceted than the original planners could have envisioned. It's a highly cosmopolitan and international city thanks to both to its legions of embassies and to the fact that thousands of new immigrants have settled here over the years, bringing their customs and cuisine with them. It's a multiracial city, one that's played an important part both in the history of jazz and the civil rights movement. It's become, in recent years, a big player in the American arts scene, with its theaters, in particular, birthing new plays that continue to live in productions across the U.S. Washington National Opera is important, too, headed by renowned tenor Plácido Domingo. And while the Mall, site of so many elegant marble monuments and memorials, is a unique treasure, the eye candy of the city doesn't stop there. This is a city of parks, grand and small, and of flowering trees and shrubs and lush green lawns. In spring, a kaleidoscope of blooms carpets the city. When the leaves turn in fall, they offer up a grand foliage display.

What follows is just a small sampling of the city's top offerings. Since this guide is also one that proudly points you toward ways to save money, we'll include some of the top ways to do D.C. cheaply in this list of the best of the best.

Statistical Washington

Founded in 1791, Washington covers 68 square miles. They were carved out of land donated to the Federal Government by the state of Maryland. The current official population numbers 582,049, according to the 2005 census. That census showed a heartening increase of 31,528 residents after a 56-year decline in population. In 1950, the population peaked at 802,178. The city is located in the heart of a metropolitan area with a population, including Washington's, of 5.42 million.

The name Washington, of course, is to honor President George Washington. District of Columbia is a nod to Christopher Columbus. The "District" in the name refers to Washington's status as a federal district, a unique designation created especially for the seat of government. It is not a state, so it is neither entitled to two U.S. senators nor the one representative its population might otherwise claim.

The primary industry is the Federal Government, followed by tourism. Trade associations, scrambling to influence national legislation, are another important industry. Washington is home to more of these lobbying organizations than any other U.S. city.

SIGHTS YOU GOTTA SEE

The grand view of the National Mall from the west steps of the U.S. Capitol It's one of our favorite views in the city, a more impressive sight than the rather unfocused vista from atop the Washington Monument. See p. 114.

The Lincoln Memorial Washington's most famous and arguably most cherished memorial (p. 97) is not only a magnificent work of art, but also played a seminal role in the civil rights movement. See p. 98.

The Vietnam Veterans Memorial Today D.C.'s *second* most famous memorial, it's gone from reviled to revered since it was unveiled in 1982. Its austere, iconoclastic look brought memorial design into the 21st century, and made an architecture star of Maya Lin, just 20 at the time she came up with the groundbreaking design. See p. 104.

The most beautiful library in the U.S. Okay, it has stiff competition. But at the **Library of Congress** you'll see what the Federal Government can do *right* when it puts its mind to it. See p. 100.

The White House If you can't snag a tour, circle it to see it from the front and back. Although you've seen the White House on the evening news, this is your chance for a close-up look. Our guess is that it will appear smaller than you imagined. See p. 89.

The Famous Faces at the National Portrait Gallery Our favorite art museum in the city, it combines the fun of reading your favorite celebrity rag (great and often gossipy wall text brings these historic figures to vivid life) with the satisfaction of seeing great art. Its sister museum, the Museum of American Art, shares its building and has some impressive treasures of its own to gawk at. See p. 119.

THINGS YOU GOTTA DO

Sit in on a session of Congress or hear arguments at the Supreme Court. The Supreme Court trumps "Law and Order" for nail-biting action and suspense as the justices interrogate the lawyers, peppering them with sharp questions (p. 99). And though you may sometimes have the odd experience of seeing a senator making a speech to an empty Senate chamber, the TV camera the only witness, if you hit it right, you might get to follow an intense debate (p. 83).

Indulge your spirit of adventure at the Smithsonian Institution's National Air and Space Museum. There's no comparable museum of space flight anywhere else. See p. 110.

Try on—in your imagination at least—a new career at two of D.C.'s best new museums. Though significantly pricier than the museums on the Mall, the **Spy Museum** (p. 125) and the **Newseum** (p. 128) do a bang-up job exploring the ins and outs of these two glamorous professions, each of which, in its own way, is intrinsic to how our government operates today.

Browse the chic boutiques of historic Georgetown. Busy throughout the week, the sidewalks spill over on Saturday and Sunday. It becomes almost a party scene, where locals show up to see and be seen. This wonderfully historic area is the preferred neighborhood of Washington's wealthier cabinet members, senators (John Kerry of Mass.), representatives, and prominent journalists. See p. 220 for shopping, and p. 197 for a walking tour.

Spend a Night at the Theater. On a par with Chicago, Minneapolis, and New York City, Washington D.C.'s theaters present a range of important new works and seriously creative revivals. Going to a show is the best way to cap off a long day of sightseeing in this artsy city. See chapter 10 for more information.

DINING FOR EVERY TASTE

Sample the hot trend in Washington dining: "small plates," aka *tapas* (from Spain) or *mezze* (of North African/Mediterranean origin). No matter the name, they allow you to graze your way through a meal, trying a bit of this and a bit of that without filling up too much. The two best in this genre are attached to wine bars; their names are **Proof** (p. 67) and **Sonoma** (p. 60). A close third is **Zaytinya** (p. 66), which plucks recipes and ingredients from across the Mediterranean. Order carefully and you can have a small feast for a small bill.

Also extremely affordable are the city's ethnic restaurants and cafes feeding a population that literally hails from all corners of the globe. The savory stews of Ethiopia are served up on 18th Street in Adams Morgan, often dubbed "Little

Ethiopia," and on the U Street Corridor. Try one of these African feasts at either **Dukem** (p. 74) or **Lalibela** (p. 75). South African cuisine is featured at the excellent **Nando's Peri-Peri** (p. 62). You'll also find world-class German, Malaysian, Indian, Belgian, Turkish, and other foods, allowing your tongue to tour the planet, so to speak, without ever leaving Washington, D.C.

Finally, eat in a restaurant that simply exudes history. When you dine at **Old Ebbitt Grill** (p. 65) or **Martin's Tavern** (p. 78), you may be occupying a seat your senator was in recently, or that a president sat in during the not-so-distant past. The interiors, lit by Tiffany-style lamps and as woodsy as Nottingham Forest, won't disappoint either. And both places are not only old-fashioned in their looks, but also in their pricing, a welcome change.

UNCOMMON LODGINGS

Many visitors put off their dream trips to Washington, D.C., for the simple reason that they don't think they can afford to go. The cost of accommodations usually takes the blame. Yet the reality is that the least expensive places to stay often yield the most exciting visits. Many D.C. residents maintain spare basement apartments or rooms expressly for the purpose of renting them to visitors. Some are located in the same areas where the most popular hotels are found, but they usually cost much less. To learn all about these "alternative accommodations," go to p. 24.

The **B&Bs** and **guesthouses** of Washington, D.C., set as they are in classic Victorian homes, are another superb option for travelers. The character's built into to every brick and board, and the folks who run these smaller accommodations are often gems as well: friendly, helpful and genuinely happy to meet people from all over the world. And because these historic homes often can't support multiple bathrooms, they usually offer several that share facilities but for deeply discounted prices.

FINEST "OTHER" EXPERIENCES

Be a spectator or participant at a **demonstration or protest** on the National Mall. You can remain silent and undemonstrative, but if a march occurs while you are in town, see what it's about. You don't have to agree with the speakers; just listen for a while. If you're really gung-ho about changing the world, you could attend a **seminar for would-be activists.** See p. 155.

Tour the **Mall by moonlight,** when the monuments and memorials are lighted and seem to possess a magical glow. National Park Service rangers are on duty nightly until midnight, but consider one of several escorted tour options—among them by bicycle or Segway. See p. 149.

Attend a concert or lecture at a **foreign embassy.** It's a great way to see the interior of some of the capital's elegant embassies, and you might get to shake hands with the ambassador. At the very least, you will learn something new about a foreign land and culture. See p. 160.

Join the legions of congressional aides preparing for the balls they might attend as part of their jobs at a festive **dance class.** It's a swell way to break the ice with locals and learn about some of the very old-fashioned rituals of D.C. See p. 152.

2 Lay of the Land

The sometimes confusing geography of Washington, the city's diverse neighborhoods, and how to get around

By Jim Yenckel

WASHINGTON IS AN EXCEEDINGLY EASY CITY TO TOUR. I'M NOT SPINNING you here. In spite of the crowds, the traffic, and the complexities of traffic circles and diagonal avenues, you are not going to have a problem getting around this city. The major reason is that much of monumental Washington—what you want to see—is clustered on or near the National Mall. And nobody is going to get lost on the Mall. Much of it is open parkland with unimpeded vistas. Look east, and the U.S. Capitol commands your view. Look west, and the Washington Monument soars skyward. You couldn't ask for two more obvious beacons to keep you from going astray.

Even venturing into more distant neighborhoods is a breeze, provided you take public transportation. The subway, called Metrorail (or, more commonly, the Metro), and public buses provide safe, clean, and reliable transportation to all but a handful of attractions cited in this guide.

You will encounter trouble—get confused, lost, or trapped in traffic—only if you insist on driving a car in Washington. Don't do it. Let me repeat. *Don't drive in Washington.* Public parking is limited, and those of us who live here have already claimed these spaces. And private parking garages will shred your budget. Typically the first hour in downtown garages is $8 or $9. Daily parking rates easily can climb to $15 to $20, and valet parking at a hotel may cost much more. Daily or overnight parking fees at many city hotels are about the same. Use a rental car only for day trips recommended in chapter 11, "Get Out of Town."

Okay, okay—you've got a car. On Saturday and Sunday mornings before the Smithsonian museums open (10am), you can find parking spaces paralleling the Mall on Independence Avenue SW between 3rd and 10th streets.

WASHINGTON'S LOGICAL STREET PLAN (AND WHY IT BAFFLES VISITING MOTORISTS)

Before there was a Washington, there was a plan. The credit goes to a French engineer by the name of Pierre L'Enfant (honored by a spacious L'Enfant Plaza just south of the Mall). George Washington, Thomas Jefferson, and other leaders in the new American government put in their two cents' worth also.

6

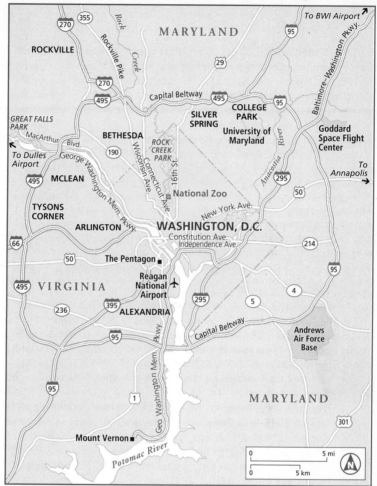

L'Enfant conceived a grid system of **numbered streets** running from north to south. Alphabetical streets run from east to west. Quite simple, so far: 1st Street, 2nd Street, 3rd Street; A Street, B Street, C Street. But then, adding character (and confusion) to the plan, he inserted diagonal **avenues** (not streets), most named for a state. Today: 50 states = 50 avenues, or almost. (California is a street; Ohio is a drive.) The diagonals carved countless triangles, circles, and mini-parks in the otherwise straightforward layout of the city. Even I, a resident of many years, can get momentarily confused negotiating a circle with multiple intersecting streets.

Not everything L'Enfant drew up got implemented. But his basic concept is in place. Here's how it works today.

Security Measures Are a Fact of City Life

Since September 11, 2001, much tighter security measures have been instituted throughout the city, primarily in local and Federal Government buildings and most museums. For sightseers, this means standing in airport-like security lines, stepping through a security machine, and—at the very least—having all purses and bags searched at many major attractions on the National Mall and elsewhere.

The list includes the White House and the White House Visitor Center, the U.S. Capitol and Senate and House office buildings, the Supreme Court of the United States, the Library of Congress, elevator access to the top of the Washington Monument, the National Archives, the Smithsonian Institution museums, the National Gallery of Art, the U.S. Holocaust Memorial Museum, the Bureau of Engraving and Printing, the State Department, the Navy Museum, the Pentagon, and the National Aquarium. Security is tightest at the White House, Capitol, Supreme Court, Pentagon, and State Department.

The security checks get tedious if you are trying to squeeze a lot of sightseeing in a day. To ease the hassle:

- **Don't carry a purse or backpack;** save your museum shop purchases for the end of the day. This will get you into the Smithsonian museums more quickly, since most only search bags and packages.
- **Empty your pockets of metal objects**—keys and coins, for example—as you would before a flight. Or keep them handy in one pocket, so you can quickly deposit them in the tray before passing through the security detector.
- **Treat the security guards with the same respect you do airport security staff.** Some are congenial; some are gruff and rude. But they have police powers, and security in the city is taken *very* seriously.
- I'm sure I don't have to remind you, but here I go anyway. **Don't carry knives, scissors, guns, replica guns, mace, or anything else that might be considered a weapon.** If you get passes for the Senate and House galleries, prohibited items also include cameras, recording devices, any battery-operated electronic device, and baby strollers.
- **Don't wear lapel pins, big belt buckles, or large metal necklaces that you know set off detector alarms.** At the White House Visitor Center, I was asked to remove my belt—one that has only a modest buckle and that has made it through countless airport security screenings without removal.

STREETS

The U.S. Capitol Building is the base point for street numbering and lettering. Picture two major thoroughfares intersecting beneath the Capitol's dome. They don't, but they come close. Like a giant "plus" sign, they cut the city into four quarters, represented in every street address as **NW** (northwest), **NE** (northeast), **SW** (southwest), and **SE** (southeast). The two intersecting streets are not numbered or lettered. The segment north of the Capitol grounds is North Capitol Street; south is South Capitol Street; east is East Capitol Street; and west is the Mall.

Got it? Okay, let's begin with the north/south numbered streets. Beginning at the west front of the Capitol, the streets number 1, 2, 3 West. The Lincoln Memorial at the west end of the Mall is 23rd Street. East of the Capitol, the numbering is the same: 1, 2, 3 East.

Now the lettered streets: From the Capitol north, they are A, B, C North; from the Capitol south, they are A, B, C South. Streets west of the Capitol become Northwest or Southwest; east of the Capitol, they are Northeast or Southeast. There are no "J," "X," "Y," or "Z" streets. At the end of the alphabet, the streets get names; as an aid, they are mostly alphabetical. Example: Euclid, Fairmont, Girard, Harvard. The first time through the alphabet, the names (with many exceptions) are limited to two syllables, as in Euclid, Fairmont, Girard, Harvard. In the second run-through, it's three syllables, as in Allison, Buchanan.

AVENUES

Other exceptions abound. Constitution Avenue, a major street paralleling the north side of the Mall, is located where you should expect to find A Street NW. Independence Avenue, the parallel street on the Mall's south side, takes the place of A Street SW. On the Mall itself, Madison and Jefferson drives link the Mall's museums. Columbia Road angles through the Adams Morgan neighborhood like an avenue but isn't.

The state-named avenues generally radiate from circles or squares in no logical order. The important ones that sightseers should know are:

- *Pennsylvania Avenue NW,* running northwest from the U.S. Capitol past the White House (in a slight jog) to George Washington University and Washington Circle to the edge of Georgetown.
- *Connecticut Avenue NW,* running north from Farragut Square (17th and K streets NW) to the National Zoological Park and on to (near) Hillwood Museum and Gardens and beyond.
- *Massachusetts Avenue NE/NW,* running northwest from Union Station to Dupont Circle, Embassy Row (it *is* Embassy Row), the Washington National Cathedral, the campus of American University, and beyond.
- *Wisconsin Avenue NW,* running north through Georgetown as one of the trendy neighborhood's two major shopping streets, and beyond.

FINDING A STREET ADDRESS

This is not too difficult on the lettered and numbered streets. For example, 1500 L St. NW is at the intersection of 15th and L streets; 1600 L St. NW is at the intersection of 16th and L streets. The numbered streets aren't quite so simple. I'll use the address of my former employer, the *Washington Post,* as an example. The *Post* is located at 1150 15th St. NW. To know precisely where to find it, you have to count up the alphabet. Between A and B streets, you find 100–199 15th St. NW; between B and C, you find 200–299 15th St. NW. The number 1150 (the *Post's* address) is therefore found between L and M streets.

GETTING AROUND IN THE CITY

My advice here couldn't be plainer: Walk and use the Metro. On foot or by Metro, you can get to all but a few of the attractions, restaurants, shopping, and nightspots described in this guide. The chief exception is Georgetown, which the Metro bypasses. But you can walk to Georgetown from a reasonably close Metro station (Foggy Bottom/GWU or Dupont Circle) or catch a Metrobus, Circulator bus, or the Georgetown Metro Connection (see below).

THE METRO

This is the best way to get around in Washington. The 103-mile subway, second busiest in the country, made its debut in 1976, the year Washington and the country celebrated America's Bicentennial. Serving Washington and the Maryland and Virginia suburbs, it proved an instant hit, and the number of lines and stations is expected to grow. The stations, which are all underground in the center of the city, remain clean, comfortable in hot or cold weather, and safe. Muggings have occurred, but they are infrequent and tend to be committed at outlying stations late at night. Metro Police patrol regularly. During the day, trains run every few minutes. As might be expected, they are crowded (and more expensive) during the morning and evening rush hours. To avoid the crush, don't use the Metro on weekdays from 8 to 9:30am or 4:30 to 6:30pm.

Lines

Metrorail operates five lines, all of which pass through downtown Washington. They are identified by color: Red Line, Blue Line, Orange Line, Green Line, Yellow Line. You can change easily between them (at no extra cost) at three central transfer stations—Metro Center, Gallery Place–Chinatown, and L'Enfant Plaza. Wall maps are posted inside every Metrorail station. Pick up a free "Your Guide to Metrorail" map at the stationmaster's kiosk at any station.

Hours

Metro begins operating at 5:30am on weekdays and 7am on weekends. It closes at midnight Sunday to Thursday; it remains open until 3am on Friday and Saturday nights. Rush hour fares are in effect from 5:30 to 9:30am and 3 to 7pm on weekdays.

During rush-hour periods, trains arrive in stations approximately every 6 minutes; every 3 minutes on the Red and Blue/Orange lines downtown. At off-peak periods, trains arrive every 12 minutes; every 6 minutes on the Red and Blue/Orange lines downtown. After 9:30pm, trains arrive every 15 to 20 minutes; every 10 minutes on the Blue/Orange line downtown.

Fares

The basic Metrorail fare is $1.35 per person (off-peak), $1.65 per person morning and afternoon rush hours, and late night on the weekends. This will get you between downtown locations. The maximum fare, which is charged during the rush hour for a ride to the end of the line, is $4.50. Children age 4 and under ride free, but you are limited to two children per adult fare. Children enter through the stationmaster's gate next to the station kiosk.

If you plan to use the Metro frequently during the day, consider buying a **1-day pass** for $7.80 per person, which is valid for unlimited rides after 9:30am weekdays and all day on Saturday and Sunday. Keep in mind, if you plan to stay close to the Mall area, you don't save money until you take your fifth ride of the day. If you have checked into a suburban hotel, you could begin saving on your third or fourth ride, depending on the distance into town.

My advice: Buy the 1-day pass if time is short and you want to see and do the most you can. Here's a possible scenario: Ride one, from your hotel to the Capitol for a tour; Ride two, from the Capitol to the Smithsonian Metro station to see the museums; Ride three, from the Smithsonian to the White House; Ride four, from the White House to Arlington National Cemetery; Ride five, back to the Mall or your hotel.

Passes are activated the first time you use them. Don't buy one for every day you plan to spend in Washington unless you have difficulty walking.

A 7-day **short trip pass** is $26.40, good for rides not costing more than $2.65 each during rush; **valid** for unlimited use any other time during 7 consecutive days. The 7-day **fast pass,** costing $39, is valid for 7 consecutive days of unlimited Metrorail travel, but runs from Sunday through Saturday only (so if your visit starts midweek, you won't be able to make this pass pay off). The 1-day pass, short trip pass, and fast pass can be purchased at Metro stations at fare/pass machines, online at **www.wmata.com/fares/purchase**, and from a sales clerk at the Metro Center Sales Office, 12th and F streets NW (Metro Center station) from 7:30am to 6:30pm weekdays.

Seniors (65-plus) living outside the Metrorail and Metrobus service area can purchase a $10 half-price discount card. Using the card, you pay half the fare charged for any ride. In the downtown area, this allows you 14 rides for the price of the card, a real bargain. A photo ID indicating your date of birth is required. **Persons with disabilities** can present a Medicare card and photo ID for the discount card also. Purchase the seniors and disability passes in person at the Metro Center Sales Office, 12th and F streets NW (Metro Center station) from 7:30am to 6:30pm weekdays.

Using the Fare Machines: You will most likely feel like a dummy the first time you try to use a Metro fare machine. Nobody will laugh; they've been there too. Often a local will step up and help. The devices are something like an automated teller machine. First consult the chart posted at every station listing the fare from there to every other station. Next deposit your money in the fare card machine. Using the indicated buttons, select the amount you want to pay; you can choose an amount for one ride or several. The machine takes coins and $1, $5, and $20 bills. But it only returns up to $5 in change, all of it in the form of coins. Finally, retrieve your card from the machine.

Metro Information

You can get details on how to get from one part of the city to another via Metrorail or Metrobus from the system's website, www.wmata.com. Or call ☎ 202/637-7000 (in English and Spanish); TTY 202/638-3780.

As I write this, Metro stations are equipped with two types of fare card machines—old and new. The original machines do not take credit cards or issue passes. The new fare/pass machines do both. Visa, MasterCard, and Discover cards are accepted. The new devices, recognizable by the credit card logos on the front, also provide recorded voice instructions if you get confused.

Insert the fare card or pass in the entrance turnstile; it unlocks the gate. It will pop up from a slot at the top of the turnstile, if your fare card is for more than one ride, so make sure you take it back. You will need it to exit the station when you arrive at your destination. **Warning:** Two people can't share one fare card. If you bought one ride, the exit turnstile will keep your fare card. If you purchased multiple rides, it will return your card.

Metro Rules

Eating or drinking on Metro trains is not permitted. Take this warning seriously. The Metro Police can pounce at any time. In 2004, a 45-year-old federal scientist was caught chewing a candy bar; she was handcuffed and jailed. In 2000, a 12-year-old girl, spotted eating a french fry in a station, got the handcuff treatment, as well, if only briefly. Remember, this is the city that makes laws for the nation; it wants them enforced.

Metro is served by some of the longest escalators in the world. (If you are physically unable to use escalators or are frightened by heights, an elevator serves each station.) The Wheaton station escalator, 230 feet in length, is the longest in the Western Hemisphere. Stand to the right going up or going down on any of them, especially during rush hour. This allows riders in a hurry to pass.

The Circulator: This is a special Metrobus network that operates bright new red buses. Regular Metrobuses sport America's flag colors—red, white, and blue. The Circulator network is particularly useful for sightseers, since it links many major downtown attractions. The buses operate 7am to 9pm daily; buses run every 10 minutes; and the fare is $1 (exact change or SmarTrip card at the front door) for each ride. Multi-ride passes, for $3 a day, are available at meters along the route. Pick up a route map at Metrorail stations or on a Circulator bus.

There are three routes (stops are indicated by a Circulator sign):

Smithsonian–National Gallery Loop (Purple on Circulator map) circles the edges of the National Mall, heading east on Constitution Avenue (north side) toward the Capitol and west (south side) on Independence Avenue past the Washington Monument to the World War II Memorial. All the major Smithsonian museums are located on this loop. Outside of walking, this is the cheapest way to get (for example) from the National Museum of Natural History to the National Museum of the American Indian.

Massachusetts Avenue–K Street Line (Yellow on map) links Union Station at its east terminus with Georgetown at its west. If you want to explore Georgetown, catch the Metro to the Farragut West or Farragut North stations, walk a block, and board the Circulator on K Street.

Convention Center–Southwest Waterfront Line (Red on map) links the Convention Center at its north terminus with the Mall (at midpoint) and the Maine Avenue riverfront at its south terminus. This line intersects the other two.

Georgetown Metro Connection: This is a two-line bus network sponsored by the Georgetown Business Improvement District to bring customers into the neighborhood from the closest Metro stops. One line serves the Foggy Bottom Metrorail station, delivering passengers to Wisconsin Avenue NW. The other line shuttles between the Dupont Circle Metro station and the Rosslyn, Virginia, station, making stops in Georgetown along M Street. They operate 7am to midnight Monday to Thursday, 7am to 2am Friday, 8am to 2am Saturday, and 8am to midnight Sunday. The one-way fare is $1.50, or 35¢ with a Metrorail transfer.

Metrobuses: A fleet of more than 1,400 buses covers 350 routes, the fifth largest bus network in the country. Because of Metrorail and the Circulator network, you probably won't find much need to use them. Of all the attractions described in chapter 5, only those on Embassy Row, including Washington National Cathedral, are best served by Metrobus—routes N2, N4, and N6. The basic fare is $1.35 cash ($1.25 if you use a SmarTrip card), and exact change is required. If you are connecting from Metrorail, you'll need to use the SmarTrip card to get a transfer; paper transfers were discontinued in January 2009. Bus-to-bus transfers using the card are free; bus-to-rail transfers get a 50¢ discount on the rail fare. Many (but not all) downtown bus stops display big colored maps showing the routes of the buses serving the stop. Scheduled arrival times also are listed.

Taxis: Taxis are readily available in downtown Washington; in the neighborhoods of Georgetown, Penn Quarter, Adams Morgan, U Street Corridor/14th Street, Foggy Bottom, and Capitol Hill; and along principal streets in outlying neighborhoods. Stand on a busy street and flag one down by waving an arm to attract the driver's attention. Taxis usually are lined up waiting for fares outside large downtown hotels.

If you haven't been to D.C. in a while, you'll be surprised to hear that cabs are now metered, making it much easier for visitors to calculate how much they'll have to pay per ride (as opposed to the previous, very confusing "zone" system). The base fare is $3, and for each rider over the first, a charge of $1.50 is added. Children 5 years of age and under ride free, however, so if you have a tot with you, make sure the driver knows his/her age. After these initial fees, you pay 25¢ for every ⅙ mile. A hard-to-calculate fee for waiting time can kick in during times of heavy traffic (it's $25 per hour, but after a minute of the cab not moving, a small portion of that is added to the fare; as I said, it's hard to calculate!). Luggage in the trunk of the car is $2 per large piece, though I've found that the driver will often ignore the charge.

Even with all these fees, riding a cab in Washington tends to be a less pricey affair than it is in such cities as Chicago and New York—about $5 seems to be the average for jaunts in downtown D.C. for one person. So though it's a splurge, it usually works out to be only a small one (unless you're heading out to the suburbs).

Two-Wheeling It in D.C.

Though not geared specifically to tourists, in 2008 a green, affordable, and highly fun new way of getting around D.C. was put into place: **SmartBikes** (www.smartbikedc.com). At key junctures around the city (see below), unmanned bike stands with spiffy, well-maintained, lightweight bicycles have been set for the use of members. These lucky folks simply insert a card to unlock one of the cycles. They then have the right to use it for as long as they like. If something is wrong with a bike, a number on the card gets them the services of a free maintenance person. When they're done with their ride, they simply drop the bike off at the nearest station.

While tourists can use these bikes, as of now there is no short-term fee schedule. All must pay an annual $40 user fee (happily, there are no additional fees after that). And you'll need to apply for a card at least two weeks in advance of your trip as it'll be mailed to you (so you can't decide once you've gotten here to SmartBike around). Still, if this type of transport appeals to you—and it should as Washington is a relatively flat, well-marked place to cycle—you might want to get the card before you come. Bikes can be found at the following stands:

- Logan Circle (14th St. and Rhode Island Ave. NW)
- Dupont Circle (Massachusetts Ave. NW and Dupont Circle)
- Shaw (7th St. and U St. NW)
- Foggy Bottom (23rd St. and I St. NW)
- Gallery Place (7th St. and F St. NW)
- Farragut Square (17th St. and K St. NW)
- Metro Center (12th St. and G St. NW)
- Judiciary Square (4th St. and E St. NW)
- McPherson Square (14th St. and H St. NW)

If you must drive: Let me repeat: During the week, trying to drive between major attractions is foolish. You will spend the day hunting for an illusive parking space. In the evening, when the suburbanites depart, and on weekends, traffic eases and you might get lucky and find on-street parking. Most (but not all) parking meters do not need to be fed on Saturday and Sunday or after 6:30pm. Your best use of a car is in the evening to get you to dinner, the theater, or clubs. Many restaurants offer valet parking, charging $5 to $10, not including a tip. Expect to pay about $10 at night in a commercial parking lot.

Keep these additional tips in mind:

- **When booking a hotel, check the rate for overnight parking.** Free or inexpensive parking may allow you to pay more for your room. Leave the car parked while you explore by Metrorail, Metrobus, and on foot.
- **If you're lucky enough to find on-street parking near the Mall or other attraction you are visiting, be careful to heed the restriction signs.** Parking during the rush hour is banned on many commuter streets, and the

chances of getting towed in this city are excellent. Parking is limited to a maximum of 3 hours during the day on residential streets in many neighborhoods; a sign will inform you that a zone sticker is required for longer parking times.

- **The city's many traffic circles confuse even those of us who live here.** Remember, vehicles already in the circle have the right of way; so yield when approaching the circle.
- **Two major downtown streets become one-way during rush hour only.** In the morning (7–9:30am), 17th Street NW is one-way south (inbound) from Massachusetts Avenue to K Street NW. In the afternoon (4–6:30pm), 15th Street NW is one-way north (outbound) from K Street to Massachusetts Avenue NW. Many other streets are one-way all of the time.
- **Three laws you should know.** In the District of Columbia, use of a cellphone while at the wheel is illegal and you are subject to a hefty fine if you are stopped. You'll also incur a $75 fee if you're stopped and you're not wearing a seatbelt (it also will earn you two points on your license—ouch!). At many intersections (most of them downtown), a right turn on red is prohibited between 7am and 7pm. Before you turn, check for a warning sign.

THE LIVELIEST NEIGHBORHOODS IN THE DISTRICT

At first glance, Washington may seem to be a city of marble monuments and memorials inhabited solely by swarms of tourists. But actually it is home to about 582,000 residents, none of whom live on the National Mall. Rather, they populate a number of distinct neighborhoods, at least one of which—Georgetown—is older than the city itself.

On the pages that follow, I direct you to seven close-in neighborhoods that rate as the city's most dynamic and fun. Enjoy the attractions, dining, and entertainment. But also take a good look around at who lives in each one. Do some people-watching. Note the varied architectural styles, a blend of old and new. Pop into a bakery, an ice-cream shop, cafe, or pub. Pretend you are one of us.

GEORGETOWN

Best for: Boutique shopping, dining, nightlife, movie theaters, classy hotels and inns, elegant old homes, gorgeous gardens, and celebrity spotting
What you won't find: Great museums, quiet streets, parking spaces
Metro: Foggy Bottom; Metrobus: 30, 32, 34, 35, 36

Once a thriving colonial port, Georgetown predates the District of Columbia. Many congressmen, arriving in the newly created nation's capital, found lodging in Georgetown. Today, it remains the place to live for wealthy politicians, at least if you're a Democrat. John and Jacqueline Kennedy resided in Georgetown before moving to the White House, and Jacqueline returned to its narrow, tree-shaded streets after the president was assassinated. Former presidential candidate Senator John Kerry lives in Georgetown as does the current secretary of state, Hillary Clinton. Occasionally a Republican finds the neighborhood's proximity to official Washington appealing. Sen. John Warner (R-VA) moved here while he was married to actress Elizabeth Taylor.

On weekends, the young and beautiful—and the rest of us—throng Wisconsin Avenue and M Street, Georgetown's intersecting shopping and entertainment streets. But the narrow tree-shaded side streets lined with expensive town houses and a scattering of mansions (the late *Washington Post* publisher Katharine Graham occupied a lovely estate-like gem at 2920 R St. NW) are as engaging in their own way. Architectural styles track American history from Federal-style town houses of the early 1800s to Victorian dazzlers to contemporary condos—many with a historic tale to tell. Sprawling Georgetown University, founded in 1789, is America's oldest Catholic institution of higher learning. President Bill Clinton graduated with the class of 1968. I focus on historical highlights in a detailed walking tour of Georgetown in chapter 8 (p. 197).

PENN QUARTER/CHINATOWN

Best for: Offbeat museums, casual dining, outdoor cafes, live theater, movie theaters, boutique shopping, arena sports, posh hotels, new luxury condos
What you won't find: Top-notch dining, shady streets, single-family homes
Metro: Archives–Navy Memorial
Fairly recently a decaying downtown strip, the Penn Quarter (and adjacent Chinatown) has sprung to life as a hip new place to live and play. Construction of a massive sports/show arena now called Verizon Center sparked the resurgence, which sort of took the city by surprise. So many museums have opened up—mostly in beautifully restored buildings—that one museum executive dubbed the neighborhood "The New Mall." Here you find the just revamped Smithsonian American Art Museum and National Portrait Gallery, the National Building Museum, the International Spy Museum, the Crime and Punishment Museum, and the Marion Koshland Science Museum. Many consider the restaurants in the immediate vicinity to be among the most exciting in the city.

Penn Quarter's main drag is 7th Street NW, running north of Pennsylvania Avenue about 7 blocks to Mount Vernon Square. Not quite so lively but still bustling are the parallel streets to the east and west. In recent decades, Chinatown has not been much more than a tiny cluster of inexpensive Chinese restaurants. Now it has all but been absorbed by Penn Quarter. Some tattered Asian restaurants remain, as does the neighborhood's distinguishing feature—the Chinatown Gateway at 7th and H streets NW. It's a soaring arch crafted in the style of the Qing Dynasty (1649–1911). A colorfully painted gift of friendship from Beijing, it reputedly is the largest single-span Chinese archway in the world. Many street and storefront signs display both English lettering and Chinese characters, helping somewhat to enhance what little Chinese flavor remains.

ADAMS MORGAN

Best for: Ethnic restaurants, funky pubs, lively nightlife, international shopping, street murals
What you won't find: Hotels, fancy dining, great museums, parking spaces
Metro: Woodley Park Zoo–Adams Morgan
Funky and scruffy best describe this diverse international/Latino neighborhood centered on 18th Street and Columbia Road NW. On the edge of downtown, it's where I first lived in Washington in a rented apartment. I walked downtown to work, an easy 20-minute stroll energized even way back then by one-of-a-kind

---

K Street Money

New York City has its Wall Street. In Washington, money and power are located in an area known as "K Street." Essentially, K Street is a street lined with bland, modern office buildings that runs west from Connecticut Avenue NW to about 24th Street NW. This is the haunt of lobby-law firms, trade associations, interest groups, and labor unions—lobbyists, in other words. Lobbying the Federal Government is a big business in the city and about 30,000 lobbyists are at work in the city, many of them former members of Congress or congressional staff aides. They are in demand because of their firsthand knowledge of Capitol Hill and, often, their first-name friendship with committee chairs and other power holders. Congressional staffers joining a lobbying law firm might easily double their salaries to $300,000 or more. Not surprisingly, in or near K Street is where you will find some of the city's most expensive, expense-account restaurants and its upscale clothing stores.

---

shops selling bargain-priced art objects, curios, and clothing from Third World countries. Aromas wafting from ethnic cafes tempted me from my own kitchen night after night. By day you will see lovely—if not always well-maintained—row houses dating to the late 19th and early 20th centuries and easy-to-spot outdoor wall murals. A giant painting of a red-headed siren with 13-foot-high breasts has advertised Madam's Organ, a blues and bluegrass pub at 2461 18th St. NW, since 1998. Elsewhere, it might be thought risqué, but not in Adams-Morgan. At first the city protested, claiming the mural was, indeed, advertising without a permit. But the owner argued successfully that it was art. At night, the neighborhood is a hot spot for music, dancing, and bars favored by young professionals in the city.

This is an edgy neighborhood where testosterone-fueled fights occasionally erupt. So don't go alone, and don't stray off the well-lighted and heavily trafficked main streets. Thousands enjoy the neighborhood's nightlife safely. But violent crimes have averaged about seven a month in recent years, primarily as inebriated revelers spill out onto the crowded sidewalks at the 3am bar-closing hour on weekends.

A historic note: Adams Morgan's name refers to two old schools located in the area, the Adams School and the Morgan School. In days of segregation, one school was restricted to white students and the other to African-Americans. In the neighborhood today, the linked names celebrate its multicultural diversity.

U STREET CORRIDOR/14TH STREET

Best for: Trendy new restaurants, soul food, live music clubs, local African-American history, spicy nightlife, vintage clothing boutiques

What you won't find here: Top-notch dining, sedate evenings, major museums, suburbanites

Metro: U Street–African-American Civil Rights Memorial–Cardozo

Washington's current hot spot for entertainment and fine-dining center, U Street is undergoing a renaissance. Yes, it still has its rough edges and for many visitors

Washington, D.C., Neighborhoods

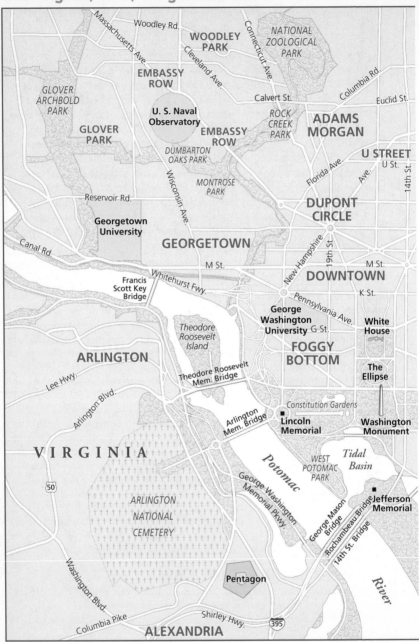

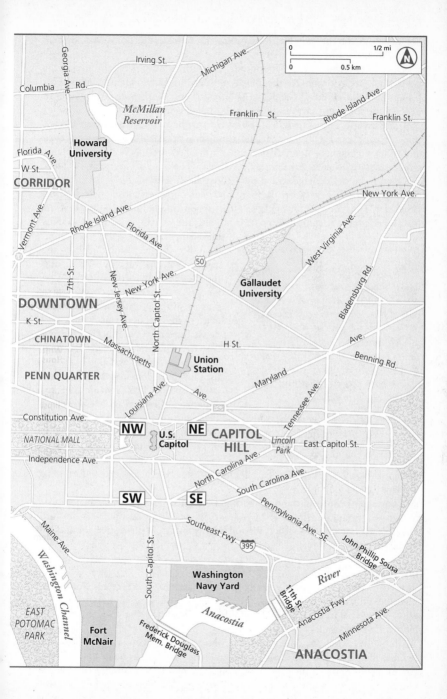

not accustomed to big-city life, it may seem threatening. But really, to come here will be an adventure.

Once U Street NW was Washington's "Black Broadway." Here the elite of the city's black society enjoyed the music of such greats as Sarah Vaughn, Cab Calloway, Billie Holiday, Nat King Cole, and Louis Armstrong. After years of decline, the street and surrounding neighborhood, centered at 14th and U streets NW, are experiencing a revival. Colorful old row houses have been transformed into offbeat shops, sophisticated (and reasonably priced) restaurants, chic bars, and other nightspots. Along 14th Street north of P Street NW, former derelict structures have been turned into luxury condos. The Studio Theatre at 14th and P is one of the city's energetic and provocative small theaters.

A must-stop for every visitor, locals and out-of-towners alike, is **Ben's Chili Bowl** at 1213 U St. NW (p. 71). It's a greasy spoon kind of lunch counter that has been serving up tasty chili half-smokes (a hot dog, really) with cheese fries and thick milkshakes for half a century. The meal is a diet disaster, but a seat at the counter will instantly thrust you into the heart of the community. Who knows? You may find yourself seated next to Washington's mayor, the police chief, or the chef of the fancy restaurant down the street. Neighboring Lincoln Theatre, a historic landmark, has been beautifully restored and put back into use showcasing local dance, theater, and musical talent. The dramatic **African-American Civil War Memorial** at Vermont Avenue and U Street NW (p. 134) honors more than 200,000 black soldiers and their white officer corps who served in the Civil War. On Memorial Day, 2009, President Barack Obama sent a commemorative wreath to be displayed at the monument.

> *In the 1940s, the corner of 14th and U was the grapevine. The cream of black society and everybody else passed through there, so if you were at 14th and U, you knew where the parties were, you knew who was in town, you knew if there was trouble. If you were at that corner, you always had the sense that something big was about to happen.*
>
> —Arthur Ashe, as quoted by 14th & U Main Street Initiative

Like Adams Morgan, the neighborhood—located just north of downtown—remains edgy, and gunfire in the wee hours, if rare, is a possibility. So don't go alone, don't stray off the well-lighted and heavily trafficked main streets, and don't overdo the booze.

DUPONT CIRCLE/KALORAMA

Best for: Cozy inns, poetry readings, art galleries, GLBT stores and some nightlife, tidy Victorian row houses, Beaux Arts mansions, small museums
What you won't find here: Wild nightlife, many children, live theater
Metro: Dupont Circle

Washington's loveliest downtown neighborhood, Dupont Circle/Kalorama, became the place after the Civil War for the city's wealthy to build grand Beaux Art mansions and elegant brick row houses. Many of the mansions now house embassies; the row houses, well preserved, are prized residences for the city's professionals and intellectuals drawn by its cosmopolitan ambiance. It is especially popular with the local GLBT community.

Art on Call

Those funky fire alarm boxes you see scattered across the Dupont Circle neighborhood once were 19th-century technological wonders, summoning the fire brigades. Now they're works of art. Twenty-two local artists each decorated one of the 22 long-abandoned sidewalk posts, which had become eyesores. The project, dubbed **Art on Call,** was organized by neighborhood citizens groups and Cultural Tourism D.C. The city originally installed the fireboxes just after the Civil War. When someone activated them, a telegraph link transmitted the box number to the fire alarm center. In the 1970s, a telephone connection made the alarm call. The 911 system, introduced in the 1990s, ended their usefulness. The refurbished boxes made their debut on September 10, 2005.

Dupont Circle, a shady urban park, is the heart of the neighborhood. Relax here on a bench to enjoy top-notch people-watching. It's a meeting place for the city's corps of young bicycle messengers; for foreign expatriates protesting their homeland government; for chess players and for dog walkers. At the circle's center, Dupont Memorial Fountain is a splashing marble tribute to Rear Admiral Samuel Francis Dupont, a Civil War hero. It was designed by Daniel Chester French, the sculptor of the Lincoln Memorial. You wouldn't be the first or maybe even the 100,000th person to soak your tired feet in its water.

Browse the shops that line Connecticut Avenue, which bisects the Circle. Kramerbooks & Afterwords Café at 1517 Connecticut Ave. NW is a neighborhood institution. Its motto: "Serving Latte to the Literati Since 1976." Then venture onto the side streets to savor the architectural treats. The Schneider Row Houses in the 1700 block of Q Street NW are a brown and greenstone fantasy of Romanesque turrets, projecting bays, and tiled mansard roofs. The neighborhood houses the Phillips Gallery, Textile Museum, Woodrow Wilson House, and Anderson House. It is the conclusion (or start, if you choose) for an **Embassy Row walking tour,** which Pauline outlines in chapter 8 (p. 208).

CAPITOL HILL

Best for: Power lunches, business hotels, an outdoor market, neighborhood cafes, political fights, scandals
What you won't find here: Spacious yards, department stores, many museums
Metro: Eastern Market

Wrapped around the U.S. Capitol, Capitol Hill is an eclectic, racially mixed neighborhood mingling congressional aides, their Senate and House bosses, federal staffers, and blue-collar workers. Oh, and did I mention the Marines? The Hill, as it is commonly called, also encompasses the Marine Barracks, the oldest continuously active Marine installation in the country (dating to 1801). Today, the Marine Band, the official White House ceremonial band, is stationed here.

Side streets east of the Capitol are lined by lovely Victorian-era houses carefully (and expensively) restored and maintained. Its principal street, Pennsylvania

Avenue SE, is a traffic-clogged commuter route, but you also will find a diverse collection of restaurants, bars, and shops. Take a look, too, at 8th Street SE, which is undergoing revitalization by an organization called Barracks Row Main Street. It was the city's first commercial street, home to the crafts workers who built Washington. The Marine Barracks (thus the name) is two blocks south.

The Capitol, the Supreme Court, the Library of Congress, the historic Navy Yard, and Union Station are the big attractions here—at least for out-of-towners. For locals, Capitol Hill's most engaging attraction is Eastern Market at 7th and C streets SE, a 19th-century emporium that was severely damaged by fire in 2007 and underwent a massive, $22-million renovation. It reopened and early reports are that the makeover is a success, retaining the historic flavor of the place but adding much-needed improvements like better air conditioning and bathrooms. Try to visit on a weekend when people flock to the market to see and be seen, and to pick up cheeses, fresh fruit, produce, meat, fish, flowers, and baked goods. On Saturday artisans and photographers display their works. On Sunday the flea market takes over. The market is open 7am to 6pm Tuesday through Saturday and 9am to 4pm Sunday.

And the scandals I mentioned—they erupt with unfortunate regularity in the precincts of the Senate and House.

FOGGY BOTTOM

Best for: River walks, boutique hotels, college hangouts, grand opera, free entertainment, volleyball matches
What you won't find here: Great shopping, vibrant nightlife
Metro: Foggy Bottom–George Washington University

Foggy Bottom is just that—a lowland adjacent to the Potomac River, where winter fogs are not unusual. Well, that's one account of the name. Another is that the neighborhood surrounds the U.S. Department of State, where foggy diplomatic language is similarly common. Whichever explanation you prefer, it's a decidedly upscale neighborhood of tiny, costly row houses, swank condo apartment buildings (the famed Watergate, for one), high-rise dorms for George Washington University undergrads, a major teaching hospital, and the massive John F. Kennedy Center for the Performing Arts.

Yes, go see all of this. But give yourself plenty of time for a lovely riverside walk. Begin where Virginia Avenue NW dead-ends at Rock Creek Parkway, just west of the Kennedy Center. Walk south on the paved walking and bicycling trail to the Lincoln Memorial. The views across the river to Theodore Roosevelt Island and Arlington National Cemetery are lovely. When colleges are in session, this stretch of the Potomac is the course for varsity shell races. Just south of the Lincoln Memorial, take in the volleyball matches that are a regular weekend and evening event from spring through fall.

North of the Lincoln Memorial, get your photo snapped sitting in the lap of Albert Einstein outside the National Academy of Science and Engineering (23rd St. and Constitution Ave. NW). He sits in bronze, a raffish, grandfatherly guy seemingly eager and open to your company. Climbing onto his outstretched leg is almost a rite of passage for a dutiful visitor.

. . . AND TWO MORE

These primarily residential neighborhoods, one poor, the other wealthy, are mentioned elsewhere in this guidebook. They generally have little to offer to the tourist except specified attractions:

ANACOSTIA

Best for: Frederick Douglass National Historic Site
What you won't find here: Fine dining, lodgings, entertainment
Metro: Anacostia

Parts of Anacostia are so troubled that many taxi drivers are hesitant to take passengers there at night, even though the law requires them to do so. Because housing tends to be less expensive, however, stable middle-class areas are on the upsurge.

FRIENDSHIP HEIGHTS

Best for: Upscale shopping
What you won't find here: Museums, memorials, monuments
Metro: Friendship Heights

Washington shares the upscale Friendship Heights shopping district with Maryland's Montgomery County on the north side of Western Avenue NW. This is the bustling mix of major department stores, boutiques, houseware outlets, cafes, and movie theaters Washington dreams of someday tempting back to the downtown core.

Four More Neighborhoods

In chapter 4 and chapter 10 we mention four other neighborhoods; here's a brief rundown of what you'll find and why we're talking about them.

- **Tenleytown** (Wisconsin and Nebraska aves. NW; Metro: Tenleytown–American University) features a small shopping district in an upscale neighborhood. Its most popular attraction is Best Buy, a large TV and other electronics discount store.

- **Logan Circle** (13th and P sts. NW; Metro: Dupont Circle and 6-block walk) marks the dividing point between Downtown and the developing 14th Street area to the north. Studio Theatre is nearby. Logan Circle was once considered part of Shaw (see below) but has become a neighborhood of its own.

- **Shaw** (just east of Logan Circle/Metro: Shaw–Howard University) is a primarily residential, African-American neighborhood undergoing gentrification. Duke Ellington was a Shaw native; several Ethiopian restaurants have sprouted on 9th Street NW between S and U streets; and the Washington Convention Center is located on the southern edge of Shaw.

- **Glover Park** (north of Georgetown and west of Wisconsin Ave. NW) is also a primarily residential area with home prices less than in Georgetown. A cluster of shops and restaurants at Wisconsin and Calvert streets serves the neighborhood.

---

3 Accommodations, Both Standard and Not

All the options, from budget digs to comfy (and affordable) suites in upscale hotels

By Pauline Frommer

IN A CITY WHERE SO MUCH OF WHAT YOU WANT TO SEE AND DO IS FREE, your biggest expense is—you guessed it—a place to stay. Washington, D.C., has the fourth highest hotel rates in the country (after New York City, Boston, and Chicago), so though nightly costs have been dropping thanks to the current recession, there are times when an overflow of lobbyists or the joyous appearance of cherry blossoms can drive prices through the roof. But bargains exist, and I'm here to help you find them. In the list that follows, I describe numerous accommodations that charge half the going rate for D.C.; at almost all, breakfast is included free of charge.

Most lodgings in the list are located in downtown Washington neighborhoods, all fairly close to each other and to the National Mall (or at most two or three stops away from it on the Metro). I have, however, added a few suburban options which you should use *only* when the city is full to the bursting (why commute when you don't have to?). And remember to not only look at hotels, but also consider the city's many apartment rental and guesthouse options, which often offer more amenities and more, well, quirky charm, for the price.

A note for parents: Many bed-and-breakfast inns discourage young children, and I've noted those that don't accept them. Most other lodgings, however, allow children to stay free in their parent's room—but the age varies from under 18 to under 12, so ask. An excellent option for families is apartment rentals, which often mimic the cost of a hotel room, but offer much more space and a kitchen to boot (helpful if you've got a picky eater in tow). You'll find a complete discussion of apartment rentals in the alternative accommodations section below.

ALTERNATIVE ACCOMMODATIONS

It's a tradition in the Pauline Frommer series to lead off with the most gracious, most revealing, and most economical way to see any city in the world. No, I'm not talking about staying with friends, although that's a terrific idea, and if you can arrange that, you're ahead of the game. No need to read any further in *this* chapter!

I'm actually proposing skipping hotels altogether. In Washington, D.C., as in many other major cities of the world, renting an apartment or a room in an apartment (or town house) offers perks and privileges far beyond what any hotel can offer. Though the rates for two people might not always be less than what you'd pay at a hotel, the advantages are many, not the least of which is the fact that you can cook some of your meals (when renting a complete apartment). That's not a knock against the local restaurant scene, which is top-notch. But having the ability to whip up a snack at will, fix a lunch to go, or stay in and cook dinner can offer significant savings. And there are many other, less tangible benefits like privacy, independence, and a chance to see what it's like to live like a Washingtonian, even if it's just for a week. Since these apartments are owned by locals—who rent only occasionally, and live there the rest of the time (filling them with comfy furniture, pictures, and other bric-a-brac that makes a home a home)—they also tend to have a friendlier ambiance than hotels.

If you're more than two, and especially if you are traveling *en famille,* the benefits of an apartment rental can be huge. Family suites can be quite costly, and the price of two connecting hotel rooms is stratospheric. With an apartment rental, you'll have more room—perhaps a door separating you from the little ones at night—and usually, walls that block out enough sound to let your neighbors sleep in the mornings if your children are being rowdy. The downside? You won't have a concierge to help you plan, or a bellman to carry bags, but these seem like small quibbles when you consider the pluses of having your own pad in the city.

In the case of "hosted rentals" or home stays, you have the pleasure of getting to know a citizen of the city. Yes, some are uncomfortable with the idea of staying in a stranger's home. And the hosts may have day jobs, so you'll probably have to work around their schedule when arranging an arrival time. Again, these are ultimately small concerns. In the best-case scenarios, your host will act as an affable advisor, helping to pave your way in the big city, and perhaps forming a friendship that lasts longer than the visit.

Beyond apartment rentals, Washington has spawned a number of congenial, reasonably priced guesthouses and small B&Bs. These offer slightly more in the way of services but retain a homey, intimate atmosphere. Set primarily in stately Victorian town houses and usually housing no more than 20 guests at a time, they can be ideal for guests who are tired of cookie-cutter hotel furnishings and want a more social experience. At these types of lodgings, you're more apt to meet your fellow guests in the lounge or breakfast room. One of the unsung perks of this sort of travel is that you meet unusually gracious, resourceful, quirky locals who serve as B&B owners. "Many of our hosts are in this business because of the people they get to meet," explains Steve Lucas, General Manager of the reservations service **Bed & Breakfast Accommodations, Ltd. of Washington, D.C.** (p. 26). "They're not making their living off of this, but they really thrive off of meeting people from all over the world. While we have a wide variety of hosts, most are in nontraditional careers—artists, writers, and the like. They are really wonderful people." The drawbacks are mostly physical: No bellmen are on duty to haul luggage, and two- and three-story guesthouses don't have elevators.

FINDING "ALTERNATIVE" ACCOMMODATIONS

Because Washington is a relatively small city, and the concept of vacation apartment rentals in private homes is still fairly new here, there's not an abundance of choices when it comes to reservations organizations. In fact, as we go to press, there's only one (count it, one) for affordable rentals and small B&Bs in the city, and one for those in the suburbs.

Because most people want to stay in D.C. itself, I'll start with the city-booker. **Bed & Breakfast Accommodations, Ltd. of Washington, D.C.** (☎ 877/893-3233; www.bedandbreakfastdc.com; AE, MC, V) is a solid organization, with a number of top lodgings in its fold. Because it's the only game in town, staff here can be quite picky when it comes to which properties they'll represent. "We check to make sure that the lodgings are offering the best welcome possible for visitors. If the closets aren't cleaned out, if there isn't a lock on the guest room door, if the shared bathroom is clearly the owner's, we don't work with them," says Steve Logan, general manager. "We also look at how often the linens are changed (our standard is a minimum of 2 towels, changed every third day). And we won't represent lodgings that are in undesirable areas of D.C." They are also quite aware that they face stiff competition from standard hotels in the city, so complaints are taken seriously. And as opposed to picking a rental via Craigslist, VRBO, or some other direct by owner source, if there's a problem, Bed & Breakfast Accommodations does all it can to re-accommodate the guest. "If we get two or three complaints about a house, we send a warning to the host that they have to change their ways, or we won't represent them any longer. It's not just their reputation, it's ours that's at stake," says Logan. "Usually, the hosts will fix any problems that come up. In the 10 years I've been here, we've only stopped working with one property."

So what kind of apartments or private B&Bs will you find through this company? The rentals tend to be fully furnished, English basement-type apartments with the host, usually the owner, living upstairs. A number are located in redbrick, Victorian-era town houses that double as bed-and-breakfast inns. The advantage they offer is that either the owner or a housekeeper is on the premises nearly around the clock, so you're not locked into a set arrival time when the apartment owner is at home; you also always have somebody right upstairs to contact if you need directions to the grocery store, or the toilet gets clogged. The B&Bs—some of which are really hosted apartments in which you are the sole guest of a resident's house—come in all shapes, sizes, and decor styles, but they do have some things in common. The guest always has a room that's far enough from the host's own room to feel comfortable and insure privacy. Although guests never have cooking privileges in B&Bs (there's actually an ordinance against it), they do get fed well and often. It's common for hosts to set out freshly baked cookies or muffins, perhaps some sherry, or another such treat in the afternoons. And because these stays are called "B&Bs" breakfast is always included, and it's usually a more generous meal than you'll get in those hotels that throw a few bagels and croissants your way in the morning. Staff visits all the homes at least twice a year, and the photos on the organization's website are updated every year and a half, so you should get a good idea of what you'll be getting from those.

Here are just a couple of examples of what you might book:

- ◆ The ultra-comfy **Aaron Shipman Apartment** is set in the basement of a B&B (if you ask nicely, you might nab some freshly baked breakfast muffins) and is furnished with a mix of antiques and contemporary pieces. If you come during cold weather, you can snuggle up in the love seat facing the wood-burning fireplace. The kitchen is quite usable, and the walls are decorated with colorful framed posters. A large shaded Victorian-style porch with comfy seating overlooks the formal English gardens out back, and secure parking ($17 a night) is provided. It's suitable for up to four people (children welcome), sleeping two in the queen-size bed in the bedroom and two in the queen-size sleeping sofa in the large living room. Rates tend to range from $85 to $125 a night but can go higher (especially with extra guests sharing the space).

◆ An elegant, chandelier-lit town house directly behind the Library of Congress, **Celia's Place** is not only extraordinarily well-located for sightseeing, but it also has as its hostess a fascinating, worldly, gregarious owner, who was once married to a congressman and now spends her time writing and teaching English literature. It's a delight just getting to know her. She rents out a little suite of rooms (suitable for 2–4 people, though they'd have to know one another as the rooms are set up railroad style, so that one must go through the other to exit). Her 150-year-old house is overflowing with artworks, and the rooms are homey in an old-fashioned way, with an antimacassar on the brass bed and lots of potted plants. Costs: from $110 low season, $155 in high.

◆ The **Guest Quarters on Capitol Hill** is an ultra-family-friendly apartment with a large bedroom in the back and a board-game and DVD-filled living room at front. Really anything your little ones could want—crayons, books, coloring books, puzzles—is set on shelves ready for use. The living room also has a comfortable fold-out couch (the hostess can provide a porta-crib for babies). In the center of the two rooms is an eat-in kitchen, fully stocked with a washer and dryer off of it. It's perfect for a family getaway—clean and cheerful but simply furnished so you don't have to worry about breaking anything. Prices start at $125 a night.

◆ The **Chester Arthur House** was once owned by the undersecretary of the treasury for that president. Its owners are two natural history writers (one writes for *National Geographic*), and they've given each room its own theme: One's Scottish with tartan draperies and framed Scottish prints on the walls, another has a frillier appeal with dusty pink walls and Sunday *Star Magazine* covers on the walls, and the third was being renovated when I visited. All rooms are oversize with a rocking chair for reading and two feature bay windows that flood the room with light. And their breakfasts are creative, ranging from egg timbales to Belgian waffles to something they call "breakfast pizza." Meals can be taken on the lovely little deck out back. Nightly rates here range from $100 to $155 in low season, up to $195 in high.

A minimum stay at all of the properties represented by this firm is 2 days, although occasionally, a single overnight is permitted. Staff is at the offices from 9am to 5pm, Mondays through Fridays, and do their best to "match-make," hooking up visitors with just the right type of accommodations for them. Booked guests get a cellphone number for one of the staff, so that they can reach them in case of any problems, 24/7. The firm charges a $10 booking fee.

Those looking for small B&Bs or home stays in the Virginia suburbs of D.C. turn to the **Alexandria & Arlington Bed & Breakfast Network** (☎ 888/549-3415; www.aabbn.com; AE, MC, V). It represents a dozen B&Bs and homes that range in price from just $70 per night all the way up to $225. Some examples of what you might get through this company:

- **Rose Hill House** in Alexandria, Virginia, is for those people who want peace and quiet for a low, low rate. The very pretty double room here (the hostess is a mosaics artist, and you'll see her work throughout the house) goes for just $60 per night for singles, $70 for doubles, year-round. A private bathroom is down the hall. Unusual for a home stay, guests are given full kitchen privileges, which can be a real money saver.
- The **Lee Retreat,** in the Old Town of Alexandria, has quite a pedigree. The furnishings here—superb English antiques primarily—are so lovely that the house was a regular on home tours of the area before the owner started accepting paying B&B guests. There's only one guest room, with two twin beds and a private bathroom down the hall, but it's a charmer and a value at $125 year-round (with breakfast). The house is surrounded by top-notch restaurants and just 1 block from a bus that will zip you to the Metro.
- **Yesteryears Treasure House** is a third choice in convenient Alexandria, Virginia. A part of the charm of staying here is meeting the hostess, Moina Ratliff. She came to Washington with her father, a four-term member of Congress from western Missouri, and went on to enjoy a 32-year career on various Capitol Hill legislative staffs (Moina's a great source for congressional gossip). In semi-retirement, she's a painter—her works hang on the walls of her 1920 Craftsman-style home, which she recently renovated. All three guest rooms are located in a brand-new second-floor add-on to the house, so everything is bright and fresh. The Junior Suite ($125 a night for two) features a queen-size four-poster bed, three comfortable easy chairs, and two large windows looking out to the garden. The Wicker Room (named for the white wicker furnishings) and Ramona's Room (named for a grown daughter) are adorned with floral print comforters. Priced at $100 a night, they share a bath. The house is about a 10-minute walk from the Metrorail station.
- Just as gracious as the choice of flower would suggest, **Magnolia House** is owned by a licensed Washington, D.C., tour guide who knows pretty much everything there is to know about the city (and shares that information generously with guests). The home is in the Tyson's Corners area, which has bus access to the center of D.C. if you're not traveling by car. Guests stay in an amenity-filled basement apartment that has cooking facilities, cable TV and VCR, and access to a flower-filled garden out back (hence the name). Nightly rates here are $125 and children are welcome.

A FEW OTHER OPTIONS FOR APARTMENT RENTALS

The chanciest option—but still viable if you do your homework—is renting a room, apartment, or house via the Internet from a **private owner.** The chancy part is that no reservation service is vetting these places for you. You deal directly with the owners and trust them to provide the fully functioning accommodations they have described.

And oddly enough, you may end up spending more doing so than you would with one of the rental companies listed above. As I searched through the listings on such sites as VRBO's in 2009, I found that the cheapest one-bedrooms tended to *start* at $150 a night, often going much higher (though occasionally I found deals, like a three-bedroom apartment for $145 a night). Some places require a minimum stay of 3 to 5 days, and you may be penalized if you depart early. A few

Questions to Ask Before Renting from an Owner

Here are the questions I think are essential to ask before renting a home from one of the "direct by owner" sites:

1. **Does the owner live nearby?** It's preferable that she does as she'll better be able to help you should you have a problem in the house. I've also found that the closer the owner is to his property, the better the maintenance tends to be. If the owner isn't in the city but you like the look of the property, make sure that there's at least some type of caretaker nearby whom you can call on if necessary.

2. **What's included in the rental fee?** You don't want to show up at a rental place for 3 days and find that there's no dishwashing soap, garbage bags, toilet paper, or other basic household goods. Most rentals do include them, but it's important to ask. Free local calls and Wi-Fi or high-speed Internet access can save you a lot of money and are standard in many rental apartments but not all, so be sure to ask about that as well.

3. **Where is it?** Sounds like a basic question, but many owners can be vague about the actual location of a home, knowing that some areas of Washington are more desirable than others. So be sure to get actual cross streets, how close the nearest police station is, and where the closest Metro stop is.

4. **What's the square footage of the home?** The more space you have, the more privacy each member of your party gets.

If you can combine the right answers to the questions above with the right prices, I say: Go for it. As with the homes rented by the agencies (which are, in some cases, the same ones being offered on such sites as VRBO.com), you're obtaining lodgings for a less expensive, more relaxing vacation.

impose a cleaning charge that can amount to as much as $100. A refundable security deposit of $150 may also be imposed. Not all owners accept credit cards. If you are a smoker, you'll likely be required to step outside.

Keeping these factors in mind, you could find a charming, well-kept apartment in one of the city's beautifully restored row houses. Several properties provide bicycles free of charge to explore the neighborhood.

The most convenient way to find owner rentals is on the websites to which many subscribe. Many owners advertise the same property on most of them. The sites are

- **Vacation Rental by Owner** (www.vrbo.com) With the largest selection, this is the one you should check first.
- **Cyberrentals** (www.cyberrentals.com)
- **Great Rentals** (www.greatrentals.com)

- ◆ **A1 Vacations** (www.a1vacations.com)
- ◆ **Rentalo** (www.rentalo.com)

There's also **CraigsList** (www.craigslist.com), but I recommend it only to those who do due diligence. Because CraigsList charges no user fees to post, it has been used by scam artists in the past, intent on separating vacationers from their security deposits. And to be frank, its message board for D.C. is a mess, with options ranging from Capitol Hill apartments to condos in Orlando and Cancun (I have no idea why they're posted on this board).

GUESTHOUSES AND B&BS

A word on our rating system: A star following the name of the lodging highlights a place that I think is especially attractive or gives you the best value for your money. Here's how the star ratings break down:

> No stars: Good
> ✸ Very good
> ✸✸ Great
> ✸✸✸ Outstanding! A must!

In each category, the accommodations are described in ascending order of cost, starting with the cheapest and moving upwards. Each listing is preceded by one, two, three, or four dollar signs, indicating its price range per double room, as follows:

> **$:** Up to $100 a night
> **$$:** $101–$125
> **$$$:** $126–$175
> **$$$$:** Over $175

Adams Morgan and Woodley Park

$–$$ Sherry in a cut-glass decanter is available at all times and in the afternoons, lemonade or hot cider with cookies is put out for the enjoyment of guests. All old-fashioned pleasures, appropriate as the 29-room **Kalorama Guest House at Adams Morgan** ✸✸ (1854 Mintwood Place NW; ☎ 800/974-6450 or 202/667-6369; www.kaloramaguesthouse.com; Metro: Dupont Circle and Metrobus 42, H2; AE, MC, V) is a sepia-toned charmer. As in so many D.C. lodgings, the house is Victorian (built in 1910), but here the illusion that you've jumped back in time is enhanced by the dozens of oval-framed photos of someone's ancestors on the walls and the dim lighting (yes, it's light bulbs, but it feels like candlelight for all the good and bad that implies). Occupying three town houses, the inn sits on a quiet, upscale neighborhood street that is a 5-minute walk from the restaurants and nightlife of Adams Morgan. Once you get into the rooms, the beds, nightstands, headboards, carpets, the works are all in good condition, having received a complete overhaul not long ago, so you will have all the modern comforts (except TVs; you'll have to go to the common room for that). Rates too are a bit old-fashioned at $69 to $95 a night for a room with a shared bath and $85 to $120 for a private bath. The largest bathless rooms (my pick if you're trying to save) are nos. 6 and 15.

Kalorama has an offshoot property that's a bit nearer to the Metro, the **Kalorama Guest House at Woodley Park** ✹✹ (2700 Cathedral Ave. NW; ☎ 800/974-9101 or 202/328-0860; www.kaloramaguesthouse.com; Metro: Woodley Park–Zoo–Adams Morgan; AE, MC, V). At that property (which now comprises two lovely houses, half a block from each other) I liked room no. 6, a second-floor haven with private bath and a private balcony (with chair swing) overlooking the quiet, tree-shaded street. Prices are the same as at the Adams Morgan property. The Kalorama "empire" also includes a couple of suites, some with full kitchens, in homes nearby their properties. Decor is similar to the guesthouses and these go for $120 to $145 a night most of the year.

By the way, all of these prices include a hearty breakfast of hard-boiled eggs, bacon, danishes, yogurt, fruit, and waffles you can pop into a toaster (plus coffee, tea, and juices, of course). The friendly hosts also stock the latest magazines and shelves of board games to keep guests amused (and making it feel even more like you're visiting a favorite aunt). On warm nights, a number of guests might gather in the garden out back of the Adams Morgan property or on the porch of the Woodley Park for sherry—it's all quite congenial. From March to June and September to December—the high season—a 2-night minimum stay is required on weekends. No elevator at any of these properties.

$–$$ I don't think the 26-room **Adam's Inn Bed & Breakfast** ✹ (1746 Lanier Place NW, 1 block west of 18th St. and Columbia Rd.; ☎ 800/578-6807 or 202/745-3600; www.adamsinn.com; Metro: Woodley Park–Zoo–Adams Morgan; AE, MC, V) has quite the vintage charm of the Kalorama houses, but its rooms—which feature large windows framed by billowing curtains—are serene, bright, and uncluttered, with shiny hardwood floors and antique pieces (a wicker chair here, an impressive headboard there). Of course, "budget" means a lack of certain amenities, such as no in-room phones or TVs. You will find them in the public rooms. They also put plastic covers on the mattresses, a big turnoff (it's worth removing them and remaking the bed, so you don't sweat all night). Since the inn was carved from three 100-year-old homes, rooms vary greatly in size with some big enough for four or five guests and others on the smallish (but not cramped) side. If you're not happy with the one you're assigned, ask to move (they're usually good about accommodating changes).

Prices are a tad higher than at the Kalorama, with single rooms going for $109 to $129 a night with shared bath (up to $149 with private). Doubles range from $119 to $169, again depending on the season and whether or not you're sharing a bath (15 of the rooms have private facilities, the rest do not). Those seeking triples and quads usually pay $10 or $20 more than the going double rate, respectively, which ain't bad; weekly rates further shave the cost (ask). And you do get some extra amenities for the extra bucks, like two comfortable reading rooms, a guest kitchen and guest-use laundry room, on-site parking ($10 extra a night), and a lovely, shady garden. Dedicated management and a great location near the Adams Morgan bar scene (close enough to stumble home easily, but far enough to be away from the noise!) add to the appeal. Continental breakfast is included; tea, coffee, and cookies are temptations anytime.

Washington, D.C., Accommodations

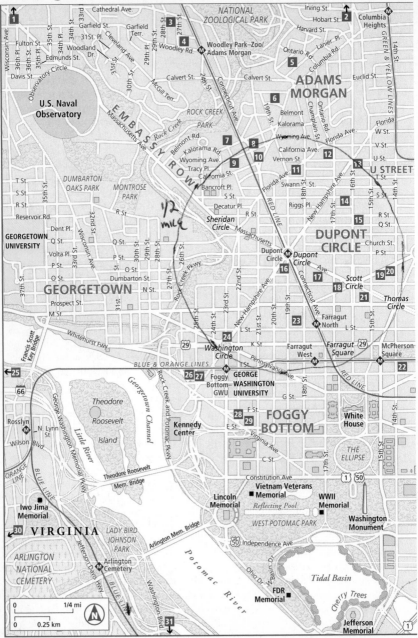

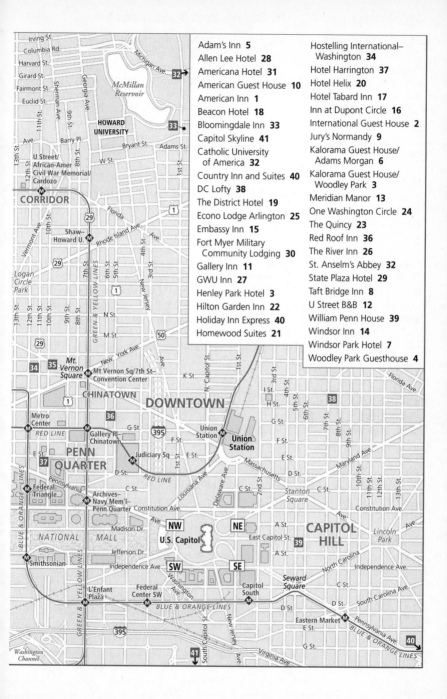

Adam's Inn **5**
Allen Lee Hotel **28**
Americana Hotel **31**
American Guest House **10**
American Inn **1**
Beacon Hotel **18**
Bloomingdale Inn **33**
Capitol Skyline **41**
Catholic University of America **32**
Country Inn and Suites **40**
DC Lofty **38**
The District Hotel **19**
Econo Lodge Arlington **25**
Embassy Inn **15**
Fort Myer Military Community Lodging **30**
Gallery Inn **11**
GWU Inn **27**
Henley Park Hotel **3**
Hilton Garden Inn **22**
Holiday Inn Express **40**
Homewood Suites **21**

Hostelling International–Washington **34**
Hotel Harrington **37**
Hotel Helix **20**
Hotel Tabard Inn **17**
Inn at Dupont Circle **16**
International Guest House **2**
Jury's Normandy **9**
Kalorama Guest House/Adams Morgan **6**
Kalorama Guest House/Woodley Park **3**
Meridian Manor **13**
One Washington Circle **24**
The Quincy **23**
Red Roof Inn **36**
The River Inn **26**
St. Anselm's Abbey **32**
State Plaza Hotel **29**
Taft Bridge Inn **8**
U Street B&B **12**
William Penn House **39**
Windsor Inn **14**
Windsor Park Hotel **7**
Woodley Park Guesthouse **4**

$–$$$$ Founded by a group of friends who met at a weekly prayer breakfast in 2001 (though there's no religious aspect to the lodging), the 18-room **Woodley Park Guest House** ✪✪ (2647 Woodley Rd. NW, a half-block west of Connecticut Ave.; ☎ 866/667-0218 or 202/667-0218; www.dcinns.com; Metro: Woodley Park–Zoo–Adams Morgan; closed mid-Dec for 2 weeks; AE, MC, V) has, even more than the others I've already mentioned, a particularly welcoming vibe. That may be because one or another of the owners always presides at breakfast, and they're a fascinating bunch, one a Lebanese émigré and contractor, another a specialist in malaria-control in the Third World—there are six altogether, and you get the feeling they're doing the guesthouse thing purely for the love of it. You can tell they found decorating the rooms a kick, too, because each is bedecked with lovely original artworks (sometimes from former guests) and pretty, valuable-looking antiques hunted from local stores. The guesthouse enjoys a prime location, half a minute from a Metro stop, close to the National Zoo, and with lots of inexpensive ethnic restaurants nearby. Quiet evenings (no TVs or radios are on the premises) and reasonable rates are the words of the day here: I stayed in room no. 125, a single/shared bath ($90/night) and it reminded me of my college dorm in its size (not decor). "City-sized" is how co-owner Laura Saba, a Washington native, describes the rooms. I'd call them small, but because occupancy is always limited to two guests per room and young children are not accepted, size may not matter as much. Doubles with private toilet and sink but shared shower start at $120 for one or two guests; if you want the entire bathroom, you're looking at $150 to $165 double most months of the year. Rates include a continental breakfast (the usual pastries and bagels plus a tasty homemade fruit salad); parking is available for another $15 a night.

$$–$$$ The reception will be a bit more gruff at the **American Guest House** (Adams Morgan, 2005 Columbia Rd. NW, just off Connecticut Ave.; ☎ 703/768-0335; www.americanguesthouse.com; Metro: Dupont Circle; MC, V); hospitality is not a strong suit here. However, if you're attending a convention at the Hilton Hotel across the street, you'll pay a lot less than your fellow conventiongoers: Room rates start at just $100 a night for a single (all rooms have private bath), $114 for a double. These same rooms can pop up to $194 when Washington is busy, and I'm conflicted as to whether I'd still recommend the place at that rate. Yes, prices include a much fuller breakfast than usual (eggs cooked to order plus a full array of cereals and fruits) and the fridge is filled with fruit juices and sodas, free for the taking. Wi-Fi is gratis, as well. And this restored 1889 mansion is certainly elegant, with its wainscoting, its carved wooden staircase (no elevator), and rooms filled with Early American antiques (or reproductions of furniture of that type). But there are the odd annoyances. Some guest rooms have no closets; rods attached to the bedroom walls make unattractive substitutes. The walls upstairs and down are plastered with tacky paper signs with seemingly endless guest dos and don'ts. And if you get a room on the top floor, the stairs will give you quite a workout. Probably my biggest bone to pick here is the service: It can be difficult to get the owners on the phone and they run the place from afar, hiring staff that seems a bit bored by their jobs. I include this one just as a decent second-choice option.

Dupont Circle

$–$$$ If I had to cut this chapter down to just one page, the **Taft Bridge Inn** ✪✪✪ (2007 Wyoming Ave. NW, a half-block east of Connecticut Ave.; ☎ 202/387-2007; www.taftbridgeinn.com; Metro: Dupont Circle; MC, V), would be the one guesthouse on it. It's that special (and since it only has 14 guest rooms which sometimes all fill up, it's lucky I can recommend more than one place to stay). A century-old Georgetown mansion—four massive columns support the portico—it's been given a vibrant makeover by its owner, a Japanese expat, who has a striking sense of style and color. Each room is painted in the deep, rich tones you'd find on a fine kimono. The sitting room, furnished in exquisite Victorian antiques, contrast with lovely modern art works on the walls. Guest rooms (some with private baths, others with shared) are spacious and luxuriously appointed, many with expensive antiques and hand-knotted Oriental rugs. A room with a shared bath is $89 for one person, $99 to $109 for two, and though these shared rooms are smaller and way up on the top floor, they make good use of the space and are quite unique (one all-wood room looks a bit like a cozy hunting lodge). Rooms with private bath range from $129 to $179 per night, depending on the season and size of the room. The rate includes a full breakfast that guests choose from a menu. The top-priced room, no. 16, features deep purple walls and opens out to a private balcony. I also like no. 17, for its size. Children are accepted on a case-by-case basis (with so many pricey things to break they try to be selective); TVs are in most but not all rooms. The inn's location near embassies and law offices draws lots of business travelers. The lively and sophisticated Dupont Circle scene, a couple of blocks south, should appeal to younger guests.

$–$$$$ The overarching theme at the **Inn at Dupont Circle South** ✪ (kids) (Dupont Circle, 1312 19th St. NW, btw. N St. and Dupont Circle; ☎ 866/467-2100 or 202/467-6777; www.theinnatdupontcircle.com; Metro: Dupont Circle; AE, MC, V) seems to be teddy bears and chintz. It makes sense when you consider that this inn, unlike many of its B&B brethren, welcomes children (it can provide a crib for babies and even stocks booster seats and baby pillows). Kids will enjoy all the toys piled here and there, the floor-to-ceiling mirrors in some rooms, and the bowls of candy in the bedrooms. Adults may think it's odd, though to be fair, the frill-factor does vary from room to room. A couple are quite pretty and refreshingly lace-free. And certainly the place's Victorian origin has bequeathed it lofty 12-foot ceilings, bay windows, white marble fireplaces, and hardwood floors. My favorite room, displaying all of this, is the front-facing Renoir Room, decorated with Renoir prints. When I last visited, every room was booked by a repeater, an impressive recommendation. Another recommendation is the delish daily hot breakfast—omelets made to order—served (in season) in the tiny backyard walled garden. The single "$" is awarded because the inn's tiny room for one, the Nook (with shared bath), goes for $95 year-round; it's a very popular choice. Off peak, other rooms (two with shared bath) go for $130 to $150 a night; in peak season, the top price is $215, the other rooms less. A four-story (no elevator) Victorian town house built in 1885, the inn was once the home of astrologer Jeane Dixon.

U Street Corridor

$$-$$$$ B&Bs have a reputation—sometimes deserved (as at the Inn at Dupont Circle, above)—of being all doilies and dried flowers. At the **U Street B&B** ✪✪✪ (17th and U St. NW; ☎ 877/893-3233; www.bedandbreakfastonustreet. com; AE, MC, V) and its sister property, the **Meridian Manor** ✪✪ (16th and U St. NW; www.meridianmanordc.com; other info same as at U Street B&B), the lace is AWOL and there's not a desiccated blossom in sight. These lodgings are as sophisticated and even hip as the up-and-coming, restaurant and dance-club heavy U-Street neighborhood they occupy. This is largely due to the efforts of co-owner Yaruslv Koporulin who, when not greeting guests and running the B&Bs, is an accomplished painter. His richly evocative paintings, and the works of other contemporary Russian artists (he grew up in Russia), fill each room. The sumptuous wall colors, bedding, rugs—indeed anything that has a color—are carefully chosen to work with the art. Beyond being eye-poppingly beautiful, the rooms, especially at the U Street B&B, are quite cozy, with top-quality mattresses on the beds and comfy chairs in each room. The decor at Meridian Manor was plainer, with furnishings and walls in all soothing neutrals. In defense of the Meridian, many of the rooms here are quite large (in fact, they might have been among the largest I've seen in Washington, D.C.); and the third floor of that house, with its two bedrooms and private living room, would be perfect for a family group. About a third of the rooms share bathrooms; these go for $90 to $115 in the low season, up to $155 when the town is busy. The "en suite" rooms (those with a private loo), go for between $105 and $155 in the low season, and $155 to $275 in the high season (though that includes the massive apartment). One final perk to staying here is an international party at the breakfast table. Because the owners speak a number of languages, they draw guests from around the world.

Bloomingdale

$-$$$ I struggled with including the **Bloomingdale Inn** (2417 1st St. NW; ☎ 202/319-0801; www.bloomingdaleinn.com; AE, DISC, MC, V), as its location is a bit, well, funky. There are no recommendable restaurants or bars within walking distance, and though the street the inn is on is safe, some of the surrounding neighborhood can get a bit dicey. Still, for those going to visit Catholic University nearby, it's convenient; and it's possible to walk 20-or-so blocks to the Mall, though at night you'd want to take a cab, bus, or drive (there's abundant free street parking nearby on a street that has no parking regulations). The two conjoined 19th-century homes that make up the inn have a beguiling history as a former church and parish house; you'll see where the prayer rails once were, and in the "Mt. Bethel" room, the sacristy is now a closet where you'll see an oddly low full-length mirror. (It was set at shoulder level so that the priest could check that his vestments were straight without indulging in the sin of pride by looking at his face.) Each of the nine rooms is different and eclectically designed, so you might have a Tiffany-style lamp here, a statue of Buddha there, and a French crystal chandelier hanging above it all. Sometimes these touches add up to an attractive, harmonious whole (as in the "Samuel Gompers Room"); other times, it looks a bit weird. On the plus side, the staff here are a friendly, helpful bunch who genuinely love their jobs . . . and that goes a long way in the lodgings biz. Plus, the afternoon snacks that are set out—cakes, cookies, and so on—are truly scrumptious. Many of the rooms share baths (and cost btw. $90–$130 a night, depending on the season); but there are some en suite options as well.

WASHINGTON HOTELS

More erratic than the stock market, Washington hotel prices seem to change by the hour, if not the minute. With the economic downturn, many are finding splendid deals through last-minute bookings. So since most hotels do not require a deposit, I'd suggest booking well in advance, but periodically checking back to see if rates have dropped. That way, you may be able to score a bargain.

I've tried to provide what is the general range you can expect to pay at each place. But the exact rate depends on the dates of your stay, with whom you booked, and sometimes the position of the stars—you just never know.

Here are other tips:

- ◆ **Alternative lodgings,** which include hostels, guesthouses, and bed-and-breakfast inns, tend to charge the same rate throughout the year. In peak seasons, therefore, they will give you the best rates.
- ◆ A hotel's **Internet site** may offer cheaper rates or special off-price packages that you won't learn about from a desk clerk. And because some hotels sell rooms in bulk to discounters, check **HotelsCombined.com** before booking. It searches such wholesalers as Hotels.com; Hotelbook.com; Quikbook.com; Travelworm.com; and AccommodationsExpress.com and more, allowing you to do just one search and get back a wide range of options. If your trip doesn't coincide with a big convention, you may find good rates at the many upscale business hotels that deal extensively with these brokers.
- ◆ If price is the first priority, make a bid on **Priceline.** You'll end up in some major chain hotel, you just won't know which one until after you've booked. (A helpful site called **BiddingForTravel.com** will clue you into what travelers have been paying on Priceline recently and which hotels they've been snagging.) You can also book specific hotels at a set price on Priceline.
- ◆ Be **flexible in your travel dates.** Travel during off-peak periods (p. 44) and on weekends, when rates are lower. If you can be flexible with your vacation dates, check rates for several days before and after your preferred dates. A convention may fill the hotel one day, emptying out the next.
- ◆ And **don't be afraid to bargain.** Never call the 800 number, though. Instead, call the hotel's local number, ask to speak with a manager, and name your price. Make it clear, in a polite and friendly tone, that you'll go elsewhere if the hotel can't match your price. You'll be surprised at how often this tactic works.

FOR YOUR COMFORT AND SAFETY Without exception, each place listed in this guide provides decent accommodations (no flophouses), and each is located in a normally safe neighborhood. Sometimes you get what you pay for, so expect cranky plumbing and worn carpeting in the least expensive places, and you won't be disappointed. Unless otherwise stated, all properties in this list offer some form of Internet link, usually Wi-Fi. If how you're staying connected is important to you, be sure to call ahead and ask. Ironically enough, usually the cheaper the hotel, the less likely you'll be charged for Internet connectivity.

DOWNTOWN

The advantage of a downtown hotel is its proximity to the Mall and most major attractions. The drawback is that the downtown area tends to empty out at night when the suburban commuters go home.

$-$$ Location, location, location are the three (and primary) reasons you choose the **Hotel Harrington** (11th and E sts. NW; ☎ 800/424-8532 or 202/628-8140; www.hotel-harrington.com; Metro: Metro Center; AE, MC, V). It's just 4 blocks from the White House and 2 blocks from the Mall—unless you have an invite from the president and first lady, it's hard to imagine a more convenient place for sightseers to stay. A Washington institution built in 1914 and still owned by the same family, it offers decent rooms at an affordable rate—nothing more, nothing less. When I last stayed there, my room was closet-size, the walls oddly nubby, and the lighting so dim I thought I might be having a stroke. However, it was clean and the mattress solid, so I started to feel silly complaining, especially when I woke up from a particularly good night's sleep. In spring, the hotel plays host to school groups—they arrive by the busload; in summer, vacationing families fill its rooms; year-round, it's a favorite with foreign students. As you might expect with all these groups, the place can get a little noisy. However all rooms have well-scrubbed private bathrooms, which are small and sport old-fashioned fixtures and black-and-white tile, and the prices are impressive: One bed goes for $99 to $109 a night (though I've seen them dip lower); with two double beds (sleeping four), $125 to $145; a deluxe family room (sleeping four or five), $155. Room no. 624, a suite with two adjoining rooms, two baths, and two TVs (great for a family of six), is $175 to $185. Usually the best rates are found right on the Harrington's own website. On-site are a diner-style restaurant and a rowdy Irish pub. Display a copy of this guide and get a 10% discount on your room, promises long-time managing director Ann Terry.

$-$$$$ It's the big and the small things that count at the 99-suite **Quincy** ★★ (1823 L St. NW, btw. 18th and 19th sts.; ☎ 800/424-2970 or 202/223-4320; www.quincysuites.com; Metro: Farragut North or Farragut West stations; AE, MC, V). Of the big things: These are among the most spacious rooms in D.C., with enough floor space to practice your putt effectively, if golf's your thing. The streamlined, almost chic furnishings (think Art Deco-esque, with accents of teal and tiger lily orange and positively plush mattresses) only enhance the wide-open feeling of these rooms. And the small things come with all the amenities guests get, from top-of-the-line toiletries (they even give you make-up remover, for heaven's sake) to the microwaves, small fridges, and coffeemakers that come with each room (more used to have full kitchens, but those have mostly been eliminated; ask if you need a real kitchen). At off-peak times, a minisuite can drop to as little as $89 through the discounter websites, an extraordinary value. At more normal times of the year, expect to pay anywhere between $150 and $269. One warning: Avoid rooms that face the alley (unless you think you'll enjoy being woken up at 4am when the dumpster there is emptied). A prime location, the hotel stands among shops, cafes, and office buildings about 6 blocks from the White House to the south and the nightlife of Dupont Circle to the north. Two other key reasons you may want to pick this one: They provide guests with free passes to the nearby Bally's gym and the staff is genuinely caring and knowledgeable.

PENN QUARTER/CHINATOWN

$–$$ When you're searching the Internet for discounts, high at the top of the list, pretty much every day of the year is going to be the **Red Roof Inn** (500 H St. NW; ☎ 800/RED-ROOF [733-7663] or 202/289-5959; www.redroof.com; Metro: Penn Quarter–Chinatown; AE, DC, MC, V) in Chinatown, which seems to go for $70 to $129 a night all year long, even when the town is busy. Why so cheap? It isn't the quality of the rooms, which are quite large, meticulously maintained, and have a cheery if corporate mien with lots of royal blue and red, plus a desk business travelers will appreciate. I'm guessing that folks are avoiding it for two reasons: It's on the outer edge of the city's Chinatown (more like "China-street"—it's that small), which is a bit seedy, though not unsafe. And to be blunt, service here is probably the worst in D.C. Behind the desk are a group of grumps who answer every request (even for directions) with a monosyllabic grunt or a "no" . . . if they stop talking with one another long enough to talk with you. I stayed here for 3 nights on a recent visit and had the misfortune to deal with them several times, at all hours of the day and night, so this is not an unsupported statement. Since most visitors won't have much contact with the staff, you can take my comments with a grain of salt; if the price is right, and prices elsewhere are wrong, this might be a good pick (how often do you end up needing the help of the desk staff?). Try **www.hotelscombined.com** to find the best rate; it usually beats going direct to the Red Roof site by a good 40% if not more. On-site is a rollicking Irish pub.

DUPONT CIRCLE

Still close in, the accommodations in this lively upscale neighborhood are close to offbeat boutiques, ethnic restaurants, and a variety of bars and other nightlife—gay and not. It will give you more of a sense of the day-to-day life residents live than the downtown area will.

$–$$$ I include the **Windsor Park Hotel** (2116 Kalorama Rd. NW at Connecticut Ave.; ☎ 800/247-3064 or 202/483-7700; www.windsorparkhotel.com; Metro: Dupont Circle; AE, MC, V) as an option for when the city is fully booked. But truth be told, there are better picks in this chapter. The service here can be curt, and the rooms are gloomy, with hard mattresses, graying blinds instead of curtains, and bland decor. True, it's not all bad news; perks include HBO, small fridges in each room, a great housekeeping staff (who keep everything spick-and-span), and low prices, especially when you go through a discounter. Apparently, Hotels.com, Expedia, and Orbitz often get allotments of rooms, and they often drop the nightly rate to as little as $88 for a double. (The desk will try and hit you up for $106–$179.) Children under 18 stay free in their parent's room. Whatever its faults, the Windsor Park occupies a choice location for those seeking good nightlife, being just 6 blocks from Dupont Circle's bars in one direction, and the hot spots of Adams-Morgan in the other.

$–$$$$ A better although often pricier pick in the immediate vicinity is the modern, attractive, and conveniently located 75-room **Jurys Normandy Inn** ✹✹ (2118 Wyoming Ave. NW, a half-block west of Connecticut Ave.; ☎ 202/483-1350; www.jurysdoyle.com; Metro: Dupont Circle; AE, MC, V). In summer, every front-facing window of the six-story boutique hotel sports a window box filled with bright red geraniums. It's the sort of welcome you would expect in, well, a small hotel in Normandy. The lobby, sitting room, and breakfast room inside are equally charming. Rooms are the standard large, well-kept boxes with tidy bathrooms that Americans expect in a good highway motel but with a touch more character. The bedspreads are of a chic, nubby hemp-like fabric and they cover plush pillow-top mattresses, offering some of the best sleeps in the city. Opposite the bed is a flatscreen TV. I would ask for a front room overlooking the street for a view of the street rather than the alley, although the rear rooms tend to be quieter. When a big convention is in town, a room for two is priced at $215 to $230. But in late summer and other slow periods, rates can plummet to as low as $89 to $109 a night. No charge for children 18 and under staying in their parent's room. In summer, Normandy guests have use of the outdoor swimming pool at Marriott Courtyard Washington Northwest, a sister hotel a block-and-a-half away.

$$–$$$$ You'll feel like you've been transported to the hippest inn in New Orleans or perhaps San Francisco, when you check into the 40-room **Hotel Tabard Inn** ✮✮✮ (1739 N St. NW, btw. 17th and 18th sts.; ☎ 202/785-1277; www.tabardinn.com; Metro: Dupont Circle; no smoking; AE, MC, V). Considered to be the oldest continually operated hotel in the city (during World War I, three Victorian town houses were linked to form the inn), the place wears its history lightly: The old-school dark wood-paneled lobby gives way to rooms that are decorated with a delightful sense of whimsy. Bright purple and canary yellow paint may cover the walls in one; a child-size chair may be set in another, just for the look; bedposts might be curlicued wrought iron or constructed from the heaviest of carved wood. No two are alike and that goes for size as well as decor. Room no. 8, which is drop-dead gorgeous, provides a sitting area furnished with a couch and two comfortable chairs. Oriental carpets cover the polished wood floors. A tinier, bathroom-less option upstairs is the size of a small pantry but so cunningly decorated, with pretty curtains closing off a small closet, you're likely not to mind. Those in the smaller rooms can spend their pre-bedtime evenings in the public sitting room off the foyer and the pub, both looking like they could have been lifted from an exclusive gentleman's club. Delightful! Singles with a shared bathroom go for $113 to $143; doubles with shared bathroom are $15 more. With private bathroom, a single is $158 to $218; add $15 again for double occupancy. Tabard's prices tend to stay pretty consistent year round. Continental breakfast is included, but the hotel's restaurant also serves up hot items (for an extra charge). The Tabard sits on a quiet side street, but busy Connecticut Avenue, a major shopping street, is a block away.

DUPONT CIRCLE NORTH

On a straight line north from the front door of the White House, these accommodations are on one of the city's loveliest thoroughfares. Their drawback is a longish walk from the Dupont Circle Metrorail station, restaurants, and nightlife. Bus service, however, is excellent, and it's a very short ride to the Mall.

$–$$$ The stately exterior, formal and attractively landscaped, suggests a foreign embassy. And in a way, the **Embassy Inn** (1627 16th St. NW, btw. Q and R sts.; ☎ 800/423-9111 or 202/234-7800; www.windsorembassyinns.com; Metrobus: S2, S4; AE, MC, V), on one of the city's most architecturally impressive thoroughfares, plays a small diplomatic role, attracting lots of foreign visitors. I wish that they

When Washington's Rooms Are Highest

As you've probably noticed, hotel rates in D.C. swing wildly from one end of the scale to the other. Here's a quick guide to when they're highest:

- **When Congress is in session:** That's when the town is flooded by lobbyists and other business travelers. Hotel rates drop when the U.S. Congress leaves town on one of its lengthy recesses; these occur in late summer, from about mid-July to the first week in September, and mid-winter, from late November (about Thanksgiving Day) to the first of February. August, of course, is summer vacation time for the legislators; December and January is the year-end holiday break. Weather-wise, both off-peak periods can be uncomfortable. August is steamy—but, of course, that's when families with kids can travel. December and January can be frigid or balmy. It's a gamble. Generally though, December is milder than January. But pack for rain, drizzle, ice, and snow.

- **During the Cherry Blossom Festival** in late March and early April. For the date of the next festival, check the festival website at **www.nationalcherryblossomfestival.org**. It also maintains a "blossom watch" that provides updates on when the trees will be at their peak beauty.

- **April and May:** Bus-, plane- and trainloads of students pour into the city during these months, filling up nearly all of the city's lower-priced rooms.

- **When a convention is in town:** In fall and spring, a big convention may fill up the city's pricier rooms, but you should be able to find a bed-and-breakfast inn or guesthouse with availability. To find out if your planned trip coincides with a big convention, check the website of the Washington Convention Center (**www.dcconvention.com**; click on "Events Calendar"; enter the dates of your proposed visit). Don't be concerned if the event is drawing only 1,000 attendees; the big conventions are what fill the hotel rooms, and these attract 15,000 to 20,000 or more.

got a better impression of the U.S. from their stay but, alas, the Embassy has declined over the years. Now the carpet in rooms is likely to be fraying, the walls scuffed, the beds potentially saggy. It's a definite third or fourth choice in the pantheon of budget lodgings, a shame as the house itself is a beaut: Built in 1910, the entryway boasts a classy marble stairway and hand-fired mosaic tiles. A standard room for one or two—snug, but larger than many—begins at $89, the off-peak rate. The maximum rate for the best room in peak season is $179, but rooms are usually less than that. (I'm almost always able to find rooms there for about $120–$140 per night.) Up to about $150, you get value for your money; much above that, and I'd opt for something a little nicer elsewhere. Take note that the

Embassy does not have an elevator. And avoid room no. 303; a single tiny window in the bedroom and bathroom invites claustrophobia. Some perks: free continental breakfast, free Wi-Fi, and free daily newspapers in the lobby.

$–$$$$ The **Windsor Inn** (1842 16th St. NW; ☎ 800/423-9111 or 202/667-0300; www.windsor-inn-dc.com; Metrobus: S2, S4; AE, MC, V) was in the midst of a re-do when I visited in early 2009, with some nice elements being added (flatscreen TVs, better mattresses) and some dubious improvements (cheap, shiny coverlets and particleboard furnishings). Sister property to the Embassy Inn (see above), it's a more modern structure so it doesn't have the same elegant bones; rooms are boxier but larger here. On the plus side, along with the makeover, are the pleasant staff, who seem a hair more with it at the Windsor than at the Embassy (odd as they have the same owner). My advice here, as with the Embassy, is to take advantage of the cheaper rates, when they're available ($89–$140) but skip it if higher prices are being charged. As at the Embassy Inn, Wi-Fi and newspapers are free here and the nightly rate includes a carb-heavy breakfast.

LOGAN CIRCLE

$–$$$$ Let's not mince words: The **District Hotel** (1440 Rhode Island Ave. NW; ☎ 800/350-5759 or 202/232-7200; www.thedistricthotel.com; Metro: McPherson Square; AE, DC, MC, V) keeps it prices low because it's on Death Row. No, there's no jail nearby. But because the owners have been planning to totally gut the place and add extra stories on top, long-term maintenance has been put on hold. Rooms can be Lilliputian (on my last visit I took the cheapest room, so there was only about 2 ft. btw. my bed and the bathroom door), scuff marks on the walls become their own form of art (I fell asleep wondering how those gray streaks happened up near the ceiling), and chipping paint is common. So why am I recommending the District? Though they haven't kept up with the big stuff, the terrific staff (they really are a lovely, helpful group) have kept what they have in top form. Linens are crisp, dust is a stranger, and you could eat breakfast off the bathroom floors. Luckily you don't have to, as breakfast—a satisfying carb feast consisting of a make-your-own-waffle bar, plus bagels, muffins, and cereals—is included in the nightly rate, as is Wi-Fi. And that rate is usually among the most reasonable in D.C., going from $70 to $175 (the latter only when the city is at its busiest). So will you arrive to find a construction site rather than a hotel? I doubt it; at this writing, the owners' loan for improvements was a casualty of the financial crisis and big changes are on hold (now maybe they'll repaint the rooms!).

FOGGY BOTTOM

A stay in this neighborhood puts you close to the Kennedy Center, walks along the Potomac River, and the youthful faces of students at George Washington University. You are near numerous restaurants, but other than Kennedy Center attractions, you will have to look elsewhere for nightlife.

$–$$ About a decade ago, I was in D.C. to write a restaurant article and I made reservations at the 88-room **Allen Lee** (2224 F St. NW btw. 22nd and 23rd sts.; ☎ 800/462-0186 or 202/331-1224; www.theallenleehotel.com; Metro: Foggy

Bottom–GWU; AE, MC, V). After checking in, I felt my way down an unlit corridor, opened the door to a room of stained carpet and concave bed . . . and worried whether or not I could leave my laptop computer there safely (some of the other "guests" I saw in the lobby looked like they might be conducting business there, if you know what I mean). It then occurred to me that if I was worried about the safety of my stuff, perhaps I should be reconsidering staying at the Allen Lee at all. I turned around and left. But times have changed, and though you'd never know if from the outside, which remains as scruffy looking as ever, the Allen Lee has been rehabbed considerably. Rooms now boast brand-new beds (some futons, some mattresses, so ask if this is important to you), new carpeting, hip-looking Googie-patterned linens, and the lobby even has two computers for guest use. So I have no worry sending you, the reader, there now, especially as rooms go for between $79 and $99 for a double with shared bathroom; $89 to $109 with private bathroom. There are similarly good rates for triples and quads. And best of all, these rates hold steady, no matter what the season. Sure there are some things they couldn't fix—many rooms are still closet-size and the walls can be thin. But where it counts—cleanliness and security—standards have definitely been raised.

$–$$$$ Just as orthopedic shoes cushion the feet, the **State Plaza Hotel** ★ (2117 E St. NW btw. 21st and 22nd sts.; ☎ 800/424-2859 or 202/861-8200; www.stateplaza.com; Metro: Foggy Bottom–GWU; AE, MC, V) offers its guests a solid if unglamorous form of comfort. All the rooms are suites, with the highly useful perk of usable, if sometimes worn-looking, kitchens (full-size fridge, burners, microwave, flatware, cutlery, and even a small table with chairs to dine at). Big enough for a family of four to share, each has two queen-size beds and a large bathroom, with the shower and toilet portion closed off from the sink by a door. The closets, too, are massive. And though the decor won't win any design awards, it's easy on the eyes, with quality, heavy wood furniture, nicely framed prints, and a soothing palette of white and beige. It's all designed for the comfort of long-term guests; the State Department is right across the street and so many visiting diplomats flow in and out that it seems almost like a mini–United Nations at times. Because the property is so massive (279 rooms), it often has to discount to stay full. I've seen rates here drop to just $69 a night, but more commonly, the rates range from $99 all the way to $225. Forget about checking in during much of the month of May. Located on the southern edge of the campus of George Washington University, the hotel fills with friends and relatives of graduating students then. On the roof is a sun deck with spectacular views; there's also a decent fitness center and on-site cafe for snacks. Less than a 10-minute walk from the Kennedy Center, the hotel is a great place for visitors who want to take in a performance. The Lincoln Memorial and the National Mall are just down the hill.

$$–$$$$ How do you choose among Washington's many downtown all-suite hotels, all roughly in the same price range? Answer: Check out the extras and, yes, even the decor. An outdoor swimming pool and contemporary flair (plus good rates) are reasons I recommend **One Washington Circle** (1 Washington Circle at Pennsylvania Ave., and 23rd and K sts.; ☎ 800/424-9671 or 202/872-1680; www.thecirclehotel.com; Metro: Foggy Bottom–GWU; AE, MC, V). It's owned by George Washington University, as is another suites hotel (George Washington University Inn) described later in this chapter. One Washington Circle is less expensive and

Off-Peak Specials at Swank Hotels that Beat the Budgets (Sometimes)

When Congress is out of town for its August and year-end holiday break, many of the city's big business hotels cut their rates substantially. If you're going to be visiting during these times, here's your chance to upgrade your accommodations at an affordable price. The following hotels charge as little as $99 to $115 a night during slow periods, for rooms that go for over $200 a night when Congress is in session or the cherry trees are blossoming.

Beacon Hotel ✪✪ (1615 Rhode Island Ave. NW at 17th and N sts.; ☎ 800/821-4367 or 202/296-2100; www.beaconhotelwdc.com; Metro: Farragut North; AE, MC, V). "Our rates change every 30 minutes," management tells me. So it goes at this spiffy 197-room property. Aimed at business travelers, the Beacon wows with flatscreen TVs, large leather-like headboards, and boldly striped coverlets. And I can personally attest to how quiet the rooms are and how sleepable the beds are. I booked it at the last minute for $109 a night in early 2009; hope you can do the same. The excellent downtown location puts you 4 blocks from the White House.

George Washington University Inn ✪ (824 New Hampshire Ave. NW btw. H and I sts.; ☎ 800/426-4455 or 202/337-6620; www.gwuinn.com; Metro: Foggy Bottom–GWU; AE, MC, V). You'll see lots of college students trooping in and out of this charming 95-room hotel, but they're only visitors. The paying guests are their parents. Owned by George Washington University, it has a lot of pluses: extra-large guest rooms and suites, many with kitchenettes; Colonial Williamsburg–inspired decor; and a quiet location on a shady street near the Kennedy Center. And hit it at the right time, and you might pay just $99 a night here, up to $113 if you opt to include breakfast.

Homewood Suites by Hilton ✪✪ (1475 Massachusetts Ave. NW at 15th and M sts.; ☎ 800/CALL-HOME [2255-4663]or 202/265-8000; www.home woodsuites.com; Metro: Farragut North; AE, MC, V). Some 175 attractive mini-apartments with all the modern convenience; each has a sitting-room

3 centuries more recent in style. Modern art on the wall and a royal blue inlaid tile slashing across the lobby's white marble floor proclaim the flair that is duplicated in the guest rooms. The hotel houses 151 suites, but the most affordable are 18 studios dubbed Guest Quarters. Quite spacious, these feature either a queen-size bed or two doubles, a large comfy sofa, and a separate kitchen—equipped with a four-burner stove, microwave, and large fridge. Large double-paned windows and a walk-out balcony give rooms an open, sunny look. Twelve years ago, the building was converted from an apartment building, which accounts for the

with a pull-out couch should you need to house kids, too. The "front" room includes a small kitchen equipped with two-burner electric stove, tall fridge, and a fully stocked cupboard. Included in the nightly rate (which has been known to drop to $125) are hot breakfasts in the lobby cafe. The convenient downtown location puts you 3 blocks from Dupont Circle's many restaurants; the White House is a 7-block walk.

Hotel Helix ✪✪ (1430 Rhode Island Ave. NW btw. 14th and 15th sts.; Metro, Dupont Circle; ☎ 800/706-1202 or 202/462-9001; www.hotelhelix. com; AE, MC, V). Decidedly sexy, the Helix boasts a vivid, Hollywood-esque decor (platform beds surrounded by sheer curtains, hot pink lights, and massive posters of surfers), a hip clientele, and 178 rooms. When I last stayed here with my daughters, they declared it the coolest hotel ever and proceeded to get sick from the bottle of free gummy bears that comes with each room. At times, rates can drop to as little as $95 per night; go for the for "Hot Dates–Great Rates" promotion.

Henley Park Hotel (926 Massachusetts Ave. NW; ☎ 800/222-8474; www. henleypark.com; AE, MC, V). Just a block from the convention center, the regal Henley Park has a baronial lobby, a clubby bar, and rooms filled with tasteful prints and Colonial antiques. Is it any surprise then that it's a landmark and member of the sniffy Historic Hotels of America? Yet in early 2009, I snagged a room here for $109 per night! Go figure.

The River Inn ✪ (924 25th St. NW btw. H and I sts.; ☎ 800/424-2741 or 202/337-7600; www.theriverinn.com; Metro: Foggy Bottom–GWU; AE, MC, V). The rooms, all suites (sleeping up to four people), are large and decorated with flair and color. The walls display evocative photos of the historic Chesapeake & Ohio Canal, which begins its 185-mile path to western Maryland just 2 blocks away. Low-season rates can drop as low as $99 but, says management, you are apt to find off-peak rates almost any time of the year, if only for a couple of days at a time, so always inquire.

roominess. Among the nice extras are an on-site fitness center and restaurant (along with the pool I mentioned above). In low season, a Guest Quarters suite, which can sleep four, generally goes for $139 to $179 (but sometimes as low as $109); in high season, you're looking at $169 to $229. Add $20 for an Executive Suite with a separate sitting room; an additional $40 for a Grand State Room with a separate dining room. The hotel overlooks Washington Circle, site of a historic equestrian statue of America's first president. The White House is 6 blocks east; lively Georgetown, 6 blocks west.

NAVY YARDS

$-$$$ Yes, you'll see the beautiful skyline of D.C. from your window at the **Capitol Skyline** ✪ (10 I St. SW; ☎ 800/458-7500 or 202/488-500; Metro: Navy Yard; AE, DC, MC, V), but take that as a clue: You need some distance to see a skyline clearly, and this hotel is located in Washington's equivalent of Siberia. There's even a free daily shuttle to take you to the sights—another big clue. You may not have to use it, however, as the hotel is just a 5-minute-walk from the Navy Yard Metro stop; and it's a safe walk—the area is a bit industrial, but no longer a slum (mostly it's populated by new, half-sold condo projects and construction sites for more of the same). Beyond the location, however, this is a pretty swell hotel for the price (usually btw. $79–$155) with all the amenities of a pricey resort—room service, bar/lounge, good gym, restaurant, and even a pool (a rarity in this city). Rooms look like a standard Best Western (unmemorable but comfortable and well maintained) as that's what this used to be, though I like the touch of having framed copies of the Declaration of Independence and other important documents as art in each room.

HOTELS IN WASHINGTON'S SUBURBS

Traveling on a budget, like life itself, can be a compromise, right? So I thought it was worthwhile to include a less than ideal solution to the high cost of D.C. lodgings: commuting into the District of Columbia. Now you might not save any money by doing so—often the prices in, say, Arlington and Alexandria are just as high as they are in the District itself. But in the lowest price category there will often be significant difference in the *quality* of accommodations. Instead of making the compromise of having less space than you'd like, or a room that hasn't been painted since the Clinton administration, you accept a bland but amenity-laden hotel at the same rate—and bring a good book (perhaps this one!) to read on that 20-minute ride into the city each morning.

Make that compromise only if all the D.C. accommodations I've scored at one or more stars are fully booked. If that's not the case, you'll want to go for those *before* the ones below just to avoid the commute. ***Note:*** that I've only covered hotels that *don't* require a car to patronize. Each is within a quarter-mile walk of the Metro.

You'll never pay more than $139 a night at the **Econo Lodge Metro Arlington** ✪ (6800 Lee Hwy.; ☎ 877/424-6423 or 703/538-5300; www.econolodge.com; Metro: Falls Church; AE, DC, MC, V), and you'll often pay just $89, which is not a bad range in a town where swings of $100 or more are common. And what you get is quite spiffy: a good-size room with a flatscreen TV, a sleep-enhancing bed, and the only Econo Lodge in the nation (I'm guessing) that has a gourmet French restaurant attached to it (La Cote D'Or). Really, this nice property could be charging more . . . well, if it weren't for one big negative: A huge apartment building is going up right next door and work starts at 6am each weekday. From the looks of it, that monster won't be up before the end of 2009, so if you're not an early riser look elsewhere (or pack earplugs).

In fact, you might look to the quirky **Americana Hotel** ✪ (1400 Jefferson Davis Hwy., Arlington; ☎ 703/979-3772; Metro: Crystal City; AE, DC, MC, V), a squat, older, family-owned motel that's a bit of an odd duck in the Crystal City area of Arlington, which is all glass high-rises (and lots of red-faced men with bristly haircuts—the Pentagon's nearby!). The Americana's the kind of place I'd expect to see in Akron, Ohio: a lovingly tended, family-run motel where you send visiting Aunt Mary when the sofa-bed finally caves in, because you know they'll take good care of her there (the staff here are real gems). Yes, the rooms are dated with their floral bedspreads and pink tiled bathrooms; and yes, the free Wi-Fi can be spotty and the pipes a bit vocal in the mornings. But heck, the beds are good quality, rooms are spotless and relatively roomy, and when other places in the area are charging $200 and up a night, you'll rarely pay more than $99 here. A key selling point: It's just a 3-minute walk from the Metro line which will get you to L'Enfant Plaza in 12 minutes flat (I timed it!).

On the first two "out of towners," the tradeoff with time on the train is pretty minor. However, at the next two, the **Holiday Inn Express** ✦✦ (5001 Mercedes Blvd. off Branch Ave., Camp Springs, MD; ☎ 888/HOLIDAY [465-4329] or 301/423-2323; www.holidayinnexpress.com; Metro: Branch Ave.; AE, DC, MC, V) and **Country Inn and Suites** (4950 Mercedes Blvd. off Branch Ave., Camp Springs, MD; ☎ 240/492-1070; Metro: Branch Ave.; AE, DC, MC, V), your commute stretches to a good half-hour and that's once you get to the station (the walk to the Metro is around 10 min.; Country Inn has a shuttle, though). Still, I had to include them because their rates are consistently excellent ($89–$129), and they're near Andrews Air Force Base so should be helpful for those visiting family members there. As for the Holiday Inn Express—hello luxury! This one is downright swanky, having undergone a multimillion-dollar renovation in 2007 that marbled up the bathrooms and added plush new mattresses, chic color schemes, and flatscreen TVs to the bedrooms. On-site are also a decent fitness room and an outdoor pool. The Homewood Inn is a bit more vanilla in its looks, but rooms are spacious, white-glove clean, and have all the amenities you get at a chain like this. Plus, there's that helpful shuttle to the Metro.

LOW-COST SPECIALTY LODGINGS

ACTIVE AND RETIRED MILITARY   The military doesn't make it easy to do, but active duty and retired military personnel and accompanying family members can enjoy comfy lodgings at a budget price from **Fort Myer Military Community Lodging** (Bldg. #50, 318 Jackson Ave., Fort Myer, VA; ☎ 703/696-3576 or 703/696-3577; www.fmmc.army.mil/sites/newcomers/lodge.asp; Metro: Rosslyn and 25-min. walk; AE, MC, V). This office handles rentals at Fort Myer, which is adjacent to Arlington National Cemetery in the Virginia suburbs, and at Fort McNair, which overlooks the Potomac and Anacostia rivers in southwest Washington. Fort Myer provides 18 one-bedroom apartments at $67 a night and 13 one-bedroom suites with separate sitting room for $122 a night. Fort McNair provides 25 guest rooms; a single with shared bathroom is $53, with private bathroom $57. A one-bedroom suite is $67. Additional guests are $3. That's the good news; now for the bad. These rooms are difficult to get from Monday to Thursday, when personnel on official business take priority. Even if you snag a 1-night rental, you may not get a second night, or if you do, you may have to change rooms. Availability eases on the weekend. And you can usually check in for all 3 nights—Friday, Saturday, and Sunday. To get a room, you must call the reservations desk at 6am the day you want the room, and then you must check back at 2pm to see if a room is free. On weekends, you go through this procedure only once; on weekdays, you must do it every day. Another hassle: Whether you're staying at Fort Myer or Fort McNair, you must check in at Fort Myer, Bldg. #50. It's not impossible to do this by Metro; I suggest using both the Metro and taxis. But if you have heavy luggage, a taxi all the way is the most practical solution. Restaurants are located within walking distance of both facilities.

Lodgings at both Fort McNair and Fort Myer are in carefully preserved historic structures. The two-story redbrick building at Fort Myer sports a Colonial look; Fort McNair's three-story is unprepossessing. But the interiors of both are furnished quite elegantly, as befits the expectations of visiting generals who often stay in them, and they are kept inspection-ready spick-and-span. Also at both, you are a short walk from dining, a swimming pool, and tennis courts. Fort McNair maintains a 9-hole golf course.

UNIVERSITY STAYS   Washington's five major universities open their residence halls in summer to interns with confirmed employment or to visitors in the city temporarily for an educational purpose. All require a minimum stay, usually 4 or 5 weeks. The school with the least restrictive rental policy is **Catholic University of America** (620 Michigan Ave. NE; ☎ 202/319-5200; http://conferences. cua.edu; Metro: Brookland–Catholic University). Catholic University requires only a 7-day stay for single or double dorm room with a shared bathroom; the rate is $29 a night for a single and $25 per person for a double. Apartments with shared bathroom require a 3-week minimum stay; the rate is $35 single and $30 double per person. Rooms are open to anyone with an educational purpose.

MONASTERY RETREATS   On a limited basis, male and female guests can stay for a few days in one of the eight guest rooms at **St. Anselm's Abbey** (4501 S. Dakota Ave. NE, Washington, DC 20017; ☎ 202/269-2300; www.stanselms.org/ guests.htm; e-mail dcabbey@erols.com; Metro: Brookland–Catholic University; closed Aug). The abbey, located on 30 landscaped acres, welcomes guests interested in the "Rule of Saint Benedict," meaning someone seeking a balance in life achieved by prayer, work, and leisure. All retreats are private and individual—no formal programs—but guests may take part in religious ceremonies. A priest is available if you request a talk. Male accommodations are in single rooms with private or shared bathroom. Most are in a Tudor-style structure with a half-timbered front built in the 1930s. Rooms line an upstairs hallway in the monastery. They are very modest, and simply furnished with bed, desk, and a chair or two. A shared bathroom is down the hall. A maximum of two women can share the Canterbury Suite, which has a parlor, bedroom with one or two beds, and private bathroom. The suggested offering is $30 a day, which includes meals. "It's the cheapest room in town," points out Fr. Hilary, the Guestmaster. Breakfast at 6am and lunch at 12:20pm are served cafeteria-style. Dinner at 6:30pm is a formal meal with the monks. Sixteen monks reside in the monastery, which conducts a day school for boys from grades 6 to 12. Some monks teach at nearby Catholic University. For reservations, contact the Guestmaster via mail or e-mail (see above). The monastery prefers to take in guests who have come for contemplative reasons rather than simply for inexpensive lodging.

HOSTELS

$ Here's a new one: a chic hostel. And if offers private rooms that are actually nicer than those in some of the surrounding hotels. That's the scenario at the **Gallery Inn Hotel** ✪✪ (1850 Florida Ave. NW; ☎ 202/234-1535; Metro: Dupont Circle; AE, DC, MC, V), which offers a mix of hostel rooms (with bunk beds housing up to six in a room) and fashion-forward private rooms, appropriate for a family as they boast a queen-size bed and a single. Each bed is set in a frame that's low to the ground, atop a merry polka-dotted rug in a room that may have a fine leather couch or perhaps a flatscreen TV. As I said, this ain't your usual hostel. Whether you go for shared accommodations or private, they come with a very nice breakfast (croissants, good muffins, and so on). And the location is terrific: right between the party-hearty Adams Morgan area and restaurant-laden Dupont Circle. The only drawbacks: the lack of a common room, kitchen, or laundry facilities. Prices are per person, not per room, and are $40 a night in a dorm room, $65 in a private room (you may be able to negotiate lower total rates if you're traveling with kids; ask).

$ In contrast, you'll be really roughing it at **William Penn House** (515 E. Capitol St. SE; ☎ 202/543-5560; www.williampennhouse.org; cash only; Metro: Union Station), but roughing it among truly impressive folks. And meeting these lovely folks, all Quakers, may be worth sleeping in a plywood bunk within sneezing distance of the guy in the bunk across from you. Yes, the dorm rooms are tight and pretty basic, even for a hostel. Its "honeymoon suite," a term they use here ironically, is the one bedroom appropriate for two people . . . but it too has a bunk bed. Still, bathrooms are mildew free, a continental breakfast is included (as is access to a kitchen), and all is kept quite tidy. Because the house was founded to give cheap beds to Americans coming to D.C. to lobby for social causes, groups have priority and take over the house about 50% of the time. Reservations for individuals are taken no more than 60 days in advance. Along with sleeps, a morning silent worship service is open to all (but not a prerequisite for staying here); and the house periodically hosts lectures, potlucks, and films. William Penn is on Capitol Hill within walking distance of the Capitol.

$ **DC Lofty** ✪ (815 7th St. NE; ☎ 202/621-6568; www.dclofty.com; Metro: Union Station; AE, DC, MC, V) is about as jaunty as the name implies, with a very collegiate vibe (perhaps it's the framed concert posters and the squooshy living room couches, which seem to be perpetually filled with some young guys arguing politics). A new lodging, all of the furnishings are fresh and of good quality from the unshakeable bunk beds to the carpeting to the surprisingly comfortable mattresses. Generally rooms go for $35 a night per person, but there are also two-bedded rooms at $45 a night. Included in those rates are free Wi-Fi and phone calls anywhere within the U.S.; free use of the laundry machines (including free detergent); and public computers that are available free of charge to guests.

$ The most typical hostel experience—for all the good and bad that implies—is found at **Hostelling International—Washington, DC** ✪✪ (1009 11th St. NW, btw. K and L sts.; ☎ 202/737-2333; www.hiwashingtondc.org; Metro: Metro Center; AE, MC, V) and it's also the most affordable at $10 a night. Rates are $25 to $45 a night in dorm-style rooms, plus a $3 "temporary membership" fee if you are not a member of HI. For that you get a bunk bed in a newly painted room that St. Francis would have found pretty monastic. But cleanliness is next to godliness and this 270-bedder is white-glove clean. You also get a lot of folks from all over the world to pal around with. The two lounges are beehives of activity with computer terminals (six of 'em), a useable kitchen and dining area, and notice boards filled with information about the nightly and daily tours that volunteers lead to all corners of the city for free. At no cost, as well, are the weekly documentary screenings and other events. Location is good, too, just up from Chinatown and walkable to the Metro.

$ Though it doesn't call itself a hostel, **International Guest House** (1441 Kennedy St. NW, btw. 14th and 16th sts.; ☎ 202/726-5808; Metrobus S2 and S4; MC, V) certainly has all the hallmarks of that type of lodging. You share a two-person or three-person room (bathroom down the hall) with strangers. Or you and your spouse can have the room to yourself. But unlike many hostels, there are no bunks, a continental breakfast is included in the price, and your digs are in a cheery, three-story yellow-brick house (sleeping a maximum of 15 guests). The price is reasonable, if not rock-bottom, at $35 per person. For children (with parents) under 15, it's $15. Children younger than 4 stay free. Drawing (but not limited to) lots of young foreign travelers, the guesthouse is a "mission" of the Allegheny Conference of the Mennonite Church USA. All staff members, who include a resident hosting couple, are volunteers who also stay here, and that's where the negatives kick in. This lodging will have a few too many house rules for some. A bell awakens you at 7:20am for a group breakfast at 8am. You must vacate your room and the bathrooms from 10am to noon for cleaning; on Sunday, it's 9am and the place shuts down entirely until 3pm so the staff can attend church. You've got to make curfew; the guesthouse locks up at 11pm. And the location is a bit out of the action; you're at least a 20-minute (non–rush hour) bus ride from the White House with no Metro stop nearby. I'd look at the other hostels above first.

4 District Dining

Great meals at an affordable price, plus where to find a quick bite on the Mall

By Pauline Frommer

WASHINGTON, D.C., MAY BE OUR NATION'S CAPITAL, BUT IN MATTERS OF food, it's anything but all-American. It's a highly international city, peopled by large numbers of immigrants and brimming with embassies; it boasts eateries from across the globe, many of which simply aren't found in other American cities. I'm talking Malaysian, Eritrean, Ethiopian, Portuguese, Belgian, and Chilean food, along with more common ethnic cuisines such as Mexican, Indian, Spanish, Chinese, and Thai. What's more, because these restaurants cater to communities of expats, they must keep their flavors authentic to stay in business. There's very little catering to American tastes in the capital; if a dish is meant to be fiery, you can bet you'll be gulping down water before you finish the plate.

This abundance of ethnic eats is great news for the budget traveler because most of these restaurants are affordably priced. So not only can travelers expand their taste horizons, eating high quality, fresh foods, but they also can do so, often, at an astonishingly low price.

Along with all this exotic fare are American restaurants that speak to the longer history of Washington, D.C., as a Southern city, a city that's long taken pride in the crispness of its fried chicken. You'll find soul food, along with crab cakes, chili dogs, and other dishes that are prized in this region. What I *won't* point you toward are the chain restaurants or notoriously touristy restaurants, such as the Hard Rock Cafe, where the teen-packed tour buses unload. (Okay, if you have a teen in tow, it's at 999 E St. NW.)

Here's how this chapter works: Before each listing, you'll see one to four dollar signs. They refer to the average price of an entree at the restaurants listed. Here's how it breaks down:

$: Most entrees under $8
$$: Most entrees from $9–$14
$$$: Most entrees from $15–$20
$$$$: Entrees above $20

You'll also see stars right after a restaurant's name. These mean:

No star: Still recommended but don't go out of your way to dine here
⭐ A solid, reliable choice
⭐⭐ Very good, highly recommended
⭐⭐⭐ The best of the best, a must, don't miss

FAQ About D.C. Dining

- **When to eat?** The busiest time for restaurants is 7 to 8:30pm. The theater crowds show up at 6pm, and a few diners—often Europeans—arrive at 9pm. Restaurants tend to empty out by 10pm. Washington isn't really a night-owl city for diners. One exception is the **Diner,** an all-night eatery (p. 70).
- **Early-Bird Specials?** Some higher-end restaurants feature a pretheater, fixed-price menu from 5 to 6:30 or 7pm. Usually, it includes salad or other starter, entree, and dessert for less than you might pay later for salad and entree alone. Among them are **Rasika** (p. 68) and **Teatro Goldoni** (p. 63).
- **What to Wear?** Only a few snooty restaurants, none of which we recommend in this guide, require male guests to wear jackets. Otherwise dress is casual but certainly not sloppy. Yes, you probably could get seated wearing a T-shirt, cutoffs, and sandals. But management wouldn't be happy, and you would look out of place.
- **Smoking?** City law bans smoking in restaurants, taverns, nightclubs, and bars. Outdoor seating is exempted from the ban.
- **Tipping?** A 15% to 20% tip is standard, with 20% gaining the edge for better-than-average service.

DINING DISTRICTS

It would be impossible for me to list every possible restaurant in D.C. If you'd like to hunt for your own find, try one of the booming restaurant areas:

- **18th Street NW north from S Street to Columbia Road** (Adams Morgan; Metro: Dupont Circle). Inexpensive ethnic restaurants, including Ethiopian.
- **8th Street SE south from Pennsylvania Avenue** (Capitol Hill; Metro: Eastern Market). A mix of chic dining spots and beer and burger pubs.
- **M Street NW from 30th to 34th streets** (Georgetown; Metrobus: 30, 32, 34, 35, 36, K Street Circulator bus, or the Georgetown Blue Bus from the Foggy Bottom or Dupont Circle Metro stations). High rents mean high menu prices, but budget diners will find burger/barbecue/pizza options also.
- **U Street NW from 13th to 9th streets** (U Street Corridor; Metro: U Street–African-American Civil War Memorial–Cardozo). Stylish new eateries that have kept prices under control.
- **7th Street NW from D to I streets** (Penn Quarter; Metro: Archives–Navy Memorial–Penn Quarter). Family dining in a blossoming theater, movie, and arena sports neighborhood.
- **14th and P streets NW, 1 or 2 blocks north, south, and west** (Logan Circle; Metro: McPherson Square). Small, stylish restaurants with innovative menus to serve the new condo units mushrooming in the neighborhood.

◆ **19th Street NW between L and N streets** (Downtown; Metro: Farragut North). Lots of expense-account dining but cheaper choices too.
◆ **H Street NW from 7th to 5th streets** (Chinatown; Metro: Gallery Place–Chinatown). Chinese and other Asian restaurants one after another.
◆ **H Street NE from 12th to 14th streets** (X2 busline from McPherson Square or Gallery Place). Washington's newest nightlife district also boasts an intriguing assortment of soul food joints and cozy taverns. It's a bit iffy after dark, so keep your wits about you if you troll for eats here.

DINING ON THE MALL

If you're like most visitors to Washington, especially as a first-timer, you're going to be spending much of your day at the museums, monuments, and memorials on the National Mall, where the choice of convenient lunch places is limited.

One solution, in the warm-weather months, is to bring a **picnic** on the Mall. The Mall and Washington's many parks lend themselves to eating outdoors. The choicest spots are along the Potomac River—for example, behind the Roosevelt Memorial in West Potomac Park. You could pick up food from one of the **kiosks** or **food carts** that dot the Mall. They offer items such as a plain hot dog ($1.50), Polish sausage in a bun ($2.50), chili dog ($1.75), slice of pizza ($2), and can of soda ($1). I recommend a kiosk hot dog over a vendor's because kiosks provide shady seating, and the food is better.

Even better is to tote along your own sandwiches or sandwich fixings, soft drinks, chips, and cookies, which can be purchased at **Marvelous Market** (www.marvelousmarket.com). The mini-chain is known for its ultra-fresh organic ingredients, made-from-scratch breads, and its fair pricing. In the downtown area, Marvelous Market has four locations:

◆ Dupont Circle, 1511 Connecticut Ave. NW; ☎ 202/332-3690; daily 8am to 9pm.
◆ Georgetown, 3217 P St. NW; ☎ 202/333-2591; Monday to Saturday 8am to 9pm, Sunday 8am to 8pm.
◆ Penn Quarter, 730 7th St. NW; ☎ 202/628-0824; Monday to Friday 7am to 8pm, Saturday to Sunday 9am to 5pm.
◆ Downtown, 1800 K St. NW; ☎ 202/828-0944; Monday to Friday 7:30am to 7pm.

Another option is the New York City–based gourmet deli and food purveyor **Dean & Deluca** (3276 M St. NW; ☎ 202/342-2500; www.deandeluca.com; daily 10am–8pm), which offers a chi-chi take on picnic goods—think smoked salmon paired with dill, or roast beef slathered in horseradish sauces.

Keep in mind, if you tote a lunch bag to any of the museums on the Mall, you will have to open it for inspection. That won't be the case when you're visiting the open-air memorials, where no security checks are made.

And here are my specific recommendations on the Mall:

$ A lunch cart, but an above-average one, **On the Fly** (right in front of the National Museum of American History; no phone; daylight hours; cash only) has as its motto: "Fresh, local, fun." It's a good summary for this bright green

Pairing Sights with Eats

Below is a chart for the major attractions on the Mall, plus eating options that are within a 5- to 10-minute walk. If you care about food, it might be worth your while to take that extra bit of time for a sit-down bite:

Attraction	Closest Good Eating Option	Other Options
Arthur M. Sackler Gallery	On the Fly (p. 53)	Teaism (p. 62)
Arts and Industries Building	National Gallery of Art Cafeteria/Garden Café (p. 55)	On the Fly (p. 53), Potbelly (p. 61), Mitsitam Café (p. 54)
Freer Gallery	On the Fly (p. 53)	Teaism (p. 62)
Hirschhorn Museum and Sculpture Gallery	National Gallery of Art Cafeteria/Garden Café (p. 55)	On the Fly (p. 53), Potbelly (p. 61), Mitsitam Café (p. 54)
Lincoln Memorial	Potbelly (p. 61)	
National Air and Space Museum	Mitsitam Café (p. 54)	National Gallery of Art Cafeteria (p. 55), Potbelly (p. 61)
National Archives	Potbelly (p. 61)	National Gallery of Art Cafeteria/Garden Café (p. 55), Teaism (p. 62)
National Gallery of Art	National Gallery of Art Cafeteria/Garden Café (p. 55)	Potbelly (p. 61), Teaism (p. 62)

"smartkart" (it runs on electricity, not gas) which offers Latino entrees (tacos, empanadas, burritos, and chili $3–$8) primarily made from organic and locally sourced ingredients that often have a dash of flair (love the chipotle *crema* on the tacos). And the guy who runs it most days has an off-beat sense of humor—enter "fun." If you're going to buy from a cart or a kiosk on the Mall, this is your healthiest, and I'd say tastiest, option.

$–$$ The standout on the Mall is the **National Museum of the American Indian's Mitsitam Native Foods Café** ☆☆☆ (p. 115 for an overview of the museum). It's trying—and succeeding—to make lunch a learning experience reflecting the nature of the museum itself. Visitors are treated to a sampling of Native American foods from throughout the Western Hemisphere. It can be a real eating adventure, with everything from fry breads to smoked duck to honey-coated beets. From South America, you could try a somewhat spicy chicken tamale in a corn husk ($7.25); salmon cakes and fire-roasted salmon cooked on a plank (both for $15) are the tasty choices from the Pacific Northwest. The last

Attraction	Closest Good Eating Option	Other Options
National Museum of African Art	On the Fly (p. 53)	Teaism (p. 62)
National Museum of American History	On the Fly (p. 53)	Teaism (p. 62)
National Museum of Natural History	On the Fly (p. 53)	National Gallery of Art Cafeteria/Garden Café (p. 55), Teaism (p. 62), Potbelly (p. 61)
National Museum of the American Indian	Mitsitam Café (p. 54)	Potbelly (p. 61)
U.S. Botanic Gardens	Mitsitam Café (p. 54)	Tacqueria Nacional (p. 62), Good Stuff Eatery (p. 56), Talay Thai (p. 57)
U.S. Capitol	Good Stuff Eatery (p. 56)	Talay Thai (p. 57)
Vietnam Veterans Memorial	Potbelly (p. 61)	
Washington Monument	On the Fly (p. 53)	The Café at the Corcoran Gallery
World War II Memorial	The Café at the Corcoran Gallery	

time I was there, I feasted on a fascinating grain and venison casserole, studded with dried berries ($14) from the Northern Woodlands. If I'm anywhere near here at lunchtime, this is where I head.

$–$$ On a cold or rainy day, the best indoor view is at the **National Gallery of Art's Cascade Café** (p. 105), located in the tunnel that links the East and West buildings. Just beyond a soaring glass wall, a cascading fountain plunges down a mini mountainside like a waterfall. Tops on the menu here are an excellent salad bar ($8.25) with dozens of choices. Soups, sandwiches, and changing entrees are also thoughtfully prepared and a cut above what you'll find in the other cafeterias on the Mall. They even have a gelato counter! Also at the National Gallery is the **Garden Café** ☆, which offers a lunch experience as elegant as the museum itself. A tablecloth drapes the table, and you sit beneath the polished marble of a Grecian rotunda. The buffet ($18) features such dishes as zucchini frittata, grilled calamari, roasted guinea hen, and arugula salad—not cheap, but the food is surprisingly good. Individual entrees—pastas and salads—go for $12 to $14.

$–$$ Kosher meals are available at the **U.S. Holocaust Memorial Museum's Museum Café** (p. 125). Located in a separate building behind the museum, the cafe offers Kosher soups, sandwiches, panini, and salads in a quiet setting.

FEDERAL CAFETERIAS Many federal departments on or near the Mall operate cafeterias or food courts. The food is standard American hot dishes, but that's not really why you are here. Once you've got your tray and table, take a look around. This is your chance to learn the truth firsthand from an actual civil servant. Engage some in conversation over the table; find out what they do. If your interest comes across as sincere, you should get a congenial response, and an "insider" look at how their particular part of government functions. Here are some of the department cafeterias that may interest you:

♦ **U.S. Supreme Court** (1st St. NE btw. East Capitol St. and Maryland Ave.; Metro: Union Station). For lawyers, law students, and fans of justice.
♦ The **Longworth House Office Building** (South Capitol and C sts.; Metro: Capitol South); **Rayburn House Office Building** (South Capitol St. and Independence Ave.; Metro: Capitol South); or **Dirksen Senate Office Building** (1st St. and Constitution Ave. NE; Metro: Union Station). All the politics (and politicos) you can stomach.
♦ **Department of the Interior** (1849 C St. NW; Metro: Foggy Bottom) and **Department of Agriculture** (14th St. and Independence Ave. SW; Metro: Smithsonian). For environmentalists.
♦ **Department of Transportation** (400 7th St. SW; Metro: Federal Center). Ever had an airline lose your luggage or delay your flight? Gripe about it to your tablemate here.
♦ **Department of Labor** (200 Constitution Ave. NW; Metro: Judiciary Square). Are you a union member? Let your tablemates know.

CAPITOL HILL

Though the U.S. Capitol soars high above, this really is mostly a residential neighborhood—albeit an upscale one with folks who love to wine and dine. Tastes are sophisticated if not all that adventurous up here, meaning that you'll be served top-quality ingredients in fairly standard preparations (the exceptions would be the restaurants mentioned below). Come here for romantic dining in trendy cafes occupying lovely old row houses.

$ Or come here for a trendy burger, served by a "Top Chef" no less. **Good Stuff** (303 Pennsylvania Ave. SE; ☎ 202/543-8222; www.goodstuffeatery.com; Mon–Sat 11am–11pm; AE, DC, MC, V), the franchise-ready effort of Spike Mendelsohn of reality TV fame, is an upscale malt shop where the ice cream is house-made and the fries are given the gourmet treatment, dusted with fresh rosemary and thyme ($2.80). The setting is a bit self-conscious, but cute, the exposed brick walls and metal heating ducts slathered with statements portending a food revolution. "We believe Good Stuff should be a way of life!" Yeah, yeah, right— and you're going to do all that on the back of burgers? Well, maybe if the burgers were a bit more moist. But here they err on the dry side. Luckily they're tarted up with everything from daikon radishes to artisanal cheeses to chipotle barbecue

> # Ahoy! Down Home Cooking
>
> I thought, as I recently sat eavesdropping on a group of young men and women in crisp Navy uniforms, that there's probably no more enjoyable place to come after long months at sea than **Levi's Port Café** ★★ (1102 8th St. SE; ☎ 202/547-6500; daily 11am–8pm; Metro: Navy Yard; AE, MC, V). An unusually welcoming, homey little place, it serves the kind of comfort food that puts mess hall grub to shame: tender pork and beef ribs ($9.95), real North Carolina barbecued pulled pork in a sandwich ($3.90) with just the right balance of vinegar and spice, collard greens without a hint of bitterness. The *Washington Post* critic has rightly praised the lasagna-rich mac and cheese as one of the top 10 finest restaurant dishes in the city. Along with meals that include a main and two sides ($5.95–$9.95) is an all-you-can-eat buffet with four different preparations of chicken and all the sides on the menu for $13. It's a swell place to pop in for lunch if you decide to visit the Navy Museum (p. 131).

sauce. My fave, and not because of my politics, is the "Obamaburger" ($6.90), which is topped with red onion marmalade, bacon, blue cheese, and horseradish sauce (a better mix of flavors than it sounds). Turkey burgers, veggie burgers, and an array of salads are available for the health conscious; beer is sold, as well. All in all, meals here satisfy though not as much as Spike, the notoriously blowhard contestant, would have us all believe. Still, if you've ever wanted to sample what these white-coated stars could actually cook, here's your chance to do so affordably.

$–$$ You'll get grub that's as tasty, but without the pretense, at **Market Lunch** ★ 🧒 (in Eastern Market, 225 7th St. SE; ☎ 202/547-8444; Tues–Fri 7:30am–3pm, Sat 8am–3pm, Sun 11am–3pm; Metro: Eastern Market; AE, DC, MC, V), an institution in D.C., in the historic Eastern Market. Guests sit at a 30-seater communal table which still bears the burn marks from a devastating fire that gutted the market in 2007 (the refurbished market reopened after a massive restoration in June, 2009). But other than that, it thankfully hasn't changed a lick. A very local crowd—cops, moms with strollers, Capitol Hill staffers—still gathers here daily to catch up on the gossip and chow down on perfectly executed regional specialties (the $12 crab cakes here, enlivened by mustard and creamy within, are legendary). Breakfast is a draw, too, from the puffy blueberry-buckwheat pancakes ($7) to the special of the house, aptly named "the brick" ($8)—a solid wedge of fried eggs, cheese, potatoes, and bun that generally suffices for breakfast *and* lunch. Chowders and sandwiches are also recommended; it's difficult to spend more than $12 for a meal here.

$–$$ Just an encyclopedia's toss from the Library of Congress, **Talay Thai** ★ (406 1st St. SE at D St. SE; ☎ 202/546-5100; www.talaythaidc.com; Mon–Sat 11:30am–3pm and 4:30–10pm; Metro: Capitol South; AE, DC, MC, V) is a bit of an odd duck. Its mismatched decor mixes somberly elegant wood-paneled walls with

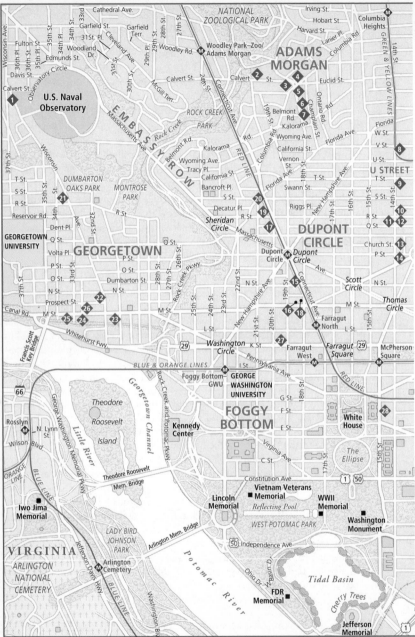

Amsterdam Falafel Shop **7**
Artfully Chocolate/ Kingsbury Confections **10**
Bar Pilar **9**
Belga Café **50**
Ben's Chili Bowl **29**
Bistrot du Coin **20**
Busboys and Poets **8**
Café Divan **21**
Coco Sala **38**
The Diner **5**
Dukem Restaurant **31**
Etete **32**
Good Stuff Eatery **47**
The Great Wall of China **12**
Jaleo **40**
Joyti **6**
Lalibela **14**
Leopold's Kafe **25**
Levi's Port Café **51**
Malaysia Kopitiam **16**
Mama Ayesha's **2**
Market Lunch **49**
Martin's Tavern **22**
Matchbox **36**
Meskerem **3**

Mitsitam Foods Cafe
Mixtec **4**
Moby Dick Kabob **15, 23**
Montmartre **48**
Nando's Peri Peri **18, 35**
National Gallery of Art Cafes **43**
Old Ebbit Grill **28**
Old Europe **1**
Oohs and Aahs **30**
Pizzeria Paradiso **24**
Posto **13**
Proof **39**
Queen Makeda **33**
Rasika **41**
Rice **11**
Saint's Paradise Cafeteria **34**
Sonoma Restaurant and Wine Bar **46**
Tackle Box **26**
Talay Thai **45**
Teaism **19, 42**
Teatro Goldoni **27**
Zaytinah **3**
Zorbas **17**

59

plastic tables splashed with day-glo colors in a tie-die pattern. Its clientele ranges from congressional aides in serious suits to protesters in sloganeering T-shirts. And its menu hits all the Thai classics—curries, satays, yum salads, you name it—but Americanizes the tastes, making the sweets a bit sweeter, the hot stuff less fiery, the sour elements less tongue curling. Usually, I'd pooh pooh this sort of treatment, but here, strangely, it works. Order a satay ($5.95) and it will come with a peanut sauce so pleasingly sugary you'll be tempted to dip everything on the table in it. Go for the Pad Thai ($7.95–$9.95), and you won't need the slice of lime that usually accompanies it: The noodles are al dente and the flavors are just sour and just sweet enough to carry the dish without that usual splash of citrus. Try a spicy dish, such as a double-starred green curry ($8.95–$13), and your tongue won't fall off. Instead, you'll taste the many levels of flavor in this creamy, satisfying stew. Add to all this quick service some of the lowest prices in the area for a sit-down meal and a convenient location, and you have an excellent alternative to the bland food courts right off the Mall (at least for when you're on this end of the Mall).

$–$$$$ I have one big beef with **Sonoma Restaurant and Wine Bar** ★★ (223 Pennsylvania Ave. SE at 2nd St.; ☎ 202/544-8088; www.sonomadc.com; Metro: Capitol South; reservations recommended; AE, MC, V): There's just too darn much lying going on here! Yes, it's a sexy place, perfect for a third date, and yes, the food can be exquisite. But the staff here, otherwise upstanding citizens, I'm sure, have been trained to push customers to over-order. "Small plates," they say, calmly ignoring the Frisbee-sized platters entering the dining hall behind them, brimming with food. Turn a deaf ear to their advice—you can always order more if you're still hungry. And starting small will help you keep your budget intact. That's important, because this is a place that can get pricey quickly, if you're not careful. A well-curated wine list of more than 40 wines by the glass tempts, though it ranges well past the vino of Sonoma. And the dishes, all crafted from fresh ingredients obtained from farmers and fishermen in nearby Maryland, Virginia, and Pennsylvania (the provenance of the food is exhaustively detailed on the menu), all sound so good you'll want to order too many. Be steadfast, and know that the Jewish-Grandmother-worthy liver pâté ($6, made, oddly enough, from "Amish" chickens) is served with an ice-cream scooper, I'm guessing, and the huge mound they give you, accompanied by fine mustards and hunks of crusty bread, is big enough for two. So are the thin-crusted pizzas ($12), topped with an assortment of treats like house-made lamb sausage (an additional $4), white anchovies, or local goat cheese. Entrees top out at $27 (for steak), but you can usually order a filling meal here for half that amount, especially if you go for one of their innovative pasta dishes, which might include a pumpkiny risotto ($13) or spinach gnocchi which dazzles thanks to a rich pork belly confit ($12). Occupying a slender row house, which means a long, slim dining area, it boasts a large, stone-topped bar at which solo travelers can dine comfortably. In the warmer weather months, pick a sidewalk table and play "guess the congressperson" as dignified men and women in suits stroll by.

$$–$$$ The look at **Belga Café** ★★ (514 8th St. SE at E and G sts.; ☎ 202/544-0100; www.belgacafe.com; Metro: Eastern Market; reservations recommended; AE, MC, V) is minimalist European—small, tightly packed tables in a sleek white room, a busy open kitchen, lots of bustle—but the menu is a mix of typical Belgian dishes (lots of sauces with beer) and what the restaurant calls Eurofusion—a blend that adds Asian ingredients. Stick with the classic Belgian dishes, as they're generally more successful than the fusions. The classic *moules et frite* ($18, mussels and french fries) comes with your choice of five preparations, including white wine, blue cheese, and curry. The accompanying *frites*, boiled and then double fried, are just as crispy and moist as you get in Belgium. Another small splurge, the Waterzooi is a classic fish stew with vegetables in a savory anise cream sauce ($20). If you're lighter of appetite, a *Gerookte Zalm Waffle* ($12), basically puff pastry cushioning smoked salmon and lying on a bed of chive cream, will satisfy. The 40 varieties of beer, including some Belgian Trappist brews rarely found in the U.S., are another big draw here.

$$$–$$$$ Every cosmopolitan neighborhood should have a good French bistro, and those on Capitol Hill are lucky enough to have **Montmartre** ✿ (Capitol Hill, 327 7th St. SE at C St.; ☎ 202/544-1244; Metro: Eastern Market; reservations recommended; AE, MC, V). The waiters bustle about, barking cheerful orders to one another in French; the food is culled from the traditional French repertoire—liver, rabbit, duck—and it's not difficult to dine here for under $20, closer to $32 if you order wine with the meal. The charm quotient is high and the food is quite "correct," as they'd say in Paris, by which I mean fresh, classically prepared, and comforting if not always groundbreaking or particularly imaginative. Set in a former post office, the big plate window at front brings in too much of the D.C. street scene for you to pretend you're in Paris. Still, when the sun warms the front tables, it's quite a nice place to be; and when the candles on the tables are lit at night, and the street is dark, it can get downright romantic.

DOWNTOWN

Downtown is not a destination dinner spot. It's filled with comforting old grills and steakhouses—places where locals can drop by and visitors can hit before the curtain rises on the theaters in the area. There are a few restaurants, however, that set the bar a bit higher.

$ And one of those, believe it or not, is a chain restaurant. Okay, I know I said I wouldn't list chains but **Five Guys** ✿ 🅺 (in the Shops at National Place, 13th St. and F St. NW; ☎ Mon–Sat 11am–6pm; Metro: Federal Triangle; AE, DC, MC, V) is a hometown success story, having been founded in Arlington, Virginia, in 1986. And they do serve a mean burger, made from meat that's never frozen, with a side of fries that come only from Idaho potatoes and still have a bit of skin showing ($4.40 burger, $1.40 fries). Looking like a diner right out of the '50s, all red-and-white tile, these are not cushy restaurants, but they are friendly with high-quality, low-cost eats. And sometimes you just want a good burger. You'll find that here and at the nine other Five Guys locations around town.

$ Another local chain so beloved that I once overheard a diner saying he flew into National rather than Dulles Airport because it had a **Potbelly** 🅺 (637 Indiana Way; ☎ 202/347-2353; Mon–Fri 11am–7pm, Sat–Sun 11am–6pm; Metro: Navy Monument; AE, DC, MC, V), this sandwichery, especially at this location, can get mighty crowded. In fact, just in from the door is a sign reassuring customers that if they're standing at that point in the line, it will be only about 7 minutes until they get to place their order (unfortunately, the line often snakes out the door; they'll need another sign on the sidewalk soon!). Regular sandwiches are $4.50, smaller (or "skinny") ones are $4, and they're composed from breads baked on the premises, chicken and tuna salads made daily, and meats that are also fresh-sliced here. Salads ($5.60) are also available, if you're avoiding carbs, as are soups. Because the first Potbelly's was an antiques store that started selling sandwiches in the late '70s, each is dolled up to look like a place Lincoln could have dined—sepia-toned photos on the walls, bookshelves, wooden booths. Another Mall-handy outlet is at 409 3rd St. SW.

$ Within walking distance of Union Station, **Taqueria Nacional** ✦✦ (400 N. Capitol St. NW; ☎ 202/737-7070; www.taquerianacional.com; daily 7am–3pm; Metro: Union Station; cash only) is a Mexican mirage. A tiny takeout counter in a brightly colored shop with traditional painted tile floors, a loud toe-tapping salsa soundtrack, and an all-Hispanic counter staff, it's tucked—oddly enough—into the courtyard of a no-nonsense, glass and steel skyscraper. Grim-faced men and women in suits on their way into Fox News gaze longingly through the doors into this little slice of Acapulco. Even more improbable, the chef behind this rustic, inexpensive little joint is Anne Cashion, a James Beard Award winner. Boy, do I wish Taqueria Nacional was open for dinner—and I say that even though the only seating it has is outdoors. But its menu features some of the best tacos I've ever wolfed down—succulent, smoke-infused pork carnitas infused, spicy chorizo, fish tacos with a lovely slaw and cream sauce, chunks of tender beef. Each goes for between $1.75 and $2.95 a pop; I found two filled me up. Fresh squeezed watermelon, hibiscus and mango juices and *horchata* are the drinks in summer here; come winter, the chili-laced hot chocolate rocks.

$–$$ The four eateries above are really grab-and-go sorts of places. But you'll want to linger at **Teaism** ✦✦ (400 8th St. NW; ☎ 877/8-TEAISM [883-2476] or 638-6010; www.teaism.com; Mon–Fri 7:30am–10pm, Sat–Sun 9:30am–9pm; Metro: Navy Memorial; AE, DC, MC, V), a D.C.–based chain of tea shops with a Zen-like decor and a broad range of bites. Breakfast offerings, for example, run from the American classics like waffles and French toast ($4.75–$5.75) to such exotic fare as cilantro-scrambled tofu ($6) and my fave, naan bread with tea-cured salmon and *raita* ($8.25, a thick yogurt and spice sauce). Lunch and dinner offerings have an even more pronounced Asian pedigree—bento boxes, curries, rice and tea soups—all darn tasty and in the $6 to $8.50 range. But most of the customers come here to wind down with a pot of tea (17 varieties, $1.75–$4.25 for the really unusual ones), a pastry (the salty oat cookies, $1.95, are addictive), and a calm, pretty place to rest their feet for a spell. In addition to this outlet, Teaism has longer hours at its outlets in Dupont Circle at 2009 R St. NW near Connecticut; and right by the Farragut West Metro station at 800 Connecticut Ave. NW at H. Street.

$–$$ **Nando's Peri-Peri** ✦✦ 🧒 (1210 18th St. NW; ☎ 202/898-1225; www.nandosperiperi.com; Sun–Thurs 11:30am–10pm, Fri–Sat 11:30am–11pm; Metro: Gallery Place–Chinatown; AE, DC, MC, V) is the poster child for internationalism. It's the first American outlet of a South African chain that cooks

Belly Up to the Bar for a Big Discount

$$–$$$$ Enzo Fargione, the Turin-born chef at **Teatro Goldoni** ✩✩✩ (1909 K St. NW at 16th St. NW; ☎ 202/955-9494; www.teatrogoldoni. com; Metro: Farragut West; AE, DC, DISC, MC, V), has made a name for himself in foodie circles by serving a carpaccio of branzino in a cigar box that, when you open it, emits a puff of aromatic smoke.

You're not going to be offered anything nearly as pretentious if you sit at the bar at Teatro Goldoni. But you will get a sampling of rustic, Alpine-Italian dishes that cost about a third of what the folks who are sitting at regular tables are paying. Lunch comes in at just $14, including a glass of vino, and dinner entrees range from just $9.95 to $16. For that, you perch on stools with backs and padded seats (quite comfortable), banter with the handsome bartenders, and have a feast. How does slow-cooked pork ribs dusted with surprisingly fiery spices and sided by stewed cabbage and potatoes sound to you? I hope it sounds delish, because it certainly is. Ditto for the perfectly seared scallops, and the saffron taglierini with duck and porcini ragu. As you can see, the selections here allow diners to roam well beyond the usual Italian staples (you'll also notice that the food's a bit heartier than you're used to, as those in the Italian Alps are more likely to use lard than olive oil). And it's the perfect pretheater choice, especially as the setting here is so theatrical: With a *Carnevale* theme, the room is bedecked with vintage masks, colorful streamers, large murals, Venetian blown glass, and harlequin photos. By the way, I've tried the raw fish in a steamy box and it doesn't deserve the accolades it's getting. (I think the bar food, for the power of its flavors, beats it!)

Portuguese chicken with spices these colonial conquerors grew fond of when they ran Mozambique. How's that for provenance? A strange cafeteria-restaurant hybrid—you order and pay at the front but a waiter then brings you your food—it's a fun place to dine, the walls covered with original art, the booths woodsy and large, and the waitstaff motivated and friendly. And the birds ($6.25 for a quarter, up to $7.75 with two side dishes) are really good. Moist, succulent, and marinated with peri-peri or bird's-eye chilis, they come with a range of sauces to sample. The original peri-peri sauce is so tasty I bought several bottles to use as stocking stuffers. I recommended blending it with their creamy garlic sauce and getting the Portuguese rice and salad on the side. Wine and beer are available, as is a children's menu ($5.25); be careful with the ice cream, though—the chocolate-chili is actually quite spicy.

$–$$ I think you'll come away from dining at **Malaysia Kopitiam** ✩ (1827 M St. NW btw. 18th and 19th sts.; ☎ 202/833-6232; Metro: Farragut West; AE, MC, V) surprised that this tasty cuisine isn't more widespread in the U.S. For those who've never tried it, it has its roots in Chinese, Thai, and Indian food, and makes judicious use of coconut milk and chilis (the two even each other out; you're never

Family-Friendly Options

Visiting families flood the city in summer, and restaurants are generally quite welcoming. Some provide highchairs or booster seats on request, create children's menus, and hand over a box of crayons to keep the youngsters occupied until dinner is served.

Among the top places to take the kids:

- **Ben's Chili Bowl** (p. 71) Give the kids a lesson in civil rights history when you take them to this historic greasy spoon. Then fill their little tummies with comfort food.
- **Café Divan** (p. 77) Though the fare is somewhat exotic, the kabobs here are straightforward enough for even the pickiest eaters. And the staff is warm and quite welcoming to children.
- **The Diner** (p. 70) Here they not only give out coloring sheets and crayons, but they also post the little darling's masterpieces on the wall. And they serve well-done diner food. What more do I need to say?
- **Levi's Port Café** (p. 57) makes the list because I feel it's important for kids to get a taste of mac and cheese that hasn't come out of a box. They'll thank you for it. That and the friendly staff and low-key ambiance make this a nice place for a family meal.
- **Nando's Peri-Peri** (p. 62) Quick service, a playful decor, and a cheap kids' menu make this a top choice for parents.
- **National Museum of the American Indian's Mitsitam Café** (p. 54) Two words: fry bread, especially when covered with chocolate sauce. Kids love it, and with that as bait, you can have them try some of the other foods on the menu here (there's a standard kids' menu, too).
- **Tackle Box** (p. 78) The young'uns will love sitting at picnic tables indoors, and the grub—fried and grilled seafood, plus a hot dog for the fish-averse—should appeal.
- **Yanni's Taverna** (p. 79), the type of cheery neighborhood place where waiters will joke with your kids and the effusive owner hugs longtime customers as they enter, is perfect for an after-zoo meal. (It's a quick stroll from the gate.) The simple, yet rich Greek food is positively addictive.

going to have overly spicy food at a Malaysian restaurant). Satays and curries are its hallmarks, but most who come to this outpost go for the meal-size soups. Steaming, bowling ball-circumferenced bowls brimming with noodles, chunks of meat or fish, and aromatic spices, they're an excellent value at $7.50 to $9.50. Of the curries, the *redang* is a standout, a long-stewed mix of coconut milk, ginger, turmeric, and either beef or chicken that's extremely tender ($13–$16). Other recommended dishes include the refreshingly tart *assam tambal* shrimp ($13) in a sauce of red onions and peppers; and the massive veggie salad ($6.95), which combines seemingly unrelated foods—hard-boiled eggs, apples, lettuce, red onions, parsley, lemon grass dressing—into one harmonious heap. You eat all these delicacies in booths ringed by authentic-looking Malaysian artifacts, in a basement dining room that grows on you as you notice the care the owners have lavished on the place. Don't be deterred if there's a wait (there often is); tables turn over quite rapidly.

$$–$$$$ Though D.C. excels in the realm of ethnic foods, I'm aware that many people who go to our nation's capital are going to want to dine on classic American fare in a setting that's as historic as the city itself. **Old Ebbitt Grill** ★★ (675 15th St. NW at F St.; ☎ 202/347-4800; www.ebbitt.com; Metro: Metro Center; reservations recommended; AE, MC, V) fits the bill perfectly. Founded in 1856 (in another building, since destroyed, unfortunately), and patronized by presidents McKinley, Grant, Harding, Johnson, Cleveland, and Teddy Roosevelt (who supposedly shot some of the animals whose heads now poke out over the bar), it's the quintessential political saloon, all mahogany woods, brass fixtures, Tiffany-style lamps, and massive oil paintings. Antique gas chandeliers dangle overhead, and deep green velvet lines the booths and banquettes. And its current location, facing both the White House and the Treasury Department, ensures its legacy as a place where bills are born and bargains struck (a lot of K St. lobbyists hang here as well). Unfortunately, the current owners have decided to update the menu, killing some of their classic dishes (like crab cakes) by adding ill-conceived Asian, Cajun, or Hispanic sauces and side dishes. Your best bets here are to stick with simple, tasty fare like the roast chicken ($13), veal stew ($13), or if you're feeling flush, a strip steak ($24).

PENN QUARTER/CHINATOWN

Penn Quarter has a mixed personality. On one hand, it's a place for pub grub, catering to the pregame crowds at the Verizon Center. It also holds the city's Chinatown, a blip of a neighborhood encompassing about 2 blocks. As in all Chinatowns, it boasts a number of Asian restaurants, none of which I find worthy of singling out. However, side by side with these less-than-exciting options have sprouted, in just the last 10 years or so, a number of downright dazzling eateries. In fact, I think it's fair to say that Penn Quarter now has the greatest concentration of innovative, foodie-friendly restaurants in all of D.C.

$$–$$$ The first celebrates an obsession with one ingredient. And since that ingredient is chocolate, I heartily approve. Most everything on the menu at **Coco Sala** ★ (929 F St. NW; ☎ 202/347-4265; www.cocosala.com; Mon–Fri noon–2am, Sat 6pm–3am, Sun 11am–6pm; Metro: Metro Center or Gallery Place; AE, DC, MC, V) uses chocolate in some way, even the savory dishes. These are divided into four categories—salad, mac and cheese, surf and turf—and portions are small, because, let's face it, eat too much chocolate and you'll get sick. Still, if you're looking for a light bite, Coco Sala may well hit the spot. The mac and cheese options ($7) are as gooey as they should be and studded with niceties like fresh sage, bacon, shrimp, and jalapenos. Salads ($7–$10) pair vegetables, cheeses, and dried fruit with chocolate vinaigrettes and chocolate nibs. After eating one you'll wonder why no one considered this use for chocolate before. Of the surf and turf options, I'm a fan of the beef slider with mole sauce ($7) and the crab cakes with a chipotle chocolate tomato glaze (market price). Finish it all up with an array of, what else, chocolate desserts and perhaps a cocktail crafted from the brown stuff. And then, with all that caffeine and sugar coursing through your veins, you may decide to stay and dance. Yup, that's why the servers here are so gorgeous, the decor so curvaceous, and the lighting so sexy: Late at night Coco Sala morphs from restaurant to hip ultra lounge.

$$–$$$$ Just as happening, though without the dancing, are chef Jose Andres' two "small plate" meccas, **Zaytinya** ✪✪ (701 9th St. NW at G St.; ☎ 202/638-0800; www.zaytinya.com; Metro: Gallery Place–Chinatown; reservations recommended; AE, MC, V) and **Jaleo** ✪ (480 7th St. NW at E St.; ☎ 202/628-7949; www.jaleo.com; Metro: Archives–Navy Memorial; reservations recommended; AE, MC, V). If Andres' name sounds familiar, it's likely you're a watcher of PBS: The chef helmed a 26-episode cooking show on that network in 2008. He's also gone *mano-a-mano* with Bobby Flay on *Iron Chef America,* written several cookbooks, and at the start of his career was apprenticed to Ferran Bulia, who's credited by many with creating molecular gastronomy (and whose restaurant El Bulli is perhaps the most praised on the planet). So are this luminary chef's prices stratospheric? Surprisingly, no. Sure, you can ratchet up a big tab with small plates if you're not careful, but it's possible to have a very filling meal at either restaurant for under $20.

   Jaleo is the more traditional of the two, its decor done in the sunny yellows and aqua blues of the Mediterranean, with clichéd scenes of Spanish life (bullfights, flamenco) depicted on murals here and there. Its food is distinctly Spanish in temperament, so you might make a meal of dates wrapped in bacon ($6) followed by an Andres original like warm Brussels sprout salad with apricots and Serrano ham (a felicitous pairing for $7) or salt cod fritters ($8). The helpful thing about tapas is if you're disappointed by one, you know there are always others coming; and while I think the ones I've listed are swell, there are some sour notes on the menu (leading me to wonder if Andres, who now owns seven restaurants in D.C., and one in L.A., is getting overstretched). At **Zaytinya,** the small plates are called *Mezze,* and they feature the flavors of Greece, Lebanon, and Turkey ranging in price from about $4 to $7.50 each. Three are plenty for one person; a couple might order five to share. The sea scallops with yogurt dill sauce ($7.25) are outstanding, as are the fried mussels smothered in a smoky walnut sauce ($7). Balance the seafood dish with grilled pork, served with an orange rind sausage and a bean stew ($5.25) or a plate of Turkish-style cured beef ($4). Maybe I've been lucky, but I've found the food to be a tad more consistent here. The setting, too, is exciting: a massive, two-story space, with floor-to-ceiling windows for primo people-watching. The bar area becomes a downright torrid pickup spot at happy hour and the crowd is among the most sophisticated in D.C.

$$–$$$ Despite its name, **Matchbox** ✪ (713 H St. NW at 7th St.; ☎ 202/289-4441; www.matchboxdc.com; Metro: Gallery Place–Chinatown; AE, MC, V) is no longer the teeny restaurant it was when it debuted in 2002. The popularity of this bistro-cum-pizzeria has allowed the owners to buy the adjoining two town houses (creating the only open-air eating space, a lovely patio, in Chinatown), plus an offshoot on Capitol Hill (at 521 8th St. SE). But the look of the place still owes much to the fact that the original building was only 15 feet wide, with a tree growing through its middle. So get ready for stairs here, as the dining rooms are stacked one on top of the other, a dumbwaiter bringing the food to each level. Though the rooms are slim, they never feel cramped thanks to the smart design that plays up the exposed brick walls with chic lighting fixtures and handsome oak booths (with nice tall walls for privacy). The feeling is trendy and young, that just about describes the crowd that hangs here as well. They come, in large part, for the pizzas ($14–$20) which are thin-crusted and cooked to a perfect light char in a custom-built brick oven. But the bistro side of the menu is solid, too. The appetizer trio of three Angus beef burgers ($8) is more than sufficient for a meal, and darn tasty. The salads ($6–$14) are generous and well dressed, the crab cakes ($14) mustardy and creamy, and such specials as honey-glazed, pecan-crusted chicken served with spinach and mashed sweet potatoes ($15) are sure to hit the spot. *Note:* Don't get confused by the Chinese characters on the awning—you're in the right place. Because the restaurant is technically in Chinatown, it's required to have them to fit in stylistically with its neighbors. But there's not a wonton or spring roll in sight.

$$–$$$$ Jaleo and Zaytinya (see above) may have debuted the small plates concept in D.C., but **Proof** ✪✪✪ (775 G St. NW; ☎ 202/737-7663; Mon–Wed 11:30–2pm and 5–10pm, Thurs–Fri 11:30am–2pm and 5–11pm, Sat 5–11pm, Sun 5–9:30pm; Metro: Gallery Place; AE, DC, MC, V) has perfected it. Formally a wine bar—it takes its name from the Benjamin Franklin quote "Wine is constant proof that God loves us"—it offers 34 wines by the glass, all of them arrayed in high-tech boxes with spigots behind the bar. The wines are smartly chosen, available in tastings of 2, 4, or 6 ounces, but unlike most wine bars, the food is the star of the show here—innovative, farm fresh, and beautifully presented. Among the standouts are a squash salad with pine nuts and bacon ($9 and superb) and a dish of spicy sweetbreads ($13) accompanied by a cool julienne of apples and celery that elicited choruses of "wow!" from my dining companions when we last tried it. Even tricky octopus ($12) is coddled into tenderness and bathed in a tangy vinaigrette. Pricing on the small plates, at $8 to $13 (which includes artisanal cheese and charcuterie plates), is higher than you'll find at its competitors, so Proof may be the meal you save for a special occasion (or go for lunch which, as is often the case, is significantly cheaper). The setting surely warrants that; it's a lovely space with plush leather banquettes, a jazz soundtrack, and monitors instead of paintings above the bar that show a rotating roster of portraits from the National Portrait Gallery (which is right across the street).

$$–$$$$ Okay, I wouldn't say I'm a groupie for Mexican chef Richard Sandoval, but whenever I head into a city that boasts one of this prolific restaurateur's places, I make a breadline, er beeline, for it. Each one is different, but they share one common strand: an egalitarian menu. Hidden among the higher-priced entrees are always several bargain dishes, and oddly enough, they often prove to be the tastiest fare. That's certainly true at **Zengo** ✪✪✪ (781 7th St. NW; ☎ 202/393-2929; www.modernmexican.com; Sun–Thurs 5–10pm, Fri–Sat 5–11:30pm; Metro: Gallery Place–Chinatown; AE, DISC, MC, V), where the Carnitas Rice Noodles ($12) is a star dish, a sinful mélange of long Asian noodles, soft-boiled egg, oh-so-tender pork shoulder, and hot-and-sour sauce that create a dish that's beyond rich—it's the Midas of noodle dishes. I also swoon for the meal-size "Give 'N Take Chicken Salad" ($10), a crispy mix of chicken, candied pecans, fine lettuces, and cabbage, lightly tossed in a zesty ginger and *piloncillo* (an unrefined Mexican brown sugar) dressing. And folks who like to try several smaller plates can easily make an affordable meal, mixing some won ton tacos (nearly raw ahi tuna with sushi rice, mango, and ginger, $11) with a heaping plate of *edamame* ($4). As you might have noticed, the menu jumps continents, combining the flavors, ingredients, and recipes of Latin America with those of Asia. The decor also has a jet-setting appeal, a chi-chi lounge with those perfect-for-canoodling low leather couches below; and its mod brown and orange dining room, its huge windows overlooking the bustling street. The only odd touch is the huge mobile that hangs above the staircase and looks like, well, flying potatoes (wait until you see it). Ah well, no place is perfect, but this one comes close.

$$$–$$$$ We finish our parade of trendy Penn Quarter restaurants with an Indian joint that may make you rethink everything you thought you knew about that cuisine. **Rasika** ✰✰✰ (633 D St. NW at 7th St.; ☎ 202/637-1222; www.rasikarestaurant.com; Mon–Thurs 11:30am–2:30pm and 5:30–10:30pm, Fri 11:30am–2:30pm and 5:30–11pm, Sat 5–11pm; Metro: Archives–Navy Memorial–Penn Quarter; reservations recommended; AE, MC, V)—its name means "flavors" in Sanskrit—quite simply ups the ante. I've had friends who've told me the black cod with cream and vinegar ($25) is the finest fish dish they've ever had. The *palaak chaat* ($8), which features fried spinach, is a lesson on how opulent salad can be, and the *tawa bangain* ($8), eggplant and potatoes with peanut sauce, can be described, truly without hyperbole, as a parade in your mouth. Chef/owner and Bombay expat Vikram Sunderam has also taken great pains to create a comfortable dining area. Furnished with ropes of ruby-colored glass, restrained pieces of Indian art, and streamlined banquettes and tables, it's easy on the eyes and back. Service can't be faulted either; there are a lot of items that need explaining on this menu, and the staff make you feel like they have all the time in the world to help you. I guess you can tell I really like this place. Rasika is located next to **Woolly Mammoth** (p. 244), so many go for its pretheater menu: three courses for $30 (a great buy). *Note:* Though it can be difficult to get a reservation here, the complete menu is also served in the lounge, and there's rarely a wait to eat there (though some folks will find the backless stools a bit uncomfortable).

DUPONT CIRCLE

One of Washington's most popular nightlife areas, Dupont Circle buzzes with cafes, boites, and bistros of all stripes. Attracting a crowd primarily in its 30s through 50s, including many gay men and women (much of Washington's gay nightlife is centered in this area), the scene has a European flair, especially in the warmer months, as crowds stroll from one outdoor cafe to another. Along with the restaurants included below, you'll enjoy tasty, affordable meals at **Thai Tanic** (1326 14th St. NW at Rhode Island Ave.; ☎ 202/588-1795; Metro: Dupont Circle; AE, MC, V), which, despite its silly name, serves quality Thai food in an airy space; and **Bistro du Coin** (1738 Connecticut Ave. NW; ☎ 202/234-6969; www.bistro ducoin.com; Metro: Dupont Circle; AE, MC, V), an oh-so-Gallic eatery. And don't forget **Teaism** (p. 62), which is also in this 'hood.

$ Every budget-conscious guide needs at least one no-fuss quick and cheap eatery where a tasty, filling meal is the cook's priority. My choice, with two Washington locations, is **Moby Dick House of Kabob** (1300 Connecticut Ave. NW at N St.; ☎ 202/833-9788; www.mobysonline.com; Mon–Thurs and Sat 11am–10pm, Fri 11am–11pm; Metro: Farragut North; and in Georgetown, 1070 31st St. NW at M St.; ☎ 202/333-4400; Metrobus: 30, 32, 34, 35, 36; MC, V). A carryout place, Moby invariably is on every "best cheap eats" list in the city. The Georgetown location is a cramped hole in the wall with tight seating. The downtown outlet is larger and has more appealing tables, including outdoor seating. Your kabobs come served on a paper plate, but they are well marinated and cooked carefully on an open grill. The pita bread is made in Moby's traditional clay oven. Sandwiches start at $6, kabob plates of lamb, ground sirloin, chicken, fish, and beef tenderloin are priced at $8 to $13 for the "super combo" (big enough for several diners). All come with rice and a chopped cucumber and tomato salad.

$–$$ Come spring and summer there are few nicer places to lounge in the sun than the outdoor patio at Zorba's ✪ (1612 20th St. at Connecticut; ☎ 202/387-8555; www.zorbascafe.com; Mon–Sat 11am–11:30pm, Sun 11am–10:30pm; Metro: Dupont Circle; AE, DC, MC, V). Set just off the main thoroughfare, it's far enough out of the hustle and bustle to be relaxing, but close enough in for great people-watching. And because there are no waiters—guests order their food at the back and then simply carry it to their tables—no one throws you evil glances if you linger too long. I like Zorba's in the winter months, too, when the bright blue-and-white decor, with its painted tiles, hanging copper pots, and of course multiple photos of a grinning Anthony Quinn as Zorba, does a very good job of channeling the Mediterranean warmth. The food is sunny too, Greek (of course) and quite toothsome, whether you go for the crisp gyro ($7.95 sandwich, $12 platter), or the lemony kabobs ($7.95–$13), both of which are sided by a yogurt sauce garlicky enough to daze a vampire. The only disappointment: bland hummus.

$–$$ I won't get into that perpetual parlor game of which restaurant has D.C.'s best pizza; there are just too many good contenders right now (see Matchbox, p. 66 for another). For those who *do* play this game, **Pizzeria Paradiso** ✪ (2029 P St. NW at 20th St.; ☎ 202/223-1245; www.eatyourpizza.com; Mon–Thurs 11:30am–11pm, Fri–Sat 11am–midnight, Sun noon–10pm; Metro: Dupont Circle; and also in Georgetown, 3282 M St. NW at 32nd St.; ☎ 202/337-1245; Metrobus: 30, 32, 34, 35, 36; AE, MC, V), remains a favorite. I think it's because they get the basics right. The crust is cooked to a nice yin-yang of crisp and chewy in a wood-fired oven. The sauce it uses isn't the usual puréed mush, but comes studded with chunks of tomato. And both locations (Georgetown more so) offer microbrews to wash the 'za down. Pies cost $9.95 to $12 for a 9-inch pizza and $17 to $19 for a 12-incher (two people can share the smaller one, up to four for the larger version). Thirty-seven toppings—fresh sliced tomatoes, pine nuts, pesto, buffalo mozzarella, mussels, you name it—are $1.25 to $2.35 each. The Dupont Circle branch, occupying a row house, is tiny, so you may have to wait awhile outside for a table. Considerably more spacious, the newer Georgetown branch looks out onto the pulsating M Street scene.

ADAMS MORGAN

This is the prime neighborhood for ethnic dining at inexpensive to moderate prices. Be sure you're dining at a place where the focus is on food, not liquor. This "party hearty" neighborhood features a number of bars that have added food as an afterthought, and the quality at these places, not surprisingly, can be dismal.

$ No alcohol is served at **Amsterdam** ✪✪✪ (2425 18th St. NW; ☎ 202/234-1969; Sun–Mon 11am–midnight, Tues–Wed 11am–2:30am, Thurs 11am–3am, Fri–Sat 11am–4am; Metro: Woodley Park–Zoo–Adams Morgan and 10-min. walk; cash only), though you may smell it on its patrons' breath. In the last 5 years, it's become *the* refueling stop for the neighborhood's barhoppers. The reason for its line-out-the-door popularity: perfectly executed, made-to-order falafel ($4.95–$6.95), and an extraordinary collection of toppings to crown your sandwich with. In all, there are 20 toppings—pickled beets, chickpeas, three types of hot sauce, yogurt, baba ganouj, Israeli salad, grilled eggplant, and on and on—and they're so good, Amsterdam's owners had to stop serving their falafels on plates, because diners were going back to the condiment bar and using it as a salad bar. Today, you're handed your sandwich wrapped in paper, perhaps accompanied by a cup of equally superb french fries (double-fried as they do in Europe, $3–$4). No need to order the larger portions; the smaller ones are huge and you want to save room for a house brownie for $3 (they joke that despite their name, *these* brownies are perfectly legal). The first time I visited here, I ended up scribbling just one word on my notepad when I bit into my first loaded-up falafel: "genius." It's my favorite place to chow down in this 'hood, despite the fact there's never enough seating in the cramped dining room or at the table out front. No matter. I'm hoping against hope that the owners take this winning formula and franchise elsewhere. I'd love to be able to get these killer falafels in my hometown.

$–$$ I love that in our nation's capital, that most American of eateries, the **Diner** ✪ (kids) (2453 18th St. NW at Columbia Rd.; ☎ 202/232-8800; www.dinerdc.com; Metro: Woodley Park–Zoo–Adams Morgan and 10-min. walk; MC, V), evokes the Declaration of Independence on its menu. "We hold these truths to be self evident, that all men and women are born with equal appetites," it reads, going on to state that its customers have "the right to eat in D.C. without breaking the bank." Amen to that! And the Diner delivers on its promise, serving up expertly prepared American classics—burgers, meatloaf, pancakes, a Thanksgiving platter with mashed potatoes and green beans—and never charging more than $15 for a dish, usually closer to $9. The restaurant itself is an airy space, a former auto parts store, with high, pressed-tin ceilings, the requisite long tile counter, and wooden booths. A look straight from the 1950s but supersized. Big windows open onto the bustle of 18th Street, adding to the festive buzz. As at most diners, there's a solid kid's menu ($5–$7); they cater further to the young ones by giving them coloring sheets and crayons and then posting the resulting masterpieces on the walls. At dinner and weekend brunch, the Diner draws big crowds, so be prepared for a wait if you come then.

$–$$$ **Mixtec** ✪ (1792 Columbia Rd. NW at 18th St.; ☎ 202/332-1011; Sun–Thurs 10am–10pm, Fri–Sat 10am–11pm; Metro: Woodley Park–Zoo–Adams Morgan and 10-min. walk; MC, V) is the sort of place you are likely to find on a street corner in Mexico City. The white-tiled walls, striped in red and green, provide minimal decoration, and tables are squeezed between the soft drink refrigerators. Piped mariachi tunes serenade, and you can see the cooks at work in the open kitchen. But this tiny eatery serves not only authentic regional Mexican dishes but also darn fine Tex-Mex, both at an affordable price (entrees range from just $5 to a high of $15). A house specialty, the rice and beans plate served with a beef and pork taco, is basic but tasty ($10). Also highly recommended is the *pescado* Acapulco ($15), shrimp sautéed in a sauce of fresh garlic, lime, and white wine. The Mexican sub sandwiches called *tortas* ($7.50)—grilled pork and guacamole with salsa—also make a filling and satisfying dinner.

$-$$$ Don't be put off by the drab exterior of **Joyti Indian Cuisine** ✪ (2433 18th St. NW at Columbia Rd.; ☎ 202/518-5892; Metro: Woodley Park–Zoo–Adams Morgan and 10-min. walk; MC, V). Inside, the look is quite spiffy, all tidy and trim and inviting. As Adams Morgan residents have discovered, the food is also appealing—not as inventive as Rasika (see above), but solid, tasty stuff. The extensive menu ($11–$17 per entree) reflects the many cuisines of India. From the south, lamb *nilgri korma* ($15), pieces of lamb cooked with cilantro, is a specialty. From the north, try lamb *saag* ($14), a lamb cooked in gently spiced spinach. Both are excellent, as is the Goan fish curry ($14).

$$-$$$ Though "Mama" is no longer reading the coffee grounds of her customers (she passed away in the early '90s), **Mama Ayesha's Restaurant** ✪✪ (1967 Calvert St. at Duke Ellington Memorial Bridge; ☎ 202/232-5431; www.mama ayeshas.com; Metro: Woodley Park–Zoo–Adams Morgan; AE, MC, V) still has a friendly exoticism that charms guests. The recently refurbished dining room sets a romantic mood with Middle Eastern tunes, ornate metal lanterns, splashing waterfalls, and colorful wall hangings. Entrees ($11–$19) include many excellent stews and stuffed dishes that will come as a surprise to those who think that Middle Eastern food begins and ends with kabobs. Try the squash stuffed with ground lamb and aromatic spices ($15) or the garlic-lemon chicken stew ($13), and you'll see what I mean. And of course, the kabobs are spot-on, cooked to your specifications in a charcoal oven. Today, the nephews and great-nephews of Mama Ayesha proudly continue her tradition of hospitality.

U STREET CORRIDOR

Soul and Ethiopian cuisine are the headliners in this neighborhood, and they make a good foil for the hopping bar scene here. Please note that U intersects with 14th Street, which also has some excellent eating options; see p. 73 for more of those.

$-$$ **Ben's Chili Bowl** ✪✪ (1213 U St. NW at 13th St.; ☎ 202/667-0909; www.benschilibowl.com; Metro: U Street–African-American Civil War Memorial–Cardozo; MC, V) has been Washington's legendary greasy spoon since 1958, a seedy-looking, cramped lunch-counter kind of place that serves nothing (well, almost nothing) good for you. Everybody goes there—especially local politicians who want to look like everyday folks—and so should you, though maybe not for dinner—the place is best for lunch, a midnight pick-me-up, or even breakfast. A chili dog smothered in onions and Ben's spicy homemade chili sauce is $3.25; a

Eat Your Heart Out at a Soul Food Buffet

$ For home-cooked soul food in a historically African-American neigh-
borhood, don't miss the **Saint's Paradise Cafeteria** ✰✰ (Shaw, 601-A M
St. NW btw. 6th and 7th sts.; ☎ 202/789-2289; Metro: Mount Vernon
Square-7th Street/Convention Center; Mon–Fri 7am–7pm, Sat–Sun
8am–6pm; cash only). Go for lunch or dinner to this find. It dishes up
crispy fried chicken, beef short ribs, pigs' feet, chitterlings, corn bread,
and much more every day of the week—and every heaping plate costs less
than $10. A Shaw neighborhood haven for budget diners for more than 4
decades, the cafeteria is operated by the United House of Prayer for All
People, a huge, sprawling church with a massive gold dome. Drawing as
many as 500 diners a day—breakfast, lunch, and dinner—it's a favorite
with the staff of nearby Howard University Hospital, neighborhood school
teachers, Washington police and firefighters, judges and lawyers from the
nearby courthouses, and conventioneers attending the Washington
Convention Center a half-block away. This is a chance to see another
Washington, well away from the Mall and entertainment centers.

chili half-smoked sausage on a bun, $4.55. Vegetarian chili and veggie and turkey
burgers are for those who don't eat red meat. Whatever you choose, you will be
hard-pressed to spend much more than $10. At that price, you get history, too.
During the 1968 riots that hit the neighborhood after the assassination of the Rev.
Dr. Martin Luther King, the cafe got permission to stay open after curfew to serve
firefighters, public workers, and activists trying to quell the turmoil. In 1985, Bill
Cosby staged a press conference at Ben's to celebrate his number-one-rated show.
A sign behind the counter celebrating that event has just been updated to read
BILL COSBY AND THE OBAMA FAMILY EAT FREE AT BEN'S. In the early days, when
U Street was known as the Black Broadway, the "Bowl's" counter served Duke
Ellington, Ella Fitzgerald, Nat King Cole, Miles Davis, and Dr. King. It still draws
top city officials and touring celebrities. If you go for breakfast (6–11am), a basic
platter—two eggs, bacon, biscuit, grits or fried potatoes—is $6.

$–$$ Bookstore, cafe, restaurant, and epicenter of the coming revolution! That
just about describes **Busboys and Poets** ✰ (2021 14th St. NW btw. U and V;
☎ 202/387-7638; www.busboysandpoets.com; Mon–Thurs 8am–midnight, Fri
8am–2am, Sat 9am–2am, Sun 9am–midnight; Metro: U Street), a restaurant you
visit as much for its mixed local crowd, its crowded events calendar, and its hip
vibe (Langston Hughes poetry on the menu) as you do for its food. Don't get me
wrong: The food is tasty and well made, a roster of American favorites from sandwiches to burgers to pizza to salads ($6.95–$11), plus a few more complete
entrees that no one ever seems to order. But what makes this place special is the
even-more-amped-than-usual political chatter at the tables, the poetry slams
and open discussions (every Sun night the topic is race; other nights you might

discuss foreign relations, poverty, or global warming). Owned by activist Andy Shallal, it really is an extraordinary melding of community center and eatery.

$$-$$$ Neither a dentist's office nor a brothel, **Oohhs and Aahhs** ★ (1005 U St. NW at 10th St.; ☎ 202/667-7142; Mon–Thurs noon–11pm, Fri–Sat noon–3am, Sun noon–8pm Metro: U Street–African-American Civil War Memorial–Cardozo; MC, V)—get it?—serves up some of the best Southern cooking in the city. Yes, it gets stiff competition from Levi's Port Cafe in Navy Yard, but it's far more convenient for most visitors and has some potent dishes in its arsenal. You may very well "ooh" over the crispness of the fried chicken ($12) and "ahh" over the nonbitter collard greens (not to mention corn bread so sweet you can feel the cavities forming). While not as dirt-cheap as its somewhat grungy looks would lead you to expect—entrees range from $11 to $25—portions are large and they have no qualms with patrons sharing food. Don't try and dine at the cramped counter where you enter; upstairs is a large room that's no better looking—its orange and blue walls, mismatched furniture, and blaring TV suggest they hired a college freshman as the decorator—but it's more spacious and reasonably comfortable.

LOGAN CIRCLE/14TH STREET

The locale of a condominium apartment boom, the neighborhood has recently sprouted a number of stylish but reasonably priced restaurants to serve the new urbanites. Expect happening restaurants, newly relocated galleries, and cute boutiques for a hipster crowd who like their choices well edited.

$–$$ And all of those urbanites are ordering in from, though not necessarily eating at, the **Great Wall of China** ★★ (1527 14th St. NW; ☎ 202/797-8888; Sun–Thurs 11am–10pm, Fri–Sat 11am–10:30pm; Metro: Dupont Circle; AE, MC, V). They're ordering in because, to be frank, this one ain't a looker. Florescent lights, metal chairs, plastic forks, a TV blaring Asian kung fu films—these are the elements that make up its anti-ambiance. But the food knocks the chopsticks off any joint in Chinatown, and most of the Chinese restaurants in D.C.'s metropolitan area for that matter. Particularly notable are the "Ma Le" selections from the Szechuan region of China, which pair unusual, flavorful peppers with chicken, shrimp, pork, tofu, or beef. I particularly like the double-cooked pork *ma le* ($11), which uses strips of bacon-like meat and fermented beans. Also tongue-worthy are the *ma le po* Tofu ($8.95) and the refreshingly cool yet fiery *ma le* cold noodles ($4.95).

$ After you've finished your plates of fiery fare at Great Wall, you may want to cool your tongue off at **Artfully Chocolate/Kingsbury Confections** ★★ (1529 14th St. NW; ☎ 202/387-COCO [2626]; www.kingsburychocolates.com; Sun 9am–9pm, Mon–Wed 10am–9pm, Thurs 10am–10pm, Fri 10am–11pm, Sat 9am–11pm; Metro: Dupont Circle; AE, MC, V), a chocolate emporium *par extraordinaire.* Case in point: The owners had the genius to pair Brie cheese with chocolate in a truffle. Beside the small counter selling house-made chocolates is the city's first "Cocoa bar," an art-laden cafe where people sip and munch different forms of chocolate as they peck away at their laptops or catch up with buddies. If

Finger Licking Good (Literally): D.C.'s Superb Ethiopian Restaurants

A recent *USA Today* article guesstimated that 200,000 Ethiopian émigrés live in the D.C. area, making it the largest Ethiopian community in the world outside of Africa. Ethiopian food has become a defining local cuisine, much as barbecue is in Memphis and salmon dishes are in Seattle.

For those who've never tried it, it's a true culinary adventure. Long-simmering stews of lamb or chicken, beef meatballs (called *keftas*) and grilled beef dishes *(tibs)* are dusted with a slow-burning spice mix called *berbere*, giving many dishes an eye-opening wallop. Onion, ginger, and cinnamon, important supporting characters, lend sweetness and depth of flavor. And because the Orthodox Ethiopian religious calendar requires numerous days be set aside for meat-free fasts, lentils, collard greens, potatoes, and other vegetables are the focus of a number of dishes, making this an excellent cuisine for vegetarians.

Most fun of all, Ethiopian cuisine banishes the fork. Instead, your dishes are served on a pizza-sized round of *injera*, a winningly sour, spongy bread, that diners use to scoop up their meals.

Platters are meant to be shared and usually come to just about $7 to $11 per person.

Most of the city's Ethiopian restaurants today sit along an eastern stretch of U Street with a number of others right off U on 9th Street. Below are my picks for the best of the best, plus a smattering of options in other areas of the city.

- **$–$$ Etete** ★★ (U St. Corridor, 1942 9th St. NW at U St.; ☎ 202/232-7600; www.eteterestaurant.com; Metro: U Street–African-American Civil War Memorial–Cardozo; MC, V). A narrow, corridor-like space seating only about 30, with exposed brick walls and pillow-covered banquettes, Etete looks like a hip American cafe. But you still dine the traditional way, scooping up bites of dinner with torn pieces of the *injera*. Here, however, the bread's a bit thinner than you'll find at other Ethiopian restaurants, which might be good for those who find the texture off-putting. And that's just the beginning of the innovations; the *doro wat* stew is made with a dash of cognac and the spicy dishes aren't quite as fiery as expected.

- **$–$$$ Dukem Restaurant** ★★★ (114–118 U St. at 12th St. NW; ☎ 202/667-8735; www.dukemrestaurant.com; daily 11am–2am; Metro: U Street–African American Civil War Memorial–Cardozo; AE, MC, V). Much larger and so popular it's spawned an offshoot deli next door and a second restaurant in Baltimore, Dukem is the Ethiopian equivalent of a dinner theater. Every night but Tuesday, singers and dancers take to the center of the restaurant in traditional costumes to put on a lively show; weekday afternoons, diners can stop by for a traditional Ethiopian coffee ceremony. It's much less hokey than it sounds, and since the cost of dining there during a show is just one measly dollar more than usual, this may qualify as one of the best values in D.C. So do they do the show to keep your mind off the food? Not at all, it's top-notch, especially the *kifto* ($10), steak tartare that's kicked up a notch with the addition of cardamom, an Ethiopian cheese, and a blend of tongue-searing spices; and the vegetarian combination ($9.50), which includes the most flavorful collard greens I've had anywhere.

◆ **Queen Makeda** ✪ (1917 9th St. NW right off U St.; ☎ 202/232-5665; daily 11am–1am; Metro: U Street–African American Civil War Memorial–Cardozo; AE, MC, V). Vegetarians are also well catered to at this two-story eatery, across the street from Etete. In particular, there's a dish here they described to me as being "chick beans" that was so hearty it tasted like a meat stew (but wasn't). Patrons here are mostly from Africa, giving it a clubhouse vibe. Diners hop from table to table, greeting one another, grooving to the reggae sound-track or even dashing behind the bar for a drink (slapping down some money there as payment). By the end of the evening, you'll likely be invited over for a drink, too. It's that kind of place.

◆ **Lalibela Restaurant** ✪✪ (1415 14th St. NW at P St.; ☎ 202/265-5700; daily 9am–11pm; Metro: McPherson Square; MC, V). I was the only woman customer in the place the first time I lunched at Lalibela. Wondering if women were welcome, I timidly asked the waitress if I could stay. She burst out laughing and explained that this was where all the Ethiopian taxi drivers eat (and none of them are female). And you know that old rule about popular truck stops having good eats? Well, it works for "taxi stops," too. Sure, the setting is diner-like, but the food is perhaps the most authentic of any I've listed here, the spices spicier, the citrus notes more sour, the honeyed wine puckerishly sweet. Besides, it's *never* a problem catching a cab when you dine here.

◆ **Meskerem** ✪ (2434 18th St. NW; ☎ 202/462-4100; www.mesekerem online.com; Mon–Thurs 11am–midnight, Fri–Sat 11am–2am; Metro: Woodley Park and then a 10-min. walk; AE, MC, V). Adams Morgan's old standby, it's probably the handsomest of the Ethiopian restaurants with two airy floors; one has western tables, but you should choose to sit at the low African stools instead (more fun). While the flavors of the food aren't quite as deep as at Lalibela or Dukem, I think you'll still quite enjoy the food here. Again, it's another good "starter" restaurant.

you want something substantial, the cheese and chocolate plate ($7.95; are you seeing a pattern here?) is quite lovely, as is the Aztec brownie sundae, which infuses chilis into the chocolate sauce ($7). Just want a sip of something? Go for the hot chocolate sampler ($7.75; your choice of three different kinds) or one of their gourmet coffees or frappes ($1.50–$4.75).

$–$$ As jammed as Great Wall is quiet and as much bar as restaurant, **Bar Pilar** ✮✮ (1833 14th St. NW; ☎ 202/265-1751; www.barpilar.com; daily 5pm–3am; Metro: U Street–African-American Civil War Memorial–Cardozo; AE, DC, MC, V) is an offshoot of Café Saint Ex down the street. Oddly enough, I think the food's more exciting here, even though the place is usually crammed elbow-to-elbow with drinkers and there are few tables at which you can actually sit down and eat the stuff. But if you can manage to get here early, before the crowds arrive, grab a bar stool at the long copper-topped bar and tuck into some seriously gourmet, but well-priced, small plates. Examples: lentils smartly paired with slices of apricot ($5); prime rib sandwich with truffle oil ($9); or the "why hasn't anyone ever thought of this before?" teaming of artichoke hearts with cured ham ($6). The menu changes nightly, so you never know what you're going to get beyond great grub, expertly mixed cocktails, and a hang with a cool, young crowd.

$$–$$$ If you're used to sweet, somewhat gloppy Thai food, get ready to shift your perspective at **Rice** ✮✮ (1608 14th St. NW at Q St.; ☎ 202/234-2400; www.ricerestaurant.com; Metro: McPherson Square; reservations not accepted; AE, MC, V). True, the majority of dishes on the menu are more "fusion" than traditional, but if you go for the "Authentic Thai" selections you'll find that though you recognize the names of the dishes—Pad Thai, Massaman curry, and so on—the flavors will be brighter, cleaner, and often *much* more spicy than usual. In fact, if you don't like fiery fare, steer well clear of those marked with a red pepper—they'll sear your tongue off. I'd suggest ordering one of the classics and then pairing it with a dish that can be found only here; a specialty is different sorts of meats, fish, and vegetables that are subtly infused with green tea. Maybe it's my imagination, but I always feel a bit more awake after I've munched on one of these; I particularly recommend the robust seared pork with tea leaves that comes slathered in a gravy so rich it tastes like it has a burgundy-wine base though it's actually made with sake ($15). Most entrees average between $14 and $16 and can easily make a meal; those with big appetites might want to add an appetizer, such as the excellent shrimp salad ($8), a yin-yang toss of shrimp with coconut and grapefruit slices, which sounds weird but works like gangbusters. One warning: Although the special "ginger" menu reads well, the ginger can be overpowering. Save this one for a special occasion. It's much chicer than your average Thai joint, each table graced with a live lotus blossom stuck jauntily in what looks like an old-fashioned inkstand.

$$–$$$$ The restaurant Tosca consistently wins a place on local "Best Of" lists for Italian food. Problem is, Tosca has prices as operatic as its name, which is why I was so pleased to hear it had birthed a lower-priced offspring. The "baby" **Posto** ✮✮✮ (1515 14th St. NW; ☎ 202/332-8613; www.postodc.com; Mon-Thurs 5:30–10:30pm, Fri–Sat 5:30–11:30pm, Sun 5–10pm; Metro: McPherson

Square; AE, DC, MC, V) is an exciting place, set in an open, high-ceilinged space that bustles with some of the most attractive people in Washington. All white, with lightboxes of vineyard scenes giving it a touch of warmth, it just feels like the place to be. Which may be the problem: Everyone wants a table, and Posto doesn't take reservations, so there's often a crush of diners waiting at the bar. Of course, you *can* dine at the bar, which features a long, communal butcher-block table. But I think that food of this quality is worth waiting to sit down comfortably for. It's an authentic take on Italian food, crafted from organic and locally sourced ingredients, and just as polished as the decor. If you want to get out without too badly denting your wallet, you can go for a pizza ($11–$14), though my favorites on the menu are the pasta dishes ($15–$17)—if it's on the menu, the cavatelli with arugula pesto and olives is quite literally spring on a plate: light, delightfully green, and toothsome. And don't skip dessert or think you have to stick with the gelato; this is that rare Italian restaurant where the desserts are as good as the mains.

GEORGETOWN (AND GLOVER PARK, RIGHT NEXT DOOR)

Along with the restaurants recommended below are two budget greats that I feature in the Dupont Circle section, but also have branches here: **Moby** (p. 69) and **Pizzeria Paradiso** (p. 69). Like many restaurants in this neighborhood, they cater to Georgetown's large (and hungry and broke) student population. But a number of extremely well-heeled Washingtonians call this neighborhood home. For them, elegant and expensive eateries conspire to make Georgetown a gourmand's treat.

$–$$$$ You can smell the spices as you step in the door of **Café Divan** ★ 🧒 (Upper Georgetown, 1834 Wisconsin Ave. NW at 34th St.; ☎ 202/338-1747; www.cafedivan.com; Metrobus: 30, 32, 34, 35, 36; AE, MC, V). That's about the only clue you'll have that this isn't another classy American bistro. (The decor, with its sleek furnishings and large showroom windows wrapping the restaurant on three sides, gives that wrong impression.) No, here you'll be dining on Turkish cuisine and at prices much more modest than the setting would suggest. Order anything that comes with the thick, creamy yogurt sauce and you'll be really happy; it truly elevates all the dishes it graces (and it's used in chicken, vegetarian, and lamb dishes, $11–$14). Beyond those entrees, all of the typical Turkish spreads—hummus, tarama, casik—are excellent and a good value at $4.50 ($5.95 for a mix-and-match plate of a number of appetizers that can easily feed three; and the kabobs ($7.25–$15) are grilled in a wood-burning oven (ask for a table away from the cooking area as it can get a tad toasty). This is a particularly good place to bring children as the waitstaff go out of their way to make them feel at home; and the food is simple enough for even the pickiest of eaters.

$$–$$$$ **Leopold's Kafe & Konditorei** ★★ (Georgetown, 3315 Cady's Alley NW behind 3318 M St. at 33rd; ☎ 202/965-6005; www.kafeleopolds.com; Metrobus: 30, 32, 34, 35, 36; AE, MC, V) is another restaurant that's a bit hard to place when you first walk in. In looks, it's vanguard Europe—white tables, sleek lines, the waitstaff dressed in black. The food, however, is all Austrian, traditional but with modern touches. That is, it tends to be lighter, without so many of the heavy sauces you get in Vienna's old restaurants. Still, you'll do well to concentrate on the Austrian classics such as the veal schnitzel ($22), a large but thinly sliced veal scallop, dipped in flour, beaten eggs, and bread crumbs and then sautéed. A slice of lemon and capers gives it its famous tang. I'll also steer you toward the bratwurst, topped with an unusual but tasty celery sauerkraut ($17). The desserts are lovely to look at but pricey; the baked chocolate mousse with hazelnut ice cream is $9. In fair weather, courtyard tables are the place to sit. They look onto Cady's Alley, a narrow lane lined by classy home-furnishing shops.

$$–$$$$ When John F. Kennedy was courting Jackie, he took her to **Martin's Tavern** ✫✫✫ (Georgetown, 1264 Wisconsin Ave. NW at N St.; ☎ 202/333-7370; www.martins-tavern.com; Metrobus: 30, 32, 34, 35, 36, or the K Street Circulator bus; reservations recommended; AE, MC, V). And today it remains *the* Georgetown spot for a first-rate, really traditional American meal. Martin's debuted in 1933 the day after Prohibition ended, and today it is run by the fourth generation of Martins. They haven't changed it much—hardwood booths, Tiffany-style lamps, and an 18-seat mahogany bar give the joint an old-fashioned warmth. It's usually full, and half the customers are regulars. Much of the staff has been around for years; they serve with efficiency and a one-of-the-family manner. The menu offers a variety of American foods, but I tend to go for the very traditional "tavern specialties" such as the Hot Brown ($11), a broiled, open-faced sandwich consisting of roasted turkey doused in rarebit sauce and topped with tomato, bacon, and Parmesan cheese. Comfy food, well prepared—and, who knows, another president-to-be may be sitting at the next table?

$$–$$$$ An offshoot of the costlier fish restaurant Hook next door, **Tackle Box** ✫✫✫ 🄺 (3245 M St. NW; ☎ 202/337-TBOX [8269]; www.tacklebox restaurant.com; Metrobus: 30, 32, 34, 35, 36; daily 11am–11pm; AE, DC, MC, V), is Washington's answer to the Maine lobster shack. Nets and buoys line its walls, diners sit at picnic tables (indoors though), and the grub here is fresh but cheap. A "Maine Meal" goes for just $13 and includes wood-grilled or fried seafood—anything from rainbow trout, bluefish, or tilapia to oysters, clams, shrimp, and bay scallops on the fried side—plus two side dishes and one sauce. It's a heckuva deal for finny food of this level and expertly cooked. The sauces, in particular the basil-walnut pesto, add just the right touch. And what would a lobster shack be without lobster rolls, right? That's the splurge, going for $19 with the house fries; in the same vein, but cheaper, are clam ($12) and shrimp ($9) rolls—yum!

$$–$$$$ **Old Europe** ✫ (Glover Park, 2434 Wisconsin Ave. NW at Calvert St.; ☎ 202/333-7600; www.old-europe.com; Metrobus: 30, 32, 34, 35, 36; reservations recommended; lunch: Sun 1–3:30pm, Tues–Sat 11:30am–3pm; dinner Sun 4–7:45pm, Tues–Thurs 5–8:45pm, Fri–Sat, 5–9:45pm; closed Mon; AE, MC, V) is schmaltzy, but that's part of its charm, and after all, it's been a Washington fixture for more than 6 decades. For old-style German dishes, this is the place to go. The setting is a traditional-looking German rathskeller; the menu is just as traditional. Sauerbraten ($18)—sweet and sour marinated slices of braised beef served with

If You Happen to be in Cleveland Park or the Palisades . . .

$–$$$ Yanni's Taverna ★ 🛢 (3500 Connecticut Ave. NW; ☎ 202/362-8871; www.yannisgreektaverna.us; Mon–Sat 11:30am–3pm and 5–11pm, Sun 11:30am–11pm; Metro: Cleveland Park; AE, DISC, MC, V) is perfect for an after-zoo meal as it's a quick stroll from the gate. Yanni's is the type of cheery neighborhood place where the waiters will joke with your kids and the owner hugs longtime customers as they enter. But even if you're new to it, you're sure to be impressed not only by the friendly service but also by the tasty food. Serving Greek food at its very richest (the *tzatziki* is as dense and creamy as crème brulée), it hits all the usual standards—souvlaki, moussaka, Greek salad—but does them all with precision and, yes, artistry. Special mentions must go to the addictive *skordalia* ($4.95), a cloud-light whip of potatoes and garlic; the moist chicken *souvlaki* ($7.95–$11, depending on sides); and the *pastistio* ($9.95), a rich "lasagna" of meat and pasta with a smooth béchamel sauce. But what I dream about when I'm away from Washington is Yanni's gyro ($7.95–$11), which has a smoky toast to it, and a spot-on blend of spices that keeps me munching, even after I'm full.

$–$$ Kotobuki Japanese Restaurant ★ (4822 MacArthur Blvd. NW, 2nd floor; ☎ 202/281-6679; www.kotobukiusa.com; take the Metro to Foggy Bottom and a bus from there to Palisades; Mon–Thurs 5–9:30pm, Fri–Sat noon–2:30pm and 5–10:30pm, Sun 5–9:30pm; MC, V on orders of $10 or more). What would you say if I told you Washington, D.C., was home to a sushi restaurant where you could gorge without guilt? Where the pieces of maki sushi were selling for only $1 a piece . . . and they didn't cause food poisoning? That's the case at this modest, second-story eatery, and though it's difficult to get to, the sushi is so good, and so darn *cheap*, that I think it's worth the trek. By using one seafood purveyor only (for many years), by making their own pickled ginger and (often) soy sauce, chef/owner Hasao Abe has managed to keep costs down. So what he spends goes into the fish, and he's not only able to serve silken, tendon-free, perfectly cut sushi, but he also often offers more unusual varieties such as white tuna, steamed monkfish liver pâté, and square-pressed mackerel sushi for next to nothing. Rolls are $2.95 to $6, and almost every piece of sushi and sashimi is $1. (Take the bus so the cost of a taxi doesn't eat up any savings you make on the food.)

potato dumplings—is prepared beautifully here. Eastern European dishes also make an appearance, such as the *bratwurst mit sauerkraut und knodel* ($18)—pan-fried pork sausage served with sauerkraut and potato dumplings. Vegetarians are accommodated with a mushroom-laden omelet ($15) or a plate of potato pancakes with red cabbage, spaetzle, and all kinds of veggies ($13). When representatives of the German tourist information office hold their press luncheons, they usually do it at Old Europe—an endorsement with clout.

5 Remarkable Sights & Attractions

The ones you definitely should see

By Pauline Frommer & Jim Yenckel

A VISIT TO WASHINGTON IS A STEP INTO THE PAGES OF AMERICAN HISTORY, a saga that is being added to daily. During your stay, it's not improbable that the White House, the Capitol, or the Supreme Court will take some action that has important national or even international impact. If you take in a session of the Court, the Senate, or the House of Representatives, you might even see it happen in person.

As the nation's capital, Washington also has become the place to honor national heroes, past presidents, victorious generals, and other notable leaders—even a few foreign leaders—whose lives have had a great and beneficial impact on the rest of us. Here George Washington, who gave his name to the city, receives his thanks in a soaring monument that is recognized around the world. The Lincoln Memorial, honoring the "Great Emancipator," has served as a stage for important moments in the history of the Civil Rights movement. Imposing statues and gleaming marble memorials recall the many sacrifices of the veterans of the nation's wars.

This is a city that is rapidly taking its place as a cultural capital. Yes, New York City holds that title, but Washington may be catching up. It is home to the Smithsonian Institution, certainly the world's most remarkable collection of museums. The "Nation's Attic," as it is sometimes called, preserves and displays a vast number of historic and cultural objects. But beyond the Smithsonian are a surprising number of top-notch art museums; historic homes that provide a wonderfully personal peephole into the past; and newer attractions that introduce visitors to the world of journalism, espionage, and more.

This chapter will introduce you to all of these options, and since there are an overwhelming number of sights to see, we're going to do it in an unapologetically opinionated manner. The "Getting Organized" section below lays out several itineraries for stays of different lengths that we feel allow visitors to get a good overview of the city. Below that, we list Washington's "iconic" attractions, those that define the city. In short, these are the sights every first-time visitor should strive to see. And because *all* of the Smithsonian Museums are extraordinary, we're giving them their own section; we think all are "iconic"; which of them you choose to visit will depend on your mood.

Below the section on the Smithsonian are seven more attractions of note. They would be defining sights in just about any city but Washington (it really is an embarrassment of riches!). Look at these as closely as you do the "iconic sights"—in many ways, they pack as great a punch!

Next up are those sights that are tailored to visitors with special interests or may be best saved for a second or third visit to the city. It's not that they're in any way second-rate—far from it!—it's just that in a city this rich and complex you have to make some choices about what you really want and need to see, so we've tried to give you some insights that will help you decide. In this category are sights like the city's historic homes, important architectural sights, and tours. Frankly, these are things you do second in D.C., especially the tours which, even more frankly, you probably don't need to do at all, unless you have mobility issues. Washington is an easy city to get around. The top sights, for the most part, are within walking distance of one another (often ranged along the Mall), so don't assume you need to zip around on a bus. With this guide in hand, you should have all the tools you need for a successful trip (we promise!). And with that, let's get started.

GETTING ORGANIZED

MAKE THE BEST USE OF LIMITED TIME, WITH 1-, 2- & 3-DAY ITINERARIES TO THE ESSENTIAL WASHINGTON

At some point on your visit, you have to face the fact that you can't see everything. To help you plan your time effectively, try the following itineraries. Thankfully, all but a handful of attractions are in Washington's central core and can be easily reached by Metro or on foot.

Note: These itineraries assume your quick trip was made more or less on the spur of the moment and you didn't have time to contact your U.S. representative or one of your U.S. senators for passes to the White House, the Capitol, and the Pentagon.

If you have just 1 day in Washington: You've got plenty of company. Business travelers from all over the country and the world are dispatched to the city to pitch their cause or product to the Federal Government. The lucky ones manage to eke out a day, at most, to look around before they hurry home. So do what they tend to do and begin your day at the major **memorials and monuments on the Mall.** National Park rangers go on duty at 8am, which gives you an early start; no lines or security checks slow you down; and you can walk from one to the other.

To get started, circle the **White House,** observing it from outside its high iron-bar fence. Note the **Department of Treasury Building** next door. Then walk a block south to the **Mall** and visit in order: the **Washington Monument, World War II Memorial, Vietnam Veterans Memorial, Vietnam Women's Memorial, Lincoln Memorial, Korean War Veterans Memorial, Franklin Delano Roosevelt Memorial,** and the **Thomas Jefferson Memorial.** This should fill a morning.

Spend the afternoon visiting two museums. We recommend the Smithsonian Institution's **National Air and Space Museum** on the Mall, since it's the best of its kind anywhere. But if art or natural history is more your speed, head to another of the Mall-based **Smithsonian Museums** or the **National Gallery.** While on the Mall, stop for a couple of minutes to take in the majesty of the **U.S.**

Capitol in the distance. Beyond these institutions, the Smithsonian's **American Art Museum** and **National Portrait Gallery,** 4 blocks north of the Mall in the bustling Penn Quarter neighborhood, are superb choices as well as museums, and American art seems most fitting on this all-American race through the nation's capital. Catch an evening performance at the **John F. Kennedy Center for the Performing Arts** (or at least the free **Millennium Stage** concert nightly at 6pm in the Grand Foyer).

If you have 2 days: On *Day 1,* duplicate the itinerary above. On *Day 2,* take a guided tour inside the **U.S. Capitol.** Reserve tickets online and in advance to make the most of your time. If you neglect to do that, be sure to get to the Capitol no later than 8:30am to get a timed ticket (as the number of unreserved tickets is limited and given out on a first-come, first-served basis). If you must wait an hour or two between the time you book the tour and the tour itself, use the delay profitably by visiting the **Supreme Court of the United States** and the **Library of Congress,** both located behind the Capitol. Foreign visitors are likely to find more of interest at the Library of Congress, which displays literary treasures from around the world. Spend the rest of the day sampling more Mall attractions, perhaps the **National Archives** or the **U.S. Holocaust Memorial Museum.** Stroll the **National Sculpture Garden,** outside the National Gallery of Art. Catch an evening performance at **Ford's Theatre National Historic Site.**

If you have 3 days: On *Day 1* and *Day 2,* follow the itineraries above. On *Day 3,* spend the morning at **Arlington National Cemetery.** Take the Metro across the Potomac River to the cemetery, where all these places are located. If you've still got stamina, return on foot across the **Arlington Memorial Bridge,** a grand ceremonial gateway to the city. Built in 1932 as a symbol of a nation reunited after the Civil War, the short span links Washington, the Union capital, with Virginia, which seceded from the Union. You can either spend the afternoon catching up with the Mall attractions you haven't gotten to yet, or spend the afternoon browsing the shops of **Georgetown,** most located on M Street NW and Wisconsin Avenue NW. Visit some of the residential streets also (we have an excellent self-guided walking tour on p. 197), perhaps stopping for a tour at **Tudor Place,** a historic home, or the lovely gardens at **Dumbarton Oaks.** Enjoy an early dinner at a **U Street Corridor** or **14th Street** restaurant and catch an 8pm performance at nearby **Studio Theatre.** Cap the evening at a **U Street** bar or club. *MUST HAVE PRINTOUT*

WASHINGTON'S 10 ICONIC SIGHTS

THE U.S. CAPITOL — *mon 5/9 ARRIVE @ 1:10pm*

In Washington, D.C., the Capitol Dome is as ubiquitous as the sun. Look up and there it is, gleaming white in the distance. That you see it from just about everywhere is no accident: By law, no building in the District can be taller than the Dome. Its importance, and the importance of Congress, is meant to be unmistakable. Incontrovertible, too, is the fact that a tour of the **United States Capitol** ★★★ 🧒 enters through the new Capitol Visitors Center, which is underground, the entrance on the East Plaza of the Capitol between Constitution and Independence Aves; ☎ 202/225-6827; Metro: Capitol South or Union Station;

Washington's Greatest Treasures

The city's many museums display a cornucopia of fascinating objects, many of incalculable monetary value and all of them of historic import. Here are some of the most notable:

- **Declaration of Independence,** one of the nation's most cherished documents. *National Archives.*
- **Dorothy's Ruby Slippers,** a pair of the magical shoes worn by Judy Garland in Hollywood's *The Wizard of Oz. National Museum of American History.*
- **First Folio of Shakespeare,** an original copy of the first collected edition of the Bard's work published in 1616. *Folger Shakespeare Library.*
- **George Washington by Gilbert Stuart,** the *Lansdowne* portrait of 1796, generally regarded as the most famous portrait of Washington. *National Portrait Gallery.*
- *Ginevra de' Benci,* the only portrait in the United States by the Florentine master Leonardo da Vinci. *National Gallery of Art.*
- **Gutenberg Bible of 1455,** one of only three still-existing copies printed on hand-made parchment. *Library of Congress.*
- **Harmony in Blue and Gold: The Peacock Room,** a complete room with floor-to-ceiling paintings by James McNeill Whistler. *Freer Gallery of Art.*
- **Hope Diamond,** the legendary 45.5-caret bluish gem found in India in the 1600s. *National Museum of Natural History.*
- **Moon Rock,** a small, smooth slice of the moon astronauts brought home to earth. *National Air and Space Museum.*
- **Star-Spangled Banner,** the War of 1812 flag that inspired America's National Anthem. *National Museum of American History.*
- **Wright Flyer,** the flimsy aircraft launched by Wilber and Orville Wright at Kitty Hawk in 1903 that inaugurated manned flights. *National Air and Space Museum.*

www.aoc.gov; free admission; 8:30am–4:30pm Mon–Sat except Thanksgiving Day and Dec 25) is a necessary stop on any first-time tour of D.C. Like the White House (see below), it's an iconic American symbol.

But more than that, when you visit the Congress, you understand, in a very visceral way, just what it means to govern a country democratically. The fights and compromises, the din of differing opinions, the necessity of creating "one from the many" *(e pluribus unum),* without trampling on the rights of that one. It's a powerful experience. And the ideals of the Congress are not just expressed in the debates on the floor of the House and Senate (though you should try to hear those

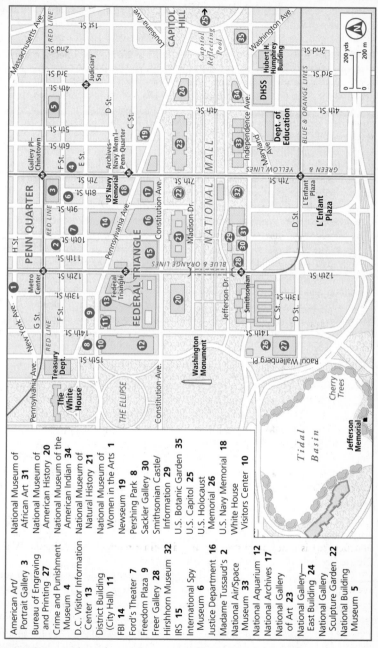

if you can; see below), but in the collection of art and artifacts that litter this massive building (the largest in the world when it was first erected).

In the course of your tour, you'll visit the **Rotunda,** the ornate ceremonial heart of the legislative branch where deceased presidents and other honorees (among them, civil rights heroine Rosa Parks) lie in state. Massive works of art on appropriately patriotic scenes give it the necessary grandeur. John Trumbull, the artist of the four massive canvases on the walls, served as an aide-de-camp to General George Washington during the war. In the eye of the Dome, 180 feet above, is a circular fresco called *The Apotheosis of Washington.* This 1865 fresco is the work of Italian-born artist Constantino Brumidi; he created similarly gorgeous, color-splashed frescoes in many of the Capitol's rooms and corridors (called the *Brumidi Corridors*). Working from 1855–1880, he completed so many, in fact, that he sometimes is called the "Michelangelo of the Capitol." At age 72, he had begun the 300-foot frieze (or ornamental band) that rings the base of the Dome when he fell, suffering a fatal injury. The frieze, completed by others, illustrates more than 400 years of American history from Columbus's discovery of the New World to the dawn of the age of aviation.

From the Rotunda, the tour continues to the **National Statuary Hall,** formerly called the Old Hall of the House. Once the site where the House met, it had notoriously bad acoustics, so Congress ordered the present House chamber built, and the representatives moved into it in 1857. The old chamber now is lined with statues of notable figures. Every state contributes two statues each. If the guide gives you a free moment, look around to see who's there from your home state. You could spot Ethan Allen of Vermont, William Jennings Bryan of Nebraska, Sakakawea of North Dakota (as her name is spelled in the Capitol), Will Rogers of Oklahoma, and Father Junipero Serra of California. Next, you'll visit the **Old Senate Chamber,** which has been restored to look as it did when occupied by the Senate from 1810 to 1859. It housed the Supreme Court of the United States from 1860 to 1935.

After the tour, be sure to make the time for the terrific new museum in the new visitor center, which holds a number of important original documents relating to the history of the Capitol along with wonderful dioramas of the city at various times in its history.

Visitors are not allowed to roam around the Capitol unaccompanied. However, you have three options for how you might do your tour:

- **The Official Guided Tour:** When Pauline did the tour, her guide rushed so quickly through his commentary it was barely understandable. Jim had a guide who talked only about how Congress works, ignoring altogether the murals and sculptures the group was passing. Our experiences, unfortunately, aren't unique; these tours tend to be rushed, the guides poorly trained. That said, even if the guides said nothing, the experience of standing inside the Capitol would be enough incentive to take the tour (and the video that starts the tour is well done, as is the exhibit that follows it). Other, better options, however, are the tours led by congressional aides (see below).

- **To book tickets:** A number of walk-in tickets are held each day for spontaneous visitors. However, you may have to wait several hours between the time you enter the new Capitol Visitors Center and the time your tour begins. During the Cherry Blossom Festival and other busy periods, folks

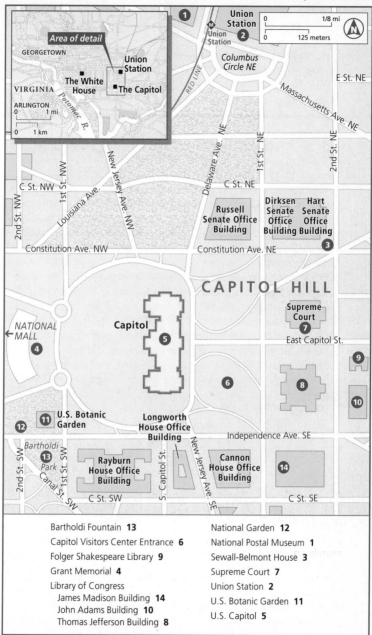

Bartholdi Fountain **13**

Capitol Visitors Center Entrance **6**

Folger Shakespeare Library **9**

Grant Memorial **4**

Library of Congress
James Madison Building **14**
John Adams Building **10**
Thomas Jefferson Building **8**

National Garden **12**

National Postal Museum **1**

Sewall-Belmont House **3**

Supreme Court **7**

Union Station **2**

U.S. Botanic Garden **11**

U.S. Capitol **5**

The U.S. Capitol from Top to Bottom

*   **The Building:** President George Washington laid the Capitol's corner-stone on September 18, 1793. As the country grew, adding more states and more legislators, the building grew with it. In 1857, a new House wing was completed, and the new Senate wing was ready 2 years later. The two additions more than doubled the length of the Capitol. This necessitated the construction of a new steel dome, completed in 1866, because the old one was now out of proportion. The most recent additions were the extension of the East Front, completed in 1962; and the new Visitor's Center below the building. Majority leader Harry Reid infamously remarked that you'd no longer have to "smell the tourists" because they'd be able to wait for their tours in air-conditioning. Alas, the geniuses who built the visitor center didn't create any sort of shelter for the area visitors wait in before they go through security. So they're probably still going to get pretty stinky.
*   **The Statue of Freedom:** Barely visible on her lofty perch, the bronze Statue of Freedom tops the Dome 288 feet above the East Plaza. Her right hand rests on the hilt of a sword; her left hand holds a laurel wreath of victory and the shield of the United States. In his original 1855 drawing, sculptor Thomas Crawford planned to place on her head a "liberty cap," the symbol of freed slaves. But Secretary of War Jefferson Davis—who 6 years later became the president of the Confederacy—objected. As a result, Freedom wears a crested Roman helmet.
*   **Transportation:** Electric subway cars connect the Dirksen and Hart Senate office buildings with the Capitol. In the pre-security past, senators shared the ride with visitors.

start lining up at 6:30am, and it's possible you may not get a spot at all on these 40-person tours. A better strategy is to go to **http://tours.visitthe capitol.gov** where you can sign up in advance for a tour date and time. Go to the site as soon as you know you'll be visiting, as these reservations can go quickly.

*   **Staff-led tours:** A second option is to join a tour led by a congressional staff member; check with your legislator to find out when one is scheduled. Though they may not be as deep on the history, on these tours you're apt to see odd nooks and crannies that these generally young staff insiders have discovered on their own. They sometimes, perhaps inadvertently, provide gossipy details about Capitol denizens that the official guides know nothing about.

♦ **Gallery visits:** Visitors who take only the two tours listed above never actually get to see the Capitol's locus of action: the floors of the House and Senate. And to be frank, these can be the most exciting areas. Though senators and congresspeople often use their time on the floor simply to speechify for C-Span (often with no other colleagues around; it's a bit surreal), watching them go through their paces, or if you're lucky, witnessing a debate, can be fascinating. Many visitors will find the tour insufficient, particularly if they want to see the chambers where the House and Senate meet. **U.S. residents** can request passes in advance to both visitor galleries from one of their senators or their representative. If you forget to plan in advance, you can also pick passes up at legislator offices, located in six buildings adjacent to the Capitol. (Offices of representatives are housed in the Cannon, Longworth, and Rayburn buildings on the Capitol's south side on Independence Ave. Senate offices are in the Russell, Dirksen, and Hart buildings on the Capitol's north side along Constitution Ave.) **International visitors** can obtain passes by presenting non-U.S.-issued photo identification (a passport) after passing through the security check.

♦ The *Washington Post* provides a daily list of Capitol Hill meetings, including when the House and Senate are in session and what committee hearings open to the public are scheduled. With a gallery pass you can attend the legislative sessions. You don't need a pass to sit in on hearings held in the House and Senate office buildings adjacent to the Capitol. But if the hearing is on a controversial topic, chances are Washington insiders will crowd you out.

THE WHITE HOUSE

We think what surprises most visitors to the **White House** ✮✮✮ 🄺 (1600 Pennsylvania Ave. NW, adjacent to the Mall; ☎ 202/208-1631; Metro: Farragut North or McPherson Square; www.nps.gov/whho; limited free tours; Tues–Sat except federal holidays 7:30am–12:30pm) is how, well, unspectacular the interior is. Sure, there are oil paintings galore, swags of fine fabrics, and plush, overstuffed furnishings. But you'll see more impressive decor, more over-the-top architectural flourishes, more bling, at other historic U.S. mansions. That's not just happenstance. Furious debate roiled the Congress when the White House was being planned about how grand the structure should be. Many felt that it couldn't be too palatial, as that would be anti-democratic. As first daughter Margaret Truman put it in her marvelously personal history of the building, *The President's House:* "The White House is the architectural equivalent of the American spirit of compromise that created the Constitution—neither too large to be undemocratic nor too small to project meaningful presidential power." A design competition was held and a relatively modest home by James Hoban was chosen. Interestingly, one of the losing entries was submitted by Thomas Jefferson (a man of many talents). No one knew he had submitted a plan, however, as he used the pseudonym T.Z.

The White House is the oldest public building in Washington, D.C. (it welcomed John Adams, the second president, as its first resident on Nov 1, 1800), and until the Taft Administration, ending in 1913, it was the open, "people's house" that the original Congress had hoped it would be. "Tourists looking around inside the White House had been allowed, when the president was absent, to go into his office and sit for a moment and bounce in his chair," reported David Brinkley in his wonderful book *Washington Goes to War*. According to Brinkley, up until 1941 it was possible to wander the grounds of the White House without answering any questions since "the White House was not yet considered much different from any other public building in the city." (The security measures surrounding World War II changed that permanently.)

What makes the building so interesting—beyond the possibility that the president or first lady could walk by at any moment!—are not so much the furnishings, but its place in history. Unfortunately, the 30-minute self-guided White House tour is light on history; you proceed quickly between roped barriers past a number of rooms used for official events, getting a quick glance and not really learning much. To help you make some sense of what you're seeing, here's a short précis of the important rooms you'll see on the tour:

- The **Library** is furnished in the style of the late Federal period (1800–20). The gilded wood chandelier with the painted red band was made about 1800 and belonged to the family of author James Fenimore Cooper *(The Last of the Mohicans)*. The silver plate lamps on the mantel were a gift of the Marquis de Lafayette. It looks elegant now, but until 1902, this was the laundry room.

- The **Diplomatic Reception Room** is where ambassadors arrive to present their diplomatic credentials. It's one of three oval rooms in the building. Franklin Roosevelt gave his "fireside chats" from this room. Beyond, Roosevelt used the **Map Room** as the "situation room" to chart the progress of World War II. When Nixon finally left the White House, the last room he was in, conversing with Gerald Ford and his wife, was the Diplomatic Reception Room. From there, he made his way outside to the helicopter, to give his infamous "peace sign" farewell.

- The **East Room,** largest in the White House, hosts receptions, ceremonies, and press conferences. Its highlight is the famous 1797 portrait of George Washington rescued by Dolley Madison during the War of 1812. It's the only object known to have remained in the White House since the Adamses moved in. The painting is a replica, painted by the artist himself (Gilbert Stuart), of the famous Lansdowne portrait that now hangs in the National Portrait Gallery (p. 119). During the Civil War, Union troops occupied the room briefly. Theodore Roosevelt's children reportedly used it as a roller-skating rink, little Tad Lincoln rode through it on his pet goat, and Ulysses S. Grant's daughter Nellie was married here. Seven presidents, including Abraham Lincoln and John F. Kennedy, have lain in state in the room at their deaths.

- The walls of the exquisite **Green Room,** a parlor for small teas and receptions, is covered with a green silk fabric chosen by Jacqueline Kennedy. On the wall to the left of the fireplace is a Gilbert Stuart portrait of Louisa Adams, wife of John Quincy Adams.

- The **Blue Room**—no doubting its bold color—has nearly always been a reception room, furnished in the French Empire style. President James Monroe chose the decor, ordering the seven gilded chairs from a Parisian cabinetmaker. The American public, or at least some of them, thought he

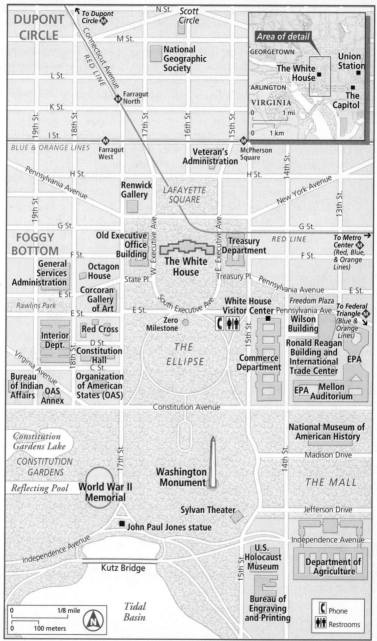

DUPONT CIRCLE

To Dupont Circle Ⓜ
N St.
Scott Circle
M St.

National Geographic Society

CONNECTICUT AVENUE
RED LINE

L St.

Farragut North Ⓜ

K St.

19th St.
18th St.
I St.
17th St.
16th St.
15th St.

BLUE & ORANGE LINES
Farragut West Ⓜ

Veteran's Administration

McPherson Square Ⓜ
14th St.

Pennsylvania Avenue
H St.

Renwick Gallery

LAFAYETTE SQUARE

H St.
New York Avenue
13th St.

19th St.
G St.

FOGGY BOTTOM

Old Executive Office Building

W. Executive Ave.
E. Executive Ave.

Treasury Department

RED LINE

G St.

To Metro Center Ⓜ (Red, Blue, & Orange Lines)

F St.

General Services Administration

Octagon House

The White House

F St.

Corcoran Gallery of Art

State Pl.

Treasury Pl.
Pennsylvania Avenue

E St.

Rawlins Park

E St.

South Executive Ave.

E St.

White House Visitor Center

Freedom Plaza
Pennsylvania Ave.

To Federal Triangle Ⓜ (Blue & Orange Lines)

Interior Dept.

Red Cross

D St.

Constitution Hall

C St.

18th St.

Zero Milestone

Ⓒ 🚻

15th St.

Wilson Building

THE ELLIPSE

Commerce Department

Ronald Reagan Building and International Trade Center

EPA

Bureau of Indian Affairs

OAS Annex

Organization of American States (OAS)

EPA
Mellon Auditorium

Virginia Avenue

Constitution Avenue

Constitution Gardens Lake

CONSTITUTION GARDENS

17th St.

National Museum of American History

Madison Drive

14th St.

THE MALL

Reflecting Pool
World War II Memorial

Washington Monument

Jefferson Drive

Sylvan Theater

■ John Paul Jones statue

Independence Avenue

Independence Avenue

U.S. Holocaust Museum

15th St.

Department of Agriculture

Kutz Bridge

Tidal Basin

Bureau of Engraving and Printing

Ⓒ Phone
🚻 Restrooms

0   1/8 mile
0   100 meters

Area of detail

GEORGETOWN

The White House ■

Union Station ■

ARLINGTON

VIRGINIA

The Capitol ■

0   1 mi
0   1 km

should have shopped at home. It was during Monroe's presidency that the burned-out White House was restored and furnished. Monroe was criticized for the extravagance of his choices.

◆ A state reception room, the **Red Room** was the scene of an aborted assassination attempt in 1891. A man with a knife was found there; two doorkeepers, with the help of President Benjamin Harrison, subdued him and tied him up with the cord from the curtains. Today, it's furnished in the American Empire style, chosen in 1962 by the Kennedys. The small round table opposite the fireplace is considered the most important American Empire piece in the White House. It was designed by French émigré and cabinetmaker Charles-Honore Lannuier. The American Empire music stand to the right of the fireplace recalls the room's use as a music room.

◆ The final room on the tour is the **State Dining Room,** which can seat as many as 140 guests. It is often the scene of gala dinners honoring visiting kings, queens, presidents, and prime ministers. Thomas Jefferson used this room as his office; inscribed on the mantel is a prayer by John Adams for blessings on the White House. You'll notice the mantel also has bisons' heads carved on it; this was at the insistence of Teddy Roosevelt, who felt that the originally planned lions' heads weren't American enough (what you see today is a reproduction of the original, commissioned by Jackie Kennedy).

If you want more background info than we provide here, consider purchasing *The White House: An Historic Guide* ($7) at the White House Visitor Center (see below). Published by the White House Historical Association, it identifies nearly every historical furnishing in both the rooms on the public tour and those that aren't. The Visitor Center also provides exhibits on White House history and decor.

GETTING A TOUR: This is a key issue. Since September 11, 2001, gaining access to the White House has become more difficult. Currently tours are limited to groups of 10 or more. U.S. residents must request passes from their senator or member of Congress. But you are not out in the cold if you are a single, say, or a couple or a family of four. Most (but not all) legislators will assemble groups of 10 people, who may not know each other. Your senator or representative might even find a spot for you in a group put together by a legislator from another state. If you call one senator and are turned down, then contact your other senator or your representative. Foreign visitors should apply through their embassy in Washington. The White House takes requests up to 6 months in advance. Tours are scheduled about a month in advance of your requested date.

Important: Remember, even if you receive a pass, a tour is not assured. Because of unforeseen events—perhaps a last-minute visit of a foreign leader—tours may be canceled abruptly. Check the phone number listed earlier in this chapter for schedule changes.

A TASTE OF THE WHITE HOUSE WITHOUT A TOUR: So how do you experience the White House if you don't have a visitor's pass? First, stop by the **White House Visitor Center** 2 blocks away at 1450 Pennsylvania Ave. NW. Open from 7:30am to 4pm daily, it serves as a museum of White House history, presenting exhibits, audiovisual displays, and ranger-led talks. And then **circle the White House on**

foot, taking in the impressive—and photogenic—views of the front and back. If you happen to be there at 11:30am, join one of the themed walks led by National Park Service rangers, which focus on the statuary, monuments, and memorials that adorn the President's Park—the name given to the encircling green spaces outside the White House fence. Other interpretive programs at the Visitor Center (9:30am and 1:30pm) include a verbal tour of the president's office in the West Wing and a slide show featuring American artists whose works are in the White House collection.

THE WASHINGTON MONUMENT

The most visually prominent of the monuments on the Mall, the **Washington Monument** ★★ 🅚 (On the Mall at 15th St.; ☎ 202/426-6841; Metro: Smithsonian station; www.nps.gov/wamo; free admission; daily except Dec 25 9am–4pm) is also an impressive record breaker: It's the tallest free-standing masonry structure in the world at 555 feet, as well as the tallest obelisk. The aluminum pyramid at the top was the largest single piece of aluminum ever cast. Like the Capitol Dome, you won't have much trouble spotting it: Just look up if you're anywhere near the Mall. At its base, 50 U.S. flags, one for each state (but not one for the District of Columbia), whip colorfully in the breeze.

In some ways the history of the structure echoes the history of the man it memorializes. Washington was a pillar of strength in a time of chaos. And out of chaos came this strong pillar. It took over 100 years from conception to completion to build the Monument. The infighting, backstabbing, and politicking required to get the thing done were intense.

The battles began in 1801 when the House approved construction of a mausoleum in pyramid shape, but the Senate objected. In 1816 and 1832, a tomb in the Capitol was proposed, but Washington's family members insisted he remain buried at Mount Vernon, as his will requested. Other cities were already constructing memorials, particularly Baltimore, where architect Robert Mills designed a 204-foot Doric obelisk, which still stands in the Mount Vernon neighborhood. Finally in 1833, a Washington National Monument Society, headed by the Chief Justice of the Supreme Court, sponsored a design competition. The winner: None other than Baltimore's Mill, who proposed, you guessed it, another obelisk (it was taller, though). Mill, who became the nation's first federal architect, designed an elaborate base with columns. But it and other features were eliminated to save money, leaving the unadorned obelisk you see.

The monument's cornerstone was laid July 4, 1848, by President James K. Polk with U.S. Representative Abraham Lincoln attending. Construction stopped for 18 years in 1858 when the monument reached 156 feet because private contributions to pay for the work were insufficient. (That's the reason the monument changes color halfway up; the initial work was done with marble from a Maryland quarry, but in the later stages, Massachusetts marble was used.) In 1876, President Ulysses S. Grant approved a congressional act to fund completion, and it was dedicated on February 21, 1885.

GOING TO THE TOP: You may be tempted, as thousands are, to ride the elevator to the top. But keep in mind that you'll first have to line up for tickets at the ticket stand (see below) and then you may have to wait a half-hour or more to get

Washington, D.C., Attractions

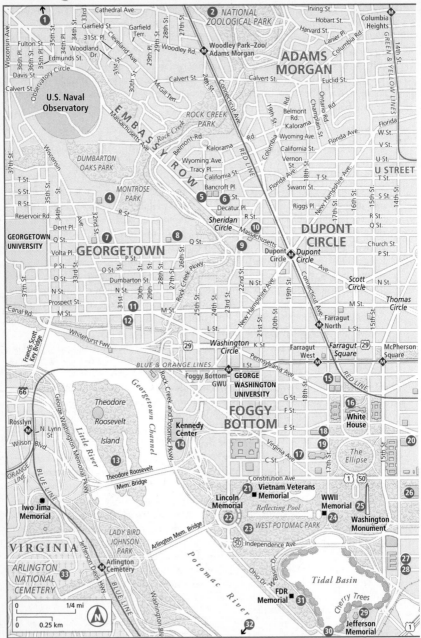

Cathedral Ave.

2 NATIONAL ZOOLOGICAL PARK

Irving St.

Hobart St.

Columbia Heights

1

Garfield St.

Garfield Terr.

31St. Pl.

Woodland Dr.

Woodley Rd.

Woodley Park–Zoo/ Adams Morgan

Harvard St.

Lanier Pl.

Columbia Rd.

ADAMS MORGAN

Fulton St.

Edmunds St.

Davis St.

Calvert Ave.

Observatory Circle

U.S. Naval Observatory

McGill Terr.

Calvert St.

Belmont Rd.

Rock Creek

Calvert St.

Euclid St.

Florida Ave.

W. St.

V St.

U St.

ROCK CREEK PARK

Kalorama Rd.

Champlain St.

Ontario Rd.

Belmont Rd.

EMBASSY ROW

DUMBARTON OAKS PARK

Massachusetts Ave.

Wyoming Ave.

Tracy Pl.

California St.

Bancroft Pl.

Kalorama

Columbia Rd.

Wyoming Ave.

California St.

Vernon St.

U STREET

Florida Ave.

T St.

4

MONTROSE PARK

5 **6**

Decatur Pl.

Sheridan Circle

10

Swann St.

Riggs Pl.

R St.

Q St.

DUPONT CIRCLE

Church St.

P St.

T St.

S St.

R St.

Reservoir Rd.

Dent Pl.

GEORGETOWN UNIVERSITY

Q St.

Volta Pl.

7

GEORGETOWN

8

Q St.

9

Massachusetts Ave.

Dupont Circle

Dupont Circle

Scott Circle

N St.

Thomas Circle

P St.

O St.

Dumbarton St.

N St.

N St.

M St.

M St.

L St.

Farragut North

M St.

Prospect St.

Canal Rd.

11

12

Rock Creek Pkwy.

Washington Circle

K St.

Pennsylvania Ave.

Farragut West

Farragut Square

29

McPherson Square

Francis Scott Key Bridge

Whitehurst Fwy.

BLUE & ORANGE LINES

I St.

Foggy Bottom– GWU

GEORGE WASHINGTON UNIVERSITY

15

RED LINE

66

George Washington Memorial Pkwy.

Georgetown Channel

Rock Creek and Potomac Pkwy.

FOGGY BOTTOM

G St.

F St.

E St.

16 **White House**

Rosslyn

N Lynn St.

Wilson Blvd.

Theodore Roosevelt Island

Kennedy Center

14

18

19

Virginia Ave.

17

The Ellipse

20

ORANGE LINE

BLUE LINE

Little River

13

Theodore Roosevelt Mem. Bridge

C St.

Constitution Ave.

26

VIRGINIA

LADY BIRD JOHNSON PARK

Arlington Mem. Bridge

21 Vietnam Veterans Memorial

Lincoln Memorial

22

Reflecting Pool

23

WWII Memorial

24

25

Washington Monument

ARLINGTON NATIONAL CEMETERY

33

Jefferson Davis Hwy.

Arlington Cemetery

WEST POTOMAC PARK

50 Independence Ave.

27

28

Iwo Jima Memorial

Potomac River

Ohio Dr.

FDR Memorial

31

Tidal Basin

Cherry Trees

29

Jefferson Memorial

30

1

Washington Blvd.

32

| 0 | 1/4 mi |
| 0 | 0.25 km |

N

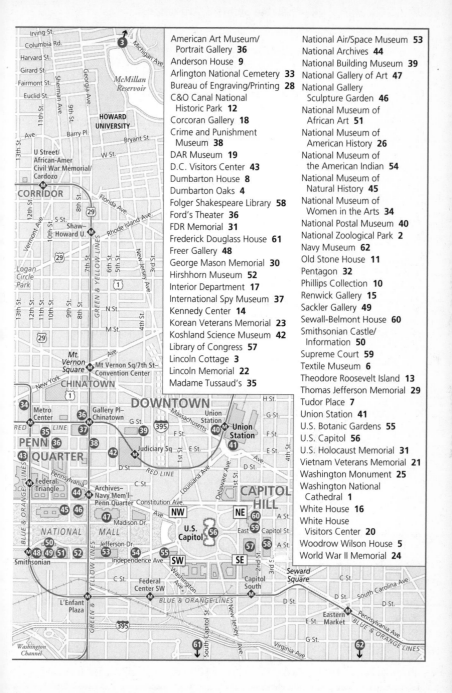

American Art Museum/ Portrait Gallery **36**
Anderson House **9**
Arlington National Cemetery **33**
Bureau of Engraving/Printing **28**
C&O Canal National Historic Park **12**
Corcoran Gallery **18**
Crime and Punishment Museum **38**
DAR Museum **19**
D.C. Visitors Center **43**
Dumbarton House **8**
Dumbarton Oaks **4**
Folger Shakespeare Library **58**
Ford's Theater **36**
FDR Memorial **31**
Frederick Douglass House **61**
Freer Gallery **48**
George Mason Memorial **30**
Hirshhorn Museum **52**
Interior Department **17**
International Spy Museum **37**
Kennedy Center **14**
Korean Veterans Memorial **23**
Koshland Science Museum **42**
Library of Congress **57**
Lincoln Cottage **3**
Lincoln Memorial **22**
Madame Tussaud's **35**

National Air/Space Museum **53**
National Archives **44**
National Building Museum **39**
National Gallery of Art **47**
National Gallery Sculpture Garden **46**
National Museum of African Art **51**
National Museum of American History **26**
National Museum of the American Indian **54**
National Museum of Natural History **45**
National Museum of Women in the Arts **34**
National Postal Museum **40**
National Zoological Park **2**
Navy Museum **62**
Old Stone House **11**
Pentagon **32**
Phillips Collection **10**
Renwick Gallery **15**
Sackler Gallery **49**
Sewall-Belmont House **60**
Smithsonian Castle/ Information **50**
Supreme Court **59**
Textile Museum **6**
Theodore Roosevelt Island **13**
Thomas Jefferson Memorial **29**
Tudor Place **7**
Union Station **41**
U.S. Botanic Gardens **55**
U.S. Capitol **56**
U.S. Holocaust Memorial **31**
Vietnam Veterans Memorial **21**
Washington Monument **25**
Washington National Cathedral **1**
White House **16**
White House Visitors Center **20**
Woodrow Wilson House **5**
World War II Memorial **24**

Plan Ahead—How Your
State Delegation Can Help You

Because of security concerns, entry into some of the major government buildings requires advance application for free passes. You get them from either of your state's two U.S. senators or from the House of Representatives delegate from your congressional district. Foreign visitors should check with their country's embassy in Washington. See more detailed discussions later in this chapter for each attraction that is affected. A little homework will save you lots of time and hassle on your visit.

Apply well in advance for a:

◆ **White House Tour:** Tours generally are limited to groups of 10, but individuals can be assigned to a group. Apply up to 6 months in advance.

◆ **U.S. Capitol Tour:** Contact a member of your congressional delegation in advance or visit his or her Washington office for a separate pass to each gallery. Also ask about joining a staff-led tour as these tend to be more lively than the official tours.

◆ **Pentagon Tour:** The Pentagon's tour office accepts applications for group tours only. Individuals must go through their Washington legislators.

◆ **Bureau of Engraving and Printing Tour:** From spring to fall, same-day tickets often are gone an hour after the ticket kiosk opens at 8am. Be smart and join a Congressional VIP Tour, courtesy of your representative. Apply up to 6 months in advance.

◆ **U.S. State Department Diplomatic Reception Rooms Tour:** Passes are available only from your members of Congress.

◆ **National Cathedral:** Special tours, often with a deeper focus, are offered to those who book well in advance through the offices of their congressional representatives.

through security. And the 70-second ride in the crowded car (there's only one) with 2 dozen other folks can be claustrophobic. If time is short, take in the dramatic city views from the monument's base and then get on with your sightseeing; you won't have missed that much. We think the view from the steps of the Lincoln Memorial is much more impressive. On its descent, the elevator allows a glimpse of some of the 193 memorial stones in the interior walls. Contributed by states, cities, and patriotic societies, each honors Washington's memory.

GETTING A TICKET: To be assured of a ticket, reserve in advance through the National Park Reservation Service (☎ 800/967-2283 or http://reservations. nps.gov). You will be charged a service fee of $1.50 per ticket plus a 50¢ handling fee per order. Free same-day elevator tickets are distributed from 8am to 4:30pm at the kiosk at 15th Street and Jefferson Drive, just down the hill from the monument. Show up early in the summer and on weekends and holidays because tickets go quickly.

THE LINCOLN MEMORIAL

When famed architect Charles Follen McKim (of McKim, Meade and White) was asked to work on the 1902 McMillan commission to reshape the overall design for the Mall, he made his views clear on what he felt would be an important addition. "As the Arc de Triomphe crowns Place de l'Etoile in Paris, so should stand a memorial erected of the memory of that one man in our history as a nation who is worthy to be joined with George Washington—Abraham Lincoln." Twenty years later, in 1922, the **Lincoln Memorial** ✮✮✮ 🄺 (On the Mall at 23rd St.; ☎ 202/426-6841; Metro: Foggy Bottom; www.nps.gov/linc; free admission; daily except Dec 25 8am–midnight) was dedicated. As the McMillan commission envisioned, it was set on a direct axis to the Washington Monument, symbolically anchoring the Mall with a monument to the nation's founding president at one end and the memorial honoring the president who saved the Union at the other.

Part of the power of the monument, of course, has to do with its placement, overlooking the long sweep of the reflecting pool. But we think it's impossible to overemphasize the impact of the work of Daniel Chester French, the sculptor hired to create Lincoln's likeness. Lincoln sits, gazing down on the visitors at his feet, the burdens of guiding the Union through the Civil War etched deeply in his face. Though 19 feet tall, the figure is eerily lifelike and exudes a fatherly compassion. Some say that his hands create the sign-language shapes for A (Abraham) and L (Lincoln), as a tribute to the fact that Lincoln signed legislation giving Gallaudet University, a school for the deaf, the right to confer college degrees. The Parks Department denies the symbolism, but it should be noted that French's son was deaf, so the sculptor *did* know sign language.

Lincoln is housed in a modified Greek-style temple of marble and limestone patterned after the Parthenon in Athens. Around it, 36 soaring columns represent the 36 states in the Union when Lincoln died at the hands of an assassin.

Another Lincoln Memorial

This isn't Washington's only monument to Lincoln. Dedicated in 1876 in Capitol Hill's **Lincoln Park** (East Capitol and 11th St. NW; Metro: Eastern Market and 6-block walk), the **Emancipation Monument** was erected by the Western Sanitary Commission of St. Louis, Missouri. Funds were collected solely from emancipated citizens declared free by Lincoln's proclamation, which went into effect January 1, 1863. The first $5 was contributed by Charlotte Scott, a freed woman from Virginia. Reportedly it was the first money she earned in freedom. President Ulysses S. Grant and his cabinet attended the dedication. Frederick Douglass, the abolitionist, gave the main address.

Before climbing the stairs to the statue, step inside the small museum at the base of the memorial. It details both its construction and, more significantly, the role the memorial has played in civil rights demonstrations and other national events. A video screen replays an excerpt of Marian Anderson, singing "My Country 'Tis of Thee" on the memorial steps after a local concert hall refused to let her appear because of her race. From those same steps, civil rights champion Rev. Dr. Martin Luther King, Jr., thundered "I have a dream," his momentous speech at the 1963 March on Washington. Those words are now inscribed in the steps leading up to the memorial. The view from the memorial steps, facing east down the length of the Mall past the Washington Monument to the U.S. Capitol, is spectacular.

An elevator inside the museum carries you up to the statue if you can't negotiate the steps. A small bookstore on the statue level sells books about Lincoln and the Civil War. Ranger talks are scheduled frequently; you often can hear a personal impromptu talk simply by asking for one at the ranger desk.

THE JEFFERSON MEMORIAL

In 1962, President John F. Kennedy invited 49 Nobel Prize winners to the White House. "I think this is the most extraordinary collection of talent, of human knowledge, that has ever been gathered at the White House," he told them, "with the possible exception of when Thomas Jefferson dined alone."

America's third president was a man of many and notable talents—scientist, inventor, architect, musician, horticulturist, political philosopher. But he is perhaps best known as the primary author of the Declaration of Independence, an achievement so dear to him that he asked that it be inscribed on his tombstone. An appreciative nation honored his many accomplishments when it established the **Thomas Jefferson Memorial** ☆ (On the Mall at East Basin Dr. SW; ☎ 202/426-6841; Metro: Smithsonian; www.nps.gov/thje; free admission; daily except Dec 25 8am–midnight). The memorial was dedicated on April 13, 1943, on the 200th anniversary of Jefferson's birth.

The memorial sports a classical look with rounded dome and multiple columns reminiscent of the Pantheon in Rome. Jefferson is credited with introducing rounded porticoes to the United States; you'll see them featured at Monticello, his plantation home in Virginia, and the original campus of the University of Virginia, which he designed. But the design of the Memorial was not without controversy. Built in the 1940s, a time when many architects were moving away from the aesthetics of classical Rome, its look elicited an angry commentary from Frank Lloyd Wright. The design, he wrote in a letter to President Franklin Roosevelt, was "an arrogant insult to the memory of Thomas Jefferson." Pauline, who finds the overall look of the memorial a bit generic and dull, thinks Wright had cause to complain.

Beneath the dome, Jefferson stands 19 feet tall in bronze. In his hand, he holds a copy of the Declaration of Independence. His gaze, unlike the Lincoln statue, seems to ignore his visitors as he looks across the lake-like Tidal Basin into the historic heart of the city he helped create. You can't blame him; the view, which takes in the Washington Monument, is grand. The statue, however, is less so. Perhaps something was lost when it was translated from plaster (its original form due to World War II shortages in metals) to bronze.

PLANNING YOUR VISIT: A visit here takes only a few minutes. The most appealing way to approach is to walk the paved trail called Cherry Tree Walk around the Tidal Basin, lined with the city's famed Japanese cherry trees (about 3 miles round-trip if you circle the entire basin). A small museum at the monument's base details its construction. A bookshop, gift shop, restrooms, and an elevator to the statue (if you can't climb the stairs) are located there also. Rangers are present to answer questions and give both scheduled and impromptu talks.

You may want to combine your stop here with a look at the FDR Memorial (p. 107), about a 7-minute walk away.

THE SUPREME COURT

All but hidden behind the U.S. Capitol, the third equal branch of the U.S. government, the judicial, is often overlooked by time-constrained visitors. But it shouldn't be. On many days, the **Supreme Court of the United States** ✿✿✿ (1st St. NE at E. Capitol St. behind the U.S. Capitol; ☎ 202/479-3030; Metro: Capitol South or Union Station; www.supremecourtus.gov; free admission; Mon–Fri except holidays 9am–4:30pm) is the most exciting place to be in town. Beginning each annual session on the first Monday in October, the nine justices hear cases and render opinions that can dramatically affect every American. Visitors are invited to sit in on arguments between lawyers for opposing sides, who are typically questioned sharply and repeatedly by the justices. It's a grand show, fast-paced, sometimes heated, and always full of weighty import. And you get a close-up seat.

Between October and April, the Court hears up to four 1-hour arguments a day on Monday, Tuesday, and Wednesday; this is done in 2-week intervals, that is, 2 weeks on and 2 weeks off. Cases are presented at 10 and 11am and 1 and

---

The Supreme Court in Brief

◆ The building was completed in 1935; for the previous 146 years, the justices sat elsewhere. Initially the Court met in New York City and Philadelphia, when the two cities were the seat of government. When the government moved to Washington, the Court got a room in the new Capitol, but it had to move periodically. From 1819, it sat in what is now called the Old Supreme Court Chamber. From 1860 to 1935, the Old Senate Chamber was its home.

◆ Busts of former Chief Justices sit either in niches or on marble pedestals along the Great Hall's side walls. A life-size seated statue of Chief Justice John Marshall is located in the Lower Great Hall. Marshall's judicial and political astuteness enhanced and confirmed the Supreme Court's power to rule on the constitutional legality of congressional legislation.

◆ Overhead in the Courtroom, sculpted figures line all four walls depicting legal themes and famous lawgivers, including Confucius and Moses.

2pm. Check the schedule in the *Washington Post* or on the Supreme Court website (see above) by clicking "argument calendar." When court is in session, two lines form in the plaza outside the courthouse. One line is for people who want to hear an entire argument; they are seated beginning at 9:30am. The other line is for visitors seeking only a 3- to 5-minute peek at the justices in action; they are shuffled in and out quietly beginning at 10am. If you have the time, try and see a case. They really are fascinating to watch, as only the most important cases ever make it all the way to the Supreme Court. If a major case is being argued, the lines for the morning sessions begin to form as early as 6am. Lines for the afternoon sessions, if scheduled, may begin to form at 9:30am.

When the Court is not in session, you can sit in on an informative 25-minute lecture about the Court and the building—designed in classical Greek style by Cass Gilbert—that houses it. The lecture Jim attended most recently was funny, gossipy, and full of insider anecdotes about the Court's day-to-day operation. Held in the Courtroom itself, the lectures are scheduled hourly from 9:30am to 3:30pm. In the **Lower Great Hall,** one floor below, exhibits provide more details on the Court's history and function.

THE LIBRARY OF CONGRESS

With memories of the Civil War finally starting to fade, the railroads cutting a swath through America, and the government expanding, Congress in the 1890s was feeling its oats. So though the **Library of Congress** ✯✯✯ (1st St. SE at Independence Ave. behind the U.S. Capitol; ☎ 202/707-8000; Metro: Capitol South or Union Station; www.loc.gov; free admission; Mon–Sat except federal holidays 10am–5:30pm) had been around since 1800, it was decided that now was the time to attempt a building that was worthy of the ambitions of this rising nation. It was to be the Federal Government's first cultural building and therefore appropriately opulent. In 1897, the new Library opened in what is today called the Jefferson building. We think it boasts the most beautiful interior in all of Washington, D.C., and one of the most beautiful in the nation. Many visitors overlook it. Don't. Not only is it eye candy of the first degree, but its curators also put on superb special exhibits and wonderfully erudite tours of the facility. It's anything but the stuffy domain of dusty legislative tomes you might expect. Really.

A bit of background first. Founded in 1800 to serve the research needs of the U.S. Congress, the contents of the Library were burned by the British in the War of 1812. Thomas Jefferson, retired as president, immediately offered his lifetime collection of 6,487 books as a replacement. Congress paid him $23,950, a fraction of what they were worth (but as always in politics, the sale was controversial with Jefferson accused of bilking the government). The number of tomes exploded after 1870 when a new copyright law, still in effect today, required that every author/publisher seeking copyright send two volumes of his or her work to the Library of Congress. Today, it's the world's largest library, receiving 22,000 items a day (it keeps about 10,000 and the rest are given away). In the collection are more than 133 million items on approximately 530 miles of bookshelves.

The Library occupies two other buildings on Capitol Hill, the John Adams (built in 1938) and James Madison Memorial (built in 1981) buildings, but it's the Jefferson you want to see.

Before you go upstairs in the Jefferson building, explore the exhibitions, take in a few minutes to gasp at the beauty of the **Great Hall** on the first floor (above the ground level, where you may enter). The ceiling, soaring 75 feet above the marble floor, is adorned with stained-glass skylights and laden with 23 karat gold. On the stairways leading up to the second level are marble putti, each representing a different profession (see if you can spot the musician, the entomologist, the pharmacist, and the farmer from the tools these babies are playing with; the Library wanted to convey that it had books dealing with these topics). You'll notice that emerging from the fancy chandeliers are plain light bulbs. This isn't an oversight: The Library was the first government building to be lit by electricity, and they were darn proud of those bare bulbs back in the day.

Also on the first floor, in the East Corridor, be sure to take a gander at the case holding the **Gutenberg Bible of 1455.** It's one of only three perfect copies printed on hand-made parchment still known to exist. Congress paid $1.5 million to acquire it at the height of the Great Depression, another indicator as to how important this document is. Across from it is a case holding the 1649 *Bay Psalm Book* by Stephen Daye, the first book printed in what is now the United States. The Library's copy is 1 of 11 that survive and 1 of 5 that are in their original bindings. Before leaving the East Corridor look up; painted on the ceiling are important Americans representing, again, the range of professions in the U.S.

Upstairs, take a peek down into the impressive main reading room, which is in the shape of an octagon. The sculptures around the perimeter are of important thinkers throughout history.

The books that would have been in Jefferson's collection form the fascinating permanent exhibition and show his interest in everything from animal husbandry to Roman history to a "how to" book on surviving if you've been accidentally buried alive (apparently a bestseller in Colonial America). Computer screens around the room allow you to read pages from books that are encased in glass in front of you.

The rest of the exhibits rotate, but you might spot a first edition of *The Wonderful Wizard of Oz,* an important map of the "New World," President Woodrow Wilson's reading script of his 1918 "Fourteen Points" address, or the contents of Abraham Lincoln's pockets the night he was assassinated. And for fun, head back down to the ground floor for the **Bob Hope Gallery of American Entertainment,** a musical tour through the age of vaudeville. The comedian's joke file, totaling more than 89,000 pages, has been digitally scanned and indexed. Visitors can call up examples to read by subject matter.

You can take a self-guided tour using a brochure distributed at the Visitors Center. Guided tours are offered Monday through Friday at 10:30 and 11:30am and 1:30, 2:30, and 3:30pm; on Saturday, the 2:30pm tour is the latest.

THE NATIONAL ARCHIVES

Of all the visitor sights in Washington, the one with the biggest inferiority complex has to be the **National Archives** ★★ (kids) (Just off the Mall on Constitution Ave. btw. 7th and 9th sts. NW; ☎ 866/272-6272; Metro: Archives–Navy Memorial; www.archives.gov; free admission; 10am–9pm daily Memorial Day weekend to Labor Day, 10am–7pm Apr 1 to Memorial Day Friday, 10am–5:30pm Labor Day to Mar 31 except Dec 25). How else to explain the overwrought introductory film

Iconic Sites in Arlington, Virginia

A trip to **Arlington National Cemetery** ✮✮✮ (Directly across Arlington Memorial Bridge from the Lincoln Memorial; ☎ 703/607-8000; Metro: Arlington Cemetery; www.arlingtoncemetery.org; free admission; Apr 1–Sept 30 daily 8am–7pm and 8am–5pm the rest of the year) should be considered as essential a visit, especially for first-timers, as anything that can be seen on the Mall. It is, quite simply, America's most important cemetery. Today more than 300,000 men and women are interred here. They include veterans from all the nation's wars from the American Revolution (reinterred after 1900) through the Iraq and Afghanistan wars. Funerals average about 28 a day. These are private ceremonies; often the firing of a funereal gun salute echoes across the shady grounds.

The cemetery is clearly visible from much of the Mall. At its summit is **Arlington House** (☎ 703/235-1530; www.nps.gov/arho). The distinctive landmark was the antebellum-style home of Robert E. Lee, which he lost when he joined the Confederate Army. Near the foot of the slope, directly beneath Arlington House, is **President John F. Kennedy's Gravesite.** At night, its famous eternal flame often can be seen flickering from river-view points on the Mall, and especially from the Lincoln Memorial. First Lady Jacqueline Kennedy Onassis is buried at his side, and brother Robert Kennedy is nearby.

Because we feel the cemetery is so important, we've devoted an entire walking tour to it on p. 184.

Arlington's second don't miss sight is the **Pentagon** ✮ (On the Virginia side of the Potomac River immediately south of Arlington National Cemetery; ☎ 703/697-1776, tour desk; Metro: Pentagon; http://pentagon .afis.osd.mil; free tours; Mon–Fri except federal holidays 9am–5pm, with advance reservations only). The headquarters for the Department of Defense is a household name known around the world. Nearly everybody who comes to Washington for the first time wants a look at it, even if it's not easy to get inside these days.

Virtually a city in itself, the huge five-sided structure (thus its name) covers 34 acres and possesses more floor space than New York's Empire

and the ludicrous slogan they sometimes use ("Adventure Into the World of Records!") in a place that should be resting on its laurels? After all, it is in its mausoleum-like **Rotunda for the Charters of Freedom** that the country's three most important documents are exhibited: the original **Declaration of Independence, U.S. Constitution,** and **Bill of Rights.** Soldiers in dress uniform stand posted in recessed nooks guarding them; though faded and nearly unreadable, they still pack plenty of emotional power. (During busy periods, expect to do some assertive wriggling to get yourself directly in front of their cases.) Other cases on

State Building. That space is occupied by 25,000 military and civilian employees. Completed in 1943 during World War II, it is threaded by more than 17½ miles of corridors. Yet Pentagon officials maintain that it is so efficiently designed that staffers can walk between any two points in the building in 7 minutes. The distinctive shape stems from the location of the originally designated site, which was bordered by five roadways. Ultimately a different site was chosen, but the design remained. Three shifts worked 24 hours a day to complete its construction in an amazing 16 months from groundbreaking.

Pentagon tours have been scheduled regularly since 1976. But you must have advance reservations to enter. Individuals can apply for a tour through their senators or representative. Visitors who are 18 and older will be asked for two forms of identification, one of which must be a photo ID. Ages 13 to 17 need only a photo ID or a parent or guardian to vouch for them.

Typically a tour lasts 45 minutes to an hour and covers about 1½ miles inside the building. The guides are hand-picked active duty personnel from the National Capitol Region's military ceremonial units. They are required to learn about 20 pages of informational material outlining the mission of each military branch.

A final choice in Arlington is the improbable **Drug Enforcement Administration Museum** (700 Army Navy Dr., Arlington; ☎ 202/307-3463; www.deamuseum.org; free; Tues-Fri 10am–4pm; Metro: Pentagon City). And no, you don't have to give a urine sample to visit it. Run as a service to the public, the museum offers a detailed look at the history of drugs in America from the time when pharmacies were selling tinctures of cocaine to help babies with teething (a standard treatment in the 1930s), through the drug wars of today. The exhibit features an eye-popping amount of paraphernalia (confiscated?), interesting wall text, and disturbing photographs. Special exhibitions on topics like prescription drug abuse also will hold your attention. This one's best for people who might have an, um, special interest in the subject matter but really, anyone who's ever lit up a doobie (and that's, what, 80% of Americans?) should find it absorbing.

each side of the Big Three display more treasured documents; in the adjacent Rotunda Gallery is one of only four originals of the **Magna Carta** of 1297, the founding document of English common law. It is the only copy permanently in the United States.

But the Archives' attractions don't begin and end with the Rotunda. We'd suggest you devote a full 2 hours to exploring the section that it calls its "Open Vaults." This area introduces visitors to the heart of the archives: its 9 billion records, covering 2 centuries worth of documents, from patent searches to genealogical records to census records, passport applications, governmental records, and more.

We know, we know: It sounds dry, but the way the curators have laid it all out is anything but. Using the very latest in interactive museum design—listening booths, computer terminals, videos, you name it—the curators have mined the material for drama (and often presented it in a very kid-friendly fashion). In an area on patents, for example, the process is turned into a game: You read the patent application and then try and guess what well-known gadget it was for. A section on immigration presents the search for genealogical data as a cliffhanger mystery, detailing the steps and missteps of several Archives users. President Nixon makes several eerie appearances: You read his resignation letter and listen to disturbing excerpts from the Watergate tapes. One of our favorite exhibits shows the letters Americans have written to the president over the years, from a 'tween seeking "federal aid" from Ronald Reagan because his mother declared his bedroom a disaster area to an overwrought fan begging Eisenhower not to cut off the sideburns of Private Elvis Presley.

The vaults are also a research center drawing thousands exploring their family histories, filming documentaries, chasing historical mysteries, or building their case in court. If you have research to do, call up for details.

And before you leave, don't forget to take a gander at the building itself. A Beaux Arts masterwork by John Russell Pope (who also designed the Jefferson Memorial and National Gallery of Art), 72 massive Corinthian columns mark the building as being one of importance. And so it is.

VIETNAM VETERANS MEMORIAL

No symbols, no patriotic words adorn the **Vietnam Veterans Memorial** ✮✩ (On the Mall at 21st St. and Constitution Ave. NW, adjacent to the Lincoln Memorial; ☎ 202/426-6841; Metro: Foggy Bottom; www.nps.gov/vive; free admission; 8am–11:45pm daily except Dec 25). Instead, the design by then 20-year-old student Maya Ying Lin is purposefully, and most would say poetically, austere: a V-shaped, 247-foot wall of polished granite with 58,245 names etched into its face, sunk down into the ground. It was dedicated in 1982.

Today, it's as beloved as the Lincoln Memorial, but when Lin's work was first revealed, its boldly iconoclastic form, its lack of the usual pieties associated with memorials, was a lightning rod for controversy. Veterans groups, looking at the design, felt this "gash in the earth" was an affront to the memory of their fallen brothers. The ruckus was so great that two more traditional memorials were added nearby: At the east end, the **Vietnam Women's Memorial** is dedicated to the more than 11,000 American women who served in the military in Vietnam. The **Three Servicemen Statue** at the west end shows a trio of heavily armed young men. Give these two works a glance, but then return to Lin's infinitely more moving, radical, and ultimately paradigm-shifting work.

Lin's goal was to design a quiet, protected place to honor American troops who died in the Vietnam War. And, in fact, as visitors descend downwards toward the center of the memorial, a hush settles on the throngs, as if in a cathedral. Architectural critic Nathan Glazer in his essay "Monuments, Modernism and the Mall" notes that the silence of the place is its most masterful stroke. "Is there any other monument that refuses to say anything at all?" he asks. "In this case the reticence of modern art also suits the subject it is dealing with. It fits our ambivalence over the war—there is nothing to be said and nothing is said. Neither that it was a victory or a defeat, nor that it was worth fighting and dying for or not, not that it was heroic or its opposite."

Some details to note:

* **The stone:** The granite was carefully chosen and shipped from Bangalore, India. The reflective quality of this particular stone, the fact that visitors can see their own faces as they're looking at the names, is meant to tie together past and present.
* **The rituals:** Many family members and other visitors leave flowers or mementos at the base of the wall; the National Park Service regularly gathers them up, cataloguing significant items and disposing of faded blooms. It is always interesting to see what mementos people leave. Many take rubbings of the names to bring home with them.
* **The names:** The inscribed names are listed chronologically from first death to last. About 1,000 names, designated by a cross, are of those who were either prisoners or missing at the end of the war and who remain unaccounted for. The memorial founders wanted the names to signify war "as a series of individual human sacrifices." To Lin, the names themselves are the real memorial. At either end of the walls is a small covered stand with a large catalog listing where on the walls a specific name is found.

NATIONAL GALLERY OF ART

The Prada, the Louvre, the Hermitage—it took centuries to amass the treasures that fill these famous collections. But in the good ole U.S. of A, well, we get things done quickly. And so it took founder Andrew W. Mellon just a few decades of a serious shopping spree to create the **National Gallery of Art** ✪✪ (On the Mall at Madison Dr. btw. 3rd and 7th sts. NW; ☎ 202/737-4215; Metro: Archives–Navy Memorial or Smithsonian; www.nga.gov; free admission; Mon–Sat 10am–5pm and Sun 11am–6pm except Dec 25 and Jan 1)—a museum that's *nearly* as great as the European ones we've mentioned. Mellon, his family, and friends bought all the art and built the buildings, but then donated the museum to the Federal Government. It continues as a private-public partnership, with the government paying for the upkeep and the security of the museum, but all works of art, even the new acquisitions, privately donated.

As for the collection, it's a wonder, containing a "Who's Who" of the art world: Jan Van Eyck, Rembrandt, Botticelli, Velazquez, El Greco, David, Ingres, Goya, Monet, Manet, van Gogh, Whistler—they're all represented. As are some rarities. The only painting in the United States by the master Florentine artist Leonardo da Vinci hangs here, as does one of the only Bosch paintings in North America, his eerie *Death and the Miser.*

The Gallery's collections are housed in two buildings, the classical **West Building,** which was the largest marble structure in the world when it opened in 1941, and the East Building, a modernistic sculptural work of art in itself designed by famed architect I. M. Pei and dedicated in 1978. They are linked by

20th-Century Heroes

Beyond the Vietnam Veterans Memorial (see above), the Mall is home to a trio of monuments to the men and women who served their nation with great honor in the last century. Each is near to a sight we'd consider more important, so we've given you ways to pair them with other sights (and thus make the best use of your time).

⬧ Dedicated May 29, 2004, the placement of the **World War II Memorial** (17th St. on the Mall; ☎ 202/619-7222; Metro: Smithsonian; www.wwiimemorial.com; free admission; daily 8am–midnight) was so controversial—it breaks the axial vista that connects the Washington Monument and the Lincoln Memorial—that it spurred Congress in 2003 to declare that the Mall was "a substantially completed work of civic art" and effect a moratorium on major new developments. This was the same Congress, however, that pushed for the completion of the project, overriding the Advisory Council on Historic Preservation, a federal agency, which had issued a formal finding requesting the design be scrapped. Congress's reasoning: The Memorial needed to be finished while veterans from World War II were still around and able to enjoy it.

Overall, we would have to agree with the Memorial's detractors—the design is old-fashioned and lacking a certain "oomph," especially when compared to the eloquent Vietnam Veterans Memorial. Oval in shape, ringing a large sunken pool, the design harks back to monuments of the past. Twin pavilions at the north and south ends of the pool commemorate the victory fought across two oceans, the Atlantic and Pacific. The 56 rectangular pillars standing smartly at attention alongside the pavilions represent the states, territories, and the District of Columbia. Along the entrance, a dozen bas-relief sculptures depict America at war. On the far side, the Freedom Wall displays 4,000 gold stars, a tribute to those who died in the war.

So yes, it's full of meaningful details, but ultimately the empty marble spaces strike us as austere and unfeeling. And we have to warn you: Plan your visit early in the morning or in late afternoon because the midday sun reflecting off the marble in summer can be brutal.

PAIR YOUR VISIT: With the Washington Monument, across the road.

⬧ It may be the least known of the National Mall's major war memorials, but the **Korean War Veterans Memorial** ✯ (On the Mall at Independence Ave. and the Lincoln Memorial; ☎ 202/426-6841; Metro: Foggy Bottom; www.nps.gov/kowa; free admission; 8am–midnight daily except Dec 25) could be the one that you remember longest—and tell the folks at home about. A very realistic representation of a squad of 19 U.S. servicemen on patrol in rugged, windblown

Korean terrain, it's cast slightly larger than life in stainless steel. The figures have the haggard, almost ghostly look of wary veterans ever alert for a hidden enemy. Heavily armed and wearing ponchos, reflecting the harsh weather, they seem actually to be moving cautiously ahead as you walk beside them—in effect joining them for a few moments on their dangerous mission.

The Korean War broke out on June 25, 1950, when communist North Korea launched a surprise attack on South Korea. A total of 1.5 million Americans served in the conflict; more than 50,000 died.

PAIR IT WITH: Lincoln Memorial, the Vietnam Veterans Memorial

◆ The rough-hewn walls, engraved with the words of the president, and sometimes spouting waterfalls, recall the look of a Frank Lloyd Wright building. They have the same from-nature, appropriate-to-the-surroundings impact and are certainly of the correct era for the **Franklin Delano Roosevelt Memorial** ✫ (On the Mall at W. Basin Dr. in West Potomac Park btw. Ohio Dr. and Independence Ave. SW; ☎ 202/426-6841; Metro: Smithsonian; www.nps.gov/frde; free admission; 8am–midnight daily except Dec 25). Overlooking the Tidal Basin, this is a subdued memorial, one not designed to awe but to invite contemplation in the many cool, quiet alcoves. The memorial is laid out in the form of four "outdoor" or garden rooms, each commemorating one of Roosevelt's four terms in chronological order.

If you go, make sure you carry this guide; otherwise the significance of what you are seeing may not be clear. At the entrance or "Prologue," a life-size bronze statue shows Roosevelt seated in a modest wheelchair (this was added in 2001, after groups of Americans with disabilities protested that there was no representation of Roosevelt's own disability). In the First Room, look for a relief sculpture depicting his first inaugural. In the Second Room, statues of a rural couple—the Appalachian Couple—and of worry-worn men standing in a 1930s bread line suggest the despair of the times. A nation beginning to regain hope is illustrated by the sculpture of a man listening to one of Roosevelt's Fireside Chats. In the Third Room, we see Roosevelt the war president, seated and wrapped in the warm cloak famous in photographs. Elsewhere, First Lady Eleanor Roosevelt is given her due in a flattering statue. In the Fourth Room, Roosevelt's death is marked by a sculptural relief of his funeral cortege.

The Roosevelt Monument offers a well-stocked gift shop, restrooms, and food.

PAIR IT WITH: The Jefferson Monument, a 7-minute walk away

◆ **Important Note:** Informative ranger talks are held at all three of the memorials.

a subterranean concourse, where you will find a delightful food court (p. 55) and gift shop. The West Building houses European art from the 13th through the 19th centuries and American painting and sculpture from the Colonial era to the early 20th century. Find modern and contemporary art in the **East Building.**

Art enthusiasts will shudder when we say that you can make a hurried survey of the West Building's Main Floor galleries in about 2 hours and the East Building in 45 minutes more. But it's true—most of what you want to see in the West Building is located on the Main Floor. (This is where you'll see the collection's works by Titian, Rembrandt, Goya, El Greco, Raphael, or Rubens, among many familiar names.) The art is conveniently grouped according to school in rough chronological order. If 15th-century Netherlandish works don't interest you, they can easily be skipped.

But first head for Gallery 6 (Italian paintings from the 13th to the 15th centuries), where the Leonardo hangs. This small painting, *Ginevra de' Benci,* dating to about 1474, is an exquisite portrait of a young, wealthy woman of Florence. Leonardo is believed to have used his hands to smooth the surface of the paint on her face. Don't neglect to look at the back of the painting; a juniper sprig is sketched there, a pun on Ginevra's name (*ginepro* is the Italian word for juniper).

The only portrait in the museum that's even more luminous (we think) is Whistler's *Girl in White.* Notice how the girl seems less corporeal than the bear's head rug she stands on; the work was considered so outré when it was created, it was refused for exhibition by the jury of the Paris Salon and had probably the greater honor of being originally shown at the 1863 *Salon de Refuses* (exhibition

(kids) The Outdoor Sculpture Garden

After racing through 7 centuries of art history, step outside to the National Gallery's delightful **Sculpture Garden** (free admission; Mon–Sat 10am–5pm and Sun 11am–6pm, except Memorial Day to Labor Day Mon–Thurs and Sat 10am–7pm, Fri 10am–9pm, and Sun 11am–7pm). Occupying more than 6 acres, a full city block, at the gallery's west end, it is a generally quiet haven for contemplation. The garden, a mini-forest of 35 varieties of decorative trees, encircles a giant pool and fountain. In winter the pool doubles as an ice-skating rink (p. 178). More than 15 modern sculptures are scattered beneath the trees. The most whimsical certainly is Claes Oldenburg's giant *Typewriter Eraser, Scale X* (1999), a stainless steel and cement rendition of a now-obsolete item. Scott Burton's *Six-Part Seating* (1985/1998) groups six red polished stone chairs in a circle, inviting you to sit and rest awhile. Yes, go ahead and do it. Youngsters will grin at Barry Flanagan's *Thinker on a Rock* (1997), a bronze takeoff of Rodin's *Thinker,* except this thinker is a giant hare with 3-foot long ears thrusting skyward.

of rejects) along with the seminal *Luncheon on the Grass* by Manet. Excuse us for pointing you to our favorite works; we're sure you'll find many of your own at this delicious gallery.

The East Building features a number of monumental works on the ground floor, all created just for this space. The building's "mascot" is the spectacular and huge red, black, and blue mobile by Alexander Calder that hangs over the stairwell. It was the last work the artist created and wasn't finished by the time he passed away. Interestingly enough, Paul Matisse, the son of famed painter Henri Matisse, was the metalworker who actually fabricated the piece. You'll see Paul's father's joyous collages on the second floor, along with works by Pollock, Rothko, Barnet Newman, and Chuck Close.

One word on I. M. Pei's architecture, and that word is: triangles. The space reserved for the building was trapezoidal, so Pei used two triangles as the basis for the shape for the East Building. But you'll see triangles everywhere: in the cut of the floor stones, the shape of the bathrooms. And in case you were wondering, Pei built the National Gallery a decade *before* he created his famous pyramid for the entrance to the Louvre in Paris.

Check at the West Building information desk for free escorted tours of the collections. If you can't catch one of those, the audio tours are the next best thing (they're actually quite well done and not too pricey at $5 per person).

THE SMITHSONIAN INSTITUTION'S MUSEUMS & ZOO

You might think that the Federal Government in its wisdom decided decades ago that the nation needed a grand national museum. But that's not how Washington got the Smithsonian. America inherited it from the proverbial "rich uncle" nobody knew existed. The Smithsonian, as we know it now, grew from an odd bequest of more than $500,000 made to the United States in the will of James Smithson. An accomplished British scientist, he never visited this country and, as far as can be determined, never corresponded with anyone here. Why he made the gift, which the government received in 1838, alas remains a mystery. Smithson's letters and journals were stored at the Smithsonian Castle and were destroyed during a fire. Perhaps he was protesting rigid British society, which discriminated against him throughout his life because of his illegitimate birth.

In his will, Smithson stipulated his legacy should be used to found "at Washington under the name of the Smithsonian Institution an establishment for the increase and diffusion of knowledge among men." Today, the Institution is a museum and research complex of 20 museums (including the zoo), two of which are located in New York City and one that is yet to be built on the Mall (the National Museum of African American History and Culture). Some resulted from bequests made by wealthy donors following Smithson's example. About 70 percent of the Institution's budget comes from the Federal Government and the rest from contributions and revenue from restaurants, gift and book shops, and theaters. The total number of objects in the Institution's many collections is estimated at more than 135 million—the bulk of them in the National Museum of Natural History. Don't fret if you can't get to all of them. You would have to live here for years.

THE CASTLE

Because it opens before most Mall attractions, the **Smithsonian Institution Building/The Castle** (On the Mall at 1000 Jefferson Dr. SW; ☎ 202/633-1000; Metro: Smithsonian; www.smithsonian.org; free admission; daily 8:30am–5:30pm except Dec 25) is the place to begin your morning, rewarding early risers. The building, built in 1855 of reddish sandstone, is a curiosity in itself. Sporting castle-like towers, it is regarded as one of the greatest examples of Gothic revival design in this country. As a sort of teaser to what's coming, the Castle displays samples from the Institution's vast collections. You might see beaded moccasins from the National Museum of the American Indian; hockey great Bobby Orr's much-battered hockey stick from the National Museum of American History, or the modernistic dining service used in flight on the Air France Concorde from the National Air and Space Museum. And if you want to pay homage to the man who founded the Institution, Smithson's remains are interred in the crypt here. Exhibits at the crypt display his portrait, will, and scientific publications. Informative hourly tours give visitors more background about the Smithsonian and the castle building itself; if one's starting, take it. Behind the Castle, the **Enid A. Haupt Garden** is a 4-acre Victorian gem, open at 7am daily except December 25.

THE NATIONAL AIR AND SPACE MUSEUM

The most popular museum in all of Washington—and that's saying a lot!—the **National Air and Space Museum** ✪✪✪ 🎒 (On the Mall at Jefferson Dr. btw. 4th and 7th sts. SW; ☎ 202/633-1000; Metro: Smithsonian; www.nasm.si.edu; free admission; daily 10am–5:30pm except Dec 25; extended summer hours determined annually) manages to tap into that most primordial of human impulses: the urge to fly. And it does so in a multilayered fashion, mixing extraordinary artifacts with IMAX movies, videos, computer terminals with quizzes, even flight simulators. So alluring is its pull that we know one family who started their sightseeing at the Air and Space Museum and then went back for 3 days running, never managing to make it to another sight in D.C. (and not regretting that choice at all).

At the heart of the collection are the historic aircraft. Dangling from the ceiling just inside the door is the original *Spirit of St. Louis,* flown by Charles Lindbergh in 1927 on the first solo transatlantic flight. While Lindbergh was still in flight over the Atlantic, officials at the Smithsonian telegraphed him in Paris asking for the airplane when he was done. They got it a year later. At the end of World War II, the U.S. Army decided to preserve a massive collection of allied and captured Axis aircraft; half of it went to the U.S. Air Force Museum in Dayton, Ohio, and the other half came here. Among the next big "gets" were the Bell X-1 *Glamourous Glennis,* the first airplane to fly faster than the speed of sound and, of course, the **Apollo 11 command module *Columbia.*** It brought back the astronauts from their visit to the moon in 1969—an artifact with wow appeal for every generation. But the awesome artifacts go well beyond planes and spaceships: Near the Columbia one of the museum's most popular items, the **Moon Rock,** a small, smooth slice of basalt 4 billion years old. Rub your fingers across it—it's permitted.

More Air & Space:
The Steven F. Udvar-Hazy Center

Aircraft too large and too numerous to display in the Mall building are now on exhibit at the Air and Space Museum's hangar-sized companion facility located near Dulles International Airport in the Virginia suburbs. Opened in 2003, it is named for the aviation businessman who contributed $60 million to establish it. Together, the two sites spotlight the largest collection of aviation and space artifacts in the world. Perhaps the Udvar-Hazy Center's most famous plane is the **B-29 Superfortress** *Enola Gay,* which dropped the world's first atomic bomb on Hiroshima on August 6, 1945. Unfortunately, there's no longer a shuttle to the center but you can get driving instructions at the museum's Welcome Center.

It's a ginormous place, so be selective and concentrate on the galleries that most interest you. The two floors of exhibits are divided between **Airplanes and Aviation** at the museum's west end and **Rockets and Spaceflight** at the east end.

If you opt for the west wing, the upstairs floor has the most to offer, especially for nostalgic older visitors. At the top of the escalator, dangling above the massive **Hall of Air Transportation,** is a Ford 5AT-Trimotor, the **"Tin Goose,"** which was the largest passenger ship when it went into commercial service on August 2, 1926. Noisy, but considered reliable—although quite cramped—it helped convince the public of flight safety. Aloft nearby is a **Douglas DC-3,** a twin-engine, 22-seat aircraft first flown in 1935; some are still in use. Reliable, inexpensive, and easy to operate, it is considered the most successful aircraft in history.

Here you'll also pay homage to the **Wright brothers,** Wilbur and Orville, whose 1903 Wright Flyer is honored (along with the Wrights) in a gallery of its own. On December 17, 1903, the duo launched the Flyer in four short but historic flights from a sand dune at Kitty Hawk, N.C. Though incredibly flimsy, it was the first manned, power-driven, heavier-than-air craft to fly. The Smithsonian acquired the Flyer in 1948 on the death of Orville Wright.

In **World War II Aviation,** you can see the actual fighter planes that dueled in the air in both the European and Asian theaters. Here are the war's legendary craft: the British Spitfire, credited with defending England in the Battle of Britain; its versatile but outmaneuvered opponent, the German Messerschmitt; the Mitsubishi Zero, Japan's primary naval fighter plane; and the North American Mustang, considered the best piston-engine fighter in the world. This is a not-to-be missed museum highlight.

But maybe your eyes and thoughts are on the future. On the first floor in the **Space Race** gallery, your questions about how astronauts live in space are answered. (You'll even learn how they go to the bathroom in space.) Upstairs, the east wing's second-floor **Apollo to the Moon** displays personal items from the early spaceflights such as razors, sunglasses, and survival gear. Back downstairs,

Rocketry and Space Flight delves into the complexities of rockets, engines, and spacecraft. All around you these amazing devices stand ready for your inspection.

And **for children:** There's the "How Things Fly" gallery, which explains many of the principals of aerodynamics in fun, interactive ways (little science experiments, really). Some of the exhibits were broken when Pauline and her family last visited, but hopefully they'll be in top nick by the time you get there.

One suggestion: On arrival, head immediately for the museum's **Welcome Center** to score tickets to the giant-screen **IMAX** show or a simulated voyage among the stars at the **Albert Einstein Planetarium.** They do sell out. Admission is $8.50 adults, $7.50 seniors (60-plus), and $7 children (2–12). Or order tickets in advance at ☎ **202/633-4629** or www.si.edu/imax; we highly recommend advance purchase if you are visiting Washington during the Cherry Blossom Festival or the busy July/August tourist season. The planetarium's **Infinity Express,** a 20-minute tour of the universe (using images from the Hubble Space Telescope and Mars Global Surveyor), departs every half-hour from 10:30am to 4:30pm. Pricing is the same as IMAX. At 5pm Tuesday, Thursday, and Saturday, the planetarium's **The Stars Tonight** 🐾 is a free tour of the night's sky.

NATIONAL MUSEUM OF NATURAL HISTORY

What the Air and Space Museum does for the history of flight, the **National Museum of Natural History** ✪✪ 🐾 (On the Mall at Madison Dr. btw. 9th and 12th sts. NW; ☎ 202/633-1000; Metro: Smithsonian and Federal Triangle; www.mnh.si.edu; free admission; daily 10am–5:30pm except Dec 25; extended summer hours determined annually) does for all things, well, natural, from mammals to dinosaur fossils to precious gems. Pauline's children were so enthralled by this museum, they insisted on coming 2 days in a row on their last D.C. visit. But the place is not just for kids. Smartly curated, with a vast collection—including the famed elephant in its glamorous rotunda—it approaches science in a sophisticated manner that's less lecture than conversation. The wall text and computer displays are constantly challenging the viewers with questions. Some are answered by the exhibit, others are ones that the scientists are still grappling with. It's an engaging way to pull in the visitor.

Of the permanent exhibits, the hall of **Geology, Gems, and Minerals** is the museum's biggest draw. It displays jewelry of exquisite cut and untold value. Awarded its own exhibit room, the legendary 45.5-carat **Hope Diamond** rotates slowly behind glass. Found in India in the 1600s, it is a surprising blue, the color the result of a minor impurity reflecting in the light. Wall text gives you the history of its supposed curse (for more on that, see p. 212). In an adjoining room are more fabulous jewels, including Marie Antoinette's diamond earrings, a gift from her husband, King Louis XVI of France.

Just as color-saturated, but fluttering, the **Butterfly Habitat Garden** offers a splendid counterpoint to the gems. It all but shimmers with these ethereal creatures. Stretching between Constitution Avenue NW and Madison Drive, the slender garden creates four different butterfly habitats: wetlands (with a small pond), meadow, woods edge, and backyard (with a guide to what you might introduce at home). About 700 species of butterflies have been recorded worldwide; about 80 have been identified in Washington.

On the first floor, the newly opened **Sant Ocean Hall** gives the National Aquarium (p. 145) a run for its sand-dollars with its multilayered, but primarily water-free exploration of life under the sea. Vast cases show samples of shimmering, pellucid jellyfish, all from the same family but as different one to the next as lions are from house cats. Nearby are the most glamorous moray eels you've ever seen. And at the heart of the exhibit is a film about underwater exploration that we have no doubt will inspire scores of future marine biology majors.

Beyond those we've featured are top-notch exhibits on **Mammals** (the Hall of Mammals) and **Dinosaurs,** as well as an aging-less-successfully section on **World Anthropology** (it can be skipped). The **Discovery Room** often features excellent activities for kids, based on whatever the temporary exhibit currently is; check the website before showing up as its hours of operation are limited.

THE NATIONAL MUSEUM OF AMERICAN HISTORY

The **National Museum of American History** ⭐ 🧒 (On the Mall; ☎ 202/ 633-1000; www.americanhistory.si.edu; free admission; Metro: Smithsonian or Federal Triangle; daily 10am–5:30pm except Dec 25) had what we'll call a "soft reopening" in November 2008. Its "Mona Lisa," the **Star-Spangled Banner,** is now ensconced in a marvelous new gallery (more on that below), but the rest of the museum still feels a bit undercooked. Iconic artifacts—like the actual Woolworth's lunch counter from the famous civil rights sit-in in Greensboro, North Carolina, in 1960, and Julia Child's studio kitchen—seem haphazardly positioned and are inadequately illuminated by the accompanying wall text. Other exhibits, like the tired *American Presidency* gallery, have the opposite problem: Crammed with cases of artifacts with War-and-Peace length wall texts, it bores with a topic that should be scintillating.

Still what the museum does well, it does extremely well. And that starts with the new Star-Spangled Banner exhibit. In it, the painful impact of the War of 1812 is brought to vivid life through sound, video, and artifacts. We'd guess most Americans don't realize just how close the U.S. came to being recolonized by Britain during that war and what the eventual raising of this massive flag in 1814 actually symbolized. They'll understand, in a very visceral fashion, after going through this superb retelling. The history of the miraculously intact flag (well, mostly intact) and the famous anthem are also explored.

We'd say, this exhibit alone justifies taking the time to see the museum, the largest history museum in the U.S., by the way, though there certainly are other treasures here, like the glistening pair of Dorothy's Ruby Slippers from the film *The Wizard of Oz;* an unflinching and quite absorbing look at the history of contraception in the United States; and for kids, an engrossing play area illuminating the principals of science on the ground floor. Train nuts will enjoy the **On the Move** gallery, which chronicles the history of American transportation (and features a number of historic choo-choos); and for pop culture fans there's Jerry's "puffy shirt" from *Seinfeld* in a case near the ruby slippers.

Bottom line: We hope the museum is better able to organize itself in the upcoming years. Right now, it's a bit of a hodgepodge, but with worthy sights to seek out. Alas, the ice-cream parlor has been removed, one of our favorite features from the pre-renovation museum.

The National Mall, America's "Front Yard"

A 2-mile-long public promenade stretching from the U.S. Capitol at its east end to the Lincoln Memorial and Potomac River on the west, the **National Mall** ✪✪✪ is a unique place. Philadelphia's Independence Mall is similar, but its focus is solely on the country's birth. The National Mall links past, present, and future. Two of the three branches of the Federal Government, the White House (executive) and the Capitol (legislative), both enjoy prominent Mall locations. The third branch, the Supreme Court (judicial), nudges the Mall from behind the Capitol.

Pierre L'Enfant, the architect who laid out the basic plan for Washington in the 1790s, envisioned the Mall as a ceremonial expanse. But for the next century, it suffered more as a national embarrassment, sporting railroad tracks, open sewers, and squalid shacks. Finally in 1902, a congressional commission chaired by Sen. James McMillan of Michigan—the McMillan Commission—began to push for change. The railroad moved out, swamps were drained, and grand marble monuments began to sprout. The Mall was on its way to becoming what it is today, a national treasure.

Lining both sides stand 10 of the Smithsonian Institution's museums, the stately National Gallery of Art, and the National Archives. Here, too, are the monuments and memorials recognized worldwide—the Washington Monument, the Lincoln and Jefferson Memorials, the Vietnam Veterans Memorial, and many more.

As America's "front yard," a term favored by the National Park Service, the Mall plays many roles. It has been and will continue to be a place of protest, drawing Americans by the tens of thousands to condemn or support a variety of nation-shaking causes. It is a place of ceremony, where citizens gather to watch a presidential inauguration every 4 years. An annual summer folk festival, a giant book fair, an annual summer movie festival, and Fourth of July fireworks enliven its festivities calendar.

As a park, it's a place to play. At noon, joggers pour from nearby office buildings. Frisbee enthusiasts hone their skills. In odd corners, local clubs compete in softball, soccer, rugby, field hockey, and volleyball on well-maintained playing fields and courts. The nonathletic can relax on a Mall bench, sipping a cold beverage and watching the passing throngs.

And the Mall is a place of beauty. Two thousand lofty American elms shade Mall pathways. The Tidal Basin's 3,000 Japanese cherry trees, fluttering with pink blossoms in early spring, glean admiration from around the world. Thousands of flowers—tulips, pansies, and annuals—decorate formal gardens and planting beds. Fountains splash, ornamental pools glisten in the sun, and the Potomac River glides swiftly past. Expect to spend much of your stay in the city on the Mall or not far away.

NATIONAL MUSEUM OF THE AMERICAN INDIAN

A splashing stream, grass-ringed ponds, simulated meadowlands, and woods encircle the Smithsonian's newest museum. They represent the landscape inhabited by the country's Native Americans, past and present. Their often sad, but compelling story is told at the **National Museum of the American Indian** ☆ kids (On the Mall at Jefferson Dr. and 4th St. SW; ☎ 202/633-1000; Metro: Federal Center–L'Enfant Plaza; www.americanindian.si.edu; free admission; daily 10am–5:30pm except Dec 25).

Stop first at the **Window on Collections.** It's probably what most visitors expect to see when they step inside. A large and colorful sampling of the museum's rich collection of Native American art and cultural objects—beadwork, dolls, arrowheads—is the largest and most diverse in the world.

But the soul of the museum really is **Our Universes, Our Peoples and Our Lives** in which 24 tribes describe their lives today, usually displaying everyday objects rather than crafts as illustration. The Saint-Laurent Metis, who live on the southeast shore of Canada's Lake Manitoba (near Winnipeg), focus, for example, on their unusual livelihood as commercial ice fishermen. To help visitors understand, their exhibit features a Lake Manitoba bombardier, a near tank-size vehicle on tracks that helps them navigate the ice. Don't miss the **Wall of Gold,** a wall hung with more than 400 gold objects, including masks. We've also been quite impressed by the films on Native American life shown in the main theater; they rotate on a regular basis, but those that we've seen have made deep impact.

The **Chesapeake Museum Store** displays handmade Southwestern pottery and other handicrafts, much of it of top-notch quality and extremely expensive. Even if you don't buy, admire the craftsmanship of tribal artisans. And the museum's **Mitsitam Native Foods Café,** which features native foods from across the Americas, is as much of a cultural experience as the museum and the best eating option on the Mall (see p. 54 for a full review).

HIRSHHORN MUSEUM AND SCULPTURE GARDEN

Bedazzled or perplexed. You may find yourself in one of these categories, or maybe both, when you step into the always stimulating **Hirshhorn Museum and Sculpture Garden** ☆ (On the Mall at Jefferson Dr. and 7th St. SW; ☎ 202/633-1000; Metro: L'Enfant Plaza; www.hirshhorn.si.edu; free admission; 10am–5:30pm daily except Dec 25). It's the Smithsonian's museum of modern and contemporary art—much of it bold and eye-catching; some of it puzzling, somber, and downbeat. The collection, housed in a giant hollow cylinder of a building wrapped around a fountain courtyard—it looks like a giant doughnut with feet—has grown from a nucleus of 12,000 works donated by American art collector Joseph H. Hirshhorn. A uranium magnate, Hirshhorn described his collecting process as intuitive, involving a "charge or energy that went straight to the heart." (For a man who made his millions finding irradiated metals, this seems appropriate.) Hirshhorn often befriended the artists whose works he collected, so this "capsule history of modern art" is also an interesting record of his distinguished social life (the museum continued to add its collection after his death in 1981). Early modernists, such as Fernand Leger and Constantin Brancuşi, are followed chronologically by the organic landscapes of Georgia O'Keeffe, who in turn

Washington for Free, a Penny-Pincher's Paradise

On a really tight budget, you easily could enjoy a week or more in the nation's capital and not spend a penny on sightseeing, recreation, or entertainment. Really.

TOURS: All the major federal institutions—the places that make the news—schedule free tours (although you may have to apply in advance for passes). At the top of the list are the **White House** and the **U.S. Capitol,** followed by the **Supreme Court,** the **Library of Congress,** the **U.S. State Department,** and the **Pentagon.** Seeing these national icons should fill 2 or 3 days.

MUSEUMS, ZOOS, AND ART SHOWS: Every one of the Smithsonian Institution's museums, including the **National Air and Space Museum** and the **National Zoo** (yes, that's a Smithsonian institution), are free, as are the renowned **National Gallery of Art** and **U.S. Holocaust Museum,** also right off the Mall. Visiting them could take another full week. But even all this doesn't exhaust the possibilities. Several embassies, including the gorgeous Canadian and Finnish embassies, host free art shows regularly.

FAMOUS BUILDINGS, CEMETERIES, AND GARDENS: The National Archives, home of the U.S. Constitution, doesn't ask for a cent. Neither do the **U.S. Botanic Garden,** the **Bureau of Engraving and Printing** (where big bucks are stacked high), **Arlington National Cemetery,** or **Ford's Theatre National Historic Site,** where Lincoln was assassinated. By now, you are probably well into a second all-free week in Washington.

MONUMENTS AND MEMORIALS: All the most-famous monuments and memorials are free—**Washington Monument, Jefferson Memorial,**

gives way to pop art. You will see works by Pablo Picasso, Piet Modrian, Joan Miró, Max Ernst, Willem de Kooning (two full galleries), and Edward Hopper. An entire gallery of small mobiles by Alexander Calder is a visual delight. Pop art is represented in part by a Claes Oldenburg textile sculpture of a 7-Up sign.

Washington produced its own school of art, also modestly represented in the museum. It's proof that politics is not the city's only creative endeavor. The school, called the Color Field, emerged in the 1950s. Inspired by earlier abstract impressionists, it's distinguished by its use of paint that is brushed, poured, or soaked onto cotton canvases. Among the standouts here are Morris Lewis' *Delta Theta* (1961) and *Point of Tranquility* (1959–60), which resembles the petals of a giant flower in full bloom.

On the Mall, the Hirshhorn's sunken **Sculpture Garden** ✮✮ (7:30am–dusk daily except Dec 25) is small but mighty, with a wonderfully varied collection of sculptures and a serenity that's unusual on the Mall (it's one of our favorite hide-

Lincoln Memorial, World War II Memorial, Vietnam Veterans Memorial. So are the lesser-known but still compelling ones—the **Iwo Jima Statue,** the **Korean War Veterans Memorial,** the **Franklin Delano Roosevelt Memorial.**

EVENING ENTERTAINMENT: The possibilities here are myriad. Tops on the list are the performances at **Kennedy Center's Millennium Stage,** every night of the year from 6 to 7pm in the Grand Foyer. Rock, pops, classical, jazz, blues, bluegrass—the program, featuring up-and-coming talent and some established favorites, changes every show. But second best is not far behind: The **Army, Navy,** and **Marine Corps bands** perform alternately at 8pm Monday through Friday on the west steps of the Capitol Building throughout the summer. The setting and the talent of these young musicians make for a very special evening. For strictly classical music, again of high quality, the **National Gallery of Art** is the venue for 6:30pm Sunday chamber concerts and solos in the gallery's West Garden Court. Performances take place from early October through June. No tickets required; just show up.

And don't forget spoken word opportunities; the city enjoys a rich (and free) literary calendar including **poetry readings, book discussions,** and **lectures.** See "The Other Washington" chapter for more on those.

Finally, free movies under the stars make Mondays from mid-July to mid-August fun. The **Screen on the Green** movie festival presents a free show of a Hollywood classic on the National Mall (btw. 4th and 7th sts.) at sundown on those nights.

The freebies list is long. Keep your eyes open while you are in town, and you are sure to add to that list.

aways in this part of town). Among the garden's more expansive works—you can't miss it—is a massive red construction of iron beams by American Mark di Suvero called, puzzlingly, "Are Years What?" Also look for Rodin's *Crouching Woman,* its shapes echoed in the abstract *Cubi XII* by David Smith across the path. A sculpture of an empty coat, a tribute to Rodin's famous likeness of Balzac, is another beautifully "echoed" work.

ARTHUR M. SACKLER GALLERY

Yet another wealthy collector donated more artworks of such value that they rate a Smithsonian museum of their own. In this case, 1,000 masterpieces of Asian art form the core of the **Arthur M. Sackler Gallery** ✭ (On the Mall behind the Castle; ☎ 202/633-1000; Metro: Smithsonian; www.asia.si.edu; free admission; 10am–5pm daily except Dec 25). Actually, the museum is beneath the Mall, reached through an elaborately decorated pavilion of Asian design situated at ground level behind the Castle in the Haupt Garden. The Mall is getting crowded, and a subterranean site helped ease the congestion. Entering the pavilion, distinguished by its multiple-peaked roof, is a form of time travel back into an exotic fantasyland of ancient art and archaeological riches.

But first, the museum introduces you to a contemporary work, *Monkeys Grasping for the Moon,* created by expatriate Chinese artist Xu Bing expressly for the Sackler in 2001. The sculpture, comprised of 21 laminated wood pieces, dangles like a chain from the sky-lit atrium to a reflecting pool two floors below. Each of the pieces forms the word "monkey" in one of a dozen languages. A Chinese fable (in which a group of monkeys, linking arms and tails, attempt to grasp the moon) is the basis for the work. The family of Madame Chiang Kai-shek, wife of the former Nationalist Chinese leader, presented the complex sculpture to the museum to commemorate her historic appearance before the Joint Session of Congress in 1943.

Other museum highlights include ancient Iranian silver, illustrated Persian manuscripts, Chinese jades and lacquer work, carved Indian ivory, exquisite Japanese folding screens, and finely crafted Cambodian earthenware. These items are scattered about in small galleries; the major display areas generally are given over to temporary exhibits and visiting shows. The **gift shop** here is one of our favorites on the Mall.

FREER GALLERY OF ART

Thanks to a wealthy donor of varied passions, a single museum houses one of the world's finest permanent collections of Asian art as well as the most comprehensive assemblage of the works of American artist James McNeill Whistler. This somewhat schizophrenic entity is the **Freer Gallery of Art** ✰✰ (On the Mall at Jefferson Dr. and 12th St. SW; ☎ 202/633-1000; Metro: Smithsonian; www.asia. si.edu; free admission; daily 10am–5:30pm except Dec 25). The founder, Detroit industrialist Charles Lang Freer, also funded the building, an Italian Renaissance-style beauty wrapped around a sculpture-filled Italianate courtyard. The Freer is connected by an underground passage to the Sackler, thus linking the Smithsonian's two big Asian collections. What is the difference between the Sackler and the Freer? The Sackler is mainly the showplace for visiting or temporary exhibits; the Freer displays only its permanent collection.

We'd suggest starting your visit to the Freer with the Whistler works, as you'll get some sense of how the collection evolved. Whistler already was collecting Japanese and Chinese artworks when Freer met him, and he credits Whistler with encouraging him to collect them as well. The purchases certainly influenced Whistler's art; an Asian influence is unmistakable in Whistler's famed **Harmony in Blue and Gold: The Peacock Room.** It is a complete room, breathtaking in its elegance and complexity, that Whistler painted for English ship owner Frederick Leyland. Its name comes from the floor-to-ceiling paintings of blue and gold peacocks. Whistler covered every inch of the ceiling and walls, creating a unique setting where Leyland could show off his prized collection of blue and white porcelain vases and an accompanying Whistler painting, *Princess from the Land of Porcelain,* which hangs over the fireplace. Interestingly, the artist and his patron had a dispute over the room before it was paid for, having to do with Whistler painting more than he was originally commissioned for, and perhaps more unnervingly, inviting friends to party in it while Leyland was away. The ship owner at first refused to pay and then settled with the artist for half the amount he requested. It's thought that the two angry peacocks, fighting over a pool of coins, is Whistler's take on the dispute. Whistler completed the room in 1877 and never saw it again.

You'll see the dreamlike, lushly pastel paintings of Whistler's contemporaries, Thomas Wilmer Dewing and Dwight William Tyrone, in nearby galleries. Though American, they also have a love for surface beauty that's characteristic in the Freer's Asian galleries.

Of all the many Asian works displayed, the most dramatic are the Japanese screens in **Gallery 5.** Don't miss them. Using screens as a canvas was seen by Japanese artists as a way to encourage an intimate relationship between the viewer and the work of art. Especially lovely is *Landscapes of the Four Seasons* (18th–19th c.), a pair of screens each with six folds. Winter is depicted on the left in a frozen snowscape, but then the countryside comes into blossom as the seasons progress across the other folds.

Freer simultaneously collected contemporary American art, including Whistler and ancient Asian art. When he bequeathed his collection to the Smithsonian, he stipulated that no more American pieces be added, but the Asian collection could grow. Among the most interesting new additions, since Freer's death, are the art films shown in two first-floor galleries. Take time to see them; they rotate, so we can't tell you what the content will be, but they usually represent an interesting take on the contemporary Asian art and cultural scene.

NATIONAL MUSEUM OF AFRICAN ART

Raising the profile and importance of African art—the art of an entire continent—is a major goal of the **National Museum of African Art** (On the Mall behind the Castle; ☎ 202/633-1000; Metro: Smithsonian station; www.nmafa.si.edu; free admission; daily 10am–5pm except Dec 25). Like the Sackler Gallery, this museum also is located beneath the Mall, reached by a second pavilion—this one with a series of roof-top domes. Ancient carved masks, sculptures, beautifully patterned textiles, beadwork, and utilitarian objects form much of the collection, but contemporary works reveal the continuing quality of African art and crafts. The colorfully subversive works of Yinka Shonibare, a Nigerian artist who's made a name for himself covering a number of unlikely objects with African cloth (a commentary on the lack of authenticity in modern African culture), will be featured beginning in November 2009.

THE NATIONAL PORTRAIT GALLERY & SMITHSONIAN AMERICAN ART MUSEUM

OFF THE MALL, BUT STILL ESSENTIAL   If you go to only one art museum in Washington, we suggest making it the two-for-one pairing of the **National Portrait Gallery** ✪✪✪ and the **Smithsonian American Art Museum** ✪✪ (8th and F sts. NW, 6 blocks north of the Mall; ☎ 202/633-1000; Metro: Metro Center/Gallery Place–Chinatown; www.reynoldscenter.org; free admission; daily 11:30am–7pm except Dec 25), which share the same building. The art is American, an apt subject for a visit to the nation's capital; much of it's young and

Civilized Museum Hours

Both the **National Portrait Gallery** and the **American Art Museum** keep later hours than their colleagues on the Mall, making them easy to fit in on most any visit. On Thursday nights, live music often plays in the interior courtyard and drinks are served. Best yet, the Reynolds is near some of the best affordable restaurants in the city (see p. 53 for more on that), making it a natural for an art stroll followed by dinner.

Nearby, the **Spy Museum** (p. 125) keeps evening hours in the summer months, making it an ideal evening outing for families. The **Crime and Punishment Museum** (p. 130) also stays open later than most, year-round, but we're not sure that's enough of a reason to patronize it.

iconoclastic, reflecting the country's modest age; and it dwells in varied ways, positive and negative, on the American Dream. Together, the museums have been dubbed the Donald W. Reynolds Center for American Art and Portraiture, named for a donor, but nobody will call them that. If you haven't heard of either, it is because both were shut down from January 1, 2000 to July 1, 2006, for a complete $298-million renovation of the historic building that houses them.

Start with the **National Portrait Gallery,** which sounds dry as dust, we know, but is anything but. Here you'll see the mugs of all those famous people who filled your high school history textbooks. In the best of the portraits, their charisma, the life-force that propelled them to fame, blasts off the canvas (or through the photograph, daguerreotypes, or sculpture; many mediums are used here). The portraits cover a vast range of Americans from a number of different walks of life. We see author Edith Wharton painted as a high society toddler; the earliest known oil painting of Native American peoples, representing four fearsome looking chieftains; Davy Crockett, dressed as a farmer. Sometimes what you think about someone is turned on its head by seeing how he or she looked. Daniel Webster and Margaret Sanger, for example, were total hotties, he looking more like a Byronic poet than a future secretary of state and she boasting the kind of looks that make sexual prophylactics necessary (luckily, she spent her career making birth control available!). John D. Rockefeller comes off in his portrait bust as having the soul of Santa Claus (of course, he was a major patron of the artist . . .).

Illuminating the works even further is what we think is the most engrossing, best written wall text in all of Washington. Usually just the right length, it offers up little tidbits of history, art history, and even gossip, that enliven the viewing. A daguerreotype of Lincoln with his wife, Mary, for example, is accompanied by insightful text on how contemporaries viewed their marriage.

To our minds some of the most interesting works in the museum are the less-lauded portraits. But the Gallery also has some blockbuster exhibits, including the nation's only complete collection of presidential portraits outside the White House ("American Presidents"). The major attraction is Gilbert Stuart's **"Lansdowne"** portrait of George Washington, generally regarded as the most famous of all Washington paintings—and Stuart's masterpiece. It was commissioned in 1796, the president's final year in office, by a wealthy Philadelphia merchant. He presented it to the Marquis of Lansdowne of Great Britain, who had supported American independence. For 3 decades, Lansdowne's heirs loaned it to the Smithsonian for display. But in 2001 they threatened to put it up for auction. Thanks to a $30-million donation from the Donald W. Reynolds Foundation, the Portrait Gallery was able to purchase it prior to the auction.

Twentieth-Century Americans is another wonderful permanent exhibit, featuring Andy Warhol's silk-screen take of Michael Jackson, video portraits of Bob Hope telling jokes to the troops while Raquel Welch dances in the background, and a painting we can only call "The Second Coming of Elvis Presley." It's that over-the-top kitschy.

The **American Art Museum** features a survey of the country's best from the Colonial era to the present. One new and contemporary work, a real mind-boggler, is Nam June Paik's *Electronic Superhighway: Continental U.S., Alaska, Hawaii* (1995), a giant neon map that outlines all 50 states and the District of Columbia. Within the boundaries of each state is a video screen, each presenting a different mini-show about the state (clips from the *Wizard of Oz* represent Kansas, the musical *Oklahoma* for Oklahoma, and less well-known, sometimes odd images rep other states). You truly have to see it to believe it. If art isn't your thing, pop in anyway to see this dazzler.

Out of the past is a dazzler of a different sort. It is Albert Bierstadt's 10-foot-wide canvas *Among the Sierra Nevada, California*. No, it isn't the real Sierra—Bierstadt painted it in London using the Swiss Alps as a model—but it does capture the majesty of the mountain range. It hangs in a room to itself, displayed as it might have been when it made a grand tour of Europe and the United States in the late 1860s.

Grandma Moses and her less-well-known colleagues are the stars of the museum's **Folk Art** galleries, a weird but wonderful trip through the world of self-taught artists. Many of the works you'll see here seem pulled intact from deep in the unconscious. Though less polished than other works in the museum, they have an undeniable power. A favorite: *The Throne of the Third Heaven from the Nations Millennium General Assembly*, a room-size altarpiece that was discovered after the death of the artist James Hampton in 1964. Despite being created entirely from aluminum foil, craft paper, and bits of glass, it's a work of intense beauty, one man's attempt to build his own personal religion.

Only part of the Smithsonian's vast collection can be displayed in the galleries. The rest hang in the **Luce Foundation Center**, three floors of glassed-in storage space open for public viewing. A second new feature is the **Lunder Conservation Center**, five laboratories and studios set behind floor-to-ceiling glass. Visitors can watch conservators at work cleaning paintings, refurbishing frames, and preserving fraying paper. It's fascinating. And don't forget to visit the Renwick Gallery (see below), the crafts offshoot of this museum.

The museums are housed in the former Patent Office, a Greek revival beauty—a work of art itself—based on the Parthenon. One of Washington's oldest public buildings, it dates back to 1836. Because of its initial purpose, it was quickly dubbed "the temple of invention."

Panda-monium at the National Zoo

The irresistibly cute family of Giant Pandas—mama Mei Xian, papa Tian Tian, and their male cub Tai Shan, born July 9, 2005—are the star residents of the Smithsonian Institution's **National Zoological Park** ✩✩ 🅺🄸🄳🅂 (3001 Connecticut Ave. NW; ☎ 202/633-4800; Metro: Woodley Park–Zoo and 3-block walk north; www.nationalzoo.org; free admission; Apr–Oct daily 10am–6pm, Nov–Mar 10am–4pm except Dec 25, grounds open at 6am year-round). There's even a "Panda-Cam" for those who want to watch the slow-moving, bamboo-munching antics of this trio from their computers at home. The zoo pays China $1 million a year to exhibit Mei Xian and Tian Tian, and the birth of their cub required an additional one-time payment of $600,000. The money goes for preservation of the endangered species in China. The zoo maintains the largest reproductive science department of any zoo in the world.

You'll find the pandas, sloths, and other animals native to Sri Lanka, Bangladesh, Bhutan Nepal, and China in the spiffy new (and greatly enlarged) **Asian Trail** at the zoo's entrance. (It's part of a $53-million overhaul of the upper end of the zoo.)

Established in 1889, the zoo is one of the oldest in America. It is a huge place, a 163-acre urban park in an upscale residential neighborhood. Plan on spending at least half a day to take in the major exhibits. And, we can't stress this enough, wear comfortable walking shoes. You will cover at least 2 hilly miles and probably more.

Beyond the pandas, the lions here are among the most active we've ever watched; and the seals delight in interacting with humans. Really, the last time we were here, they followed us along the rail, jumping up to greet us every minute or so. Olmsted Walk is the zoo's main thoroughfare, which you follow mostly in a wide loop, downhill for a mile and then back up again. Youngsters will enjoy the **Kids' Farm,** a zoo of cows, donkeys, and goats in a 2-acre mock farm at the zoo's farthest end. Before you set off, check in at the Visitor Center for special scheduled programs, such as panda interpretation, elephant bathing and training, seal and sea lion training, and octopus feeding.

THE RENWICK GALLERY

Outrageous, comical, and often supremely elegant describe the modern American handmade crafts from the 20th and 21st centuries exhibited in the **Renwick Gallery** ✩✩ (1661 Pennsylvania Ave. NW at 17th St.; ☎ 202/633-1000; Metro: Farragut West; www.americanart.si.edu/renwick; free admission; daily 10am–5:30pm except Dec 25). Really, this is a museum you're going to laugh out loud in. Though the artworks are exquisitely crafted, many are oddball, which makes for entertaining viewing. A small space, you can do it justice in 45 minutes. A popular work is *Game Fish, 1988* by Larry Fuente, a fantasy sculpture depicting a giant sailfish flamboyantly bedecked in colorful buttons, beads, coins, and even a Superman doll. Another fine work is *Ghost Clock* by Wendell Castle, a grandfather clock draped in the delicate folds of a carved white shroud.

Though not part of the crafts collection, the upstairs Grand Salon, a lavish and spacious Victorian room from the Civil War era, merits a peek. On its walls hang two giant landscapes by Thomas Moran, *The Chasm of the Colorado* and *The Grand Canyon of the Yellowstone*. We also recommend spending some time with the 506 portraits of Native Americans in the George Catlin's Gallery, the artist's attempt to save, at least on canvas, a way of life that was tragically disappearing. See it *before* you look at the bizarre crafts in the other room, or you may be inclined to giggle inappropriately at some of the names of the people in the portraits (*He Who Puts Out and Kills,* portrait number 294, is next to *How Did He Kill.* We know this is meant to be serious, but was the person who arranged the portraits getting a bit of a laugh? We think so.)

A branch of the American Art Museum (see above), the Renwick collections are housed in a French Second Empire–style building that was Washington's first art gallery.

NATIONAL POSTAL MUSEUM

"Uh, oh," you might think, "the history of mail sure sounds pretty dry to me." Not at all! The **National Postal Museum** ✪✪ 🄺🄸🄳🄢 (On Capitol Hill at Massachusetts Ave. and 1st St. NE; ☎ 202/633-1000; Metro: Union Station; www.postal museum.si.edu; free admission; daily 10am–5:30pm except Dec 25) tells exciting tales, sure to earn a youngster's rapt attention. In America's early years, delivering the mail in fair weather and foul often proved a life-threatening adventure. Learn about the challenge of posting a letter in pre-Revolutionary America, a near-roadless wilderness; ride with the Pony Express across the vast and lonely Great Plains; witness (via video) the now bygone skill of mail car clerks who tossed and snatched up mail bags from a fast-moving train. Stamp collectors will want a look at the "Rarities Vault," which features two new exhibits each year. The museum occupies the Old City Post Office Building, a classic Beaux Arts–style structure that complements neighboring Union Station.

MORE WORLD-CLASS ART MUSEUMS

In addition to the Smithsonian member museums we've mentioned, check out the oldest private art collection in Washington, D.C., opened in 1874, the **Corcoran Gallery** ✪✪ (500 17th St. NW, 1 block from the White House; ☎ 202/639-1700; Metro: Farragut West; www.corcoran.org; $8 adults, $6 military/seniors 65-plus, $4 students; Wed–Sun 10am–5pm, Thurs 10am–9pm, open on holiday Mon, closed Thanksgiving, Dec 25, and Jan 1). It occupies an enviable position just opposite the White House. (A pairing of the two makes for a wonderfully varied morning.) As a consequence of its age and the somewhat haphazard way in which it grew—yes, the tastes of another Gilded Age tycoon, William Wilson Corcoran, are at its heart—its collection is quirky and eclectic and its holdings vast. The Corcoran is the proud owner of some 14,000 objects from the 6th century B.C. through today. And though it's already moved once to make room for its displays—its original home is the splendid building that today houses the Renwick Gallery—there's only enough room to put a small fraction of these holdings on display.

Of these permanent pieces, the Gilbert Stuart portrait of George Washington and the mythic American scenes (*Niagara Falls* by Frederic Edwin Church and Albert Bierstadt's *Last of the Buffalo* from 1888 plus works by Whistler, Sargent, Eakins, Winslow Homer, and Mary Cassatt) may be the most famous. But to our minds they don't have the aesthetic wallop of the European works donated by Senator William Andrews Clark. We know of no better way to brighten up a rainy day than wandering among the Barbizon landscapes, the Salon Dore (an intact and deliciously opulent Louis XVI–era room), and the 13th-century stained-glass windows and tapestries of the Clark wing.

The building itself, designed by Ernest Flagg and opened in 1897, is a splendid example of the Beaux Arts style, especially the soaring interior atrium galleries and rotunda.

Opened in 1921, the **Phillips Collection** ★★ (1600 21st St. NW; ☎ 202/387-2151; Metro: Dupont Circle; www.phillipscollection.org; donation suggested weekdays, varied weekend fee in range of $12 adults, $10 students/seniors 62-plus, under 18 free; Tues–Sat 10am–5pm, Thurs 10am–8:30pm; Sun 12–7pm except June–Sept Sun 12–5pm, closed all federal holidays), is considered America's first museum of modern art. Duncan Phillips, a steel and banking heir from Philadelphia, founded the museum in his home. Not so unusual, but unlike other mansion-based museums, this one was actually opened to the public *while* the family was still living in it. This gives the Phillips, in its older areas at least, a quirky hominess and personality. Many rooms are still set up as the family originally had them.

Duncan Phillips's (and the museum's) most famous acquisition is Renoir's *Boating Party.* Phillips purchased it in 1923, considering it "one of the greatest paintings in the world." Completed in 1880, it pictures a group of 14 Parisians at lunch on the balcony of a restaurant on the Seine near Paris. Among those 14 are his future wife Aline Charigot (holding the dog), and Gustave Caillebotte, an important art patron and painter (he's seated in the lower-right corner). Along with the light-hearted and festive *Boating Party,* the small, intimate museum, full of odd nooks and corners, displays other Impressionist works by van Gogh, Degas, and Cezanne. They are a must-see for art lovers.

The museum opened a new addition in 2006, greatly increasing its gallery space. Here you find the new **Rothko Room.** It's a rectangle designed to the exact specifications that artist Mark Rothko and Phillips concluded in 1960 was needed to best display four of Rothko's bold blocks of color. Pauline finds it the most meditative space in the city and is drawn back there again and again (so look for her if you go!).

Beyond the art, the Phillips has a busy schedule of events. Gallery talks are held Thursday at 6 and 7pm. Classical concerts Sunday at 5pm in the Music Room feature emerging artists and have been a museum tradition for 60 years. Talks and concerts are included in the admission fee.

It's surprising to learn that the **National Museum of Women in the Arts** ★ (1250 New York Ave. NW; ☎ 202/783-5000; Metro: Metro Center; www.nmwa.org; $8 adults, $6 students/seniors (60-plus), under 18 free; Mon–Sat 10am–5pm, Sun 11am–5pm, closed Thanksgiving, Dec 25, and Jan 1) is the only one of its kind in the world. But it makes a good case that the old boys club of painting and sculpture isn't the be all and end all for arts appreciation. Women artists, from such famous names as Georgia O'Keeffe and Mary Cassatt, to such surprise artists as the actress Sarah Bernhardt (who was also an accomplished sculptor) bring their own oomph to the mix. And this handsome, former Mason's Hall has something no other Washington museum has: a painting by Frida Kahlo. It's a cocky self-portrait she gave to her reputed lover, the Russian revolutionary Leon Trotsky, during his time in Mexico. Many make the pilgrimage just to see Kahlo's defiant sensuality. In addition to the permanent collection, the museum always has two or more temporary exhibitions (its recent one of female photographers literally had us stopping in our tracks every few feet, arrested by the immediacy of the works on display). It's a nice bite-size gulp, even for those who might be feeling museumed-out.

FOUR MORE EXCELLENT MUSEUMS

In any other city, the following museums would be star attractions. But D.C. has such an embarrassment of riches that these four, while top-notch, can't be considered "iconic" experiences. That said, depending on your own interests, you might enjoy some of them *more* than some iconic sights.

That certainly might be the case with our next pick. True or not, it has been claimed that more spies prowl Washington's streets than any other city in the world. We always feel like we might meet one, on a busman's holiday, at the **International Spy Museum** ✿✿ 🧒 (800 F St. NW, 4 blocks north of the Mall; ☎ 866/spymuseum or 202/393-7798; Metro: Gallery Place–Chinatown; www.spy museum.org; $15 adults 12–64, $12 children 5–11, $14 seniors, military, and spies (employees of the FBI and CIA are admitted free, as well as employees of our allies' intelligence services); Apr–Oct 10am–8pm daily, Nov–Mar 10am–6pm daily, closed Thanksgiving, Dec 25, and Jan 1), an imaginative, surprisingly scholarly examination of this shadowy profession.

At the outset of a visit, guests assume a spy's identity, one of many kid-friendly touches (small video screens test you on how well you remember your cover throughout the museum). More computer games and videos games follow, teaching you the tricks of the trade: how to blend in, make "drops" of important information, tap phones, and change your look. Spy gizmos—umbrellas with poison tips! A James Bond–type car with hubcaps equipped with flashing blades! Cameras in every place possible!—fill the cases in the next rooms. And then you get to the meat of the museum: an in-depth, interest-grabbing examination of the "secret history of the world"—how spies have shaped hundreds of major historic events from the D-day battle of World War II to the leaking of the secrets behind the creation of the atomic bomb. A favorite: the videos recounting the tales of master spies who've been caught over the years.

Plan to spend a minimum of 2 hours, longer if you've got kids with you (Pauline had to drag her two daughters kicking and screaming out of this one, something she can't say about any other museum). Summer lines can get long, so consider purchasing timed tickets in advance from Ticketmaster, ☎ 800/ 551-7328; www.ticketmaster.com.

Much of what you come to Washington to see is inspirational or at least entertaining. The **U.S. Holocaust Memorial Museum** ✿✿✿ (Adjacent to the Mall at 100 Raoul Wallenberg Place SW, but use the entrance at 14th St. and Independence Ave.; ☎ 202/488-0400; Metro: Smithsonian; www.ushmm.org; free admission; 10am–5:30pm daily except Yom Kippur and Dec 25), essentially detailing

The Country's Most Infamous Theater

A shot rang out in the theater, and the president slumped in his seat, mortally wounded. Stunned, the audience witnessed the assailant leap from the presidential box onto the stage. Injured, he stumbled away to the alley and fled on horseback. And in a split second, the course of history shifted.

Because of their importance, Ford's Theatre and the presidential box where President Abraham Lincoln was fatally wounded on the night of April 14, 1865, have been preserved as **Ford's Theatre National Historic Site** (511 10th St. NW, 3 blocks north of the Mall; ☎ 202/426-6924; Metro: Metro Center or Federal Triangle; www.nps.gov/foth; free admission; daily 9am–5pm except Dec 25). And believe it or not, the theater has been back in business for quite some time now. The most evocative way to see it is to attend a matinee or evening performance. Ford's puts on a full schedule of plays and musicals featuring locally based as well as nationally known actors, designers, and directors (p. 249). The redbrick Victorian building has been restored inside and out to look as it did on the night of the assassination. Like patrons that evening, you will sit on hard-backed chairs, though they now have cushions. Above on the right is the box where Lincoln and his wife Mary Todd Lincoln sat with two guests watching *Our American Cousin,* a comedy. The box is furnished with reproductions except for the red damask sofa where one of the guests, Major Henry Reed Rathbone, was sitting; he was stabbed in the left arm. The engraving of Washington hanging on the front of the box also is original.

a multiyear atrocity—the murder of six million Jews and others—is horrific and emotionally draining. What makes a visit endurable are the strength and courage displayed by the survivors, who recall their experiences in heart-wrenching detail. They offer up their awful trial in the hope that no other people will suffer as they did. In June of 2009, the museum was the site of a terrible attack by a white supremacist and Holocaust denier that left a security guard fatally wounded.

Of the many museums we describe in this guide, the Holocaust Memorial, which opened in 1993, is the one you cannot visit in a rush. To absorb the lessons of the Permanent Exhibition, presented in numerous audiovisual exhibits and seemingly miles of printed text, plan to spend a minimum of 2 hours. For your sake and that of other visitors, don't bring children under the age of 11. They may be frightened by what they see, which includes graphic images of brutality and death.

No passes are necessary for entering the Museum building, special exhibitions, the interactive Wexner Learning Center, and other Museum resources. Passes are required for visiting the Permanent Exhibition—The Holocaust—March through August. These passes, which are issued for a specific time during the day, can be obtained at the museum on a first-come first-served basis on the day of your visit. You can also order passes from **Tickets.com** at ☎ **800/400-9373.** A "convenience" fee of $1.75 per ticket and a "processing" fee of $1.25 per order are charged.

We challenge you to make it through the performance without glancing up at the box again and again, wondering, "What if . . . ?"

If you can't see a show, Ford's still makes a short (30-min.) but illuminating stop on your sightseeing itinerary. The theater's basement is a museum detailing the assassination, the subsequent hunt for actor John Wilkes Booth, who fired the shot, his death at the hands of his pursuers, and the trial of alleged fellow conspirators. You see such historic items as Lincoln's overcoat, the dagger Booth used to stab Rathbone, and Booth's left boot and spur. Entangled in the decorations of the presidential box, Booth broke a small bone in his left leg in the jump. Dr. Samuel Mudd cut the boot from Booth's foot when Booth sought Mudd's medical help during his flight. You can peek into the theater and the fatal box if a rehearsal or performance is not underway.

The assassination story continues just across the street at the Petersen House, 516 10th St. NW, the **House Where Lincoln Died**, a four-story redbrick home. Lincoln received immediate medical attention from a young doctor in the theater audience, and then he was carried unconscious to the home of William Petersen, a tailor. Visitors are shunted through the Front Parlor, where Mary Todd Lincoln waited out the night; the Back Parlor, where Secretary of War Edwin Stanton began the initial investigation of the crime; and the Back Bedroom, where Lincoln died at 7:22am on April 15. Furnishings are not original, but they are of the period.

Passes are not required to simply enter the museum building, and if you are in a hurry there are a few exhibits that won't take much time. Youngsters under age 11, as well as adults, will hear a sample of the memorial's message in **"Remember the Children: Daniel's Story"** . It is the Holocaust from the perspective of a young boy growing up in Nazi Germany. About 20 minutes.

The **Permanent Exhibition** begins with an elevator ride to the fourth floor. There the Holocaust story unfolds chronologically with the rise of Nazi Germany, illustrated with grainy film clips of Adolph Hitler exhorting thronged supporters and of massed, goose-stepping troops on parade. It ends, two floors below, with the Allied liberation of the death camps. You will step into a railroad box car used to transport Jews under inhumane conditions to killing centers. You will see prayer shawls, umbrellas, piles of shoes, and artificial limbs confiscated by the Nazis. Perhaps most horrifying, you will view a scale-model re-creation of the killing process at a death camp, where the assembled victims had no idea of their approaching fate. Here and there are spirit-boosting exhibits, such as the small vessel on display, along with its sister ships, that helped smuggle nearly all of Denmark's Jews to safety in neutral Sweden. Ultimately, the memorial is a reminder, as the museum suggests, of our "responsibilities as citizens of a democracy" to never acquiesce to another holocaust.

With newspapers closing every other week, it seems, a visit to the **Newseum** ✮✮✮ 🅺🅸🅳🆂 🏆 (555 Pennsylvania Ave. NW; ☎ 888/NEWSEUM [639-7386]; www.newseum.org; Metro: Archives–Navy Memorial; $20 adults, $18 seniors, $13 youth ages 7-12; daily 9am–5pm except Thanksgiving, Christmas, and New Year's Day) takes on not just added poignancy, but may raise feelings of alarm. That's because at the core of this entertaining yet erudite enterprise there's an important message: Journalism is an integral part not just of democracy, but of civilization itself. And the museum makes its case in a much less heavy-handed way than we just have, while at the same time acknowledging the myriad of ways that journalists can screw up. In a town of absorbing museums, this one more than holds its own. Trust us, you won't want to move on.

Which is why you'll want to set aside at least 4 hours to see the Newseum, which is huge (about 250,000 sq. ft.). Do it from top to bottom, so the story gets told in the right order. It starts, believe it or not, with town criers and smoke signals, acknowledging the need for journalists even in pre-literate societies (who'd have thunk it?), and then zooms through 500 years of reported news, with absorbing artifacts from a 3,000-plus-year-old cuneiform brick from Sumeria to newspapers from the time of the French Revolution to TV, radio news, and even blogging. To handle issues of journalistic ethics, such as how reporters deal with their own biases and when it's okay to use anonymous sources, they've enlisted the help of such heavyweights as Dan Rather, Brit Hume, and Cokie Roberts, among others. These bolded names star in a series of hard-hitting videos, in small theaters off the main galleries.

Our favorite exhibit was the **Running Towards Danger** gallery, which featured a moving documentary about the reporters who ran *toward* the Twin Towers on 9/11, just as everyone else was running away. The gallery of **Pulitzer Prize** photos is also mesmerizing. Each year's award-winning photo is here, and it brings back a rush of memories. They're accompanied by absorbing accounts of what was happening in and around the split second when the shutter snapped. Don't forget to bring the kids. They won't be bored, we promise. Each floor has interactive elements for them, whether it be a pop quiz on journalistic ethics, or oddball bits of video to view. And they'll *love* the interactive newsroom, where they can see what it's like to stand in front of a camera and report the news (you can then download the video off the Internet for $5). As well, there's usually something playing in one of the museum's 15 theaters that's either geared toward the younger set or appropriate for kids.

MUSEUMS & ATTRACTIONS FOR VISITORS WITH SPECIALIZED INTERESTS

ANTIQUES

A half-block off the mall, the **Daughters of the American Revolution (DAR) Museum** (1776 D St. NW; ☎ 202/628-1776; Metro: Farragut West; www.dar.org/museum; free admission; Mon–Fri 9:30am–4pm, Sat 9am–5pm except federal holidays and 2 weeks in July) boasts a collection of 30,000 decorative and fine arts objects made or used in America prior to the Industrial Revolution. They are displayed in two galleries and 31 period rooms that include an 18th-century

Georgian tavern and a 19th-century Tennessee parlor. We'd say this collection has a dusty, lavender-scented charm—if antiques are your thing, by all means stop by. Guided tours are offered on the hour and half-hour from 10am to 2:30pm weekdays and 9am to 4:30pm Saturday; it's also possible to wander through on your own with a self-guided tour booklet if you prefer.

The skilled craftsmanship of early America's finest artisans is spotlighted in the eighth-floor **Diplomatic Reception Rooms** ✦ (23rd St. btw. C and D sts. NW; ☎ 202/647-3241; Metro: Foggy Bottom–GWU; http://receptiontours.state.gov; free admission; Mon–Fri except federal holidays) at the U.S. State Department. The elegant collection of antiques, including silver by Paul Revere and Chippendale furniture from Philadelphia, literally furnishes the setting for some of the country's most important diplomatic meetings. Reservations for a 45-minute escorted tour of the rooms are required at least 90 days in advance. They can be made at the website (see above) or through your representative or senators. Tours are scheduled for 9:30, 10:30am, and 2:45pm. Children younger than 12 not admitted.

ARCHITECTURE

Oddly, the building that houses the **National Building Museum** (401 F St. NW; ☎ 800/222-7270 or 202/272-2448; Metro: Judiciary Square; www.nbm.org; $5 suggested donation; Mon–Sat 10am–5pm, Sun 11am–5pm, closed Thanksgiving, Dec 25, and Jan 1) is of as much interest as the museum itself. Constructed in 1887 in Italian Renaissance style for the U.S. Pension Bureau, it's a redbrick fantasy that often is used for gala events such as inaugural balls and campaign fundraisers. The ornate **Great Hall,** almost the size of a football field, boasts eight massive columns rising 75 feet from the floor of the hall; they're among the tallest interior columns in the world. Building tours are scheduled 12:30pm Monday to Wednesday; 11:30am Thursday to Saturday; and at 12:30 and 1:30pm Sunday.

As for the exhibits, they tend to be temporary and can be a bit hit-or-miss in their execution, tackling such topical issues as managing suburban growth, preserving landmarks, and revitalizing urban centers. One long-term display zeros in on seldom-seen architectural details—for example, the tops of skyscrapers high above a viewer's eye (building buffs will enjoy viewing all these odd scraps, for the rest it's a bit of a yawn). Another better-curated hall examines how the monument-filled city of Washington grew from swampy land on the Potomac River. Children will enjoy the special play area, complete with building blocks (lots of 'em) and special, age-appropriate classes on architecture and engineering (check the website).

CELEBRITY WAX LIKENESSES
(YUP, MADAME TUSSAUDS IS IN D.C.)

In 2008, **Madame Tussauds** 🧒 (1025 F St. NW at corner of 10th St.; ☎ 202/942-7300; www.madametussauds.com/washington; Metro: Metro Center; Sun–Thurs 10am–4pm, Fri–Sat 10am–6pm; $18 adults, $15 seniors, $12 children) joined the city's overpopulated museum field, trying to draw in visitors with its minimalist re-creation of the Oval Office (hey, you can sit in the chair for photos, something they aren't going to let you do in the real White House!). We don't think that's enough reason to make room for it on your schedule, though kids do get a kick out of trying to make the wax figures blink (or at least Pauline's did), and you might work it in as a peace offering to your over-museumed offspring. As at its other venues, you'll find movie stars and sports hero mannequins (some startlingly lifelike) with ones that speak more directly to the history of the city (politicians mostly). Kudos to whoever decided to pair Nixon with George W. Bush—they make an oddly appropriate couple.

CRIME

The new **Crime and Punishment Museum** (575 7th St. NW near F. St.; ☎ 202/ 393-1099; www.crimemuseum.org; Mar 20–Aug 31 daily 9am–9pm, Sept 1–Mar 19 10am–8pm; $18 adults, $15 seniors, law enforcement officials, and kids 5–11, active military and veterans enter free on Tues, Wed, and Sun with ID; Metro: Gallery Place–Chinatown) has a lot of both going on. The crime here is that they've taken an inherently fascinating subject and unnecessarily tarted it up with such gimmicks as shooting ranges and car chase rides (uh, isn't this supposed to be a "museum"?). Punishment comes from the fact that though some of the wall text and interactive exhibits are intriguing and quite well done, containing surprising pieces of memorabilia (like an actual electric chair), you have to wade through a lot of dross to get to them. We're sure gore-obsessed 14-year-old boys will enjoy it (and maybe some bloodthirsty adults, too) and for TV fans, *America's Most Wanted* films episodes in the basement and those who show up at the right time (which is not advertised in advance) will get to see a taping. But we found the glorification of serial criminals, and the idea of looking at horrific crime scenes for the fun of it, more than a bit disturbing. In a town with this many superb museums, you can do better.

EXPLORATION

It's a sign of the riches of Washington, D.C., that the **National Geographic Discovery Center** ✿ ☺ ⓚⓘⓓⓢ (1145 17th St. NW; ☎ 202/857-7588; Metro: Farragut North; www.nationalgeographic.com; free admission; Mon–Sat and holidays 9am–5pm, Sun 10am–5pm, closed Dec 25) isn't better known. Though it consists of just one large room, it brings the considerable resources of the National Geographic Society to bear in creating its exhibits, often partnering with top institutions around the globe. Don't believe us? China's famed Terra Cotta warriors will not be displayed at the National Gallery or Smithsonian when they come to Washington in November 2009; they will be here. When we last visited, the topic was whales, an exhibition created in New Zealand and containing massive skeletons, interactive displays on whale behavior, and even the model of the whale head that was used in the film *Whale Rider*. You never quite know what you'll get here, but it's usually kid friendly (at the whale exhibit, along with computer games, kids were given free coloring/work books to enhance their experience). Lectures and workshops (p. 154) are also an important feature here.

IMPRESSIONIST ART

David and Carmen Kreeger collected art, especially Impressionist works, with eager enthusiasm and a whole lot of money. And they displayed them in their home, a postmodern architectural jewel designed by Philip Johnson to show off the 200-work collection. Today the house and the collection form the intimate **Kreeger Museum** (2401 Foxhall Rd. NW; ☎ 202/338-3552; D6 bus from P and 22nd sts. NW to Foxhall and Reservoir rds. NW with half-mile walk; www.kreegermuseum.org; $10 adults, $7 students and seniors 65-plus; tours Tues–Fri 10:30am and 1:30pm by appt., self-guided tours Sat 10am–4pm without appt.). Impressionist works include paintings by Monet (nine, including the lovely *Meadows at Giverney*, 1884), Renoir, Sisley, and Pissarro. Four Picassos, highlighted by the vibrant and bold *Man with Golden Helmet* (1969), hang in the library. Washington's notable Color Field school is represented by an abstract construction from Sam Gilliam and the multicolored and wavy stripes of Gene Davis. Despite its many virtues, the museum should be considered a lagniappe, something a little extra (and worthy) for art lovers with time to spare—especially with such a surfeit of art elsewhere in the city. Children under 12 are discouraged from the weekday tours, which last about 90 minutes.

LATIN-AMERICAN ART

Impressively, the government-sponsored **Art Museum of the Americas** (At 18th St. and Constitution Ave. NW; ☎ 202/458-6016; Metro: Farragut West; www.oas.org; free admission; Tues–Sun 10am–5pm except federal holidays) does not shy away from controversy. Its blockbuster show in 2008/2009 featured moving responses from artists in Argentina, Colombia, Guatemala, Brazil, and Chile to the disappearance of their countrymen over the years. The works were unflinching, angry, and at times, quite moving. A member of the Organization of American States, it's a small art museum so space can be tight. The works on display, either from the permanent collection or in special shows, change frequently. Mostly they are bold and colorful and well worth a quick look.

MARITIME HISTORY

The sprawling exhibit hall that is the **Navy Museum** 🧒 (Washington Navy Yard, 9th and M sts. SE; ☎ 202/433-4882; Metro: Eastern Market, connecting to N22 bus to the entrance gate; www.history.navy.mil; free admission, but phone reservations required 24 hr. in advance; Mon–Fri 9am–5pm, weekends and holidays 10am–5pm, closed Thanksgiving, Dec 25, and Jan 1) covers Navy history from the Revolutionary War to the present with plenty of military hardware, including a massive World War II anti-aircraft gun, a submarine chamber with operating periscope (the kids will want to take a look), and a Navy fighter plane suspended from the ceiling. And lots and lots of ships, of course; dozens of historic models fill the hangar-like museum and the Navy destroyer *Barry* is moored outside on the Anacostia River. You are welcome to go aboard. And the Navy Yard itself, where the museum is located, is a historic site; the service's oldest shore establishment, it dates to 1799.

Is this enough to make you want to travel the 40 minutes or so it takes to get there from downtown? It depends. Certainly, the museum is for a "must-see" for military buffs. For everyone else, we think it's something to do after you've covered all the major sights. If you do decide to go, try to visit on a Wednesday when a retired admiral leads wonderful tours of the place. Then pop by **Levi's Port Café** (p. 57) afterward for a soul food feast.

MONEY

On August 28, 1862, a whopping 9,000 types of state-chartered notes were being traded in the United States as money. Many were worthless because of the failure of the issuing banks. On August 29, 1862, the Federal Government cleaned up the situation. On that date, it got into the manufacturing business itself, authorizing the creation of the **Bureau of Engraving and Printing** 🔵kids (14th and C sts. SW, adjacent to the Holocaust Memorial and the Mall; ☎ 202/874-2330 and toll-free 866/874-2330; Metro: Smithsonian; www.moneyfactory.com; free admission; 8:30am–3pm Mon–Fri except federal holidays and Dec 25–Jan 1). Overnight, it stabilized the economy (well, for a little time at least) and today, that Bureau continues printing up money, taking its marching orders from Congress, which tells them how much replacement cash will be needed each year (paper bills only; coins are the province of the U.S. Mint).

You can easily see this "Money Factory" (the official nickname) on a quick half-hour tour of a glassed-in corridor above the factory floor. You'll learn a bit, but not much, about security procedures (for obvious reasons) and a whole lot about paper stock, inks, and designs. Don't be afraid to ask questions: The tour is most interesting when the guides veer away from their canned spiel. It's kinda fun, especially for kids. They get a real kick out of guessing how much moolah they see temptingly spread out before them. A 5-foot-high stack of sheets of $1 bills (as tall as most kids) is worth $320,000 when trimmed. If $100 bills are being printed, the same stack of sheets is worth $32 million. As might be expected, nobody gets close enough to snatch a few samples.

The ticket booth, inconveniently located at the tour exit at Raoul Wallenberg Place and Independence Avenue SW, opens at 8am, but during busier times of the year, lines form as early as 6:30am, and tickets may all be gone by 9am. You'll need to line up there if you visit between the first Monday in March and the last Friday in August. At other times of the year, you can simply go right into the visitor center to take the tour (no tickets required due to smaller numbers of visitors). *Insider tip:* To avoid standing in line in spring and summer, join a Congressional VIP Tour (p. 96). You can apply for a ticket up to 6 months in advance by contacting your U.S. senator or representative.

SCIENCE

Science research plays a role in public policy decisions. This is the message of the small, high-tech **Marion Koshland Science Museum of the National Academy of Sciences** (6th and E sts. NW, 3 blocks north of the Mall; ☎ 202/334-1201 or 888/567-4526; Metro: Judiciary Square; www.koshland-science-museum.org; $5 adults, $3 students/military/seniors 65-plus; Wed–Mon 10am–5pm, closed Thanksgiving, Dec 25, and Jan 1). Interactive exhibits tackle such issues as global warming, use of DNA in criminal investigations, and tracking the origins of SARS (a quickly contained epidemic threat). Be prepared to concentrate; this is serious stuff, seriously presented. You can't just breeze through and expect to make any sense out of what you see. Children under 13 not admitted.

SHAKESPEARE

English majors take note. The world's largest and finest collection of Shakespeare's printed works is maintained and displayed (some of it, anyway) at the **Folger**

Shakespeare Library ✫ (201 E. Capitol St. SE; ☎ 202/544-4600; Metro: Capitol South; www.folger.edu; free admission; Mon–Sat 10am–5pm, closed all federal holidays). Curators delve into the literary riches two or three times a year to stage major exhibitions in the **Great Hall,** itself a paneled gem reminiscent of Elizabethan England. But always on display is a **First Folio of Shakespeare,** the first collected edition of his works. Put together after his death in 1616 by a pair of fellow actors, the First Folio is the only source of 18 plays, including *Macbeth, Julius Caesar,* and *The Tempest.* A computer program called **"Turning the Page"** allows you to examine a few pages of its *Romeo and Juliet.* Another rarity that attracts lots of attention when it is displayed is Queen Elizabeth's "gift roll" of 1585, a list of Christmas gifts she gave and received that year. She and her courtiers proved rather generous. On your way out, take a peek inside the adjacent **Elizabethan Theatre.** With its half-timbered facade, it suggests the courtyard of an inn, which might have served as a playhouse for a traveling group of actors. A regular season of plays is presented here. Outside, visit the **Elizabethan Garden** on the museum's east end and the fountain topped by a statue of **Puck** on the west side.

TEXTILES

Preserving and displaying rare handmade fabrics, including ancient apparel, from around the world is the mission of the small but renowned **Textile Museum** (2320 S St. NW; ☎ 202/667-0441; Metro: Dupont Circle; www.textilemuseum.org; $5 suggested donation; Tues–Sat 10am–5pm, Sun 1–5pm, closed federal holidays and Dec 24). The museum claims to be one of the world's foremost specialized art museums. A bold claim, but in fact its exhibits are exquisite. See an 18th-century Chinese "Dragon Coat" of meticulously embroidered silk; a 13th-century striped tunic from Peru; a dashing red scarf from 20th-century Bali; Oriental rugs; Japanese kimonos; tapestries; banners; colorful burial wraps; and more. Housing 17,000 objects, the museum occupies a pair of adjoining mansions dating to the early 1900s. They are representative of the museum's fashionable Kalorama neighborhood, located just off Embassy Row. Before you leave, be sure to take a walk through the formal gardens in the rear.

FIVE MORE MEMORIALS YOU'LL WANT TO SEE

It's hard to believe, but almost in the city's heart is a 91-acre near-wilderness where you can escape from urban hubbub—Theodore Roosevelt Island in the Potomac River. This peaceful retreat is the site of the **Theodore Roosevelt Memorial** 🄺🄸🄳🅂 (On the Potomac River at the Virginia end of the Theodore Roosevelt Memorial Bridge; ☎ 703/289-2500; Metro: Rosslyn and a 20-min. walk; www.nps.gov/this; free admission; dawn–dusk daily). Preserving forest, marsh, and swamp, the island was dedicated in 1967 to America's 26th president as a memorial recognizing his love of nature. Two and a half miles of island trails invite easy hikes. In the center, a 17-foot-high statue of Roosevelt soars to treetop height. He is dressed in frock coat, his right hand raised in a vigorous gesture representative of his famous enthusiasm. Four large stones are inscribed with his comments on nature, mankind, youth, and government. To read more about the park, see p. 170 in chapter 7.

You may well walk over the next memorial without quite realizing what it is. Set right off Pennsylvania Avenue, the **U.S. Navy Memorial** (Pennsylvania Ave. btw. 7th and 9th sts. NW; ☎ 202/737-2300; Metro: Archives–Navy Memorial;

www.lonesailor.org; free admission; always on view) is right off a busy street and easy to overlook. You'll know you're there when you see the statue of the U.S. Navy bluejacket—he looks somewhat like a figure out of a Calvin Klein–goes-military ad. The 7-foot-tall statue called "The Lone Sailor" is the focal point of the memorial. He is posed as if waiting to board ship. At his feet is a huge world map inlaid in granite. Bas reliefs on an amphitheater wall highlight various Navy units, such as the Seabees, and the contribution of Navy families at home. The bronze for the statue was mixed with metal artifacts taken from eight Navy vessels representing more than 200 years of naval history. Art critics and Pauline give thumbs-down to the memorial as unimaginative, but Jim disagrees. He finds the Lone Sailor, boldly confronting an uncertain future, to have a very personal impact. Immediately behind the outdoor memorial, the **Navy Heritage Center** (free admission; daily 9:30am–5pm, except closed Nov–Feb Mon and most federal holidays) features a small, limited museum called the Gallery Deck and the Ship's Store, selling nautical merchandise. Click on "Plan of the Day" on the website (see above) for the schedule of concerts and other events. Unless you come from a Navy background, you can skip the center.

At the end of the Civil War in 1865, the Grand Review of Troops marched down Pennsylvania Avenue in Washington. Not invited to participate were 156 African-American units who also fought for the victorious Union cause. In 1998, they received belated recognition with the installation of the **African-American Civil War Memorial** (Vermont Ave. and U St. NW; ☎ 202/667-2667; Metro: U Street–African American Civil War Memorial–Cardozo; www.afroamcivilwar.org; free admission; always on view). A bronze statue called **"Spirit of Freedom,"** centered in a granite-paved plaza, depicts uniformed black soldiers and a sailor, armed and alert. Behind them, the **"Wall of Honor"** lists the names of 209,145 members of the United States Colored Troops (USCT), which includes 7,000 white officers. Two blocks west of the memorial, the **African-American Civil War Memorial Museum** (1200 U St. NW; free admission; Mon–Fri 10am–5pm, Sat 10am–2pm) houses a modest collection of photographs and documents chronicling the African-American role in the Civil War. U Street, the location of both memorial and museum, was once known as Washington's "Black Broadway." Undergoing revitalization, it's emerging again as one of the city's hot dining, shopping, and entertainment areas. Before you hoist a beer at one of the street's trendy bars, detour a block or two to ponder the memorial.

Two tree-lined "pathways of remembrance" border blue-gray marble walls. Inscribed on the walls are the names of more than 16,500 of America's federal, state, and local law enforcement officers who have been killed in the line of duty since just after the Revolutionary War in 1792. The walls, set in a 3-acre park called Judiciary Square, form the **National Law Enforcement Officers Memorial** (E St. btw. 4th and 5th sts. NW; ☎ 202/737-3400; Metro: Judiciary Square; www.nleomf.com; free admission; always on view). At the entrance of each pathway, the bronze sculpture of a lion and her cubs symbolizes "the protective role of our law officers." Approximately half of the officers listed on the walls were shot to death. Another 28% died in traffic-related accidents. Each year in May, new names of the fallen are dedicated in a huge **Candlelight Vigil** at the memorial. Currently exhibits at its **Memorial Visitor Center** (2 blocks east at 605 E St. NW; Mon–Fri 9am–5pm, Sat 10am–5pm, Sun noon–5pm, closed major holidays)

In the Shade of the Democracy Tree

Perhaps Washington's least known monument—though it shouldn't be—is the **Democracy Tree.** A 25-foot-tall shady elm, it stands at 21st Street and New Hampshire Avenue NW, a few blocks north of the White House. Look for it curbside ringed by a small fence. A bronze plaque placed at the tree's foot in 2001 protests Washington D.C.'s lack of a voting senator or representative in the U.S. Congress. Sponsored by the Foundry United Methodist Church, it is an anguished appeal for redress:

"This tree is dedicated to the more than half-million veterans, taxpayers, and citizens of the District of Columbia who, despite fighting in foreign wars, paying their full measure of taxes, and faithfully serving their country, continue to have no voting representation in the Congress of the United States of America. Taxation without Representation is Tyranny."

Most anyone who calls Washington home agrees. Jim certainly does.

explain the memorial's history and significance. A video kiosk allows you to call up the name and photograph (where available) of anyone whose name is inscribed on the walls.

As bold as it is graceful, the **National Air Force Memorial** (Southwest of the Pentagon; ☎ 703/247-5808; www.airforcememorial.org; Metro: Pentagon and half-mile walk; free admission; Apr 1–Sept 30 8am–11pm daily, Oct 1–Mar 31 8am–9pm daily) was dedicated on October 14, 2006. It pays tribute to the millions of men and women who have served in the U.S. Air Force and in its predecessor organizations—the Aeronautical Division of the U.S. Signal Corps; the Division of Military Aeronautics, Secretary of War; the Army Air Service; the Army Air Corps; and the Army Air Forces. The Air Force, which has suffered more than 53,000 combat casualties in the country's wars, was the only branch of military service without a memorial in the Washington area. The memorial features three stainless steel spires that soar skyward 270 feet. In an interview with the *Washington Post,* architect James Ingo Freed said his inspiration came when he saw TV footage of Air Force jets performing their bomb-burst formation. Several planes shoot skyward in unison and then peel off, creating high-rising vapor trails that curl at the top. While honoring the sacrifice of American Air Force men and women, the memorial also was conceived as a tribute to America's formidable air power. The site, a promontory called the Naval Annex, enjoys a grand and unobstructed view of Washington and its monuments.

HISTORIC HOUSES & THE FASCINATING FOLKS WHO LIVED IN THEM

Washington has been home to many people who have played an important role in shaping the nation. Their homes, now open as museums, serve as a memorial to their accomplishments—and, often, to their idiosyncrasies. A few houses also exhibit important decorative arts collections. Each should provide a refreshing break from the crowds on the Mall. They are quiet and uncrowded, and several display lovely gardens. Note that descriptions of **Dumbarton House, Dumbarton Oaks Mansion and Garden, Old Stone House, Tudor Place,** and **Anderson House** can be found in chapter 8. (See "Walking Tour 2: Georgetown" on p. 197.)

Marjorie Merriweather Post, heir to the Post cereal fortune, was a business-woman, philanthropist, and art collector—though she is more popularly remembered as a wealthy socialite, known in her day as "the Queen of Washington." As a collector, her most notable achievement was assembling one of the most important collections of Russian imperial art outside Russia today. It is on view along with her also impressive French decorative arts collection in the 40-room home she bequeathed to the pubic as a museum, officially **Hillwood Museum and Gardens** ✫✫ (4155 Linnean Ave. NW; ☎ 202/686-5807; Metrobus: L1 or L2 Connecticut Ave. to Tilden St. and walk east on Tilden to Linnean Ave. and turn left; www.hillwoodmuseum.org; by reservation only, $12 adults, $10 seniors 65-plus, $7 college students, $5 students 6–18, under 6 not admitted; Tues–Sat 10am–5pm, closed Jan and most holidays; reservations required). Rooms are furnished with outstanding examples of Russian Fabergé, ceramics, glass, textiles, and metalwork. Post acquired these objects when her third husband, Joseph E. Davies, served as U.S. ambassador in Moscow from 1937 to 1938 during Stalin's reign of terror. In the turmoil, imperial art went on the market with the approval of the Soviet government in need of cash, which Post readily provided. Treasures include a portrait of another empress, Catherine the Great of Russia, in the entry hall and two chests of drawers (called commodes) flanking the library door made by the official cabinetmaker to Louis XVI and Marie Antoinette.

Surrounded by woodlands, the 25-acre estate on which Hillwood sits is land-scaped with "pleasure gardens." Audio tours and guided tours are available, but we think the best way to see the house is to simply pick up a copy of Hillwood's complimentary 25-page tour and souvenir booklet and go at your own pace through the house and gardens. Though advance reservations are required to enter the estate, you can arrive at any time of the day and take as long as you want to explore.

Mary McLeod Bethune, a child of former slaves, became the most celebrated African-American figure of the New Deal era. Her Logan Circle town house, where she lived for 6 years from 1943, honors her work. It is now a National Park Service museum called the **Mary McLeod Bethune Council House National Historic Site** (1318 Vermont Ave. NW; ☎ 202/673-2402; Metro: McPherson Square; www.nps.gov/mamc; free admission; Mon–Sat 9am–5pm, closed Thanksgiving, Dec 25, and Jan 1). The house also served as the first headquarters of the National Council of Negro Women, which Bethune founded. A tireless activist, she served as an advisor on African-American affairs to four presidents. When President Franklin D. Roosevelt appointed her director of the Division of Negro Affairs of the National Youth Administration, it was the highest position in the Federal Government ever held up to that time by an African-American woman. A visit to the tidy Victorian-era home begins with a 25-minute film. From it, you learn Bethune was the 15th of 17 children—the first child born in freedom in her family. As a youngster, she helped her parents farm cotton. But she was determined to go to college and later founded a school for girls in Daytona Beach, Florida, that she built into a college.

Stephen Decatur, born to a prominent Philadelphia family, joined the new U.S. Navy in 1798 and quickly earned fame for his heroism in 1804 during the Barbary Wars in the Mediterranean. After more valiant service in the War of 1812, he and his wife became celebrity residents of Washington. Their home is now the **Stephen Decatur House Museum** (1610 H St. NW; ☎ 202/842-0920; Metro: Farragut West; www.decaturhouse.org; donation requested; Mon–Sat 10am–5pm, Sun noon–4pm, closed Thanksgiving, Dec 25, and Jan 1). Escorted tours lasting about 40 minutes begin at 15 minutes after the hour. The three-story, Federal-style brick mansion, built around 1818, is one of only three surviving residences designed by Benjamin Henry Latrobe, known as the "Father of American Architecture." Its location 1 block from the White House overlooking Lafayette Park made it a very fashionable residence. The tour focuses on the city's social life of the period and on Decatur's exploits, including his duel with a political enemy that cost him his life at the age of 39.

Born a slave in Maryland, Frederick Douglass secretly learned to read and managed to escape to New York City when he was 20. There he founded an anti-slavery newspaper, wrote books, and made good use of his oratorical skill to press the abolitionist cause. In 1877, he was named U.S. Marshall of the District of Columbia. He and his wife purchased a hilltop home in the city's Anacostia neighborhood. Dubbed Cedar Hill, it is now a National Park Service museum called the **Frederick Douglass National Historic Site** (1411 W St. SE; ☎ 202/426-5961; Metro: Anacostia and B2/Mt. Rainier bus; www.nps.gov/frdo; free admission; daily Apr 15–Oct 15 9am–5pm, Oct 16–Apr 14 9am–4pm, closed Thanksgiving, Dec 25, and Jan 1). An escorted tour of the white-brick house, with a 17-minute film, begins at the Visitor Center at W and 15th streets SE at the foot of the hill. Among Douglass's personal artifacts on exhibit is Abraham Lincoln's cane, a gift from Mary Todd Lincoln after her husband's assassination. If you take public transportation: The B2 bus stops in front of the house. But to reach the Visitor Center, walk a half-block down W Street to 15th Street. Note that Anacostia is a low-income neighborhood where crime remains a problem. If you have safety concerns, consider taking a taxi to the museum; you can summon a return taxi from the Visitor Center. This is the only attraction in this guide to which we are in any way uneasy about sending you. Another option is to go by Tourmobile. A special 2½-hour tour departs at noon daily from the Washington Monument and Arlington National Cemetery from June 15 through Labor Day. Tickets ($7 adults; $3.50 children 3–11) should be purchased at least 30 minutes in advance from either departure point.

Alice Paul, a lifelong activist for women's rights, founded the historic National Women's Party in 1917 to pressure Congress and the White House for the right to vote. The organization's headquarters and Paul's home for 43 years was the **Sewall-Belmont House** (144 Constitution Ave. NE; ☎ 202/546-1210; Metro: Union Station; www.sewallbelmont.org; $5 donation suggested; Tues–Fri 11am–3pm, Sat noon–4pm except federal holidays). Inspiring 60-minute tours, given on the hour, spotlight Paul and early suffragist leaders—Susan B. Anthony, Lucretia Mott, Elizabeth Cady Stanton—who fought long and hard to get the vote for their gender and to obtain equal legal rights for them.

Two Presidential Homes

You don't have to take a White House tour to walk in the footsteps of a U.S. president. The homes of two of America's most complex, important presidents are open to visitors (and much easier to get into than the White House nowadays!).

The first is the 28-room home of America's 28th President—the **Woodrow Wilson House** ★★ (2340 S St. NW; ☎ 202/387-4062; Metro: Dupont Circle; www.woodrowwilsonhouse.org; $7.50 adults, $6.50 seniors 65-plus, $3 students 7-plus; Tues–Sun 10am–4pm except major holidays). Its story is a tragic one. Wilson had had a stroke a year before he left office and was too ill to attend the inauguration of his successor. Instead he was driven to his new home, a 1915-built mansion, in the prestigious Kalorama neighborhood. With little money of their own, his wife used the cash from Wilson's Nobel Peace Prize and the donations of friends to buy and furnish the home. Since presidents back then were allowed to keep the gifts they received while in office, the home was decorated with a number of remarkable objects. A mosaic of St. Peter hangs in the Drawing Room, a gift from Pope Benedict XV when the Wilsons toured Europe at the conclusion of World War I. On another wall in that same room, a token from the French government, a priceless Gobelins tapestry hangs; it's so massive the bottom of it has to be rolled up. A complete samurai outfit, presented by Emperor Hirohito, can be seen in the library.

Alas, Wilson's ability to enjoy his opulent home was limited. He never recovered from the stroke (in fact, there's speculation that for the last year of his presidency, it was his wife who was calling the shots) and died just 36 months after moving in. His wife Edith lived here until her death, many years later, but kept the home looking exactly as it had when Wilson was alive. In a way, it's very much a time capsule for high living in the early 1920s: You'll see what was then a state-of-the-art icebox in the kitchen, and a pantry filled with boxes of "Kellogg's Pep" and other goods from that era. But more poignantly, you'll learn about the difficult final years of a man who may well have been one of the country's most intellectual and idealistic presidents.

Guided tours lasting about 60 minutes are scheduled on the hour; you can reserve on the website (above) or join as a walk-in visitor.

A major strength of the Wilson tour is the remarkably intact nature of his home. **President Lincoln's Cottage** ★ (in the Soldiers Home at the intersection of Rock Creek Rd. NW and Upshar Rd. NW; ☎ 800/514-ETIX; www.lincolncottage.org; Mon–Sat 10am–3pm, Sun noon–4pm; $12 adults,

Paul's organization had a particularly tough time. Its members marched, picketed the White House, got arrested, and were repeatedly sent to jail, where they staged hunger strikes and suffered abominable conditions. Their nonviolent tactics are seen as a precursor to the later civil rights movement. At the same time,

$5 children, $10 members of the military; Metro: Georgia Ave.–Petworth and then the H8 bus or a 10-min. walk), which sits on the ground of the Soldier's Home and was used for many purposes over the years, has not a stick of furniture that Mary or Abe might have rested a weary hand on. The curators, aware of this deficiency, have turned to audio and video displays to re-create some sense of authenticity. And because of the strength of the tale they have to tell, their methods work remarkably well.

The Lincolns moved into the cottage the summer after their son Willie passed away in 1862. The White House in summer was oppressive (Lincoln's secretary John Hay wrote that the odor coming off the nearby swamps at that time of year was like "ten thousand dead cats") and Mary Todd Lincoln was worried that the air and polluted water could be danger-ous for her other son, Tad. She was probably right; modern historians think Willie died from a typhoid-like illness caused by pollution in the canal that served as the White House's source of water.

So, the family moved up to this house on a hill, cooled by breezes all year long. Lincoln made a perilous commute through a dense forest each day from there to the White House. Despite this, the family enjoyed being away from the White House so much that they ended up extending their stays well beyond the summer months. All in all, the Lincolns lived here for a full quarter of the time he was in office. Lincoln was at the Cottage the day before he was shot.

On the tour, you'll hear about the daily life of this Civil War first fam-ily and about the informality of this "mini–White House" where tourists would stop by just to chat with Abe and soldiers gathered in the kitchen for a snack. You'll learn how his living here might have changed the course of the war; removed from the fishbowl of the Presidential Mansion, Lincoln was able to talk more directly with the soldiers who surrounded him. He also often met wounded soldiers on the way back from the front on his daily commute. He never failed to stop and talk with them about what they had witnessed.

Like the Wilson tour, a visit to the Lincoln Cottage will introduce you to a side of the president of which you were probably unaware. For Lincoln fans—and doesn't that include just about all of us?—this makes for a moving and at times powerful pilgrimage.

Note: Advance reservations are essential. Since the site opened in 2008, its tours often sell out.

Paul trained novice female lobbyists in the Sewall-Belmont House to present the organization's case to Congress. In 1920, the 19th Amendment granting women the right to vote was ratified.

But Paul fought on for equal rights for women, writing the original Equal Rights Amendment in 1923. The fight for an amendment, as yet unratified, continues. But the National Women's Party no longer lobbies; it has transformed itself into a public education organization. The Sewall-Belmont House, a museum recalling and reaffirming the organization's goals, displays political cartoons, banners, and photos of the fight for the right to vote.

The house itself, a grand Georgian-style mansion set in the heart of Capitol Hill, is one of the oldest in the city, built in 1800. Robert Sewall was the original owner but he rented it to Albert Gallatin, treasury secretary under presidents Jefferson and Madison. As a tenant, Gallatin drafted the financial details of the Louisiana Purchase in the house. The Belmont in the name is Alva Belmont, who bought it for the National Women's Party in 1929.

WASHINGTON'S ARCHITECTURAL STANDOUTS

Washington's first major buildings were the **White House** and the **Capitol,** begun in 1793, a full 7 years before the city became the seat of government. From the outset, talented architects and designers accepted the challenge to create monumental structures for the capital city of a new nation. Often the designs reflected the marble domed and columned models of ancient Greece and Rome, a way of giving the new city a grandeur it had yet to earn. Sometimes they goofed, bequeathing the city "standouts" reviled by critics and citizens alike.

We have cited many admirable buildings already. But other structures, perhaps not serving such notable public uses, also merit the attention of visitors interested in urban architecture. We list seven additional "standouts" in order of their potential to interest visitors to the city—their "wow" factor, as it were.

Completed in 1908, the mammoth marble **Union Station** (Massachusetts and Louisiana aves. NE; ☎ 202/289-1908; Metro: Union Station; www.union stationdc.com; always open) was designed to serve as a triumphal gateway to the city. At the time, it was the largest train station in the world. The enormous **Waiting Room** sprawls beneath a barrel-vaulted ceiling gilded with 72 pounds of 22-karat gold leaf; the **Grand Concourse** was patterned after the Baths of Diocletian in Rome. At 760 feet in length and 130 feet high, it is one of the largest public spaces built in the country.

A bit of a curiosity, the **Old Post Office Pavilion** (12th St. and Pennsylvania Ave. NW; ☎ 202/289-4224; Metro: Federal Triangle; www.oldpostofficedc.com; free entry; Mar–Aug Mon–Sat 10am–8pm and Sun noon–7pm, Sept–Feb Mon–Sat 10am–7pm and Sun noon–6pm) was the city's first "skyscraper," its first steel-framed structure, and the first government building to have its own electric power plant. Built in 1899 in Romanesque revival style, and looking entirely out of place among its neoclassical neighbors, it once was home to the U.S. Post Office and the D.C. Post Office. But just 15 years after its debut, it was regarded as dated and faced demolition. Then the Depression intruded, and later preservationists stepped in to save it as an architectural monument. Today it houses shops and a food court. You can ride to the top of the 315-foot-high **Clock Tower** (second-highest viewpoint only to the Washington Monument) for a 360-degree view of the city. In the tower are the **Congressional Bells,** a bicentennial gift from Great Britain to the U.S. Congress. They were modeled after the bells of Westminster and ring on holidays. Practice rings can be heard at 6:30pm on many Thursdays.

Notable for its unusual shape, the result of an odd triangular-shaped lot, the **Octagon** (1799 New York Ave. NW; ☎ 202/638-3221; Metro: Farragut West; www.theoctagon.org) also takes its place in history as the temporary residence of President James Madison and his wife Dolley. This lovely brick building, dating to 1801, houses the architectural and design museum of the American Architectural Foundation. The Madisons moved in after the British burned the White House in the War of 1812. The Treaty of Ghent, ending the war with Great Britain, was signed in the second-floor parlor on February 17, 1815.

Despite its name, the Octagon is not eight-sided. The name may derive from its round entrance hall, a type that in the 18th century was often constructed with eight angled walls and called "octagon salons." Architect William Thornton, first architect of the U.S. Capitol, actually conceived a three-story, six-sided structure incorporating a circle, two rectangles, and a triangle.

Even so, visitors (except large groups) at press time (the Octagon is in the final phase of an extensive exterior restoration including replacement of the main roof, restoration of the unique coal vault and related archaeological testing, stone repair, and portico roof restoration), take a walk around the building—initially a private residence—to admire its appearance. It is considered one of the best examples of Federal period architecture in the country. The style is an adaptation of the work of Robert Adam, a fashionable Scottish architect of the era who broke away from the rigidity of formal Georgian architecture. Visit the website for updates on construction, and when tours will resume.

Known as the "Church of the Presidents," **St. John's Episcopal Church** (Overlooking Lafayette Sq. at 16th and H sts. NW; ☎ 202/347-8766; Metro: McPherson Square; www.stjohns-dc.org; Mon–Sat 9am–3pm for visits) claims that every president since James Madison has worshiped here. Madison chose pew 54, paying the customary rental; since then #54 has been the presidential pew. Architect Benjamin Latrobe designed and built St. John's in 1816. A block away across Lafayette Square is Decatur House (see Historic Houses), which he also built. Initially the church was simple in design, taking on the shape of a cross. But later, architects added a Roman-style portico with six tall columns over the entrance. After it came a triple-tiered steeple, which gives the building something of a top-heavy look, like legendary Brazilian entertainer Carman Miranda hefting a pile of fruit on her head. Inside, take a look at an 18th-century prayer book in the president's pew autographed by a number of chief executives.

Washington's most historic lodging is the **Willard Hotel** (14th St. and Pennsylvania Ave. NW; Metro: Metro Center). A hotel has stood on this site since 1816; it acquired the name Willard in 1850 and the present 12-story building was completed in 1904. No other local hotel can match its legendary heritage. Julia Ward Howe wrote the "Battle Hymn of the Republic" in her room in the previous Willard during the Civil War. In 1963, the Rev. Dr. Martin Luther King, Jr., composed his "I Have a Dream" speech in the current Willard. The term "lobbyist," an important (if often criticized) profession in the nation's capital, was born in the Willard's lobby, where influence-peddlers lurked in search of anybody with political clout. Henry Hardenbergh, who designed New York City's famed Plaza Hotel, came up with the plans for the Willard also. Predating the Plaza by 3 years, it bears stylistic similarities and is more fanciful than most major buildings in the city. On your way down "Peacock Alley" (the hotel's block-long promenade), check out the lobby, decorated with 35 different types of marble.

The Grandeur of Gothic:
Washington's National Cathedral

A Gothic dazzler, nearly a century in construction, the massive Episcopalian **Washington National Cathedral** ✪ 𝙠𝙞𝙙𝙨 (Wisconsin Ave. at Massachusetts Ave. NW; ☎ 202/537-6200; Metrobus: N2, N4, N6 from Dupont Circle; www.cathedral.org/cathedral; Sun 8am–6:30pm, Mon–Fri 10am–5:30pm, Sat 10am–4:30pm; suggested donation $3 adults, $2 seniors, $1 children) looks like something out of 14th-century England. That is, until you notice that one of the gargoyles on its facade is Darth Vader, the *Star Wars* villain (he glares down in the company of 3,000 hand-carved gargoyles and other statuary). A popular contest asked the general population what modern monsters should be added, and Vader was a winner.

Despite this detour into pop culture, the cathedral is generally regarded as the country's finest example of Gothic architecture, built of grayish Indiana limestone with flying buttresses, a trio of soaring towers, sparkling stained glass, pointed arches, ribbed vaulting, and lots of wrought iron. It's the sixth largest cathedral in the world. If you've never been to Europe, the cathedral provides a taste of what you've missed.

Before you enter, take a close look at the front of the building. Extending from the exterior walls are those fabulous gargoyles. Above and on the left of the left-hand door is the Greek god Pan, portrayed as a curly-haired faun with his pipes. All but impossible to see without binoculars is that sculpted head of Darth Vader. These creatures are part of the cathedral's gutter system, built to keep rainwater from running down the walls. (They project the water away from the walls through pipes.)

Keep in mind as you progress through the building that the theme of all the decorative elements—glass, iron, polished wood, statuary, and embroidered fabrics—is the Christian story of creation. The carved works just above the three main entrance doors at the **West Facade** show the creation of day, the creation of humankind, and the creation of night. The story continues the length of the cathedral to the **High Altar,** where 110 small figures of men and women exemplifying the highest of Christian ideals surround the figure of "Christ in Majesty."

On entering the cathedral Nave, turn and look behind you and up to the west window, called the **Creation Rose.** The window is 26 feet in diameter and contains more than 10,500 pieces of hand-blown glass. Many

Political knavery thrust fame on the **Watergate** (2500–2700 Virginia Ave. NW; Metro: Foggy Bottom-GWU). This modernistic complex of buildings, another "eccentric" design, gained notoriety after the break-in that ultimately resulted in Richard M. Nixon's resignation as president. The hapless intruders actually entered the Virginia Avenue office building. But the complex also includes the Watergate Hotel, the Watergate condominium apartments, and another office pieces are faceted to produce a sparkle, especially when the midafternoon sun beams through. The cathedral claims, justifiably we think, that it is one of the finest 20th-century rose windows in the world. The window tells the story of creation in the abstract. A center of white glass represents the biblical phrase, "Let there be light." Panels of red, gold, and blue radiate from the center, suggesting to parishioners that all creation comes from the Christian God. More than 200 stained-glass windows adorn the cathedral. A handout at the information desk describes each set of windows in detail.

As you proceed toward the altar, take note of the 16th-century tapestries in **St. Mary's Chapel** on the left. They tell the story of David and Goliath. Opposite it on the right side is the **Children's Chapel,** where everything is built to the scale of a 6-year-old. The mini-chapel's kneelers feature embroidered baby animals, and wrought-iron figures depict fantasy creatures. At the **Canterbury Pulpit,** between the two chapels, the massive piers soar nearly 100 feet to the vaulting. The sculptured figures on the pulpit portray people and scenes involved in translating the Bible into English. Stones for the pulpit came from Canterbury Cathedral in England.

On the right of the Nave is the cathedral's **Great Organ.** Brief demonstrations are given Monday and Wednesday at 12:30pm. Those sitting in the lovely carved dark oak choir stalls are apt to get blasted if the organist plays a rambunctious piece.

On the right side of the cathedral, visit the **Bishop's Garden,** modeled on a medieval walled garden. Within the walls are two herb gardens, a rose garden, perennial borders, and medieval architectural elements. Guided tours are offered at 10:30am Wednesday from April to October, starting in the adjacent Herb Cottage.

Tours: Escorted 30-minute tours ($3 adults, $1 children) are offered Monday through Friday from 10 to 11:30am and 12:45 to 4pm, Saturday from 10 to 11:30am and 12:45 to 3:15, and on Sunday from 1 to 2:30pm. One-hour "Behind the Scenes Tours" ($10) are scheduled 10:30am and 1:30pm Monday through Friday. If you simply want to enter and walk around, there's a suggested visitor donation of $3 for adults, $2 seniors, $1 children. It's open Sunday 8am to 6:30pm, Monday through Friday 10am to 5:30pm, and Saturday 10am to 4:30pm.

building around the corner on New Hampshire Avenue. The clustered buildings are wrapped around a sunken courtyard with a cascading fountain that doubles as the Foggy Bottom neighborhood's shopping mart. Architectural critics struggle to define the Watergate style. Baroque is one suggestion. The buildings are curved; balcony-like platforms jut seemingly haphazardly from some floors, and here and there stretch rows of teeth-like crenulations, as if the structure is waiting to chomp down on anyone approaching too closely. The name is a puzzle. Some suggest it derives from a 1930s plan to build a ceremonial gate to the city close by. Others note that a block away, Rock Creek and the Chesapeake and Ohio Canal converge and empty into the Potomac—a water gateway to the city.

ESPECIALLY FOR KIDS

Washington, D.C., is a top city for families. Museums and other cultural organizations regularly present programs for children, but even those that don't are sure to appeal to the youthful curiosity of, well, youngsters. Below are our picks for the best family sites for all ages.

WHERE TO GO FOR CURRENT KIDS' PROGRAMS

Two good sources provide a current list of special programs for children and their parents:

⬥ Look for family programs presented by the many **Smithsonian museums** at www.si.edu/events/kids/asp. Check this one out before you leave home. The schedule generally includes performances and classes up to 4 months in advance. Most are on the Mall.

⬥ Once you reach Washington, take a look in the Friday "Weekend" section of the *Washington Post*. It prints a list of "For Families" programs for the upcoming week in the city and suburbs.

And one final tip: At each Smithsonian museum, ask at the Information Desk for a special kid/family guide to the exhibits.

TOP MUSEUMS & OTHER ATTRACTIONS
FOR THE YOUNGER SET

The **Museum of Natural History,** particularly the O. Orkin Zoo, is full of creepy, crawling things—many alive, some mounted. Younger kids also will be thrilled (and maybe a little frightened) by the **Hall of Mammals** and the **Sant Ocean Hall,** where mounted animals and fish are posed in natural habitats. The preteen crowd will appreciate **Reptiles: Masters of the Land,** the museum's giant dinosaur show. At the **FossiLab,** they can watch the staff preserving and assembling a recent dinosaur find. And be sure to see if anything fun is happening in the **Discovery Room,** which features interactive activities based on whatever temporary exhibits are going on. This museum is tops for kids; Pauline's children would sleep here if they could! See p. 112.

The **National Air and Space Museum** is better for older children and teens who will enjoy the technical stuff; take the younger kids to the museum's giant-screen **IMAX Theater,** where they can choose from four action-packed shows. See p. 110.

The **Bureau of Engraving and Printing** has a 45-minute escorted tour that is short enough not to weary the young ones. And after all, who isn't thrilled to see a money factory? See p. 132.

The **U.S. Botanic Garden** (On the Mall; ☎ 202/225-8333; Metro: Federal Center SW; www.usbg.gov; free admission; daily 10am–5pm) comes complete with its own **Jungle,** a damp, leafy tropical rainforest that grows, it seems, almost to the sky—or nearly up to the 93-foot-high dome anyway. In season, the staff gardeners also nurture two live-growing tunnels—one of green willows and another of flowering vines. Intrepid young explorers are invited to crawl inside. See p. 168.

The **Smithsonian's National Zoo** is a natural for youngsters, especially the **Kids' Farm,** a 2-acre mock farm, sporting a big barn and a silvery pond, which is home to cows, donkeys, and goats. See p. 122.

The **National Postal Museum** demonstrates that as improbable as it may seem, delivering the mail has been a sometimes adventurous, even dangerous, undertaking down through the decades. This aspect of derring-do, plus a multiplicity of kid-friendly high-tech audiovisual devices and computer games, makes this museum a good bet for kids. See p. 123.

The **National Aquarium** (14th St. btw. Constitution and Pennsylvania aves. NW; ☎ 202/482-2825; Metro: Federal Triangle; www.nationalaquarium.com; $7 adults, $3 children 2–10, $6 military/seniors 60-plus; daily 9am–5pm except Thanksgiving and Dec 25) is a great place to take museum-weary youngsters. Stop here after you have toured the White House; it's just around the corner. This is a small aquarium, the ideal size to entertain but not tire the young folks. Here, they can get their hands wet, plunging into the simulated tidal pool called the **Touch Tank.** The hall's layout is convenient; you make a large loop, moving from one glass case to the next up one aisle and back another. Each tank represents a particular aquatic area of the country. The giant **loggerhead sea turtle** lives in a simulation of Gray's Reef, a limestone outcropping off Georgia's coast. **Leopard sharks** glide ominously through a kelp forest, the kind found off California's central coast at Monterey. **Channel catfish,** eerie-looking creatures, float almost motionless in the Great Lakes. Try and be at the aquarium at 2pm for an aquarium keeper's talk and a **creature feeding.**

SUITABLE TOURS FOR KIDS

Children often get restless on guided tours. And who can blame them? Many can be quite dull and involve too much sitting. But **Bike the Sites** (p. 147) and **Washington Walks** (p. 150) schedule family tours of the city that take into account the shorter attention spans of 4- to 9-year-olds. **C&O Canal Boat Rides** (p. 148) and **DC Ducks** (p. 147), each offering a mini outdoor adventure, also rate as kid-friendly.

Around & Around We Go

When the kids hit history overload, take time out for recess. For a real change of pace, treat them to the old-fashioned **Carousel of the Mall** 🧒 (In front of the Smithsonian's Arts and Industries Bldg.; Metro: Smithsonian; $2 per ride; Mar 1–Aug 31 10am–5:30pm daily, 11am–5pm rest of year). The music box sings a merry song; the colorfully painted horses maintain a lively canter, and the ride lasts about 5 smile-filled minutes. Restrooms are available inside the "Castle" behind the Carousel.

SHOWTIME FOR KIDS OF ALL AGES

Many local cultural organizations, including the Smithsonian, schedule programs aimed at youngsters and their parents. Check out your show options and order tickets well in advance of your trip to Washington. (These performances are also popular with those of us who live here.)

The Smithsonian's **Discovery Theater** (☎ 202/357-1500; www.discovery theater.si.edu; $6 adults, $5 children), located on the Mall, features puppets, storytellers, dancers, artists, musicians, and mimes in 300 performances from September to May.

Saturday Morning at the National (1321 Pennsylvania Ave. NW; Metro: Metro Center; ☎ 202/783-3372; www.nationaltheatre.org; free admission, tickets first-come, first-served; 9:30 and 11am) is a weekly program from September to April highlighting magicians, storytellers, actors, and musicians in shows aimed at children ages 4 and older.

The **Kennedy Center's Performances for Young Audiences** (at the Kennedy Center; www.kennedy-center.org; Metro: Foggy Bottom–GWU), the center's newest stage, features an annual series of family-oriented entertainment. The ongoing schedule includes theater, dance, puppetry, and opera for young people and their parents, often featuring the best children's theater performers and companies from around the world. Even the National Symphony Orchestra pitches in, with winning and informative programs about music for youngsters. In 2008, the center debuted an orchestra theater piece it commissioned based on E. B. White's *Trumpet of the Swan.* Dates and prices vary for programs.

Stages for All Ages provides free tickets to live performances at more than 20 Washington-area theaters for students 17 and under. The deal is that you get one free ticket for every full-priced ticket purchased. Tickets are limited to age-appropriate shows. Many are recommended for age 13 and older, but some will also suit the 4-to-8 crowd. Keep in mind that some of the theaters are in the suburbs, which poses a transportation problem if you don't have a car. Get details at ☎ 202/334-5885 or www.lowt.org.

CLASSES FOR KIDS

Several museums offer regularly scheduled education programs for children and their parents.

Art-experience classes during which children study the artworks on view and then are given the opportunity to create their own pieces, are available at the **Arthur M. Sackler Gallery** (p. 117), **Washington National Cathedral** (p. 142; stone carving and stained glass-making classes are featured), and the **National Gallery of Art** (p. 105; it also offers a children's film program).

Remember the Children: Daniel's Story presents the story of the Holocaust from the perspective of a young boy growing up in Nazi Germany. It is a permanent exhibit at the **U.S. Holocaust Memorial Museum** (14th St. at Independence Ave. SW; ☎ 202/488-0400; Metro: Smithsonian; www.ushmm.org; free admission; daily 10am–5:30pm except Yom Kippur and Dec 25). The museum recommends the 30-minute program for elementary and middle school students, assuring parents that "it presents the history of the Holocaust in ways that children can understand." Child development professionals and educators helped in its development, and three child psychiatrists (described as "eminent") reviewed all details.

Family Programs offered by the **National Building Museum** (401 F St. NW; ☎ 202/272-2448; Metro: Judiciary Square; www.nbm.org; free admission; Mon–Sat 10am–5pm, Sun 11am–5pm) focus on the fundamentals of architecture. See the website for details; even on days when there aren't formal classes, the Museum hands out "family tool kits" that introduce the kids to the principles of engineering, physics, and architecture through games and building projects.

WASHINGTON BY ESCORTED TOUR, INCLUDING SOME OFFBEAT WAYS TO GO

To stay within your budget (and if you have strong legs), you don't need to pay for a guided tour to see Washington. It's really not necessary. The city seems to have been laid out to make sightseeing easy for out-of-towners. Most of what we've described in this chapter is on the Mall, which is in the heart of the city. If you want more information than this guide provides, free information brochures are handed out at almost every attraction, especially National Park Service sites and Smithsonian museums. Many also provide free tours.

But if you have difficulty getting around on foot, Washington is amply serviced by bus tours. Crave a little fun while learning? Then join a bicycle, Segway, or Duck tour. Guided walking tours provide in-depth insights into selected neighborhoods. A Potomac River cruise/tour makes a refreshing break from museum-going and takes you to the few areas that would be more difficult to attempt on foot.

AMPHIBIOUS TOURS

DC Ducks 🧒 (Union Station; ☎ 202/832-9800; Metro: Union Station; www.dcducks.com; $28 adults, $14 children 4–12; mid-Mar to early Nov) offers a not-so-serious look—let's make that a hokey look—at the city close-up and from the water that the youngsters will appreciate. A "duck," or more properly DUKW, is an amphibious military personnel carrier dating back to World War II. The firm's restored 1942 Ducks take you on a 90-minute tour—1 hour is spent "waddling" on the Mall and 30 minutes are devoted to gliding somewhat more gracefully on the Potomac River. Tours depart every 30 minutes from 9am to 4:30pm daily. Go for the offbeat experience, not for any insights into historic Washington.

BIKING TOURS

Just one choice here: **Bike the Sites** ✪ 🧒 (Old Post Office Pavilion, Rear Plaza, 12th St. and Pennsylvania Ave. NW; ☎ 202/842-2453; Metro: Federal Triangle; www.bikethesites.com; tours range from $30–$40) organizes several different bicycling itineraries. Before we go any further, though, we have to issue a warning: D.C. has heavy traffic and rude drivers. We recommend these tours therefore *only* if you're an adept cyclist and familiar with driving in urban traffic. Tour hours are seasonal, with the most frequent tours during the summer months. Because the routes are generally flat, they don't require much stamina. The *Capitol Sites Tour* ($40 adults; $30 children 12 and under; daily 10am–1pm) is its most comprehensive, covering 7 to 8 miles from one end of the Mall to the other. Three family bike adventures, for children ages 4 to 10 with an adult, feature a combined ride and stroll lasting 2½ hours.

BOAT TOURS

Taking you not only on the water, but also back to the 1870s, the **C&O Canal Boat Rides** ✪ 🐾 (C & O Canal Visitor Center, Georgetown, 1057 Thomas Jefferson St. NW; ☎ 202/653-5190; K St. Circulator bus to 30th St. NW; www.nps.gov/choh; $5, free for children 4 and under; Apr–Oct Wed–Sun) ply the historic Chesapeake and Ohio Canal, a national parkland that parallels the Potomac River for 185 miles from Georgetown in Washington to Cumberland, Maryland. You board a mule-drawn, open-air barge for a 1-hour round-trip ride; the "big excitement" comes when the barge enters one lift lock and is raised 8 feet from one canal level to the next. Park rangers don period clothing to add to the time-travel effect, using stories and music to outline the canal's history. Progress is at a mule's pace— for many, a tedious mule's pace—so more active members of your family may want to walk with the mule tender on the towpath. May through October departures are Wednesday to Sunday 11am, 1:30, and 3pm; in April the boat runs only Wednesdays and Sundays at those times.

Capitol River Cruises (Washington Harbour, Georgetown, 31st and K sts. NW; ☎ 800/405-5511; Metro: Foggy Bottom; www.capitolrivercruises.com; $13 adults, $6 children 3–12; Apr–Oct daily on the hour from noon to 7 or 8pm) operates the *Nightingale* on 50-minute cruises from Georgetown to the Mall and back. The *Nightingale* is a small tug-like vessel with minimal frills and a pug-ugly look. But hey, it's cheap and it gets you on the water. You will find a beverage and snack bar aboard. *Tip:* If you buy tickets online at the website, the price is $10 adults/ $5 children.

For river cruises to Mount Vernon, see p. 271.

BUS, TROLLEY & TRAM TOURS

These are the conventional tours, doing the city once-over-lightly to see the highlights. You don't really need to take a tour to see and enjoy Washington. But not everybody is up for long walks, especially in the heat of summer. Beyond these more standard offerings, be sure to consider the **Scandal Tours** (p. 150) and the bus tours led by the terrific walking tour company **Washington Walks** (p. 150), which will offer you wheels with quirkier commentary.

Tourmobile Sightseeing ✪ (☎ 202/554-5100, www.tourmobile.com) is the only commercial tour company authorized by the National Park Service to provide point-to-point service on the Mall. Its *American Heritage Tour* is offered daily except December 25 and January 1, making 20 stops at 40 major historic attractions on the Mall and at Arlington National Cemetery. You hop on and hop off its 85-passenger red, white, and blue trams at any stop throughout the day, from 8:30am to 4:30pm April through September and 9:30am to 4:30pm October through March. Adult tickets are $27; children (3–11) pay $30. Board and buy tickets at any Tourmobile stop. *Note:* The Mall is 2 miles long from the Capitol to the Lincoln Memorial, a daunting distance under a hot, humid summer sky. To its credit, the Tourmobile will help you save energy for those miles of corridors in the Smithsonian's museums. If your time in Washington is short, this is the tour to take because it focuses on the capital's major sights.

Tourmobile also schedules seasonal tours to *George Washington's Mount Vernon Plantation* (noon departure by motor coach from Washington Monument or Arlington National Cemetery; 4 hr.; $30 adults, $15 children); and to *Frederick*

Douglass National Historic Site (noon departure from Washington Monument and Arlington National Cemetery; 2½ hr.; $7 adults, $3.50 children).

Old Town Trolley (Union Station; ☎ 202/832-9800; Metro: Union Station; www.trolleytours.com; $35 adults, $18 children 4–12; daily 9am–5:30pm except July 4, Thanksgiving, Dec 25, Sun of Memorial Day weekend, and Marine Corps Marathon Sun in Oct) is another hop-on, hop-off tour. This one operates green and orange trolley-type cars on rubber wheels, covering considerably more territory than the Tourmobile. The trolleys ply three separate loops stopping at 16 attractions, and you can switch from one loop to another and back. They are the *National Mall and Downtown Loop;* the *National Cathedral, Uptown, and Georgetown Loop;* and the *Arlington National Cemetery Shuttle.* To make the best use of your day's ticket, begin the day on the National Cathedral Loop, hopping off only to visit the cathedral. Make the rest of the loop, which amounts to a quick ride through several upscale neighborhoods, including Embassy Row. Then hop on the National Mall Loop, making the complete circuit before doubling back to visit one or more of the Mall museums. At midafternoon, catch the Arlington National Cemetery shuttle.

Martz Gold Line/Gray Line (Union Station; ☎ 800/862-1400; Metro: Union Station; www.graylinedc.com; daily except Thanksgiving, Dec 25, and Jan 1) operates 47- and 55-passenger motor coaches on a series of 4-hour and 9-hour tours daily. Take these tours if you want comfy seats, onboard restrooms, and air-conditioning. Study the tour descriptions carefully (see the website above) for a short list of attractions that you actually will visit and the much longer list you will see only from the bus window. Tours depart from Union Station.

Their most comprehensive offering is *Tour DC, All-Day Combination,* which includes Washington, Arlington Cemetery, Mount Vernon, and Old Town Alexandria, Virginia (8:30am, 9 hr., $66 adults, $34 children). The company has too many variations to list here.

SEGWAY TOURS

Yup, these are those dashing vehicles featured in the film *Paul Blart: Mall Cop.* Still, Pauline can tell you from personal experience that they're a heckuva lot of fun to ride, easy to master, and how much trouble can you get into? The ones you'll be renting here go at a maximum speed of about 12 miles per hour. If you haven't seen the film, these differ from a scooter in that you navigate standing up rather than sitting. A first-time training lesson takes about 10 minutes; a helmet is provided. Two firms schedule Segway tours in the city. Minimum age for both is 16; weight limit, 260 pounds.

Segs in the City (Old Post Office Pavilion, Pennsylvania Ave. btw. 10th and 12th sts. NW; ☎ 800/734-7393; Metro: Federal Triangle; www.segsinthecity.net) operates a 2-hour tour from the Capitol to the White House ($70) at 10am, 2:30 and 7pm daily; a 1-hour tour around the Capitol and Supreme Court ($45) at 12:30 and 5pm daily; and a 2-hour tour of Embassy Row ($70) at 5:15pm on Saturday and Sunday. The Embassy Row tour impresses us as the most suitable for Segway sightseeing due to the minimal number of intersecting streets, the lengthy uphill distance covered, and because most of the sights (40 embassies) can be seen only from the outside anyway. Tours are limited to 6 people; this is probably the one to take if you are a Segway novice.

City Segway Tours (1455 Pennsylvania Ave. NW; ☎ 877/734-8687; Metro: Federal Triangle; www.citysegwaytours.com; Apr 1–Nov 30) organizes a 4-hour tour exploring the length of the Mall ($70) at 10am and 2pm daily. Um, 4 full hours zipping around? Frankly that seems a bit long to us, but diehard Segway fans may enjoy it.

SCANDAL TOURS

A witty and irreverent motorcoach jaunt, **Scandal Tours/Gross National Product** ✫✫ (Warehouse Theater, 1017 7th St. NW; ☎ 202/783-7212 or 800/979-3370 for reservations; Metro: Mt. Vernon Sq.–7th St. Convention Center; www.gnpcomedy.com; Apr 1 to Labor Day Sat 1pm; $30 adults, $25 seniors, $20 students; reservations required) is led by members of a local comedy troupe. They hit the U.S. Capitol, the White House, the Watergate Office Building, and even the Tidal Basin, where Thomas Jefferson keeps watch. The commentary can get racy, so parents beware. However, it's actually a highly informative tour through the dark side of the country's legislative history. If you're going to do a motorcoach tour, this is the one to pick.

SCOOTER TOURS

City Scooter Tours ✫ (Old Post Office Pavilion, 12th St. btw. Pennsylvania and Constitution aves. NW; ☎ 888/441-7575; Metro: Federal Triangle; www.cityscootertours.com; $75; Wed 1–4pm and Sun 10am–1pm; reservations required) provides a relaxed tour of the National Mall in self-operated electric convenience/mobility vehicles. They are aimed at people age 10 and older who have difficulty walking. Companions without a mobility problem can accompany the tour on bikes from Bike the Sites (see above). Children under 16 must be accompanied by a parent or guardian. The firm provides electric headsets so you can hear the guide's commentary.

WALKING TOURS

Beyond the tours mentioned below, please keep in mind that there are splendiferous self-guided walking tour itineraries in chapter 8 of this guide, as well as information on self-guided tours you can download off the Net. If you prefer having a guide along whom you can pepper with questions, the following two tour companies are tops:

Talented, loquacious guides—local teachers, actors, retired lawyers—offer up a witty, insider's view of the city on **Washington Walks** ✫✫✫ (☎ 202/484-1565; www.washingtonwalks.com; $10; Apr–Oct only). These tours are very popular with locals, a sign you're going to get in-depth information, not some pat overview. From spring into fall, the organization offers a crowded weekly schedule of walking tours. Most last about 2 hours; call in advance for reservations. Topics covered include: *Arlington National Cemetery, Embassy Row, the White House Un-Tour* 🔳, *Movable Feast* (a snack-a-thon), *D.C.'s Most Haunted Houses, Before Harlem There Was U Street,* and *Memorials by Moonlight.* The company is now also offering bus tours to the area's Civil War sights and Jazz Age sights; these cost $30 to $42/person, depending on the itinerary. Check the website above for tour hours and location; most depart from the nearest Metro station and cover an easy 1 mile in distance.

A specialty for those who enjoy James Bond, or perhaps just want to become better snoops, **Spy Tours of Washington** ✪ (www.spiesofwashingtonontour.com; $12 per person; dates and times vary, see website) introduces visitors not only to the areas of D.C. where feats of espionage derring-do took place, but also to the methods spies use today to get the information they're seeking. Your tour guide is the deceptively normal-looking Carol Bessette, the former president of the National Military Intelligence Association, who has at her fingertips a lot of the secret history of the city.

The 'Other' Washington

Where you meet Washingtonians & share the experiences that make them such enthusiastic residents

By Jim Yenckel

IN DUBLIN, I CRAWL THE PUBS. IN RIO, I GAZE AT THE SLEEK BODIES strolling Copacabana. In Amsterdam, I bicycle. That's what the locals do, and because part of the fun of travel is trying to live like I'm a local, if just for a short time, I like to join them in their everyday pastimes whenever I can. It's also one of the best ways to meet the people who actually live in the place you are visiting.

So how do you go about meeting my friends and neighbors in Washington? I'll introduce you to a variety of ways. For example: Attend a book reading by a Washington author. Catch the always-bustling after-work happy hour scene. Participate in a protest march.

I realize you have plenty to see and do on your limited time in Washington. But try at least one or two of the activities I suggest. You will discover the "other" Washington, the city beyond the monuments, memorials, and museums of the nation's capital. It's the Washington most visitors never get the chance to enjoy.

HOW WE LEARN

The nation's capital attracts new residents from all over, who arrive intent on getting things done. They are movers and shakers, always looking for ways to increase their knowledge—for fun, for profit, for political advantage. Whatever, they are the folks you will meet at these popular learning experiences.

DANCE LESSONS

In Washington, getting ahead socially and politically means knowing how to dance. This is a city of countless charity balls, embassy balls, an occasional White House dinner dance (depending on the style of the incumbent president), and, every 4 years, the inaugural balls. Young dynamos climbing the ladder to the top don't want to look like klutzes, so they take dance lessons. You can too. Several Washington institutions provide inexpensive dance lessons on a regular basis, an opportunity for local folks to get to know each other and for you to get to know us.

Every Tuesday night, the **Jam Cellar** (Josephine Butler Parks Center, 2437 15th St. NW; ☎ 202/558-0338; www.thejamcellar.com; Metro: Woodley Park–Zoo and 10-min. walk) hosts a free, 30-minute beginners swing-dance lesson from 9 to 9:30pm. Afterwards, a swing-dance party bounces until midnight to DJ tunes ($6). The center is in a restored Italian Renaissance–revival mansion. Once the home of both the Embassy of Hungary and the Embassy of Brazil, it features a 4,000-square-foot grand ballroom with 14-foot high ceilings, French doors, and a gleaming oak parquet floor.

Go Bollywood! Consider it another aspect of Washington's rich international life; the metropolitan area has a large Indian population. If you saw the lively dance parties in such India- and Indian-themed movies as *Monsoon Wedding* and *Slumdog Millionaire,* and you dreamed of joining in, now you can. Twice weekly, **Dhoonya Dance School** (Coors Dance Studio at Flashpoint, 916 G. St. NW; ☎ 856/625-8406; www.dhoonyadance.com; Metro: Gallery Place–Chinatown) provides introductory lessons to the energetic Bollywood style—a sort of shoulder, wrist, and hip step that works up a sweat. Introductory lessons are taught at 1pm Sunday and 8:30pm Thursday. The price is $20.

Washington is said to have one of the largest gay and lesbian populations in the country. To meet this segment of the city's culture, take in a country-style GLBT function. A square-dancing group, **D.C. Lambda Squares** (www.dclambda squares.org; National City Christian Church, 5 Thomas Circle; Metro: Dupont Circle) promenades and "doe-see-does" with Mainstream, Plus, and Advanced steps. Beginners are welcome on Mondays, with a new series of classes starting about every 3 months.

READINGS & SIGNINGS, BOOK DISCUSSIONS

Washington is full of issue advocates with a message, and many of them put their arguments in print. Local bookstores are full of thick tomes by local authors—fiction and nonfiction; they and a steady influx of writers from beyond the Beltway appear regularly at bookstores, libraries, nonprofit think tanks, and university campuses to read from their latest opus, to talk about their work, and (they hope) autograph a copy for you. Invariably, these events are free.

Before you arrive, check the websites of the individual bookstores. Once you're in town, pick up a free copy of the *City Paper,* and look for upcoming events in the Books section. On Thursdays, the District insert in the *Washington Post* lists book functions in the "Community Events" column.

In 2009, newscaster Gwen Ifill discussed politics and race and novelist Carl Hiassen met his younger fans at **Politics & Prose** (5015 Connecticut Ave. NW; ☎ 202/364-1919; www.politics-prose.com; Metro: Van Ness–UDC). Olga Grushing, one of the top young novelists, read a chapter from her latest at **Chapters** (445 11th St. NW; ☎ 202/737-5553; www.chaptersliterary.com; Metro: Metro Center). There's frequently an emphasis on nonfiction works arguing politics, international affairs, national and economic questions, and other issues confronting the country and the world. In a single week in February 2009, you could have heard Congresswoman Barbara Lee discuss her book *Renegade for Justice & Peace;* U.S. Air Force veteran (and former lead interrogator in Iraq) Matthew Alexander read from his new tome *How to Break a Terrorist;* Robert G. Keiser, one of the esteemed thinkers at the *Washington Post,* ruminate on the corrosive effects of lobbying on the U.S. government; and Christopher Dickey of *Newsweek* delve into his latest book on the New York Police Department and its expanded national security responsibilities.

Other bookstores (all downtown or close by) with author events include:

♦ **Kramerbooks & Afterwords Café & Grill** (1517 Connecticut Ave. NW; ☎ 202/387-1400; www.kramers.com; Metro: Dupont Circle)

♦ **Borders Books** (1801 L St. NW; ☎ 202/466-4999; www.borders.com; Metro: Farragut North; and 600 14th St. NW; ☎ 202/737-1385; www.borders.com; Metro: Metro Center)

♦ **Barnes & Noble** (555 12th St. NW; ☎ 202/347-0176; www.barnesand noble.com; Metro: Metro Center; and Georgetown, 3040 M St. NW; ☎ 202/965-9880; www.barnesandnoble.com; K St.)

LECTURES & TALKS

I've said this in other ways elsewhere in this guide, but it bears repeating. A sizeable percentage of Washingtonians savor intellectual pursuits. They form the receptive audience for a variety of scholarly lectures and other programs organized by the Smithsonian and other museums, local universities, think tanks (right, left, and independent), and federal and city departments and other agencies. Often (but not always) free, they are generally listed in the *City Paper* and the *Washington Post* in the same section as author readings (see above). In advance of your visit, you can check out Smithsonian and other museum events on their websites (see chapter 5). Hours vary from morning into evening.

In a single week in 2009, you could have heard a talk about the long-term ramifications of Lincoln's assassination at the **Library of Congress** (p. 100), about African-American pioneers in aviation at the **National Air and Space Museum** (p. 110), on promoting democracy in the Middle East at **Catholic University** (p. 48), on plants in American history at the **U.S. Botanic Garden** (p. 168), on the use of light and color in Renoir's painting *The Boating Party* at the **Phillips Collection** (p. 225), on the sexual habits of animals ("Woo at the Zoo") at the **National Zoo** (p. 122), and on the history of iron at the **Navy Memorial.** Lecturers include diplomats, professors, museum curators, military and government officials, and scientists, among others—many the leading experts in their field.

The **Phillips Collection** (p. 225) hosts a weekly arts talk called **Artful Evenings** (1600 21st St. NW; ☎ 202/387-2151, ext. 260; www.phillipscollection. org; Metro: Dupont Circle). They are held at 6 and 7pm every Thursday. Sessions are free, but you must pay the museum's admission fee, which varies. Talks tend to focus on the museum's current shows. Usually, the museum's curators or the education staff lead the talks, but occasionally guest lecturers are invited to provide expert insights into a particular painting or a show.

Among the liveliest and most unusual offerings are those put forward by the **National Geographic Society** 🄺 (Downtown, Grosvenor Auditorium, 1600 M St. NW; ☎ 202/857-7700; www.nglive.org; Metro: Farragut North). Throughout the year, the famed magazine presents live educational lectures and films 1 or more evenings a week. Many make excellent, affordable family entertainment. Often a series of lectures (single tickets available) focus on subjects such as adventure travel, conservation, photography, and exploration. In 2009, lecturers took the audience deep under the ocean's surface, to the Victorian-era search for the "lost civilization" of the Amazon, and to the North Pole, among dozens of places. Many of the lecturers are authors of stories that have appeared in the *National*

Geographic magazine. Tickets for nonmembers of the society tend to average $18, but can be more, depending on the lecture. Travel films alternate with the lectures. Tickets range from $5 to $10. Most presentations begin at 7:30pm.

SOCIAL ACTIVISM

In a city of issue-oriented achievers, it's no surprise there's a school for activists, offering a wide selection of one-session, 2-hour classes for as little as $10 to $50. Called **SALSA (Social Action & Leadership School for Activists;** 1112 16th St. NW; ☎ 202/234-9382; www.hotsalsa.org; Metro: Farragut North), it's a program of the Institute for Policy Studies. A liberal think tank, the Institute lists entertainer Harry Belafonte and *The Nation* editor Katrina vanden Heuvel on its board of directors.

In the winter/spring of 2009, some of the offerings at SALSA included "Hip Hop as Mass Media," "Grassroots Advocacy," and "Climate Change, Movement Building and You." The classes attract lots of issue-oriented folks. They include people who work in nonprofit organizations, social justice groups, environmentalists, community leaders, union officials, and such do-gooders as volunteers in rape crisis centers. The advice tends to be more practical than theoretical, and lots of give and take between leader and class is typical.

PHOTOGRAPHY

In this photogenic city, visitors aren't the only ones carrying cameras. Professional photographers, a majority of them working for national and international news organizations, ply the byways of government, capturing the news of the moment. You, too, can learn how best to portray Washington in photos at **Washington Photo Safari** ✦ (Renwick Gallery, 17th and Pennsylvania Ave. NW; ☎ 877/ 512-5969 or 202/537-0937; www.washingtonphotosafari.com; Metro: Farragut West). The organization schedules three or four half-day and full-day photo sessions every week. A staff of eight professional photographers, led by architectural photographer E. David Luria, instructs in the art of photographing the city's memorials, monuments, and museums, interior and exterior. The basic course, Monuments and Memorials, is recommended for first-timers. Luria, whose photos have appeared in more than 100 publications including *Time* magazine, leads this one himself. With more than 30 magazine covers to his name, Luria also has led numerous photography tours for the Smithsonian's Resident Associates program. The Monuments and Memorials session (starting at $79 for a half-day, $139 for a full day), starts at the Renwick Gallery and concentrates on memorials but also includes the White House and Union Station. There are other "themed" safaris and technique classes, as well as trips farther afield to shoot photos in Baltimore, Annapolis, and Frederick, Maryland, as well as in Northern Virginia.

STARGAZING

Federal workers are said to be clock watchers; at the **Naval Observatory** (Observatory Circle, Wisconsin Ave. NW; fax 202/762-1467; www.usno.navy.mil/ USNO; daily 9am–5pm; see website for information about tours; Metrobus: N2, N4, N6), this definitely is true. Its primary mission, an important one, is keeping the United States on time. In this increasingly complex technological world, knowing

The Best Source for Current Schedules

To participate in some of the meet-the-locals activities described in this chapter, you are going to have to make reservations or other arrangements well in advance of your trip. I'll tell you when advance reservations are necessary; phone numbers and websites are provided for this purpose.

Once you have arrived in Washington, the most thorough listing of current activities aimed at Washington residents—athletic, cultural, kids, nightlife—is found in the **City List** pages of the *City Paper*. A hefty tabloid, the free publication is distributed weekly on Thursday in news boxes, coffeehouses, and neighborhood markets throughout the city. You also can search the City List online at www.washingtoncitypaper.com.

Other sources include the *Washington Post*'s Thursday **District Weekly** insert and its Friday **Weekend** section, or visit the "Going Out Guide" online at www.washingtonpost.com/gog. GLBT events and programs are listed in the **Community Calendar** of *Metro Weekly*, a 60-plus page free magazine distributed citywide in news boxes on Thursday. The Community Calendar also is available online at www.metroweekly.com.

---

the precise time around the globe is critical—for example, in coordinated military action or space shots. The observatory achieves this by making regular observations of the sun, moon, planets, selected stars, and other celestial bodies to determine their positions and motions and by using the data obtained to maintain a master clock. The popular tours of the facility and a second-stargazing program in Rock Creek Park allow Washingtonians an opportunity to learn more about the observatory's important function and about the night sky. It's one of the little-known activities of the government, and you can see it happen. Individual and group tours must be reserved in advance. You can reserve online at the website above, and are strongly urged to do so as far in advance as possible. In 2009, the Observatory will be participating in a number of national and international programs associated with the International Year of Astronomy, commemorating the 400th anniversary of Galileo's first use of a telescope to explore the universe.

As an aid to their education, the *Washington Post* regularly alerts readers to what constellations will be appearing overhead. You, too, can stargaze with the astronomers. Public tours are offered from 8:30 to 10:30pm on selected Mondays. You will be briefed on the observatory's timekeeping assignment and get a look at the night sky through its telescope. Reserve free tickets online or by fax (202/762-1489). For 50 years, a program called **Exploring the Sky** (Rock Creek Park Nature Center, Military and Grover rds. NW; ☎ 202/895-6070; www.nps.gov/rocr/planyourvisit/expsky.htm; Metrobus: S2, S4) has encouraged residents and visitors to see the stars and planets through telescopes. Sessions are held shortly after sunset once each month on Saturday from April through November. Beginners, including children, are welcome. Instruction is provided by National Park Service rangers and members of the National Capital Astronomers. For a schedule, check the website.

HOW WE WORK

The primary work of Washington is governing. The watchdog press and foreign embassies each have a role in the process. This is the home, to borrow a word from former president George W. Bush, of the "deciders," at least on matters of national and international concern. Much of the action takes place in sprawling office buildings behind closed doors. The city is full of big secrets, at least until a whistle-blower leaks a controversial item to the *Washington Post* or *New York Times*. But since the United States strives—we hope it does, anyway—to nurture a government "of the people, by the people, and for the people," a lot of what Washington does is required to take place in public. Below, I'll show you where to see the nation's leaders at work. And you will get a peek at the press, foreign embassies, and organizations involved in the governing process.

VISIT A MEMBER OF CONGRESS

U.S. senators and representatives need the votes of American citizens to keep their jobs. The Republican Party, which took a big thumping in the 2008 congressional and presidential elections, learned that lesson the hard way, and saw many of its members evicted from Capitol Hill. So, if they are savvy, they are receptive to meeting and greeting residents of their home jurisdictions. Of course, the warmth of your welcome—a polite nod or a hearty handshake and pat on the back—may be determined by whether you belong to the same political party or have made a big contribution in time or money to their election. Don't just drop in—although that is always an option. You will get a better reception if you make an appointment. Legislators are busy people, often out of the office at committee meetings or voting on the floor of the Senate or House. With an appointment, you stand a good chance of being ushered into the legislator's personal office, where you can talk with your representative about whatever's on your mind. Even without an appointment, drop by the office to pick up gallery passes. You must have the passes to see the chambers (one pass per person for each chamber) where the Senate and House meet or to sit in on a session of either body.

Senate offices are located in the Russell, Dirksen, and Hart buildings. The three are clustered just north of the Capitol grounds at 1st Street and Constitution Avenue NE. Offices of the representatives are housed in the Cannon, Longworth, and Rayburn buildings, similarly clustered on the immediate south side of the Capitol grounds at New Jersey Avenue and Constitution Avenue SE. You must go through a security check to enter, but no pass is required. To contact the staff of your legislator, call the main number of the **Senate** (☎ 202/224-3121) or the **House of Representatives** (☎ 202/225-3121). You can also get the contact information (address, phone, and e-mail) for every elected representative (including state governors and legislators) at www.usa.gov/Contact/Elected.shtml.

SIT IN ON A MEETING OF THE SENATE OR HOUSE/ ATTEND A CONGRESSIONAL HEARING

You don't need a pass to sit in on a congressional hearing. Often the hearings are more interesting than sessions of the full Senate and House. At a hearing, you are sitting up close to the action, which can get heated. Legislators ask nitty-gritty questions, sparring verbally with each other and outside witnesses. This is where you hear real debate, senators attacking each other over such issues as presidential appointments to the Supreme Court, tax cuts or hikes, changes to Social Security, or balancing the federal budget. The senator from Missouri, Harry S Truman, my personal political hero, propelled himself into the Vice Presidency and ultimately into the White House as the hard-working chairman of a special Senate committee investigating waste and mismanagement in defense spending prior to World War II. He and his committee traveled the country searching for evidence of waste and then summoned government, corporate, and union officials to its Senate committee room to answer probing questions that touched off occasional angry exchanges. The committee's findings resulted in a major overhaul of spending procedures just as America entered the war. Truman biographer David McCullough writes that "no one could remember congressional hearings being handled with such straightforwardness and intelligence." Keep this is mind when you watch the nation's current crop of legislators in committee.

On a personal note, my wife likes to tell this story about a House committee meeting she sat in on. It illustrates the impact these committee hearings can have on individual citizens. For several years, she was a lobbyist for a national insurance association. One day she was on the Hill for a committee "mark-up" session on a tax bill that interested her association. A "mark-up" is when the committee goes line by line through a bill to make sure it's accurate; this comes after the debate but before the vote. Before my wife's part of the bill was discussed, the committee took up a provision allowing homeowners to claim tax deductions for expenses involved in renting a house to a family member. Previously, no deductions were allowed for rentals within the family. Sandy's ears perked up because at the time we rented a house to my parents. We were, she learned that day, to become the unsuspecting beneficiaries of a piece of legislation working its way through the House process.

If an issue being tackled is controversial or of momentous importance—maybe universal health care someday—you may be crowded out by Washington insiders with a vested interest in the outcome.

You do need a pass to watch the **House and Senate in action.** Sparks can fly on the floor of either chamber, but ponderous oratory is more common. You may be surprised when stepping into the Senate or House gallery that only a half a dozen legislators are present on the chamber floor and another seated with a gavel at the desk on the podium. A lot of what the two bodies do in session is perfunctory. A representative praises the noteworthy achievement of a constituent; a senator makes a statement for the record citing an important development in his or her home state. These are not nation-shaking events that require the presence of all 100 senators or 435 representatives. Even during periods of debate, legislators who don't plan to speak may skip the session; more than likely they have heard all the arguments in committee meetings many times before. When it's time for an important vote, they come hurrying when summoned. If you are lucky enough to be present during a vote, you should spot many of the familiar faces you see on the TV news. If a tie in a Senate vote is expected, the Vice President, whose constitutional function is to serve as president of the Senate, may preside and cast the winning vote. In both the Senate and House chambers, an aisle divides the desks of Republicans and Democrats. From the vantage of the presiding Vice President or the Speaker of the House, Democrats are seated on the right and Republicans on the left. You will note, however, that nobody stays seated very long. When debate is raging, legislators mingle with fellow party members plotting strategy or duck out to antechambers to consult aides. Those young men and women scurrying about on the floor are likely congressional pages delivering messages or otherwise running official errands for their bosses.

The busiest days on Capitol Hill, at least for public events, are Tuesday, Wednesday, and Thursday. Many legislators like to spend the weekend in their home states, skipping out of Washington on Friday and returning on Monday. This doesn't necessarily mean they are playing hooky: Keeping in touch with their constituencies is important if they want to be reelected. Representatives, with their 2-year terms, are especially hard-pressed to raise campaign funds for the next election, which is always impending. As campaign costs soar, they must spend more time at fundraising events back home. At the same time, they run the risk of being accused of contributing to what the voters may see as a do-nothing Congress.

The *Washington Post* prints a daily list of Capitol Hill events, listing public committee and nomination hearings and if and when the Senate and House are meeting. You also can check the websites of the **Senate** (www.senate.gov) and the **House of Representatives** (www.house.gov). Most committee hearings are held in the morning; but afternoon hearings are frequent too. The Senate and House, when meeting, usually are called into session at noon. Sessions can last into the night and early morning hours if a controversial issue is at stake. To sit in on a session of the Senate or House you need to obtain a gallery pass. You can apply for passes in advance of your arrival or in person at your legislator's office. The passes are not dated, so you can choose what day or time you want to use them. On some days, only a handful of legislators may be on the floor handling routine business, and you won't have any difficulty getting a seat. When an important vote is pending, nearly every senator or representative shows up, and gallery seating may be tight.

WATCH THE SUPREME COURT IN ACTION

By the time a court case reaches the Supreme Court its outcome often can affect the way Americans live. You may hear lawyers pro and con debate issues involving criminal justice, environmental protection, taxes, business management, health, and more. The nine Justices of the Court hear cases from October to April. We outline the procedures for attending in a more detailed description of the Court in chapter 5 (p. 99).

WATCH OR JOIN A PROTEST MARCH

No, I'm not being facetious. Washington is the national leader as the site for protest marches and demonstrations. Some are organized in Washington itself; others descend on the city from elsewhere. As the national capital, Washington provides any demonstration, even a poorly attended one, a certain status. And the presence of a large national and international press corps all but insures plenty of publicity. Depending on the issue, Washingtonians—an assertive population—fill the ranks of the protesters, often as leaders. I have marched more than once in front of the White House to support a cause in which I believe strongly.

Some protests are organized weeks or months in advance, and you will know about them before you arrive in Washington. Among the most historic in recent decades are the Vietnam War protests, when the city air was scented by tear gas; the civil rights March on Washington when the Rev. Dr. Martin Luther King, Jr., gave his "I Have a Dream Speech" on the Mall; marches in support of both sides of the abortion issue; and demonstrations against the financial policies of the World Bank at its headquarters in Washington.

More common, though, are small demonstrations outside a foreign embassy, challenging one or more of the home country's actions or policies. Unless you are a member of the organizing group, you are not likely to know in advance where and when the protest is scheduled. But if you are lucky enough to chance upon one—not at all unlikely—don't be shy. Hear what the group has to say, read the materials they hand out, and ask questions. In many cases, you will be talking to exiles or expatriates acting to bring about political reforms in an abusive home government.

VISIT A FOREIGN EMBASSY

In chapter 8, we guide you on a walking tour of Embassy Row, which is lined by numerous foreign embassies. You see them from the outside—which in itself is quite interesting. But try also to get an inside look behind the scenes. An amiable way to step inside an embassy is to attend a public function there. Many are quite lovely, built or decorated in a style illustrating national customs. The new Italian Embassy is a modernistic take on a Tuscan palazzo. Inuit sculpture from the territory of Nunavut adorns the interior of the Canadian Embassy. Consider a visit a sort of mini-trip abroad. Several embassies feature art galleries displaying native works; a few host music recitals and lectures. Look for a listing of current exhibits in the Galleries column of the free weekly *City Paper* or in the Friday weekend section of the *Washington Post*. These functions are part of the embassy's everyday work in promoting the national image—to increase tourism; to obtain economic or military aid; or—for a few—to counter negative publicity, such as a bad report about human rights abuses.

Let me give you an example of what you might see. One week in the not so distant past, the *City Paper* listed an exhibit of surreal paintings at the **Embassy of Chile;** a photography display at the **Embassy of the Czech Republic;** and "Impressions of Estonia," a show of artworks at the **Embassy of Estonia.** All were free events. In addition, the Embassy of Estonia scheduled "An Elegant Evening Affair." It featured a traditional Estonian buffet and a sampling of Estonian beers for $50. The Czech Embassy hosted a free reading of Joseph Topol's *Cat on the Rails*. The **Embassy of Austria** presented a free recital by a soprano and pianist. To join in, do a thorough search of the events listings in the two newspapers cited above. These events tend to draw well-traveled Washingtonians; often they have either been to the hosting country or plan to visit soon.

WATCH THE MEDIA REPORT THE NEWS

The media—newspapers, newsmagazines, TV news shows, and major political blogs—isn't one of the three formal branches of the Federal Government. But the Founding Fathers considered freedom of the press crucial to democracy, enshrining it in the First Amendment in the Bill of Rights. As the source of major news year-round, Washington is home to on-site bureaus representing major media outlets nationally and internationally. The **Newseum** (p. ###) chronicles the role of the press in American society.

To see an offshoot of the press at work, take a behind-the-scenes **Voice of America Tour** (330 Independence Ave. SW; ☎ 202/203-4990; www.voanews.com; Metro: Federal Center; Mon-Fri except federal holidays noon and 3pm; reservations recommended). The Voice of America is a 24-hour, international multimedia news broadcasting facility. On the tour, you will see VOA's bustling Newscenter, which operates 24 hours a day, 7 days a week. The news staff broadcasts news reports live on radio, television, and the Internet in 44 languages. You are likely to see and hear several broadcasts, although you may not understand what is being said at many of them. Advance reservations are recommended; children age 7 and older are welcome. While at the Voice of America, take a look at the historic mural, *The Meaning of Social Security*, by artist Ben Shahn. It was commissioned in 1940 for the Cohen Building, which houses VOA, to commemorate the 1935 Social Security Act. The legislation was a part of President Franklin D. Roosevelt's sweeping social reforms during the Great Depression. You can make reservations online, or by phone at ☎ 202/203-4990.

If you can put together a group of 10 to 30 people (extended family, two families), tour the almost always busy newsrooms of the *Washington Post* (1150 15th St. NW; ☎ 202/334-7969; www.washpost.com; Metro: Farragut North; free admission; Mon only 10-11am and 1-2pm). One of the country's most important newspapers, the *Post* often can be an exciting place to be—especially if news is breaking. This is the newspaper that broke the Watergate story. Its coverage brought fame to reporters Bob Woodward and Carl Bernstein and led to President Nixon's resignation. If you saw the movie *All the President's Men*, which portrayed the events of Watergate, you saw a replica of the *Post*'s main newsroom where reporters pecked away at typewriters with piles of copy paper at their side. Computers have replaced typewriters and copy paper at today's *Post*, but otherwise the newsroom looks much the same. On a hot story like Watergate, the newsroom—the command center for city, suburban, national, and foreign news—takes on the look of controlled chaos.

My advice, as a former editor and writer, is to take the latest tour in the day. On a morning newspaper, even a major one, the day gets underway slowly and gradually builds to a wild crescendo. Reporters return from their assignments in the afternoon and start writing frantically to beat the early evening deadlines. Many of the editors get to work at about the same time, pondering what stories to headline. If you visit at 10am, the earliest tour, you are apt to see only a few sleepy editors downing coffee at their desks. The tour takes about 45 minutes. Tour reservations are required; and it is recommended you make them 1 or 2 months in advance. Children must be age 11 or older.

GET BRIEFED ON THE GLOBAL ECONOMY

Given America's world status, Washington not surprisingly plays host to major international organizations, including three that tackle the challenges of the global economy: **International Monetary Fund** (IMF), **Organization of American States** (OAS), and **World Bank.** In recent years, meetings of both the IMF and the World Bank have been targeted by mass demonstrations protesting against a globalization that is corporate-led and marginalizes large numbers of people around the world. To see and learn how they and the OAS operate—and to hear what if any changes the protests have achieved—take the **IMF, OAS, and World Bank Walking Tour** (IMF Center, 720 19th St. NW; ☎ 202/623-7001; http://siteresources.worldbank.org/EXTABOUTUS/Resources/tours.pdf; Metro: Farragut West; free admission; second Thurs of every month 10am and 2pm). Advance reservations are required; complimentary snacks are served.

The tour begins at the IMF, which has 184 member countries. You will hear a briefing and participate in a question-and-answer session. Briefings are very much a part of the Washington scene: The president gets one daily and its impossible to imagine how the Pentagon would function without briefings. It's how busy people with lots of responsibility keep tabs on what's happening. So picture yourself as an international bigwig being updated on the work of these three organizations. The briefers will tell you about the work of each, maybe outlining a current program or concern. Before you leave the IMF, take a look at the "Money Wall," which displays world currencies. You move on to the **OAS** (17th St. and Constitution Ave. NW), which has 35 members, for another briefing. While here, view the impressive Hall of the Americas, which features a tropical patio ringing a fountain suggesting Mayan, Aztec, and Zapotecan art. The **World Bank** (1818 H St. NW), the final tour stop, occupies a spare, modernistic building that its designers see as an architectural glimpse of the future. Here you get a third briefing and the opportunity to visit the InfoShop, which markets books, publications, and souvenirs related to the economy.

HEAR THE BIG BOSSES TAKE A BEATING

The **Capitol Steps** (Ronald Reagan Bldg., 1300 Pennsylvania Ave. NW; ☎ 202/312-1555; www.capsteps.com; Metro: Federal Triangle; $35) bash the leadership at 7:30pm every Saturday and Sunday. With a strong and loyal Washington following, they've been at it for more than 25 years. Along the way, they have recorded 26 albums, including "I'm So Indicted."

The group made its debut in December 1981 when three staffers for Sen. Charles Percy of Illinois were assigned to plan entertainment for a Christmas party. The story they tell is that at first they wanted to stage a nativity play, but in all of Congress they couldn't find three wise men and a virgin. So they turned to the headlines of the day to create song parodies and skits that let their bosses have it smack between the eyes. They were a hit, and the show goes on.

Many of the Steps have quit their day jobs on Capitol Hill, and not all current members are former Hill staffers. But taken together, the cast has worked in 18 congressional offices, and they have 62 years of collective Senate and House staff experience. They know where the bodies are buried. Attend a performance, and get an insider's view of how Washington really works.

TAKE A PEEK INTO THE MOVIE INDUSTRY

Movies are an important aspect of the city's cultural and working life. Seemingly year-round, film crews are barricading streets to film a script set in the nation's capital. Years ago, I walked into the afternoon editor's news conference at the

Washington Post and sat down next to Dustin Hoffman, who was researching his role as Watergate reporter Carl Bernstein in *All the President's Men,* the Watergate movie. Robert Redford, who played Bob Woodward, sat across the room.

So many movies have been made on location that a tour company called **On Location Tours** (Departing from near Union Station, Massachusetts, and Louisiana aves. NE; ☎ 212/209-3370; www.screentours.com/tour.php/dc; Metro: Union Station; $34; Saturdays at 10am) is now offering escorted tours to location sites. The 3-hour bus tour takes you to the location of movies filmed in Washington. You will, the tour company promises, stand on *The Exorcist* stairs at Georgetown University, visit the bar used in *St. Elmo's Fire,* and see locations for *Forrest Gump.* Clips from the movies shot at the locations add to the experience. And you will hear lots of historic trivia about the sights visited.

The Motion Picture Association of America, the lobbying arm of the American film industry, is located in Washington, where it can push for anti-film-pirating legislation. Film stars testify regularly before congressional committees in support of issues they back, and then they're spotted on the bar scene in Georgetown or Adams Morgan. Until recently, the **American Film Institute,** charged with rescuing and preserving America's fast-disappearing film heritage, was headquartered at the Kennedy Center. But when it moved, it didn't go far—to Silver Spring, Maryland, where it continues to feature movies for the movie buff. Art films, documentaries, and short subjects are screened daily beginning at 1pm (until 10pm daily) at the American Film Institute's **AFI Silver Theatre and Cultural Center** (Silver Spring, 8633 Colesville Rd.; ☎ 301/495-6720; www.afi. com/silver; Metro: Silver Spring and 2-block walk; administrative offices weekdays 9am–5:30pm). The institute also schedules lectures and discussions by directors and actors. I listened to a charming, articulate Olivia de Havilland recall the troubled filming of *Gone With the Wind.* Though it was sad to see AFI leave the Kennedy Center, the move took it from an auditorium designed for live performances to its more appropriate location in a restored movie house.

LEARN HOW SECURITY AGENCIES NAB SPIES

Spies and traitors have lurked in the city's shadows in the past, and we can assume they are still around today. The Federal Bureau of Investigation has shut down its tours, which touched on spy tracking. But a good alternative is **Spy City Tours** (Departing Union Station, Massachusetts and Louisiana aves. NE; ☎ 800/GRAY-LINE; www.spymuseum.org/special/spycity_tour.php; Metro: Union Station; $59; Tues and Sat 10am). Organized by the **International Spy Museum** (p. 125), the 2-hour bus tour takes you to 25 of Washington's notable espionage sites. You will see the pub where traitor Aldrich Ames, a CIA agent doubling as a Soviet KGB mole, revealed the names of 25 American spies (all Russian citizens) in the Soviet Union—10 of whom were then shot in the back of the head. Ames's arrest in 1994 badly embarrassed the CIA. Along the way, you will learn a few spy techniques—how to maintain a fake identity, for example, or how to pass along secret files and participate in an undercover operation. You play the new recruit, and you will be tested on your skills of observation, evasion, and code-breaking. This is a fun tour on a serious subject.

HOW WE RELAX

CHESS ACTION

Some of Washington's finest chess players can be seen in action at **Dupont Circle Chess in the Park** (Metro: Dupont Circle), where 10 permanently affixed tables with benches for four are reserved for them. You can watch or, if you think you are good, let the players know you are interested in a match. The George Washington University Chess Club cites the Dupont Circle tables as a recommended training ground for beginners and an excellent way to become acquainted with the Washington chess community. International chess players from Embassy Row are frequently on hand. If you decide to play, the club notes that almost all games are touch-move and you may be playing speed-chess against the clock. It warns members to beware of the occasional hustler: "Don't play for money unless you genuinely think you have good odds of winning." You can catch the matches most weekday evenings and all day Saturday and Sunday from spring through fall, weather permitting.

WITH LAZY DAYS

When we locals have an idle weekend, we don't spend all of it watching football on TV. You will find crowds of us:

- **Browsing the boutiques of Georgetown** (M St. and Wisconsin Ave. NW; K St. Circulator bus). We aren't necessarily intent on buying anything. But we want to be in the know—au courant, in the loop. We want to check out what's new in fashion or in the galleries. We want to bump into friends, maybe to share a beer or a late lunch. We want to see and be seen.
- **Strolling the Chesapeake and Ohio Canal towpath** (Georgetown, Thomas Jefferson St. NW at Lock 4; K St. Circulator bus). The path is wide, the terrain gentle, and after a few minutes you have the Potomac River on the left and the canal on the right. Joggers and bicyclists race past, but most people are out for an easy amble, enjoying the water views and breezes. Take note as you stroll that this invaluable recreational and scenic asset almost became a vehicle parkway. Historic preservation and environmentalism are ongoing issues on Capitol Hill. The canal and towpath, saved from destruction as a national parkland, is a lesson in what the stakes are.
- **Visiting a 19th-century open market** (7th St. and North Carolina Ave. SE; www.easternmarket.net; Tues–Sat 7am–6pm, Sun 9am–4pm; Metro: Eastern Market). A Capitol Hill institution and neighborhood town center since 1873, Eastern Market is the last of Washington's 19th-century markets to remain in continuous operation. As we go to press in June 2009, it's about to reopen after an extensive renovation, following a disastrous fire in 2007. On weekends, farmers show up to display their produce. Every Saturday there's a crafts fair (10am–5pm) and on Sunday a flea market draws the bargain hunters (10am–5pm). This is small-town America in the heart of the nation's capital. The term "Inside the Beltway" tends to be derogatory and often is used to mean a place where people have lost touch with reality. Take in Saturday morning at Eastern Market, and you'll see we're not really all that weird.

AFTER-WORK HAPPY HOURS

Mostly the realm of young and unattached professionals, the 5-to-7pm happy hour at downtown bars and pubs is a thriving segment of the local social whirl. Every big city has a happy hour, but in Washington it's an important part of the workday. Sure, it's a pickup opportunity, but it's also one way for singles in high-pressure jobs to let off steam, get to know their coworkers, or maybe to network (an always important activity in the nation's capital). If they are newly employed from out of town, as many are, they may be looking to build a family of friends over a brew or two. Many places cut drink prices and provide free nibbles to attract the 20- and 30-something crowds. Thursday has become the best night of the week for deals. If this is your milieu, join in. Among the popular and affordable happy hour choices:

- The **Front Page Restaurant & Grill** (1333 New Hampshire Ave. NW; ☎ 202/296-6500; www.frontpagerestaurant.com; Metro: Dupont Circle). A bustling Dupont Circle watering hole for 2 decades, it sports a newspaper theme and a rustic heavy wood and brick decor that gives it a comfy ambiance. Happy hour is Monday to Friday from 4 to 7pm. For $2.75, you can get a house wine, rail drink, or a lite beer (or Front Page Ale). On Thursdays, it's $2, Miller Lite and Corona, 4pm to close, and the Taco Bar serves three tacos for $1 from 5 to 7pm.

- **Lucky Bar** (1221 Connecticut Ave. NW; ☎ 202/331-3733; www.lucky bardc.com; Metro: Dupont Circle). Happy hour runs from 3 to 8pm, Monday to Wednesday and Friday, with draft beer from $2.50 to $3.75, and well drinks $3.50. (Thurs is "Do the Deuce," an all-night drink special.) Meet the bike messengers, the muscular crew that threads city traffic to hand-deliver important documents demanding immediate attention. Cheap food and drinks are what draw them to this Dupont Circle hangout, now a decade old. Students, interns, and soccer fans congregate here too (they serve English breakfasts to soccer fans who get up early to watch the European games on the telly!).

- **Hawk 'n' Dove** (329 Pennsylvania Ave. NW; ☎ 202/543-3300; www.hawk anddoveonline.com; Metro: Capitol South). On Capitol Hill, this big noisy bar—which claims to be the oldest Irish bar in town—has been drawing Capitol staffers since 1967. So the story goes, it's a place where the folks who do the real work, Democrat and Republican alike, gather to gripe about their bosses. To preserve their jobs, they refer to the senator or representative who employs them only as "my member" should anyone be eavesdropping. Happy hour specials are offered from 4 to 7pm on weeknights with domestic beer $1.95 a bottle and well drinks $2; on Thursday, happy hours at the other bars along this strip (p. 257) can also be worthwhile.

GALLERY HOPPING ON FIRST FRIDAY

Washington is home to artists and artisans from around the world, so the art scene is quite active. Visit the galleries; maybe talk to the artists. The most convenient way is to participate in First Friday. More than 25 **Dupont Circle art galleries** (Metro: Dupont Circle) host a free open house from 6 to 8pm on the first Friday of every month. Many serve food and wine; often a musician is on hand to serenade; and some decorate with lanterns to provide a festive look. Washington arts lovers move from gallery to gallery, mingling and meeting, and so can you. Most galleries are located in close proximity on Connecticut Avenue and on R Street NW. The works are varied. The **Washington Printmakers Gallery** (1732 Connecticut Ave. NW; ☎ 202/332-7757; www.washingtonprintmakers.com) displays etchings, aquatints, and lithographs. **Studio Gallery** (2108 R St. NW; ☎ 202/232-8734; www.studiogallerydc.com) is the city's oldest cooperative gallery with diverse shows. **Gallery K** (2010 R St. NW; ☎ 202/234-0339) focuses on contemporary art. The quality of works generally is first-rate, but prices can be high because of the city's high cost of living. Go to browse, people-watch, and, maybe, find a bargain. For a list of participants, pick up a free copy of *Galleries Magazine* in any gallery. A list of many Dupont Circle galleries also can be found at **www.artlineplus.com**.

FOREIGN CULTURAL CENTER PROGRAMS

Many foreign nationals, perhaps assigned to work in their homeland embassy, call Washington home, at least temporarily. Several countries sponsor cultural centers, where American citizens can meet people from abroad and learn about them and their native land. Lectures, concerts, and art shows are among the programs presented. Many are free.

In a single week in 2009, you could have attended a lecture on Japanese Animation at the **Japan Information and Culture Center** (1155 21st St. NW; ☎ 202/238-6949; www.us.emb-japan.go.jp/english/html/index.html; Metro: Dupont Circle); heard a lecture on Hamas and the Palestinian people at the **Palestine Center** (2425 Virginia Ave. NW; ☎ 202/338-1290; www.palestine center.org; Metro: Foggy Bottom); viewed new German documentaries on globalization at **Goethe-Institut** (812 7th St. NW; ☎ 202/289-1200; www.goethe.de/washington; Metro: Gallery Place–Chinatown); and learned about how changing methods of census gathering are affecting international relations at **Meridian International Center** (1630 Crescent Place NW; ☎ 202/667-6800; www.meridian.org; Metro: Dupont Circle), an American organization sponsoring cultural exchanges. Look for current listings in the free Thursday *City Paper*.

Other cultural centers regularly organizing events include:

- **Alliance Francaise** (2142 Wyoming Ave. NW; ☎ 202/234-7911; www.france dc.org; Metro: Dupont Circle). It hosts French wine-and-cheese-tasting sessions, films, art exhibits, recitals, and lectures.
- **Asia Society, Washington Center** (1575 I St. NW, Ste. 325; ☎ 202/833-2742; www.asiasociety.org/visit; Metro: Farragut North). Founded to foster understanding between more than 30 Asian nations and the United States, the organization sponsors about 50 public programs annually on contemporary affairs, trade and investment, and arts and cultures. You don't need to be a member to attend many functions.
- **Brazilian-American Cultural Institute** (4719 Wisconsin Ave. NW; ☎ 202/362-8334; www.bacidc.org/us; Metrobus: 30, 32, 34, 35, 36). Concerts, movies, art shows, and samba lessons.
- **Instituto de Mexico en Washington, D.C.** (2829 16th St. NW; ☎ 202/728-1628; http://portal.sre.gob.mx/imw; Metrobus: S2, S4). Occupying a beautiful mansion, the institute presents a year-round program of films, art shows, concerts, and lectures.

7 Outdoor Washington

Parks, active pursuits, & major league teams

By Jim Yenckel

WASHINGTON IS CALLED A CITY OF MOVERS AND SHAKERS, AND THIS APPLIES not only to workday achievements but equally to off hours. Local folk really do move, pursuing athletics of all sorts with remarkable vigor. Hometown puffery, you think? Not at all. Let me cite a fairly creditable source agreeing with me: *Men's Health Magazine* in its "MetroGrades 2009," ranked Washington as America's number one city for fitness, for both men and women. Along with temperate weather for much of the year (even though the summers can be pretty sizzling), much of the city—nearly one-fifth—is devoted to parks, more than in any other major city. A city that plays sports apparently also likes to watch them. Fans in the metro area support major league baseball, football, basketball (men's and women's), hockey, and soccer teams. This chapter is a guide to spectator sports and to recreational activities and the parks in which to enjoy them. I've divided the city's parks into two categories—places where you can run, hike, bike, or otherwise maintain your aerobic schedule, and places where you simply can relax, enjoy the setting, and watch the passersby.

OUTDOOR SPACES FOR ACTIVE PEOPLE

Washington is the center of a metropolitan area that claims a population of more than five million. But in the city itself you won't feel like you're being crushed by the crowds. The reason is its abundance of green spaces—parks and playing fields—many of them conveniently located adjacent to National Mall or not far away. These are the major outdoor spaces that those of us who live here value highly.

PARKS ON OR NEAR THE MALL

Two miles long and 5 blocks wide, the vast green expanse of the **National Mall** ★★★ (☎ 202/426-6841; www.nps.gov/nama; Metro: Smithsonian; daily until midnight) gives downtown Washington plenty of needed breathing room. Its gravel paths attract runners and strollers throughout the day; its green lawns teem with Frisbee tossers. In spring, the annual Kite Festival, traditionally a part of the National Cherry Blossom Festival, fills the sky with dancing color (see "Events" in chapter 12, p. 281). For more on the Mall itself, see chapter 5, p. 114).

An adjunct of the Mall, **West Potomac Park** ★ (On the Mall; ☎ 202/426-6841; www.nps.gov/nama; Metro: Smithsonian; daily during daylight hours) is a sports playground with great Potomac River views. Administered by the National Park Service, it is tucked between the Tidal Basin on the east and the Lincoln Memorial on the west. Go here to watch or join pickup soccer, softball,

167

A Museum of Plants

Long before anyone thought to worry about "invasive species," the Congress of the United States created the **U.S. Botanic Garden** ✪ kids (On the Mall at Maryland Ave. and 1st St. SW; ☎ 202/225-8333; Metro: Federal Center SW or Capital South; www.usbg.gov; free admission; daily 10am–5pm except Dec 25) with the express purpose of importing plants that might improve American agriculture. That was way back in 1820 and after a couple of fits and starts, the current structure with its eye-catching greenhouse was constructed in 1934 (and just recently renovated). No, you're not going to see your senator gathering seeds and saplings to send back home to constituent farmers. Just as the structure changed over the years, so did its mission, and now this is a dedicated "museum of plants" with flora representing different ecosystems and species around the globe. One gallery is devoted entirely to orchids; the **Desert** is a sun-baked landscape of exotic and prickly cacti; the **Jungle** simulates a tropical rainforest soaring above an abandoned and decaying plantation. It's the sort of spooky setting that delights youngsters. Trees shoot up three stories beneath the glass.

And you (or at least your kids) don't just have to look at it all: The **Children's Garden,** an open courtyard within the Conservatory, offers tykes a potting bench, garden tools, and, usually, a potted plant or two to transplant.

For gardening enthusiasts, **Bartholdi Park,** just across Independence Avenue, features a demonstration garden for home landscapers. And in 2006 the 3-acre **National Garden** debuted. The latest addition to the Mall also features a formal rose garden; a water garden (in honor of the first ladies—and I don't know why); a terraced butterfly garden; and a display of native trees, shrubs, grasses, and flowers from the Mid-Atlantic region.

Strolling through these various gardens and environments is a soothing change from the hustle and bustle of the Capitol building and nearby Smithsonian Museums. Take some time out for it if you can.

—*Pauline Frommer*

rugby, field hockey, and lacrosse matches. Once, full-fledged polo matches, galloping horses and all, were staged on its broad grass-covered fields, but sadly they have disappeared in recent years.

East Potomac Park ✪ (Adjacent to the Mall; ☎ 202/426-6841; www.nps.gov/nama; Metro: Smithsonian; daily during daylight hours) offers opportunities for inexpensive golf and tennis. Located just east of the Tidal Basin and the Jefferson Memorial, the park is all but hidden by the complex of vehicle and railroad bridges linking Washington with Virginia across the Potomac River. From behind the Jefferson Memorial, follow Ohio Drive (on foot or bicycle) past the George Mason Memorial. This will get you under the bridges and into this large and lovely peninsula jutting into the Potomac. Run, bike, or stroll the 3.2-mile loop around the peninsula with water and monument views every step of the way. At Hains Point, the tip of the peninsula, check out the massive sculpture called *The Awakening*. The head and hands of a giant male figure arise from beneath the ground. (For details on golf and tennis, see p. 179.)

Unlike the two Potomac parks, the 45-acre **Constitution Gardens** ✪✪ (On the Mall; ☎ 202/426-6841; www.nps.gov/nama; Metro: Smithsonian; daily during daylight hours) is formally landscaped; it's a quiet place of shaded walks. In one corner, the Vietnam Veterans Memorial is its most noted attraction. Nearby, a footbridge leads to a little island in the pond where you find a small memorial to the **56 Signers of the Declaration of Independence.**

No way you can see it all, but take a look at a bit of one of the country's most unusual parks. Beginning in the heart of Georgetown, the **Chesapeake and Ohio Canal National Historic Park** ✪✪ (Rock Creek Pkwy. at 28th and K sts. NW; ☎ 202/653-5190; www.nps.gov/choh; Metro: Foggy Bottom–GWU; daily during daylight hours) stretches northwest for 185 miles alongside the Potomac River to Cumberland, Maryland. Built between 1828 and 1850, the canal served until 1924 as an important shipping route between the farms in the West and the factories in the East. Mules towed the barges, treading the towpath that parallels the canal. Barge captains and their families lived their entire lives on the canal, and lock tenders operated the 74 lift locks that carried the barges from near sea level to an elevation of 605 feet. A few stone structures that housed the tenders still stand. As a west-bound barge glided up to a lock, the tender closed two giant swinging doors behind it. This enclosed the barge in a mostly watertight chamber. Then the tender pumped water into the chamber, lifting the barge like an elevator to the next level. Then the tender opened the lock's forward doors, and the barge moved on. The park preserves the canal and many of its structures. A small **visitor center** (1057 Thomas Jefferson St. NW, btw. 30th and 31st sts. south of M St.) on the canal in Georgetown tells the historic story. For the first mile, the canal and towpath edge past homes and shops in an urban parklike setting, and then they start their long climb through the green countryside. Many hikers and bicyclists travel the full length over a period of several days, camping in the park or staying in motels and inns adjacent to it. However, day hikers tend to turn back at Fletcher's Boathouse at the 3-mile point (water, snacks, and restrooms). For details on seasonal barge rides, see chapter 5 (p. 148).

PARKS AWAY FROM THE MALL AREA

Unless visitors go to the National Zoo, they often miss **Rock Creek Park** ✪ (☎ 202/895-6070; www.nps.gov/rocr; daily during daylight hours). Though it covers more than 1,700 acres within the District of Columbia and virtually cuts the city in half from north to south, most of the park is tucked away in residential neighborhoods. President John Quincy Adams delighted in roaming the woods before it became a park; he called it "a romantic glen," where he could listen "to the singing of a thousand birds." Still a semi-wilderness of forest and meadow (coyotes have been spotted since 2004; deer are everywhere), the park begins at the Potomac River, opposite the Watergate complex in the 2600 block of Virginia Avenue NW. Initially it is draped across a slender gorge cut by Rock Creek. But the green spaces widen as it winds north for about 15 miles to the

Bonsais, Hiking & Tram Rides: Discovering the National Arboretum

Is it a park, a garden, or a museum? Take your pick, because the **United States National Arboretum** ✪✪✪ (3501 New York Ave. NE; ☎ 202/245-2726; www.usna.usda.gov; Metro: Union Station, connecting to Metrobus X6 on weekends only; free admission; daily 8am–5pm except Dec 25) qualifies on all three counts. Covering 450 rolling acres along the Anacostia River, the arboretum is, indeed, a living museum where trees, shrubs, and herbaceous plants are cultivated for scientific and educational purposes. The result is a beautifully landscaped garden in nearly constant bloom from early spring to early winter. My quandary is whether the arboretum should be listed in this guide as an "outdoor space for active people" or a "park for the not so active." Since it could be either, I've sandwiched it between the chapter sections.

Active: Many local folks enjoy bicycling or hiking its 9 miles of paved roads. More unpaved hiking trails explore groves of trees and sloping meadows.

Not so active: You can explore the arboretum by car or climb aboard a 48-passenger tram for a 35-minute escorted tour. The tram operates weekends and holidays from early April to mid-October. Departures are 10:30 and 11:30am and 1, 2, 3, and 4pm. There is a fee: $4 adults, $3 seniors, $2 children (4–16).

Perched on one of Washington's highest points, the arboretum has been landscaped into numerous gardens. The **Azalea Collection** draws visitors in the spring, when thousands of bushes turn the park's Mount Hamilton into a blaze of color. Mid-autumn is the season for the 13-acre

Maryland border (Western Ave. NW) at Chevy Chase. The **Zoo** (see chapter 5, p. 122), located within the park, is near the southern tip. Also, **ranger-led programs** focusing on aspects of nature and the park are scheduled regularly at the Nature Center. Many are aimed specifically at children. To reach the Nature Center, take Metro to the Friendship Heights station and transfer to the E2 Metrobus. Get off at the intersection of Glover and Military roads NW, and walk south on the trail up the hill (about 100 yd.). Free and ticketed outdoor concerts and theater productions are presented in the summer at the park's Carter Barron Amphitheatre (16th St. and Colorado Ave. NW), but it is advisable to attend only if you can go by car. Keep in mind you will be competing for limited seating with Washingtonians who live in the neighborhood.

It's hard to believe, but almost in the city's heart is a 91-acre near-wilderness where you can find escape from urban hubbub—Theodore Roosevelt Island in the Potomac River. This peaceful retreat is the site of the **Theodore Roosevelt Memorial** ✪ (On the Potomac River at the Virginia end of the Theodore

Asian Collection's camellias clinging to steeply sloping terrain. Don't miss the **National Grove of State Trees,** a 30-acre woodland featuring the state tree of nearly every state. The District of Columbia is represented by a scarlet oak; California sent (what else?) a California redwood; from Kansas came a cottonwood tree. The **National Herb Garden** is the largest in the country, containing annual, perennial, and woodsy herbal plants.

The **National Bonsai Collection and Penjing Museum** (10am–4pm only), housed in three large pavilions, is also a must-see. The Japanese art of bonsai is the cultivation of dwarf trees in which the placement of branches, the styling, and even the pot the tree occupies carry deep symbolism. Penjing is the Chinese precursor to bonsai. The bonsai collection began when the Nippon Bonsai Association of Japan donated 53 bonsai to the people of the United States in honor of the 1976 Bicentennial. Since then, the collection has grown to more than 150 plants.

Unfortunately, getting to the arboretum, which is on the eastern edge of the city, is inconvenient. By car, take New York Avenue east as if leaving Washington for Baltimore or New York City. It's by far the ugliest gateway to the capital. Turn right onto Bladensburg Road at the traffic light, and go 4 blocks to R Street. Make a left turn on R Street and continue 2 blocks to the arboretum gate. By public transportation, catch the X6 Metrobus from Union Station. With a Metrorail transfer, the fare is 25¢; the return is $1.25. The bus operates only on weekends and holidays; departures from Union Station are every 40 minutes from 7:55am to 4:35pm. Return trips from the arboretum are 8:16am to 4:56pm.

Roosevelt Memorial Bridge; ☎ 703/289-2500; www.nps.gov/this; Metro: Rosslyn and a 20-min. walk; free admission; daily dawn–dusk). Preserving forest, marsh, and swamp, the island was dedicated in 1967 to America's 26th president as a memorial recognizing his love of nature. Two and a half miles of island trails invite easy hikes. In the center, a 17-foot-high statue of Roosevelt soars to treetop height. To some, the statue is an intrusion on the semi-wilderness. It does seem out of place, as if it had tumbled from a truck hauling it to a more fitting location on the Mall. Still, I think Roosevelt would approve. From the Rosslyn Metro station: After exiting, turn left on Moore Street and go to the end of the block. Turn right on 19th Street and go 1 short block to Lynn Street. Cross Lynn and turn left. In 2 more blocks you will see a sign to the **Mount Vernon Trail.** Follow the trail to the island. The island is at the northern end of the Mount Vernon Trail, an 18.5-mile paved trail that winds south along the Potomac River to George Washington's Mount Vernon Plantation.

OUTDOOR SPACES FOR THE NOT-SO-ACTIVE

Step into a bit of France and Italy at **Meridian Hill Park** ✫✫ (16th and W sts. NW; Metrobus S2, S4; www.nps.gov/rocr/cultural/merid.htm; daily during daylight hours). Laid out in formal design with lots of statuary, the 12-acre park was modeled after the Renaissance and Italian gardens that adorn many of the world's capitals. Begun in 1914, Meridian Hill Park was acquired in 1933 by the National Park Service and completed in 1936. Occupying a slope, it is gently terraced; its most dramatic feature is a series of 13 cascading pools, spilling from one to the next down the hill. Above the pools rides Joan of Arc, as represented by the city's only female equestrian statue. It's a bronze replica of the Paul Dubois work that stands before the Cathedral of Rheims in France. Erected on the Great Terrace, the statue divides the French-influenced upper portion of the park (a long grassy mall) with the lower Italianate portion. President James Buchanan, who spent 4 tumultuous years in the White House prior to the Civil War, is remembered with a less vigorous statue. He is seated, a robe draped across his lap. Befitting the lower park's Italian theme, Dante Alighieri, the 13th-century Italian poet, scholar, and diplomat, stands 11 feet tall in flowing bronze robes. His statue was a gift from an Italian-American newspaper in New York City on behalf of Italian Americans.

Yes, it's a traffic circle, but a special one. **Dupont Circle** ✫ (Intersection of Connecticut, Massachusetts, and New Hampshire aves. NW; Metro: Dupont Circle) doubles as Washington's friendly back porch, a place where urban dwellers pause for a few minutes to chat with their neighbors. Ringed by park benches, it's a place to sit and read or watch the city flow past. Almost in the city center, it's the focal point of the Dupont Circle/Kalorama neighbor (see chapter 2, p. 20).

Four other block-size downtown parks with shady trees and benches tempting you to relax are **Lafayette Park** ✫✫ (Opposite the White House, 16th and H sts. NW; Metro: McPherson Square); **Franklin Square** (14th and I sts. NW; Metro: McPherson Square); **McPherson Square** (15th and I sts. NW; Metro: McPherson Square); and **Farragut Square** (17th and I sts. NW; Metro: Farragut North or Farragut West). All are accessible daily until nightfall. Summer concerts, usually some form of rock performed by local artists, interrupt (or relieve, depending on your point of view) the quiet at Farragut Square from noon to 2pm on Thursdays. Note that in late afternoon, many of the city's homeless gather at McPherson Square, where a mobile kitchen provides dinner.

My favorite downtown park, an ideally located rest stop for tired sightseers heading back to their hotels, is little **Pershing Park** ✫ (Opposite the White House Visitor Center at 15th St. and Pennsylvania Ave. NW; Metro: Federal Triangle; daily during daylight hours). A sunken retreat, its shade trees tempt you down its terraced sides to below street level, at least partially hiding busy Pennsylvania Avenue. At the bottom, a large pool nearly half a square block in size suggests (use your imagination here) a lake tucked into a mountain valley. At one end a waterfall cascades down the slope. I'm not sure summer temperatures are any cooler in the park, but it certainly seems like it. In winter, the pool becomes an ice-skating rink (p. 178).

THE CITY AS OUTDOOR SCULPTURE GARDEN

If you want to honor a national leader or hero with a statue, where do you put it? In Washington, D.C., of course. As a result, the city is bedecked with statues, so many in fact, that its many parks, circles, and squares are virtual outdoor sculpture gardens. Keep your eyes open for the ones I list below, or plot a walking tour of your own; they all are situated in locations you are likely to pass on your sightseeing excursions.

Out of hundreds of possibilities, I've spotlighted 10 of artistic, historic, and particular whimsical relevance. The historic statues, those born of the Civil War for example, put faces on names in the history books. If for no other reason, stop for a moment when you pass one of the city's statues and see whom it honors. They all have an interesting story to tell.

For the history behind each statue, I'm indebted to James M. Goode, the former curator of the Smithsonian "Castle" and author of *The Outdoor Sculpture of Washington, D.C.*, published in 1974 by the Smithsonian Institution Press. Sadly, little information about individual statues is provided on the site of the statues.

ON CAPITOL HILL

The Civil War's victorious commanding general is honored with one of the city's most important statues, known as the **General Ulysses S. Grant Memorial** ★ 🧒 (Union Square, east end of the Mall in front of the Capitol; Metro: Capitol South). Overlooking the almost lake-size Capitol Reflecting Pool, the bronze portrait of Grant, who went on to be elected president, sits astride his charger, Cincinnatus. The sculptor, Henry Merwin Shrady, a relative unknown at the time, studied Grant's life mask to get the face correct. The horse used as a model was provided by the New York Police Department. Shrady is said to have turned a water hose on his equine model to observe the ripple of the muscles. On Grant's right (north) is the Cavalry Group, seven horsemen charging onto the battlefield. Critics regard it as one of the most dramatically exciting statues in the country, the horses and their mounts seemingly alive and in full gallop. One horse, however, has fallen and taken his rider down with him. Using a mirror, Shrady sculpted his own face as the rider's. Military posts staged cavalry drills so he could get the troop movements correct. On Grant's left (south) is the Artillery Group, another action-packed tableau depicting three powerful horses pulling a caisson with cannon and three riders. In a brief stroll around the memorial's large marble platform you can sense the courage, tragedy, and chaos of battle. Endorsed by Congress, the statues were dedicated in 1922 on the 100th anniversary of Grant's birth. A military parade marched from the White House down Pennsylvania Avenue to the memorial, where Vice President Calvin Coolidge was among the principal speakers. Sadly, Shrady died 2 weeks before the ceremony. Note on the Grant statue the single word, GRANT. In 1922, he needed no other identification.

NEAR THE WHITE HOUSE

Leading the long parade of equestrian statuary, **Major General Andrew Jackson** (Lafayette Square; Metro: McPherson Square), or at least his statue, enjoys what may be the most prestigious site for an honoree in Washington—directly across Pennsylvania Avenue from the White House. Over the years, attempts have been made to move Jackson elsewhere, since every other statue in Lafayette Square is a

JFK to the Rescue

Directly across from the White House, Lafayette Square is a 7-acre park lined by attractive row houses that give the park its 19th-century flavor. In the 1960s, those houses were threatened by demolition and were destined to be replaced by the 10-story National Courts Building on the east side of the square and the New Executive Office Building on the west side. But President John F. Kennedy opposed the scheme, which would completely change the character of what once was called "the President's Park." Instead, he asked the architectural firm of John Carl Warnecke & Associates to come up with a plan that preserved the square's charm. What emerged was an innovative design that saved the row houses but allowed the construction of the office buildings behind them. At street level, the taller buildings intrude very little on the setting. This "fusion" of old and new has been duplicated elsewhere in Washington and across the country.

Revolutionary War figure. But Jackson, another general who became president, remains, and has since the dedication in 1853 on the 38th anniversary of the Battle of New Orleans. The work, the first equestrian statue cast in the United States, commemorates the general's victory in the final battle of the War of 1812. He is shown reviewing his troops, his hat raised high in salute, and his horse rearing as if to charge. The sculptor, Clark Mills, was self-taught and, when he got the job, had never seen an equestrian statue. But he had studied European prints of such sculptures and set about establishing America's grasp of the art. A crowd of 15,000 turned out for the dedication; leading the way was President Franklin Pierce and his entire cabinet. The sculptor, when asked to say a few words, struggled to overcome his emotion but reportedly didn't manage to get out a single utterance.

Although he lost out to Jackson for the prime position in Lafayette Square, **Major General Marquis Gilbert de Lafayette** (Lafayette Square; Metro: McPherson Square) was well compensated by having the entire square named after him. Many visitors hurrying through the park take a glance at Jackson and rush on thinking they have seen Lafayette, the boy general who served as Washington's aide-de-camp at Valley Forge and fought on until the war's end at Yorktown. But the marquis stands heroically in the square's southeast corner, one of four Revolutionary War leaders each occupying a different corner. (The others are generals Thaddeus Kosciusko, Friedrich Wilhelm von Steuben, and Comte Jean de Rochambeau, all foreign imports like Lafayette aiding in the American war.) He is posed atop a tall marble pedestal, dressed as a civilian petitioning the French National Assembly to assist the Americans in their fight for independence. At the pedestal's base, a cloak-draped female figure symbolizing America looks up at him while holding out a sword as if urging him to grasp it and join the fight. The Lafayette statue was unveiled in 1891 to commemorate the service he and his French compatriots provided in the war. Lafayette's full name is quite lengthy, but his officer buddies knew him as Gilbert; thus the statue's official name.

You might want to tote along binoculars to better examine the **General William Tecumseh Sherman Monument** (15th St. and Pennsylvania Ave. NW; Metro: Federal Triangle). It stands on a prominent site where Sherman reportedly reviewed victorious Union troops at the end of the Civil War in 1865. In 1903, the spot, just outside the south White House fence, must have seemed appropriately prestigious for the Union's second most famous general. It's still an excellent location, but new security barriers sometimes impede access. You can still get to the statue, acclaimed as one of the city's most elaborate, but only after negotiating a maze of fencing. Sherman rests astride his horse, his right hand holding a pair of field binoculars as if ready to view a battle. Horse and rider are placed atop a high pedestal, almost too high for anyone to view clearly; thus the need for your own visual aid. More evocative of the war are four life-size troopers, who stand alone at each corner at the pedestal's base. They represent Infantry, Cavalry, Artillery, and Engineers, all branches of the Union military. They are so realistic, the urge is to step up and ask them about their battlefield experiences. Two other groups of statues about midpoint on the pedestal represent War (two vultures attack the body of a dead soldier) and Peace (a woman and three children). Eight bas-reliefs depict aspects of Sherman's military career, among them his controversial but victorious march through Georgia.

As handsome in bronze as he was in life, **Alexander Hamilton** (15th St. NW at Pennsylvania Ave. NW; Metro: Federal Triangle) stands at the south entrance to the Department of Treasury Building. A heroic general in the Revolutionary War, he served as the country's first treasury secretary, creating the department and guiding the young nation to financial credibility and relative stability. James Earle Fraser, who completed the statue in 1923, was one of America's leading sculptors. He also produced the statue of Albert Gallatin, Hamilton's able successor, which stands at the north entrance to the Treasury building. Hamilton is dressed formally in the 18th-century attire of a gentleman. By most historic accounts, he was a brilliant man, high-spirited, affable, charming, and good looking. Fraser captured these characteristics nicely. President Warren G. Harding presided at the dedication, creating something of a mystery when he mentioned an unidentified donor who provided funds for the work. Newspapers of the day suggested it may have been a woman who wore a veil.

Count Casimir Pulaski (Pennsylvania Ave. and 13th St. NW; Metro: Metro Center) cuts the most dashing figure of any of the city's equestrian subjects, decked out in the ornate uniform of a Polish marshal, a flowing cape draping elegantly from his shoulders. Pulaski's bronze portrait occupies a corner of Freedom Plaza, a venue for official ceremonies, entertainment, and other events sponsored by the government of the City of Washington. So who was this guy who merits such prominent recognition? A Polish nobleman, he began his military career as a Polish freedom fighter, earning the rank of marshal general. But he was inspired by America's fight for independence. He sought the help of Benjamin Franklin, then on diplomatic duty in Paris, and Franklin recommended him to George Washington. His courageous service in the Battle of Brandywine in 1777 prompted Washington to commission him as a brigadier general in the American cavalry. A brilliant commander, respected by his troops, he suffered a fatal wound in the Battle of Savannah in 1779 and died at the age of 31.

The Boy Scout Memorial 🧒 (On the Ellipse at 15th St. btw. E St. and Constitution Ave. NW; Metro: Federal Triangle) is a natural stop if there are any Boy Scouts, former Scouts, or Scout leaders in your group. But the tribute offered is not to the Scouts themselves but to their parents and others who work on behalf of American youth. Financed by the contributions of Scouts and unveiled in 1964, it is located on the site of the First National Boy Scout Jamboree in Washington in 1937. Unfortunately, the statue has not been a critical success. In the center stands a young Scout in full uniform, hiking boots on his feet, and a walking stick in his hand as he strides off. He looks like the ideal Scout, and nobody has a problem with him. But he is greatly overshadowed by the two giant allegorical figures behind him, a male and female only partially clothed in wind-blown drapery. They represent American Manhood and Womanhood. All well and good, except when you see the threesome for the first time, you're apt to wonder why the kid's parents are nearly naked. I mean no disrespect to Scouts—I was one myself—but sometimes sculptors goof.

NEAR THE WORLD WAR II MEMORIAL

Numerous nations have bestowed statues on Washington of their homegrown champions of liberty. Prominent among them is **General Simon Bolivar** (18th St. at C St. and Virginia Ave. NW; Metro: Farragut West), who is credited with liberating much of South America from Spanish rule. He is represented in bronze with what may be the largest equestrian statue in the world. The designer, Felix W. de Weldon, also sculpted the Iwo Jima Memorial. Bolivar, astride his horse, lifts a sword high above his head. My historical source says he is urging victory. But his formidable gaze is directed at the Art Museum of the Americas and at the rear of the Pan American Union building just beyond. One might easily think, instead, that he is launching a military charge against the two buildings and the Organization of American States, which they house. Around his neck he wears a bronze replica of a gold medal given to him by Lafayette. The statue, erected in 1959, was a gift of Venezuela, one of the countries Bolivar liberated.

PENN QUARTER

At first glance, the **Temperance Fountain** (Pennsylvania Ave. at 7th St. NW; Metro: Archives–Navy Memorial) is a puzzler, an endearing oddity that amuses the locals and befuddles visitors. It stands on one of the most prominent corners along Washington's ceremonial avenue, the route of the inaugural parades from the Capitol to the White House. The structure resembles a small temple, its canopy supported by four granite pillars, one at each corner. Beneath it is a pair of entwined dolphins, their rear flippers lifted rakishly in the air. Atop the canopy, an elegant water crane on stilt-like legs silently observes the daily hubbub around him. The impish dolphins once spouted drinking water. A San Francisco dentist, Henry Cogswell, gave the fountain to the city so people could quench their thirst with water rather than alcohol. A man who made his fortune in the California gold rush, Cogswell donated similar fountains to other cities in the 1870s and 1880s, but most have been removed. A U.S. senator once tried to convince Congress to get rid of the one in Washington. He's long gone, but the fountain is still here.

RECREATIONAL SPORTS

If you need a break from the museums of the Mall, don your athletic gear and get outdoors. I describe a variety of ways to stretch your muscles.

ON FOOT Sometimes it seems as if the whole city is toting up the miles on a morning, noon, or evening run. President Bill Clinton was occasionally spotted on Washington pathways leading his security detail on a merry chase until knee problems sidelined him to his bicycle. President George W. Bush also ran regularly, maintaining a creditable speed for a non-racer. On your first visit to the city, **run along the Mall** ✮✮, simply for the thrill of running in the shadow of the White House, U.S. Capitol, Washington Monument, and other memorials. You won't find as historic a running trail anywhere else in the country. If you want company when you run, join the free 5-mile Fun Run organized at 9am every Sunday by **Fleet Feet Sports** (1841 Columbia Rd. NW; ☎ 202/387-3888; www.fleetfeetdc.com; Metro: Woodley Park–Zoo/Adams-Morgan). Routes vary, and are usually partly through the city streets and partly through Rock Creek Park. A couple dozen runners go at a pace from 7- to 12-minute miles.

The quietest, least urban trail is the towpath of the **Chesapeake and Ohio Canal** ✮✮, which runs uninterrupted (if you're up to it) 185 miles west alongside the Potomac River to Cumberland, Maryland. The gravel towpath begins on the Georgetown waterfront, a few steps from the Thompson Boat Center at the west end of Virginia Avenue NW. You can reach it from the Mall via the Lincoln Memorial and the Kennedy Center. Water and restrooms are available at the 3-mile point. I trained for the Marine Corps Marathon on the towpath, running 9 miles out and then doubling back. Running here involves all pluses and no negatives.

ON WHEELS Two-wheeled touring is a great way to recover from museum overdose. If you have the foresight, you could sign up with SmartBike (p. 14), but since that involves a fee that's only realistic if you rent for several days, also look into the rentals at **Thompson Boat Center** (2900 Virginia Ave. NW, on the Potomac River at the intersection of Rock Creek Pkwy. and Virginia Ave. in Georgetown; ☎ 202/333-9543; www.thompsonboatcenter.com; Metro: Foggy Bottom–GWU), a National Park Service concessionaire. The bike rental center is open from 8am to 6pm daily from mid-March through September. All-terrain bikes (21-speed) rent for $8 an hour or $25 a day. But who needs them? Unless you are bicycling up Embassy Row, the terrain is mostly flat. Single-speed cruisers are $4 an hour or $15 a day.

From the center, cycle the nearly level towpath of the **Chesapeake and Ohio Canal** ✮✮, passing a number of canal locks. For strong of leg, a prime destination is Great Falls on the Potomac, 14 miles one-way, where you will find an impressive waterfall and a visitor center with restrooms and water.

Or point your way downriver, following the 19-mile **Mount Vernon Trail** ✮✮ south from the Virginia side of Arlington Memorial Bridge to George Washington's Mount Vernon Plantation. This is a paved trail, mostly paralleling the Potomac and occasionally bridging marshlands. I've bicycled both many times; they can get busy on weekends, but either is worth the effort.

ON THE WATER   See the river; get on the river. It's a great way to cool off and still take in those historic Washington views. **Thompson Boat Center** (see "On Wheels" above) rents two-person canoes, singles and doubles kayaks, and (if you are properly certified) rowing shells and Sunfish sailboats. From its dock, you can go **upriver** past Georgetown to Fletcher's Cove; **downriver** to Arlington Memorial Bridge at the Lincoln Memorial and **across the river and around Theodore Roosevelt Island.** Haul out your vessel and tour the island. The distance from Memorial Bridge to the cove, the area to which renters are restricted, is about 3.5 miles—lengthy enough to satisfy most recreational paddlers. Remember, the Potomac is a powerful river, and the current is strong. If you paddle downriver, save your strength for the return. Rentals are available from 8am to 5pm. The season begins when the water temperature reaches 55°F; it ceases at the end of October. A canoe for two rents for $8 an hour, $22 a day; a singles kayak, $8 an hour, $24 a day; doubles kayak, $10 an hour, $30 a day; single racing/recreational shells, $13 an hour; double racing shells, $26 an hour; sailboats, $10 an hour.

Paddling a canoe on the Potomac is muscle work. Pedaling a paddleboat on the Tidal Basin is, well, for softies. But fun, and something you can do as a couple or with the kids. Yes, they're called paddleboats, but you pedal to propel them across the water. Check in at the dock for **Tidal Basin Paddle Boats** ✰ (☎ 202/479-2426; www.tidalbasinpaddleboats.com), located just north of the Jefferson Memorial on the Mall. Boats are rented 10am to 5pm daily from March 15 through Labor Day; from Labor Day until Columbus Day Weekend, Wednesday to Sunday. A two-passenger boat rents for $8 an hour; for four passengers, $16 an hour. At least one passenger must be 16 years old. Anyone who fits properly into a life vest can ride in a boat.

ON HORSEBACK   Saddle up and ride through Rock Creek Park, a 1,700-acre woodlands that stretches from the Potomac River north to the Maryland state line. Slicing through the heart of residential Washington, it's the National Park Service's oldest urban park, dating back to 1890. The **Rock Creek Park Horse Center** (5100 Glover Rd.; ☎ 202/362-0117; www.rockcreekhorsecenter.com) schedules hour-long guided rides alongside splashing Rock Creek 5 days a week, in season. Rides are held Tuesday, Wednesday, and Thursday at 6pm in June, July, and August; and on Saturday at 9:30 and 11am and Sundays at 11am and 12:30pm from April through October. The cost is $35 per person; reservations are required; and 12 is the minimum age. Kiddies at least 30 inches in height can go for a 15-minute pony ride ($20) on those same days of the week (weekdays in summer at 3 and 3:30pm, weekends Apr–Oct from 1–3:30pm). To reach the Horse Center, take Metrorail to the Friendship Heights station. Transfer to the E2 Metrobus line, which runs east toward the park along Military Road, Missouri Avenue, and Riggs Road. Get off at the intersection of Glover Road (also called Oregon Ave.) and walk south on the trail up the hill to the park's Nature Center (about 100 yd.).

ON ICE SKATES   Once the cold weather sets in, two open-air ice-skating rinks add a jolly note to downtown D.C. The largest and prettiest is the **National Sculpture Garden Ice-Skating Rink** ✰ (☎ 202/289-3360; www.nga.gov/ginfo/skating.shtm; Mon–Thurs 10am–9pm, Fri–Sat 10am–11pm, Sun 11am–9pm;

$7 adults, $6 seniors, students, children), located right on the Mall between the National Museum of Natural History and the National Gallery of Art. The rink occupies what in other seasons is a large fountain and pool. A few blocks west, the **Pershing Park Ice Skating Rink** ✯ (15th St. and Constitution Ave. NW; ☎ 202/737-6938; Mon–Thurs 10am–9pm, Fri–Sat 10am–11pm, Sun 11am–9pm; $7 adults, $6 seniors, students, children) neighbors the White House. It too offers rentals, snack service, and restrooms. Skate rental at both is $2.50 with a form of ID.

ON THE COURTS   Two large public tennis complexes welcome visitors, although reservations usually are necessary. The **East Potomac Tennis Center** (East Potomac Park; ☎ 202/554-5962; www.eastpotomactennis.com; 7am–10pm daily) provides 24 courts—10 clay and 14 hard—and offers lighted night play. The facility is located at Hains Point at the tip of the park; flag a taxi to get there, and call for a pickup when your match is over. A hard court is $8 an hour; clay, $15. The **Rock Creek Park Tennis Center** (16th and Kennedy sts. NW; ☎ 202/722-5949; www.rockcreektennis.com; daily 7am–11pm) maintains 25 outdoor tennis courts—10 hard and 15 clay—and 5 indoor courts during the winter. From downtown, catch the S2 or S4 Metrobus north on 16th Street to Kennedy Street.

ON THE LINKS   It's not Pebble Beach, but visitors can get in a round of golf with great water views at the **East Potomac Golf Course** (Ohio Dr. at Hains Point; ☎ 202/554-7660; www.golfdc.com; daily 6:30am–6pm except Dec 25), a 10-minute taxi ride from most downtown hotels. And, in contrast to a private club's exorbitant rates, greens fees here range from a piddling $9 to $20 for 9 holes and $26 to $30 for 18 holes. Golf cart rental is $13 for 18 holes; rental clubs, $12. Three courses and a driving range comprise the golf complex; the Red and White courses each offer 9 holes and the Blue course boasts an 18-hole (6,303-yd.) championship course. **Rock Creek Golf Course** (16th and Rittenhouse sts. NW; ☎ 202/882-7332; www.golfdc.com; daily 6:30am to dusk except Dec 25) features another bargain-priced 18 holes in a lush park setting. The rate for 9 holes is $16 to $19; for 18 holes, $23 to $28. Cart rental is $13 per person for 18 holes. Club rental, $12 for 18 holes. Catch the S2 or S4 Metrobus north from K Street on 16th Street to Rittenhouse.

ON THE LANES   We also cover **Lucky Strike Lanes** (701 7th St. NW; ☎ 292/347-1021; www.bowlluckystrike.com; Metro: Gallery Place–Chinatown) in the nightlife chapter (p. 260) because it's become such a truly hopping nightspot after dusk. You'll find 14 lanes, 3 pool tables, and 3 big-screen TVs. The rate is $4.95 to $7.95 a game per person. Shoe rental is $3.95. This is not your typical strip mall alley; Penn Quarter is an upscale neighborhood dotted with luxury condos, and Lucky Strike Lanes reflects this.

SPECTATOR SPORTS

Athletic or not, Washingtonians are big sports fans, supporting six professional teams. You can catch one or more of them almost any time of the year.

BASEBALL

In 2005, Washington got its first baseball team in 34 years. The **Washington Nationals** ✯ (Nationals Park, 1500 S. Capitol St. SE; ☎ 888/632-6287 for ticket purchase; www.nationals.com; Metro: Navy Yard; Apr–Oct; AE, MC, V) formerly the Montreal Expos, moved to a city that had been bereft of baseball since the Washington Senators packed up and moved to Texas back in 1971. A long run of injuries and the defection of key players have meant disappointing seasons since the move, but ever-hopeful locals have been keeping their fingers crossed. The team now plays in a multimillion-dollar, brand-spanking new ballpark south of the U.S. Capitol, **Nationals Park** (opened in 2008). As the Nationals build a following, sellouts are rare (unless a team with a big star or the World Champions visit the District). Single tickets in the lofty top rows (aka "the Grandstand") are $5 per person every game; the price climbs in easy stages from $10 to about $75 as you work your way closer to the field (and then jumps to $175–$335 for the "Diamond" and "Presidents" luxury box seats). And, for the games where they don't expect a huge crowd, deemed "value" games, the tickets other than Grandstand are discounted by $5. A fan favorite during the fourth inning of each game is the "President's Race," where costumed mascots wearing huge foam heads in the likeness of the presidents on Mt. Rushmore (Washington, Jefferson, Lincoln, and T. Roosevelt) careen around the field to the urging of the fans. If you're keeping track, Honest Abe has won the most times, and poor T.R. hadn't come in first at all (like the Nationals), as of the end of 2008.

BASKETBALL

Until 1997, the **Washington Wizards** (Verizon Center, 601 F St. NW; ☎ 202/661-5050; www.washingtonwizards.com; Metro: Gallery Place–Chinatown; Nov–Apr; AE, MC, V) were known as the Washington Bullets, an unfortunate name for a city with troubling crime statistics at the time. The team was born as the Chicago Packers in 1961, moved on to Baltimore for a few years, and landed in the nation's capital in 1974. After a string of losing years, playoff appearances in recent seasons have sparked new interest in the team, and the 20,000-seat Verizon Center (also known as "the Phone Booth") often does sell out (so call well in advance if you'd like to see them). A limited number of cheap seats at the top of the arena behind the baskets go for $10 per person, and you get what you pay for. Still, they sell out fast when put up for sale, usually a month before the game. The next-cheapest seats are $40, and prices climb to more than $100. To be assured of a lower price, buy online in advance.

Summer visitors can enjoy pro hoops as well. Soon after the Wizards end their season in spring, the WNBA takes to the Verizon Center court from May through September. The "W" is represented locally by the **Washington Mystics** (Verizon Center, 601 F St. NW; ☎ 202/266-2200; www.washingtonmystics.com; Metro: Gallery Place–Chinatown; AE, MC, V). The team has had a roller-coaster history, and despite lots of high draft choices from finishing near the bottom of the league, has yet to make it to a league championship (or even an Eastern Conference championship). Despite this, Mystics fans are among the most loyal in the league, and the team consistently has some of the league's highest attendance figures (drawing around 9,000 fans a game in 2008). The Mystics play 17 home games, and walk-up tickets at the box office should be readily available. The cheap seats, high and behind the baskets, go for $15 per person. Better seats are $20 to $70 per person. Courtside seats can be had for $115.

FOOTBALL

Washington goes wild every season for the **Washington Redskins** (FedExField; 301/276-6060; www.redskins.com; Aug–Dec). Taking in a game is the social thing to do for the well-heeled and the well-connected. Everybody else catches it on TV. The Redskins, of course, have won a few Super Bowls, but not since 1991. Still, the fans pay big bucks and undergo incredible traffic jams to watch in person at FedExField in suburban Prince Georges County, Maryland. Most home game seats go to season ticket holders, and they have sold out annually since 1966; there's a long waiting list to buy. Your chance of scoring a single ticket at the box office is next to nil, and the cost places an afternoon at a game in the big-splurge category. But if you really, really want to go: Some tickets are set aside for the visiting team; if these don't sell out, the visitors return them to the FedExField Box Office. (See phone number above.) Typically, this occurs the Thursday before a Sunday game. Of course, every Redskin fan knows this, and priority goes to fans on the waiting list to buy season tickets, so good luck. And, of course, you can try your luck online at such sites as **StubHub, eBay,** and **CraigsList.** Box-office prices (when available) range from $35 to $130 per person. The Redskins play eight regular season home games, as well as a couple at home in the pre-season. To reach FedExField (lucky you), take Metrorail to the Landover Metro Station. From there, shuttle buses make the run to the stadium ($5 round-trip). Shuttles begin operating 2 hours before the 1pm game time and run until 2 hours after the game.

HOCKEY

Hockey is the third major sport to make use of the conveniently located and always busy Verizon Center. In Washington, the National Hockey League is represented by the **Washington Capitals** (Verizon Center; 601 F St. NW; ☎ 202/397-7328 for tickets; 202/266-2200 for executive offices; www.washingtoncaps.com; Metro: Gallery Place–Chinatown; Sept–Apr; AE, MC, V), a division winner in the 2008 season and perennial contender for the Stanley Cup. The team first took to the ice in 1974–75. Getting a ticket at the door isn't a problem. The cheap seats in the goal zone are $25; for a seat in ice chip distance of the action, get ready to shell out $175 (and there are many options in between).

MEN'S RUGBY

The Washington area has become one of the main sources for rugby talent in the country. Embassy staffers from Europe, where rugby got its start in 19th-century England, formed clubs, stirring local interest. Now nearly a dozen teams are fielded during the fall-to-spring season. I'm featuring the **Washington Renegades** (Stead Field, 17th and P sts. NW; www.dcrugby.com; Metro: Dupont Circle) because of their convenient downtown practice field. After a match, teams and spectators head for a nearby pub.

MARINE CORPS MARATHON

It's your choice, spectator or participant? An annual event for more than 3 decades, the **Marine Corps Marathon** ☆ (☎ 800/RUN-USMC; www.marinemarathon.com; fee $94; AE, MC, V) attracts thousands of spectators and runners alike. TV talk-show host Oprah Winfrey completed the 26.2-mile loop through downtown Washington in 1994. I did it in 1995. In 2008, some 20,000 participants earned

Gay & Lesbian Athletic Events

Washington has a large gay and lesbian community, which has formed an impressive network of athletic teams and clubs. Events are listed weekly in the Community Calendar of *Metro Weekly*, a free magazine distributed citywide in news boxes. Out-of-towners are welcome at most. Washington is one of four finalists to host the international Gay Games in 2014.

- For a listing of dozens of GLBT sports teams, clubs, and events, head for **www.teamdc.org**, a site for all the sports-related happenings in the D.C. community, with information on sports from adventuring to ultimate Frisbee, with any number of others in between, from kickball to cheerleading.
- Go rowing with the **D.C. Strokes Rowing Club** (www.dcstrokes.org), the oldest gay and lesbian rowing club in the United States. Recreational row (weather permitting): 6 to 7:30pm Monday, Wednesday, and Thursday.
- Play water polo with the **Washington Wetskins** (www.wetskins.org), the longest continuously operating water polo team in the United States to openly welcome individuals who identify as gay, lesbian, bisexual, or straight. Practice: Wednesday 7:30 to 9pm and Sunday 3:30 to 5pm; Takoma Community Center Pool, 300 Van Buren St. NW; Metro: Takoma.

a finisher's medal. Held on a Sunday morning in late October (the date varies), the race is almost as exciting for the folks who line the route from beginning to end. The winners complete the course in under 2½ hours; the laggards trail by 3 or 4 hours more. As a spectator, you can admire the athletes' stamina and cheer on the determined plodders. The race begins just south of the Iwo Jima Statue at the north end of **Arlington National Cemetery** (Metro: Rosslyn). It ends back at the statue, which is perched at the top of a small hill. For many runners, that hill seems almost like Mount Everest. The route streaks through Georgetown, tackles a part of Rock Creek Park, and covers much of the Mall.

SOCCER

Since the debut of major league soccer in 1996, **DC United** (RFK Stadium, 2400 E. Capitol St.; ☎ 202/587-5000; www.dcunited.com; Metro: Stadium–Armory; Mar–Oct; AE, MC, V) has garnered more domestic and international awards than any other American team. It took the Major League Soccer Cup championship in 1996, the club's debut year, and again in 1997, 1999, and 2004. Washington's large soccer-hungry international community has sparked loyal fans. DC United plays 16 home games. You can buy tickets online (see above), but you will pay extra for mailing and service fees. Save bucks and buy at the gate; you should have no problem scoring a ticket unless a championship is in question. Depending on the game, single tickets range from $22 to $50. There are discounts for children and students with ID.

8 Walkabouts

Three history-rich, self-guided tours:
Arlington Cemetery, Georgetown,
& Dupont Circle/Embassy Row

By Pauline Frommer & Jim Yenckel

DARE WE SAY THIS? YOU COULD SPEND AN ENJOYABLE AND REWARDING WEEK in Washington and never step inside a museum. Simply walk the city's streets and you'll find that Washington is draped in layers of history. Monuments surprise around many corners and iconic buildings loom. Look to the left and you might see the site of an important protest march or even riot, to the right the spot where a political figure was outed in a scandal or a famed jazz musician played. Though it sounds trite to say so, Washington itself is a living museum, as impressive as anything you'll see indoors.

And by seeing the city on foot, you'll have a chance to drink in the wonders of D.C. at a human pace. The bus tours that zip around the city simply go too fast to take it all in. In the pages ahead, you supply the feet and the eyes, and we'll supply the commentary. We've picked three neighborhood walks that will envelop you in the sweep of the city's history, architecture . . . and gossip. A stroll through Arlington National Cemetery is a reminder of the contribution America's military men and woman have made to the country's defense and of the ultimate cost of war. Georgetown, the city's oldest neighborhood, has been home to the country's movers and shakers since the city's birth. It's also an architectural delight. The tour along Embassy Row, lined with dozens of foreign embassies and statues of foreign leaders, highlights America's important role in world affairs. Its "Gilded Age" history should also fascinate.

And if you were hoping to go on a self-guided walking tour of an area not covered in this book, head to the site of **Cultural Tourism DC** (www.cultural tourismDC.org). It publishes a series of free "Heritage Trail" booklets. Seven in number and growing, they guide you into parts of the city you might not otherwise visit. Online copies can be downloaded at the website; printed copies can be ordered online. They also may be available (but don't count on it) at the **D.C. Visitor Information Center** (Ronald Reagan Bldg. & International Trade Center, 1300 Pennsylvania Ave. NW; Metro: Federal Triangle; Mon–Sat 8am–6pm).

Walking Tour 1: Arlington National Cemetery

Start: Visitor Center (take Metrorail to the Arlington Cemetery station).

Finish: Iwo Jima Statue/Rosslyn Metrorail station.

Time: 2 hours, not including time spent at Arlington House and Tomb of the Unknowns.

Best times: 8am to noon daily from late spring to early fall to avoid midday heat. Anytime from 8am to 5pm daily the rest of the year.

Worst times: Noon to 5pm in July and August because of the oppressive heat.

Hours: April through September 8am to 7pm; October through March 8am to 5pm.

The best known of the nation's military cemeteries, Arlington National Cemetery is the last resting place for veterans from every American war. In rank, they range from private to five-star General of the Army. One of the country's most important national shrines, its rolling green hills above the Potomac River also shelter the remains of two U.S. presidents, numerous Supreme Court justices, and a few celebrities, boxer Joe Lewis, actor Lee Marvin, and mystery writer Dashiell Hammett among them. More than 300,000 servicemen and women, their families, and certain dignitaries are interred in the cemetery's 624 acres. Officials conduct an average of 28 burials every weekday.

You can join an escorted Tourmobile tour of the cemetery, as we outline in chapter 5 (p. 148). But if you have the time and the legs, this walkabout is a much better way to see the cemetery. The paid tour stops at the major sites, as does this walking tour. But it whisks you past almost everything else. On foot, you can read the gravestones; study the statuary and memorials; and pay homage to historic figures not mentioned on the formal tour. As you walk past the endless rows of headstones, noting the youth of many, they seem to take on greater meaning.

Military cemeteries originated as a result of the traditional duty of commanders to care for battle casualties. In 1864, when the number of Civil War deaths overwhelmed the capacity of hospitals and burial grounds near Washington, the Army's Quartermaster General, Montgomery Meigs, proposed the use of 200 acres on what was the 1,100-acre plantation of the Robert E. Lee family before the war.

This tour will visit Arlington House, the Lee family home, which the Federal Government seized when Lee chose to fight for the Confederacy. By war's end, 16,000 graves were clustered near the house. In 1882, Lee's eldest son, Custis Lee, disputed the government's ownership, and the Supreme Court ruled in his favor. But because of the presence of so many graves, he accepted $150,000 in lieu of the return of the property to the Lees. Like his father, Custis Lee graduated from West Point and served in the Confederate army, attaining the rank of major general. In 1870, he succeeded his father as president of Washington and Lee University in Lexington, Virginia.

Note: The free map of the cemetery distributed at the Visitor Center uses the word "drive" when naming the streets. The street signs themselves use the word "avenue." I have chosen to use the word "drive" in this text for consistency.

Walking Tour: Arlington National Cemetery

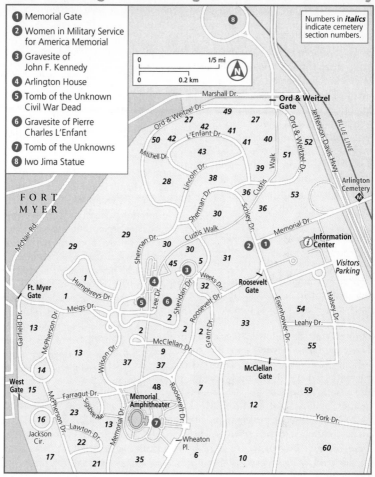

1 Memorial Gate

2 Women in Military Service for America Memorial

3 Gravesite of John F. Kennedy

4 Arlington House

5 Tomb of the Unknown Civil War Dead

6 Gravesite of Pierre Charles L'Enfant

7 Tomb of the Unknowns

8 Iwo Jima Statue

Numbers in *italics* indicate cemetery section numbers.

FORT MYER

1 Visitor Center

A large, modern structure with lots of natural light, the Visitor Center bustles like a busy railway station as sightseers line up at the ticket windows for the Tourmobile. You're walking, so you skip the lines. Be sure to take a look at the current exhibits, which do change. Pick up a copy of the cemetery brochure at the Information Desk; you may find its map useful. This itinerary does not return to the Visitor Center,

ending about a 20-minute walk away. Restrooms and water fountains are located at other major stops on this tour. No food is available at the cemetery, and picnicking is prohibited.

Exit the Visitor Center toward the tour vehicle plaza. At Eisenhower Drive at the end of the plaza, turn right to:

2 Roosevelt Gate/Schley Gate

The large wrought-iron gate in front of you, called Roosevelt Gate, honors

President Theodore Roosevelt, who led the Rough Riders up San Juan Hill in Cuba in the Spanish-American War. Across Memorial Drive is its iron double, Schley Gate, a tribute to Admiral Winfield Scott Schley. His naval force defeated the Spanish fleet at Santiago Harbor in Cuba during the war. A gold wreath is displayed in the center of each gate. Inside each is a shield bearing the seals of the military services. The Army and Marine Corps seals adorn the Roosevelt Gate; the Navy and the Coast Guard seals are represented on Schley Gate. So where is the Air Force seal? The Air Force was a branch of the Army when the gates went up. Parties attending an Arlington burial who arrive by vehicle enter the cemetery through Roosevelt Gate.

Pass through the Roosevelt Gate to:

❸ Memorial Drive

Look to your right down the length of Memorial Drive. Beyond the traffic circle, it continues across Arlington Memorial Bridge. The bridge and the drive were designed by the famous architectural firm of McKim, Mead, and White as a single project to provide a grand entrance to the cemetery. They were dedicated on January 16, 1932, by President Herbert Hoover. The bridge is a symbolic link between the Lincoln Memorial and Arlington House, the Robert E. Lee Memorial—a reuniting, as it were, of the North and the South following the Civil War. Behind you, the huge Hemicycle, a semi-circular retaining wall, marks the ceremonial terminus of Memorial Drive. Within the huge niche at its center is a bas-relief of the Great Seal of the United States. Stairways on either side of the niche climb to a terrace, where you get an even more impressive view of the drive, the bridge, and the Lincoln Memorial.

Enter the Hemicycle at the Roosevelt Gate end. Before you, you'll see the:

❹ Women in Military Service for America Memorial

More than 2.5 million women have served in military roles since the founding of America. A memorial to honor them, completed in 1995, could not have been placed in a more prestigious location in Arlington National Cemetery than at its ceremonial entrance. Their story is told in films and in changing exhibits in 14 alcoves that line the Hemicycle's spacious marble interior. More than 1,000 women joined the organization during World War II to fly noncombat missions, many of which had a definite element of danger. They delivered planes from the factories to the airfields. They pulled targets for antiaircraft gunnery training. And they tested planes to determine if they had been properly repaired. The Memorial's newest exhibit chronicles the ongoing story of women serving today in Afghanistan and Iraq.

Continue to the far end of the memorial and exit to Schley Gate. From the Hemicycle, cross Schley Drive to the footpath and turn left. Pass the first set of stairs and climb the second set on the left. Head to the:

❺ President William Howard Taft Memorial & Gravesite

The 15-foot-high shaft or stele of pink granite marking Taft's gravesite and that of his wife Helen is a fairly discreet remembrance of the *other* president buried at Arlington. His wife is the only *other* first lady here also.

A hefty 300-pounder, Taft was the weightiest person to occupy the White House. His achievements matched his size. After leaving the presidency, he was named Chief Justice of the

Many Memorials

Arlington National Cemetery is the site of many more memorials than any single walking tour can visit. The free cemetery map pinpoints the sections or grids where these memorials can be found. Those you may want to seek out on your own might include:

- **Tomb of the Unknown Dead of the War of 1812,** 14 soldiers in a mass grave whose bodies were uncovered in a construction site in 1905. Section 1, Grid N—33/34.
- **USS *Serpens* Memorial,** honoring the 250 lives lost when the Coast Guard ammunition ship exploded on January 29, 1945, at Guadalcanal in the South Pacific. Section 34, Grid XY—17.
- **Lockerbie Memorial Cairn,** for the 270 victims of the bombing of Pan American Flight 103 over Scotland on December 21, 1988. Section 1, Grid NO—33/34.
- **Nurses Memorial,** dedicated to the nurses who have served in America's armed forces. Many are buried near the statue of a military nurse. Section 21, Grid M—19/20.
- **War Correspondents Memorial,** in memory of journalists who died while covering wars for the American public. Grid OP—23/24.

Supreme Court, the only person to hold both positions. Sports fans may know he was the first president to throw out the first baseball of the season. The occasion, which inaugurated the yearly tradition, was a game between the Philadelphia Athletics and the Washington Senators in 1910.

Soon after Taft was buried in 1930, the War Department ordered a headstone to be topped by a Latin cross. No one knows whatever became of it; it simply never showed up. In its place, Helen Taft privately commissioned the odd-looking headstone rising before you. It is topped by a palmette motif, based on the fan-shaped leaves of a palm tree. The design was considered a hallmark of taste in neoclassical urban architecture. But it also may refer to Taft's work for the U.S. government in the tropical Philippines early in his legal career.

Double back to the first set of stairs, and begin climbing them. Near the bottom of the grass-covered hillside between the two sets of stairs is a cluster of tombstones marking the graves of several World War II generals. On the far right, you'll find the:

6 Gravesite of Gen. Omar Bradley

The highest ranking of the group, Omar Bradley's tombstone displays the engraved five-star wreath of a General of the Army. Following the successful D–day Landing in Normandy on June 6, 1944, Bradley commanded the largest force ever headed by an American field officer—1.3 million men whom he led across Europe into Germany. Because of his concern for his troops and their morale, he became popularly known as "The GI General." Gen. George C. Marshall, another five-star-wearer who served as Army Chief of Staff, dubbed Bradley "the finest Army group commander" in the U.S. Army.

Four other five-star World War II leaders are buried at Arlington: General George Marshall, who following World War II was named secretary of state and conceived the Marshall Plan; Admiral William D. Leahy, Chief of Staff to President Roosevelt; Air Force General Henry H. Arnold, chief of the Army Air Corps; and Admiral William F. Halsey, who commanded naval forces in the South Pacific. Only two men outrank them—World War I General of the Armies John J. "Black Jack" Pershing, who is buried at Arlington; and George Washington, who received his promotion posthumously. He is buried at Mount Vernon.

Climb the stairs, called Custis Walk, nearly to the top. It's a slog getting there, but inside the shady grove of holly trees on the left, you can rest and recover while contemplating:

7 The Tomb of Robert Todd Lincoln

Robert Lincoln, the eldest son of Abraham Lincoln, reportedly pondered the question frequently of what would have happened if he had joined his father and mother at Ford's Theatre the night the president was assassinated. Invited by his father, young Lincoln, then 21, declined because he had planned another engagement with friends. Could he have thwarted the attack, saving his father's life? When he learned of the shooting, he joined his mother at the Petersen House, across the street from the theater, where the president died the next morning.

History books note one of the ironies in Robert Lincoln's life. As a young man, he came close to falling beneath the wheels of a train at a railway station. But he was rescued by actor Edwin Booth, brother of the man, John Wilkes Booth, who later killed his father. He was also present when Presidents James Garfield and William McKinley were assassinated, a coincidence that greatly troubled him. Robert and Mary's son Abraham died of an illness at the age of 17 in England, where his father was minister to Great Britain.

Robert had expected to be buried at his father's tomb in Springfield, Illinois. But his wife Mary reportedly preferred an Arlington gravesite, figuring her husband had achieved significant distinction to warrant a site independent of his father. Robert had served briefly in the Civil War after leaving college, and he once held the position of secretary of war, both of which qualified him for Arlington.

Along with Robert Todd Lincoln's remains, buried in the tomb are also Robert's wife Mary, and their teenaged son Abraham Lincoln II. Their home is Stop 6 on Walking Tour 2: Georgetown.

Continue the climb to the top of Custis Walk, and turn left on Sheridan Drive. Look on the right for a large, semicircular tombstone with the name WEEKS:

8 Gravesite of Thurgood Marshall

Marshall, whose life was devoted to public service, became the first African-American to sit on the U.S. Supreme Court, a position he held for 24 years.

His dark gray tombstone is on the hillside behind the Weeks memorial, along with those of several other Supreme Court Justices. Prior to his court appointment, he spent 25 years as legal counsel for the National Association for the Advancement of Colored People. In that position, he argued numerous cases before the Supreme Court, including *Brown v.*

Board of Education. The court's landmark 1954 decision for Marshall and the NAACP declared separate but equal to be an unconstitutional justification for school segregation.

Nearby are the gravesites of other Supreme Court luminaries: Chief Justice Warren Earl Burger and Associate Justices Harry Blackmun, Potter Stewart, William J. Brennan, William O. Douglas, and Oliver Wendell Holmes, Jr. Among the judges rests Admiral Hyman G. Rickover, "Father of the Nuclear Navy." An ornamental chain fence keeps you off the grass, so you don't get a close-up view from the front at this stop. At Stop 9, some of the tombstones will be closer.

John Wingate Weeks, by the way, was an influential Massachusetts senator, secretary of war in the Harding and Coolidge administration, and failed candidate for the Republican nomination for president in the election that put Woodrow Wilson in the White House.

Continue on Sheridan Drive to the intersection of Weeks Drive. Turn right onto the approach to the Kennedy Gravesite and bear right onto the curving "handicap" access. Look to the right for Holmes and other justices:

⑨ Gravesite of Oliver Wendell Holmes, Jr.

An American aristocrat, Holmes, a future Supreme Court Justice, grew up in a family whose friends included such New England literary heavyweights as Ralph Waldo Emerson, Henry Wadsworth Longfellow, Herman Melville, and Nathaniel Hawthorne. Graduating from Harvard (he was class poet) as the Civil War raged, he received a lieutenant's commission. Often in the heat of battle, he was wounded three times—in the chest at

the Battle of Ball's Bluff near Leesburg, Virginia; in the throat at Antietam in Maryland; and in the foot at Chancellorsville in Virginia.

Holmes survived these wounds to experience another dramatic event during the war. James Edward Peters, author of *Arlington National Cemetery,* a guide to notable figures interred here, provides the details. In July 1864, Confederate General Jubal Early was ordered to attack Washington in the hope of drawing Union troops away from Lee's beleaguered army. As Early's troops approached Fort Stephens on the outskirts of Washington, President Lincoln rode out to take a look. Climbing onto a rampart, Lincoln and his stovepipe hat drew Confederate fire. The general accompanying him suggested Lincoln take cover, but his advice was ignored. Finally, an exasperated Holmes, who was present, shouted at Lincoln, "Get down, you fool!" This time the president listened and obeyed, later thanking Holmes.

An influential legal career led to his appointment at age 61 to the Supreme Court, where he served for 29 years. One of the court's most respected jurors, he became known as "the Great Dissenter" because of his astute legal opinions. His often quoted remark about taxes—"Taxes are what we pay for a civilized society"—is inscribed on the building housing the Internal Revenue Service in Washington.

Continue up the curved walkway to the:

⑩ Kennedy Gravesites

Adorned by the Eternal Flame, this may be the best-known gravesite in the country. It continues to be the one most visited in Arlington National Cemetery. Interred here with President John F. Kennedy, assassinated on

November 22, 1963, are his wife Jacqueline Kennedy Onassis, who died in 1994; their infant son Patrick, who died 2 days after his birth on August 7, 1963; and their unnamed daughter who was stillborn on August 23, 1956. The body of Robert F. Kennedy, attorney general in his brother's administration, was placed a few steps to the left of the other Kennedy graves following his death by assassination. It is marked with a simple white cross. Excerpts from his speeches are inscribed on a fountain wall to the rear.

Initially, the former president was buried in a small hillside plot ringed by a white picket fence. But the size of the crowds—as many as 3,000 an hour in the months following the funeral—overwhelmed the site. Cemetery officials and the Kennedy family decided a more suitable memorial should be built. A 2-year project, it was completed in 1967. The Kennedy family and the government shared the cost. The memorial, including the imposing circular walkway by which you arrived, the elliptical terrace (with its fine view of Washington), and the wall bearing inscriptions from Kennedy's words, now occupies 3¼ acres. The memorial, one of Arlington's most elaborate, easily handles the now diminished throngs.

At Kennedy's death, it was thought he would be buried in Brookline, Massachusetts, since most presidents lay at rest in their native states. Asked her opinion, the first lady replied, "He belongs to the people." The slab of stone chosen to cover the grave, however, comes from Cape Cod, President Kennedy's favorite place. Mrs. Kennedy also wanted to mark the site with a flame similar to that of the French Unknown Soldier in Paris. It is thought she may also have been influenced by the Eternal Light Memorial at Gettysburg National Military Park in Pennsylvania, which she and the president visited shortly before his death.

Burning from the center of a circular granite stone, the Eternal Flame required specially designed apparatus created by the Institute of Gas Technology in Chicago. Should rain extinguish the flame, a constantly flashing electric spark near the tip of the nozzle relights the gas. The fuel is natural gas, which is mixed with a controlled quantity of air to produce the flame's shape and color.

Retrace your path back via Sheridan Drive to Custis Walk and continue climbing the stairs almost to the top where you'll find the:

⑪ Gravesite of Mary Randolph

On the left, surrounded by a brick wall, is the oldest grave in Arlington. Mary Randolph, believed to be a direct descendant of Pocahontas, was a cousin of Mary Lee Fitzhugh Custis, wife of the builder of Arlington House, George Washington Parke Custis. Robert E. Lee and Thomas Jefferson were among her other many cousins. She is thought to have been the godmother of Mary Anna Custis Lee, the wife of Robert E. Lee. The author of a popular how-to guide about household management, her many family connections brought her often to Arlington House, a place she regarded fondly. At her death in 1828, George Washington Parke Custis permitted her to be buried on his estate. The stone, its inscription barely legible, was a gift of her youngest son, Burwell.

Continue up the stairs to the walkway and turn left:

⑫ Lookout Point/Gravesite of Pierre Charles L'Enfant

This expansive terrace directly below Arlington House provides a fine view down the hillside to the Kennedy graves, a limited view of the Pentagon to the right, and a panorama of Washington across the Potomac River.

Uphill behind you, the tomb to the left of the flagpole marks the remains of Pierre Charles L'Enfant, the Paris-born engineer entrusted by George Washington to design the new American capital city. A captain in Washington's Revolutionary War army, he was one of the founding members of the Society of the Cincinnati, an organization of officers who served in the war.

L'Enfant incorporated ideas from the great cities of Europe, drawing up plans for a grand mall linking the Capitol and the "President's House," wide avenues and squares, circles and triangles. But in 1792, Washington dismissed him because of his excessive fees and the highhanded manner in which he pursued his design. In 1825, he died penniless in Maryland and was buried there.

But the city he envisioned took shape, and in 1909 Congress acknowledged his contribution by giving him the honor of lying in state in the Capitol building. Afterward, he was buried with full military honors at a site that offers a grand view of Washington. Two years later, President Taft dedicated the white marble memorial, now very much weathered. Inscribed within a circle on the monument is his plan for the city.

Climb to the top of the stairs to:

🔳 Arlington House

Resembling a Greek temple, this multi-columned mansion was the pre–Civil War plantation home of General Robert E. Lee and his wife Mary Custis. Six of their seven children were born here. Your stop includes a 10-minute self-guided tour of the house

itself, a peek into the slave quarters, a visit to the Lee Museum, and a walk through the garden.

This historically significant house is closely linked to George and Martha Washington. George Washington Parke Custis, who built it between 1802 and 1818 on land his father John purchased, was the grandson of Martha Washington and grew up in Mount Vernon. Martha's first husband was Daniel Parke Custis with whom she had her son John and daughter Martha. She and George had no children. George Washington Parke Custis fathered a daughter, Mary Anna Randolph Custis. She married Robert E. Lee at Arlington House. Got it?

It may seem odd that the Confederate Army's commanding general is honored with a memorial overlooking Arlington National Cemetery, where so many Union troops lie. This was done in 1925 in recognition of his dedication to peace and reconciliation after the Civil War.

Currently, **Arlington House** (www.nps.gov/arho; daily 9:30am–4:30pm except Dec 25 and Jan 1; free admission) is devoid of furniture, thanks to a renovation which is supposed to be finished in 2010. It is still open to visitors, though it may be closed on certain days due to construction, so check the website first before heading to Arlington. Through its columned portico, the room on the right off the entrance hall is the **Family Parlor,** which because of all the youngsters was often in disarray. Usually, a charming portrait of Mary Custis, painted in 1831 just before her marriage to Lee, hangs in this room. Adjoining it is the **Family Dining Room,** where—so family tradition maintains—Lee frequently placed a rosebud on the plate of each woman present for breakfast.

Upstairs (following the designated tour route) are the bedrooms, each one opening to the upper hall—used as a summer sitting room because it caught the breezes. Lee wrote his letter of resignation from the U.S. Army in the master bedroom, located at the top of the stairs on the far side of the hall. Back downstairs, the **White Parlor** is traditionally furnished with Victorian furniture the Lees purchased in 1855. A huge painting in the adjacent **Morning Room** depicting the Battle of Monmouth, one of Washington's Revolutionary War victories, will be returned to the space when work is done. Mary's father was the painter. It once hung in the U.S. Capitol and was protected during the Civil War at Tudor Place, the Georgetown mansion built by Martha Custis (granddaughter of Martha Washington; sister to the builder of Arlington House) and her husband (p. 206).

Exiting the house, move on to the Slave Quarters, the humble structures to the rear. In one room, a display introduces some of the plantation servants, focusing on their lives just before and after the war. Among them, Selina Gray, personal maid to Mary Lee, is credited with rescuing many artifacts belonging to George and Martha Washington left behind when the Lees departed. (George Washington Parke Custis brought them to the mansion from Mount Vernon.)

Though George Washington Parke Custis considered slavery "the mightiest serpent that ever infested the world," he kept 60 slaves at Arlington at his death in 1857. In his will, he stipulated that they be freed if the estate were free of debt. Otherwise, their freedom should be delayed for 5 years. Lee, executor of the estate, found the property seriously in debt. Five years later in

1862, he gave the slaves their promised freedom, writing from the battlefield.

Of particular note is the model of "Freedman's Village," a planned community created on the Lee estate in 1863 for former slaves. A temporary refuge, it had closed by 1900. Another former slave structure on the opposite side of the yard houses a bookstore, restrooms, and water fountain. Beyond it, a path leads through the Kitchen Garden, patterned after the original, to the **Robert E. Lee Museum.** Exhibits trace his life from boyhood to military commander to college president. Personal objects include the Colt revolver he received at the end of his tour of duty as superintendent of the U.S. Military Academy at West Point and the mess kit with folding silverware that he used throughout the Civil War.

Double back past the Slave Quarters to the **Flower Garden.** Mary Lee took great pride in the hilltop garden, shaping its formal design. Destroyed in 1864, it has been restored.

Walk a few steps to the right of the garden. A nearly hidden brick path on the left leads through a tall hedge to the:

🅮 Tomb of Unknown Civil War Dead

The large monument, set in what was the Lee family's rose garden, marks the mass graves of about 2,111 unknown soldiers killed in the Civil War, perhaps including Confederate casualties. It was Arlington's first monument dedicated to troops killed in the fighting. In this way, their sacrifice was honored, but the monument also served a less noble cause. Reportedly, Quartermaster General Montgomery Meigs ordered that the bodies be buried at this specific site, figuring the graves would deter the Lees from ever returning to their home.

Follow the sidewalk alongside Meigs Drive to McPherson Drive and turn left. At the divide, keep to the left and continue past Farragut Drive. Turn right at Jackson Circle. While on Meigs Drive, keep an eye to the right for the gravesite (it's a mini Washington Monument) of Abner Doubleday, the Civil War officer who returned Union fire in the Confederate bombardment of Charleston's Fort Sumter on April 12, 1861. This marked the start of the war. Doubleday is also credited with being the "Father of American Baseball."

⑮ Confederate Memorial

The 32-foot-tall Confederate monument, designed by a Southern veteran of the Civil War, is ringed by the graves of 482 Southerners, including soldiers, their wives, 15 civilians, and 12 unknowns. The pointed headstones, different from others at Arlington, are said to stem from a Confederate legend that the points would "keep Yankees from sitting on them."

When the war ended, Southern families sought to decorate the Confederate graves, but often permission was denied because of the animosity between former enemies. But in 1906, William Howard Taft, then secretary of war, granted the request of the United Daughters of the Confederacy to erect a major monument. President Woodrow Wilson spoke at the unveiling in 1914, a symbolic ceremony symbolizing the continuing reconciliation of North and South.

Sculptor Moses Ezekial placed a woman at the top of the monument to symbolize the South. In her left hand is a laurel wreath; in her right is a pruning hook resting on a plow stock. At her feet are inscribed these explanatory words from the Bible: "And they shall beat their swords into plow shares and their spears into pruning hooks." The four embossed urns on the base represent the 4 years of war; the 14 shields signify 13 Confederate states and the state of Maryland, which offered support to the South. Six vignettes—in one an officer kisses his infant child—recall the war's impact.

This is the stage of the walkabout you are most likely to encounter burial ceremonies. Be mindful to keep a discreet distance.

Double back on McPherson Drive to Farragut Drive and turn right. At Sigsbee Drive, turn right.

⑯ Mast of the USS *Maine*

"Remember the *Maine*!" was the rallying cry at the outset of the Spanish-American War. The vessel's main mast, standing upright atop a massive monument, is an emphatic reminder of what those words meant. On a diplomatic assignment to Cuba, the warship *Maine* exploded in Havana's harbor on the night of February 15, 1898, killing more than 250 officers and sailors. In the heated journalism of the day, the press blamed Spain, which governed Cuba. Some modern historians think the explosion might simply have been an accident.

While war with Spain raged, the dead whose bodies could be recovered were buried in Havana. In 1899, at war's end, most were reburied in Arlington. Eleven years later when the *Maine* was raised from the harbor, 66 more bodies were recovered and buried at Arlington. The mast was transported here as well. The ship itself was towed out to sea and scuttled with honors.

A total of 229 *Maine* victims are buried in the area encircled by Sigsbee Drive. All but 62 are unknowns. The two bronze cannons were captured

Who Can Be Buried at Arlington?

Space is tight at Arlington National Cemetery, and authorities have imposed eligibility restrictions. Those who may be buried include:

- Any Armed Forces member who dies while on active duty.
- Any veteran retired from active duty.
- Any veteran retired from the Reserves over age 60 who served a period of active duty.
- Any Armed Forces member separated honorably for medical reasons prior to October 1, 1949. Must be certified 30% disabled on day of discharge.
- Any Armed Forces member receiving Medal of Honor, Distinguished Service Cross (Navy Cross or Air Force Cross), Distinguished Service Medal, Silver Star, Purple Heart.
- The president of the United States and past presidents.
- Anyone who served on active duty and who has held the position of Chief Justice or Associate Justice of the Supreme Court and certain other high government posts.
- Any former prisoner of war who died after November 30, 1993.
- Spouse, minor child, or permanently dependent child of the above eligible veterans.
- Certain spouses and minor children, including the widow or widower of someone buried or lost at sea or declared missing in action.

Eligibility is not quite so limited for those whose ashes are placed in the cemetery's Columbarium. Check the cemetery website for full details at **www.arlingtoncemetery.org**.

from the Spanish. Sigsbee Drive is named for Admiral Charles Dwight Sigsbee, who as a younger captain commanded the *Maine.*

Descend the walkway on the far side of the monument, and turn left at the bottom of the slope where you'll encounter:

⑰ Three memorials

Three separate monuments stand side by side: the **Space Shuttle *Challenger* Memorial,** honoring the seven astronauts who died when the Challenger exploded on takeoff on January 28, 1986; the **Iran Rescue Mission** **(Operation Desert I) Monument,** dedicated to the eight military personnel who died in the failed rescue attempt in April 1980 of the 53 Americans held hostage in Iran; and the **Space Shuttle *Columbia* Memorial,** remembering the seven astronauts who died when their ship disintegrated on return to earth on February 1, 2003.

Return to the downhill walkway and turn right on Memorial Drive. Turn right onto the flagstone walk to the:

⑱ Gravesite of Audie Murphy

Before his 21st birthday, Audie Murphy (later a successful Hollywood actor) became American's most-decorated soldier. Wounded three times, he received the Medal of Honor for gallantry and 27 other medals. His modest, government-issued tombstone, like those of thousands of others buried at Arlington, was too small to list all of his commendations. A small U.S. flag flies alongside it. The baby-faced Texas farm boy who would become a legend was rejected by the Marines and paratroopers because he was too short. But the Army infantry took him, sending him first to Sicily, where his ability in combat eventually brought him promotion to major.

Back home after the war, he got a hero's reception and his photo on the cover of *Life* magazine. Actor James Cagney urged him to go into films. He made 40, the best of which, critics say, was *Red Badge of Courage,* based on Stephen Crane's Civil War novel. He starred as himself in a movie based on his autobiography, *To Hell and Back.* He died in 1971, age 46, in the crash of a private plane near Roanoke, Virginia.

Cross Memorial Drive to the Memorial Amphitheater, setting for official ceremonies, and circle it to the right where you'll find the:

⓳ Tomb of the Unknowns

The body of the Unknown from World War I lies in the white marble sarcophagus. Beneath the terrace to the rear of it, indicated by the three rectangular slabs, are the Unknowns from World War II and the Korean War. For a time, an Unknown from the Vietnam War was buried also. But DNA testing later identified him, and the place now is kept vacant.

You will want to wait for the Changing of the Guard Ceremony, an amazing performance of precision marching and manual of arms. The tomb is guarded 24 hours a day, every day of the year. From April 1 to September 30, the ceremony takes place every half-hour; the rest of the year and at night, it's every hour. The Tomb Guards, all volunteers, are members of the 3rd U.S. Infantry. They must be trim, tall, and possess an unblemished military record.

Note that the Tomb Guard marches 21 steps down the mat behind the Tomb, turns east for 21 seconds, turns north for 21 seconds, and then takes 21 steps back up the map, repeating the process throughout his time on duty. The number 21 reflects the 21-gun salute, the highest ceremonial military honor that can be bestowed. Restrooms and water fountains are located in the Memorial Amphitheater.

Take the path at the right of the Tomb, and circle downhill to the left past the steps leading up to the Tomb. Just beyond the steps, note a small sign pointing right to Section 7A. Near the end of the path, look right toward the:

⓴ Gravesite of Joe Louis

Joe Louis, the "Brown Bomber" and heavyweight champion of the world longer than any fighter, did not technically qualify for burial in Arlington—although he had served in the Army in World War II. At Louis' death in 1981, 3 decades after his final bout, President Ronald Reagan waived the technicalities, and "the Champ" received full military honors. As an Army sergeant, Louis was assigned to a segregated unit, fighting 96 exhibition matches before more than two million troops. Actor **Lee Marvin,** a Marine private wounded during the battle of Saipan in June 1944, is buried next to Louis.

You can complete the tour now by following Roosevelt Drive (just ahead, turn left) back to the Visitor Center and the Arlington Metrorail station. Or you can continue on this tour to the Netherlands Carillon and Iwo Jima Memorial, a 20-minute walk through the cemetery. If you decide to go on the longer tour, at Roosevelt Drive, turn left and follow it to Roosevelt Gate. Proceed through it and Schley Gate, continuing on to Custis Walk. Take the walkway downhill to the right. At Ord & Weitzel Gate, take the uphill path to the left where you'll find the:

㉑ Netherlands Carillon

The 50-bell carillon, the modern rectangular structure ahead, was a gift to the people of the United States in appreciation for the liberation of Holland on May 5, 1945, during World War II. It stands just outside Arlington Memorial Cemetery, located officially in parkland alongside George Washington Memorial Parkway. You can climb to the top for the views from 2 to 4pm on Saturdays. Summer concerts (June–Aug) are held from 6 to 8pm Saturdays. In May and September, they are held 2 to 4pm on Saturdays.

Follow the path north, bearing right into the grove of trees at the divide.

㉒ U.S. Marine Corps War Memorial

The Iwo Jima Statue is its popular name. But the official title is the **U.S. Marine Corps War Memorial.** One of the country's most famous (and most photographed) statues, it's a bronze re-creation of the historic moment when five Marines and a Navy hospital corpsman raised the U.S. flag on Mount Suribachi on the Pacific island of Iwo Jima on February 23, 1945. It is dedicated to all Marines who have given

their lives in defense of the country since 1775. Actually, there were two flag raisings on 550-foot-high Mount Suribachi that momentous day. Marines initially hoisted a small flag at 10:30am, thrilling U.S. forces all over the island. The statue depicts the raising of a second, larger flag that afternoon, when the slopes had been cleared of the enemy. News photographer Joe Rosenthal snapped the second flag-raising, and his inspiring photo went on to win a Pulitzer Prize and lasting fame. Three survivors of the event, Private First Class Rene A. Gagnon, Private First Class Ira Hayes, and Pharmacist Mate Second-class John H. Bradley, posed for the sculptor, Felix W. de Weldon, who modeled their faces in clay. The other three subjects died in subsequent fighting on Iwo Jima. To model the faces of the deceased, de Weldon collected their physical statistics and old photos. The figures stand 32 feet high; the bronze flagpole is 60 feet long, and a cloth flag flies from it 24 hours a day. The memorial is the traditional finish line of the annual Marine Corps Marathon in October. A Marine in uniform drapes a "Finisher" medal over each entrant who makes it (Jim has one), shakes hands, and offers congratulations.

Continue past the monument, bearing left on the paved path uphill. Turn right on Lynn Street across the bridge. On the far side of the bridge, bear right, and go past Fairfax Drive to Wilson Boulevard. Turn left 1 block to North Moore Street, and then right a half block to:

㉓ Rosslyn Metro Station

Rosslyn is a busy commercial center, with many options for reasonably priced food and drink along Wilson Boulevard and adjacent streets.

Walking Tour 2: Georgetown

Start: Old Stone House (3051 M St. NW); Metrobus 30, 32, 34, 35, 36, or K
Street Circulator Bus or Metrorail, Foggy Bottom/George Washington
University followed by a ½-mile walk.

Finish: Old Stone House, following a wide loop itinerary.

Time: Approximately 90 minutes, not including time spent at historic houses or
lingering in an outdoor cafe.

Best times: From 10am daily (after morning rush hour) until 5pm (before evening
rush hour).

Worst times: Before 8am when very little is open; during rush hour periods; and after
dark, when architectural details can't be seen.

If you are seeking a typical Washington neighborhood, Georgetown isn't the
one. Nothing is typical about Georgetown. Many of the local folks are famous
newsmakers. Its houses, even the tiny ones, are expensive; mansions sell in the
multimillion-dollar range. Its shops and restaurants cater to decidedly upscale
tastes. It's also the city's most historic, liveliest, and prettiest neighborhood.

Settled primarily by Scottish immigrants in the early 1700s, Georgetown
(named for King George II of England) became a busy seaport long before
American independence and the establishment of the new nation's capital on its
doorstep. Tobacco was the main product, brought to warehouses and wharfs from
Virginia and Maryland plantations for shipment to England. By 1791, when the
site for Washington was chosen as the seat of government for the United States,
Georgetown may have been the country's busiest tobacco market. Wealthy traders
built mansions on the high bluffs overlooking the Potomac River. Soon senators
and representatives flocked to join them. Georgetown was a short coach ride from
the considerably more humble town of Washington then under construction.

Even today, Georgetown, roughly a square mile in size, seems like a village
entirely separate from Washington—although at a decent pace you can walk from
the White House to the Old Stone House (start of this tour) in 20 minutes. It
enjoys its own thriving commercial center, drawing throngs of weekend window-
shoppers; its own modest port, dispatching a river tour boat; and blocks of shady
neighborhood streets lined with charming 18th- and 19th-century houses.

The tour we've outlined here, a wide loop, takes in all the aspects of
Georgetown that have made it Washington's most-desired place to live: gorgeous
old streets; the developing, modern waterfront; historic homes and gardens; residences of some of the rich and famous, including Jack and Jackie Kennedy; and
its lively shopping lanes.

While we indicate stops at significant sights, don't limit your sightseeing only
to them. Keep your eyes open to the architectural details of the elegant old
homes that line almost every step of this route. Note the fine details such as flickering glass lamps, wrought-iron gates, ornate brickwork, whimsical front porch
statuary, beautifully carved doors, and the well-tended gardens with cobblestone
walkways.

The predominant architectural style is that of the Federal period (about 1790–1830), typically a boxlike structure with an elegant door and windows arranged in strict symmetry. But you will see homes resembling Greek temples and a few Victorian "painted ladies" looking like visitors from San Francisco.

① Old Stone House

As Washington's oldest known structure still standing, the unassuming little stone house makes an appropriate beginning for a Georgetown tour. Completed in 1765, it was built of solid hewn oak boards and blue fieldstone, quarried about 2 miles up the Potomac River. A succession of owners ran businesses out of the house or rented it. Initially a one-room residence for the family of Christopher Layman, a cabinetmaker, in later years it acquired a second floor and rear kitchen. In 1953, when the Federal Government bought the house, it served as a used car dealership. The cars were displayed on a paved lot that has since been transformed into a lovely English-style garden. Be sure to see it.

The house occupies a potentially pricey piece of real estate, and it might well have been torn down. But it has been spared over the decades. A myth might be responsible.

As an on-duty National Park Service ranger tells the story, a sign once hung over the front door proclaiming "George Washington's Headquarters." Not true, as park historians now know. What really happened: In 1791, President George Washington and Pierre L'Enfant, who designed Washington's street layout, stayed at Suter's Tavern in Georgetown. Later, John Suter, Jr., son of the tavern owner, opened a clockmaker's shop in the Old Stone House. The Suter name linked to George Washington and the Old Stone House gave birth to the misconception that it served as Washington's office,

and nobody dared tear down a house with these presidential credentials.

The house is open noon to 5pm daily. The garden is open from 9am to 4pm daily. There is no charge. If you start this walkabout before noon and the house hasn't yet opened, complete the itinerary and then take a look inside.

Walk a half-block south toward the Potomac on Thomas Jefferson Street NW. Immediately in front as you step from the Old Stone House is:

② Lock 4, Chesapeake & Ohio National Historical Park

Lock 4 is where the canal boat, the 80-passenger *Georgetown*, departs on 1-hour canal cruises Wednesday through Sunday from early April to late October. The first cruise each day is at 11am; if you are there by 10:45am, you can watch the crew, dressed in 19th-century costume, harness the pair of mules that provides the locomotion. It's a bustling scene from out of the past as the boat loads its passengers and the otherwise docile mules try to snatch one more mouthful of hay before going to work. To board now, purchase cruise tickets at the **Canal Visitor Center,** across the street to your left at 1057 Thomas Jefferson St. (restrooms inside). But we recommend continuing on this walkabout and returning to take a later cruise. By then, you will be ready for a relaxing—and cooling—ride into the countryside. See "Boat Tours" in chapter 5 (p. 148) for more details on hours and prices. In season, you can view the canal boat, an authentic reproduction, between tours at Lock 4.

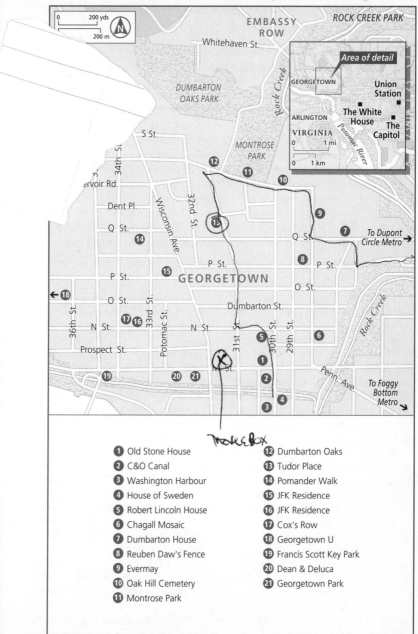

1 Old Stone House	**12** Dumbarton Oaks
2 C&O Canal	**13** Tudor Place
3 Washington Harbour	**14** Pomander Walk
4 House of Sweden	**15** JFK Residence
5 Robert Lincoln House	**16** JFK Residence
6 Chagall Mosaic	**17** Cox's Row
7 Dumbarton House	**18** Georgetown U
8 Reuben Daw's Fence	**19** Francis Scott Key Park
9 Evermay	**20** Dean & Deluca
10 Oak Hill Cemetery	**21** Georgetown Park
11 Montrose Park	

Georgetown's Other History

In its early years, Georgetown was the hub of a major slave trade, buying and selling captives taken from Africa and slaves from plantations in Maryland and Virginia. In 1862, while the Civil War raged, President Lincoln signed a local law freeing Washington's slaves months before his Emancipation Proclamation. Seeking freedom, African-Americans from the Confederacy poured into Georgetown, creating a large black working class. But many lost their jobs when port operations declined. And when real estate prices began to soar, they moved away, leaving only a small population today. But the **Mt. Zion United Methodist Church** (1334 29th St. NW), the oldest African-American church in Washington, is still in operation. Many in its congregation, widely dispersed in the metropolitan area, are descendants of Georgetown's earlier residents. The church was founded in 1816; the current brick structure was built in the 1870s. To see the church, detour north on 29th Street between stops 6 and 7 on this walking tour.

The C&O Canal was conceived during the period of the late 1790s and early 1800s when America experienced a canal-building boom. More than 3,000 miles of canals were constructed. In a mostly roadless landscape, they carried manufactured goods and settlers inland to places that riverboats could not reach, returning with lumber, grain, hay, and coal for the increasingly industrialized East. The heyday of the canal era lasted until the mid–19th century when railroads began to replace them. Most of the canals have crumbled into oblivion. But a few, including the C&O, remain to tell the story of the canal boatmen, the lock tenders, their families, and their unique way of life.

President John Quincy Adams broke ground for the canal and towpath on July 4, 1828. Though he and its investors were unaware, the canal already was on its way to becoming obsolete. On the same day, construction began on the Baltimore and Ohio Railroad in Baltimore, and over the years it would prove a tough and eventual victorious rival in the interior trade.

The initial plan, called the "Great National Project," envisioned a 460-mile canal linking Georgetown with Pittsburgh. The cost was estimated at $3 million and completion was anticipated in 10 years. It didn't happen that way. Disease epidemics, money problems, and labor troubles slowed work for 22 years until 1850. By then, the cost had mushroomed to $13 million, and even then the canal fell far short of its original terminus, reaching only 185 miles to Cumberland, Maryland. Still, it managed to continue operating for 74 years until 1924, when massive flooding forced it into bankruptcy. While it was in business, the canal routinely lifted boats from near sea level to an elevation of 605 feet at Cumberland using 74 lift locks similar to Lock 4. On its tour, the *Georgetown* is maneuvered through a lock to demonstrate how they operated.

In the 1950s, transportation planners suggested turning the canal and its 12-foot-wide towpath into a Potomac River auto parkway. But Supreme Court Justice William O. Douglas, a conservationist, led a march on the towpath to convince the government, public, and press that the canal should be preserved for its scenic and historic value. The entire canal and towpath from Georgetown to Cumberland was established as a national historic park in 1971. The canal's recreational uses are detailed in chapter 7 (p. 169).

Now walk 2 blocks south to where Thomas Jefferson Street dead-ends at the Potomac. Cross K Street, which runs beneath the elevated Whitehurst Freeway. The freeway, a major commuter route, is Georgetown's most obvious eyesore. Movement is underway to remove it, perhaps by channeling traffic in a tunnel beneath K Street. We'll see.

❸ Washington Harbour

A fantasy of splashing fountains, terraced outdoor cafes, offices, and condominiums, the Washington Harbour complex is Washington's version of the Riviera—a waterside playground for the rich and famous and their wannabe onlookers.

Its designer, Arthur Cotton Moore, faced the task of blending old Georgetown's adjacent Victorian neighborhood with the nearby classical monuments on the Mall. What he came up with, to quote a generally appreciative review by the American Institute of Architects, was a postmodern assemblage that "borders on the eccentric," adding that it was "easily the most talked about building of the 1980s." Much of Washington's Potomac shoreline has been treated well, kept open by parks and pedestrian lanes that welcome the public. But Georgetown's waterfront, blighted by the overhead Whitehurst Freeway, developed as an industrial area. This 1980s project was a big step in opening up this stretch of the river to the neighborhood and the city, a process that continues.

From the boardwalk alongside the river, the Kennedy Center to the left makes a tempting snapshot. That dense woodland directly across the river is Theodore Roosevelt Island, preserved as a memorial to the former president. Look to your right to spot the ticket booth for Capitol River Cruises, which offers daily 50-minute cruises beginning at noon.

Walk 1 block past Thomas Jefferson Street, and turn left at the giant sundial to 30th Street. On your right, the soaring, six-story glass sculpture is the:

❹ House of Sweden

A novel concept for a foreign embassy, this building was completed in September 2006. Under one architecturally dramatic roof are located the Embassy of Sweden; organizations and companies with a Swedish-American focus; a trade exhibition area; a conference center; and two floors (the top ones) of luxury river-view apartments. Costing $34 million, the building is Sweden's way of boosting its profile in the United States and assisting Swedish trade delegations to this country.

Five top Swedish architects submitted entries in a design competition for the building. A jury chose the work of Gert Wingardh and Tomas Hansen of Wingardh Architects of Gothenburg. The exterior of the building is clad in screened glass interspersed with a framework of wood—the kind of building materials used in Sweden.

Continue north on 30th Street across the canal and busy M Street to N Street, and turn left for a half-block to:

❺ Robert Todd Lincoln House (3014 N St. NW)

Now a private residence, the site of many fashionable parties, the large red-brick house was for many years the residence of Robert Todd Lincoln, the eldest son of President and Mrs. Abraham Lincoln. Built about 1799, it was initially the home of a wealthy tobacco merchant from Scotland. Lincoln purchased it in the early 1900s, residing there and at a second home in Vermont until his death in 1926. He added substantially to the original building.

A college student during much of the Civil War, Lincoln at age 21 received a captain's commission in February 1865 near the war's end and served on the immediate staff of General Ulysses S. Grant. Following the war, he earned a law degree in Illinois, where he had been born in 1843, and embarked on a quite distinguished career as lawyer, diplomat, and company president. As the slain president's son, he was held in high esteem by the American public.

From 1881 to 1885, he served as secretary of war under Presidents James Garfield and Chester Arthur. President Benjamin Harrison named him minister to Great Britain, a position he held from 1889 to 1893. He retired in 1922 as president and chairman of the board of the Pullman Palace Car Company. The only one of the Lincolns' four sons to reach maturity, Robert Todd Lincoln was present at the dedication of the Lincoln Memorial in 1922. He is buried in Arlington National Cemetery along with his wife Mary Harlan and their teenaged son Abraham Lincoln, Jr. The gravesite is a stop on the Arlington cemetery walkabout.

Double back on N Street to 28th Street. En route, note the row of fine Federal period houses at nos. 2806, 2808, and 2812, all believed to have been built in the early 1800s. The Federal-period house at no. 2812 is often referred to as the Decatur House, because the widow of Stephen Decatur is said to have lived there after her husband's death. Read more about the Decaturs in chapter 5 (p. 137). Its door is especially lovely.

6 Chagall Garden Mosaic

At no. 2726, on the next corner, you will have to strain to see the Marc Chagall mosaic tile artwork over the garden wall alongside 28th Street. It is a large work (10 × 17 ft.), placed at the far end of the backyard garden on a brick wall adjoining the neighboring house. Chagall was a friend of the owners, art patrons and collectors, and stayed often as a guest at their house. Chagall, who loved Georgetown's small-town feeling, promised his hosts that one day he would do something for their garden. And in 1969, he showed them a drawing of the mosaic he planned. The upper half features figures from Greek mythology; the lower half depicts refugees from abroad arriving in "the land of skyscrapers." Chagall was a World War II refugee himself. On the owner's death, the mosaic was bequeathed to the National Gallery of Art. For the best view, stand on your tiptoes on the sidewalk across the street from the garden.

Continue east on N Street to 27th Street, which parallels Rose Park. Go north on Q street to:

7 Dumbarton House and Garden (2715 Q St. NW)

Joseph Nourse served as Register of the U.S. Treasury for the first six U.S. presidents. He was apparently close to the first ladies as well: Dolley Madison took brief refuge in the house on August 24, 1814, when she was forced to flee from the White House as the British were approaching during the War of 1812. This 1796 Georgetown

Beloved Bison

If you're up to it, detour 3 blocks east on Q Street to see the **Buffalo,** four massive creatures that mark the approaches to Dumbarton Bridge. They are life-size, each 7 feet high and realistically fashioned in bronze in 1914. We cite them because they have been fondly adopted by generations of Washington residents. They are well worn, sometimes (unless freshly scrubbed) bedecked in a patina of green but still majestic (and, well, loveable). The bridge, which links the Kalorama neighborhood to Georgetown across Rock Creek, is an interesting structure itself, designed to resemble a Roman aqueduct. The juxtaposition of buffalo (really bison) and ancient Rome prompted the American Institute of Architects to comment: "It's a bit like watching Buffalo Bill's Wild West Show trundle across the Ponte Vecchio." Artistic curiosities like these enliven the city's generally more serious sculptural heritage. Double back to Dumbarton House to continue the walking tour.

mansion is a fine example of the Adamesque style made popular by a fashionable Scottish architect of the era named Robert Adam. It now houses the headquarters of the National Society of the Colonial Dames of America. They open it to the public as a museum of Federal period furniture and decorative arts (☎ 202/337-2288; www.dumbartonhouse.org; $5 adults, free for students with valid ID; escorted tours Tues–Sat 10:15, 11:15am, 12:15, and 1:15pm; closed all federal holidays). A tour of the seven museum rooms lasts about 45 minutes.

The spotlight is on the Federal period furnishings (roughly 1790–1830), but you get insights into the upscale Georgetown lifestyle and a brief history of the early owners of the property. If decorative arts are your passion, you don't want to miss this site. If not, we'd suggest skipping the tour and strolling through the lovely walled garden. Take a walk along its graveled paths, which the organization landscaped in 1991 to celebrate its centennial.

Continue west on Q Street to 28th Street and turn left. At P Street, turn right where you'll see:

8 Reuben Daw's Fence

As you negotiate this short jog, note the Federal-style house at no. 1511 28th Street that sports an Asian look. The black iron fence in front of the trio of P Street houses was the idea of Daw, a locksmith, who is said to have used Mexican War muskets that he purchased in a pawn shop to erect it. Dean Acheson, secretary of state in the Truman administration, lived at no. 2805, hosting a luncheon here for the president on his final day in office.

Return to 28th Street, and turn left. Walk to 1623 28th St. otherwise known as:

9 Evermay

Privately owned, this huge Georgian mansion on the right dating to the early 1790s is one of Georgetown's finest homes. You can't see much of it, because it is mostly hidden behind a tall wall that secludes the 3.5-acre estate. But the spacious front yard and entrance drive give you an idea of its grandeur. Samuel Davidson, a Scottish immigrant who made a fortune in real estate, purchased the site and built the house with proceeds he earned in a sale of land that is now occupied by the White House and Lafayette Park. Davidson, who is buried in Oak Hill Cemetery (Stop 11), bequeathed the property to a nephew in Scotland (wouldn't we all like a rich uncle like this?). But he stipulated conditions: His nephew had to move to Georgetown, and he had to change his name to Davidson. The nephew, no fool, did both and lived in the house until his death. The fifth owner, an architect and diplomat, restored the house in 1924.

Continue north on 28th Street to R Street and turn left to 30th Street until you reach:

⑩ Oak Hill Cemetery

This historic 15-acre cemetery, dating to 1849, doubles as a beautifully landscaped garden in the natural 19th-century Romantic style of England. Terraces dotted with fountains and statuary stair step down a steep slope. The burial stones and monuments are mostly from the 19th century and particularly from the Civil War. Edwin Stanton, Abraham Lincoln's secretary of war, is buried here. Most of the plots were sold years ago, and until recently the few burials still permitted were limited to spaces in old family lots. But the cemetery is installing underground crypts, making new burial spaces available. Visitors are welcome; you can purchase a $3 guide to who's buried where at the office just inside the entrance gate. The grounds are open (no charge) from 10am to 4pm Monday through Friday, except during burials and on national holidays.

W. W. Corcoran founded the cemetery, purchasing the acreage along Rock Creek from a great nephew of George Washington. He is the same Corcoran, a wealthy banker, who established the Corcoran Gallery of art in what is now the Renwick Gallery (more on both at p. 122 and 226). James Renwick, Jr., architect of the Smithsonian "Castle" and the Renwick Gallery, designed the cemetery's iron enclosure and the little Chapel, visible on the right. He patterned it after the old Gothic chapels of England.

Dean Acheson, whose residence was noted at Stop 9, is buried at Oak Hill. Other notables include the Peter family, owners of Tudor Place (ahead on Stop 14); John Howard Payne, who wrote the words to "Home Sweet Home"; John Nicolay, Lincoln's White House secretary and noted biographer; General Joseph Willard, proprietor with his brother of the Willard Hotel (p. 141); and Peggy O'Neal Eaton. Eaton, one of the prettiest women in Washington in her day, was a tavern keeper's daughter who married Senator John Eaton of Tennessee. Her alleged conduct—was she unfaithful to her first husband, who committed suicide?—caused a split in the cabinet of President Andrew Jackson. Jackson stoutly defended her reputation, as did Martin Van Buren, his secretary of state, but the gossip raged. Legend has it that she wanted her tombstone to read, "She was never dull." But, sad to say, she has no tombstone at Oak Hill.

The cemetery also holds the remains of two Confederate spies, both women. Antonia Ford Willard fell in love with her captor, General Joseph Willard (of the Willard Hotel above), and later married him. Bettie Duval Webb secreted messages in her abundant hair; she was part of a famous spy ring.

Continue west on R Street a few steps to:

⑪ Montrose Park

This park, which feeds into Rock Creek Park, was the site of Parrott's Ropewalk in the early 19th century. Richard Parrott manufactured rope and rigging used on sailing vessels docking at Georgetown. It was called a "walk" because strands of hemp to be woven into cordage were laid out in long parallel segments like raised railroad tracks, and workers walked back and forth the length of the strands as they wove the rope. At the western end of the park, a sign points to the right down a shady walkway to Dumbarton Oaks Park. The walk is called **"Lovers Lane,"** a pleasant stroll. When Robert and Mildred Bliss purchased Dumbarton Oaks in 1920, they gave 27 acres to the National Park Service, most of which forms Dumbarton Oaks Park.

Continue west on R Street to 31st Street to:

⑫ Dumbarton Oaks and Garden

When the prominent Washington family, the Blisses, bought Dumbarton Oaks in 1920, the grounds had been neglected. Derelict farm buildings stood on its steep slopes, and cow paths wandered among them. Mildred Bliss's goal, a 20-year project, was to transform the land into a distinctively original garden yet one that displayed elements of the traditional English, French, and Italian gardens that she loved. She chose as her landscaper Beatrix Jones Farrand, who had worked on the private gardens of John Rockefeller, Jr., and the grounds at Yale University. The two aimed for informality, beauty, and interest in winter as well as in summer, and spaces for outdoor living.

A 30-minute stroll takes you through the 1810 Orangery, its wall covered by a fig planted before the Civil War; the Rose Garden, a Bliss favorite with nearly 1,000 roses; the Fountain Terrace with its 18th-century fountain; and the Pebble Garden, which covers the former tennis court. The garden is open March 15 through October 31 from 2 to 6pm and November 1 through March 14 from 2 to 5pm; it is closed Monday, all federal holidays, December 24, and during foul weather. Admission is $7 adults, $5 seniors (60-plus) and children (2–12) from March 15 to October 31. There is no fee the rest of the year.

The house is of historic interest as well: Two international meetings held

---

Why So Many Dumbartons?

A tract of land that includes much of today's Georgetown once was called Rock of Dumbarton. One of Georgetown's earliest settlers, a Scotsman named Ninian Beall, had opposed England's Oliver Cromwell, who temporarily ousted the monarchy. Beall was taken prisoner at the Battle of Dunbar in 1650 when Cromwell invaded royalist Scotland. Dispatched as a prisoner to Barbados, he eventually made his way to what is now Georgetown, a part of the English colony of Maryland. He is said to have named the land he acquired on the bluff overlooking the Potomac River the "Rock of Dunbarton" after a rock outcropping near Glasgow. Dumbarton was a later spelling change. Along with the park, there's Dumbarton House (Stop 8) and Dumbarton Oaks and Garden (Stop 12).

at Dumbarton Oaks laid the foundation for the establishment of the United Nations. Now a property of Harvard University, a gift from Robert and Mildred Bliss, the estate's museum displays the couple's renowned collection of Byzantine and pre-Columbian artifacts, many of them gold (p. 136).

Turn left 1 block on 31st Street to:

13 Tudor Place (1644 31st St. NW)

This beautiful mansion, occupying a full square block, was owned by Martha Custis, granddaughter of Martha Washington, and her tobacco merchant husband Thomas Peter. If you have time, we recommend taking the 45-minute tour of the house; it's full of objects George and Martha Washington used in Mount Vernon. Details of the house and tour appear in chapter 11 (p. 265). Even if you don't enter the house, step up the entrance walkway for a good look at the exterior. The house is regarded as a premier example of American neoclassical architecture. Its 19th-century American silver collection is regarded as especially outstanding. Tudor Place remained in the Peter family until 1984.

Take a Break

As you make your way to Stop 15, you cross busy Wisconsin Avenue, one of Georgetown's two major commercial streets. Detour downhill a couple of blocks for lunch at Georgetown's most historic restaurant. Family-run since 1933, it's **Martin's Tavern** (1264 Wisconsin Ave. NW at N Street; ☎ 202/333-7370; www.martins-tavern.com). John Kennedy courted Jacqueline here, and it's still a favorite of Georgetown residents. The menu is American and moderately priced. Some outdoor tables are available, weather permitting. But at lunch, you may prefer the air-conditioned interior.

At 31st and Q streets, turn right on Q. Proceed 2 blocks to Wisconsin Avenue. Jog left a half-block and then right onto Volta Place. A half-block past 33rd Street, the alleyway on the left is:

14 Pomander Walk

The 10 tiny pastel-colored houses, five on each side of the lane, date from 1885. Occupying what was once a notorious slum area housing former slaves freed in the Civil War, they are an example of some of Georgetown's humbler structures that have been restored to charming, albeit pricy homes. Note the appealing features such as double-door entrance alcoves, flower boxes in the windows, and gas lights. But would you want to live in a house tucked into a narrow alley, without any kind of decent view to speak of? For lots of Washingtonians, the lure of Georgetown and its urban attractions is strong. They are close to work, restaurants, shops, movies, and nightspots. If they want a view, the Potomac River is a 10-minute walk away, and the towpath of the C&O Canal transports them into the countryside in only a few more minutes.

Take Volta Place west to 34th Street; turn left to P Street; and turn left again to:

15 3271 P St. NW

Individually and as a couple, John and Jacqueline Kennedy often chose Georgetown as their residence. The future president, then a U.S. senator, lived in this 1818 Federal-style house in 1953 while courting the future first lady, at the time "The Inquiring Photographer" for the *Washington Times-Herald* newspaper. It was here, one presumes, that they made many of the plans for their wedding in Newport, Rhode Island. After the wedding, they rented a larger town house at

3321 Dent Place, which is not on this tour. Note that for a few blocks P Street is paved with bricks, and abandoned streetcar tracks still remain. In the 1950s, the city shut down its streetcar lines and substituted buses, a decision that many longtime residents regret.

Double back on P Street to 33rd Street, and turn left. At N Street, turn right to:

16 3307 N St. NW

Another Federal-style house and another Kennedy home, this one was a gift from John to Jacqueline in 1957 after the birth of their daughter Caroline. John, Jr., was born while they lived here. This was the Kennedy residence during the presidential campaign. The double living room, redecorated three times in their first year of residence—one can only speculate why—proved an excellent place to host intimate political gatherings because of its spaciousness. After Kennedy's election, the press gathered outside the door day and night for 2 frosty months before the inaugural hoping for news of cabinet choices and other developments. Helen Montgomery, who lived across the street, graciously invited members of the press inside from the cold, serving them coffee and sandwiches. A bronze plaque on the house commends her hospitality.

Continue on N Street to:

17 Cox's Row (3327–3339 N St. NW)

The American Institute of Architects cites this row of five town houses, built between 1815 and 1818, as "among the finest and purest examples of Federal-era architecture in a city known for its Federal-era buildings." Such distinctive features as sunken panels, arched doorways, and leaden swags (a form of ornamentation above the doorway and windows resembling bunches of evergreen branches) reflect the Federal style—only slightly altered by later modest touches of restoration. The row has historic as well as architectural significance. Colonel John Cox, the builder, was a successful Georgetown merchant. He married an heiress, whose dowry included the land on which nearby Georgetown University sits. In time, Cox was elected mayor of Georgetown, a position he held for 22 years. When Lafayette returned to Washington in 1824, Cox invited him to stay at no. 3337, and Lafayette accepted. Cox and his wife lived next door at no. 3339. Note the whimsical polished brass fox head adorning the fence outside no. 3327.

Continue on N Street to 37th Street and turn right for 1 block:

18 Georgetown University, 37th and O streets NW

Founded in 1789 with just 12 students, Georgetown University is the oldest Catholic and Jesuit university in the United States. Today it enrolls 13,000 students in four undergraduate schools, the graduate school, and professional schools of business, law, and medicine. Its School of Foreign Service is one of the largest schools of international relations in the world and the oldest in the United States. More than 60 buildings dot the 104-acre campus.

This walkabout does not include a campus tour, but of course you can explore the campus on your own. If you do here are some highlights to hit:

As you enter the Main Gate, pause at the old stone gatehouse on the left, which serves as an information booth. You should find pamphlets with a map of the campus placed in front of the window. The seated gentleman directly ahead of you is John Carroll, the university's founder and the first archbishop of Baltimore.

The imposing gray granite fortress with multiple spires behind him is Healy Hall, the campus centerpiece completed in 1879. Named for Patrick F. Healy, the first African-American president of a major university who served from 1873 to 1882, it houses administrative offices and classrooms. Its loftiest tower soars 300 feet above the Potomac River. Riggs Library, occupying the tower on the left, is one of the last cast-iron libraries in the United States. A money-saving architectural phase, library stacks (where the books are shelved) were made of cast iron and are part of the building's support. The big drawback is that the stacks can't be moved.

Behind Healy Hall is the Quadrangle, scene of presidential addresses from George Washington to Bill Clinton, a 1968 graduate. Overlooking the Quadrangle from behind Healy Hall is Old North Hall, completed in 1793 and the oldest structure on the campus.

Also on the Quadrangle is Dahlgren Chapel of the Sacred Heart, which has served the campus since 1893. The chapel's stained-glass windows and pipe organ make it a favorite for weddings. The cross suspended over the main altar dates to the earliest days of Colonial Maryland.

Exit the Georgetown campus to 37th Street and head right 2 blocks to Prospect Street. Turn left to 36th Street. On the right, descend 75 steps to M Street. Go left to 34th Street, and cross M Street to the park.

🔟 **Francis Scott Key Park and "The Star-Spangled Banner" Memorial**

Key is remembered as the man who wrote the words for the National Anthem the night an English force bombarded Baltimore's Fort McHenry in the War of 1812. A prominent lawyer, his home at the time was located 100 yards west on M Street. But it was dismantled when Francis Scott Key Bridge, just to your right, was constructed in 1923. A bust of Key is easy to miss beneath the park's shady arbor. Information signs provide more details of the British attack of September 13 and 14, 1814, when by the dawn's early light the huge star-spangled banner still flew above Fort McHenry.

Walking Tour 3: Dupont Circle & Embassy Row

Start:	Dupont Circle.
Finish:	The Finnish Embassy (3301 Massachusetts Ave.; see below for public transportation instructions) appropriately enough.
Time:	Approximately 2 hours not including time spent at touring the inside of historic homes, should you so choose.
Best times:	Weekdays during normal office hours to catch glimpses of foreign dignitaries, sometimes in their native dress, and to step inside churches and a mosque.
Worst times:	At night, when everything of interest shuts down.

Think of the Dupont Circle/Embassy Row area as Newport, Rhode Island, with an international twist. Once a favored seasonal haunt of Gilded Age millionaires, today its impressive mansions house the world's embassies, from Togo to Brazil to

Finland. The story of this neighborhood transformation forms the basis of our walking tour.

And the tale begins on an improbable note. At the end of the Civil War, the elegant area you'll be exploring was a wasteland. A swampy creek snaked through its heart, and the mud literally ran with blood, as what is now Dupont Circle was the setting for a large slaughterhouse. But a combination of land speculation and urban works projects in the 1870s began the facelift and by the 1890s the Dupont area was home to some 100 over-the-top mansions. The era's oil barons, gold rush magnates, and other tycoons of industry made these homes part of their yearly circuit: They spent summers in Newport, autumns in Washington, D.C. (where they sought to influence public policies), and winter/spring in New York City. Most of the extravagant mansions you'll see on this tour sat empty for two-thirds of the year.

The stock market crash of 1929 put an end to this high society roundelay. Fortunes were lost and with them, most of these properties. At the inception of World War II, some were lent or rented to the government to use for war agencies, others became boardinghouses, and eventually a number were sold to nations seeking embassies in Washington.

That's why few of the embassies you'll see on this tour reflect their national character in the design of their buildings. And the dichotomy between the actual financial status of some of these nations and the grandeur of their embassies can be startling. Some nations, fallen on hard times, have allowed their buildings to deteriorate to a sad state; it's not uncommon to see flaking paint, sagging steps, or boarded-up windows in this otherwise wealthy neighborhood. And because these buildings are not covered by D.C. property codes—they're diplomatic properties after all—there's nothing the neighbors can do to push for repairs. The quiet demeanor of the neighborhood is also frequently broken by the chanting voices and banging drums of a political or diplomatic demonstration. Typically, a crowd of angry expatriates or students is protesting some policy of their homeland government. The TV cameras zoom in for close-ups, and the Metropolitan Police keep alert. If you chance upon a protest, take a moment to find out what the hubbub is about. At other times, fleets of limos clog the avenue when an embassy—usually celebrating a homeland holiday—throws a big party and invites everyone (even those grumpy neighbors!).

As for food, you won't find much of it as you wander along. Better to pick up a picnic at **Teaism** (2009 R St. NW near Connecticut Ave; see p. 62 for more) and stop in one of the garden areas along the way to nosh.

① Dupont Circle

We'll start in the center of the traffic circle so you can get a good look around. Dupont Circle is one of the most famous place names in D.C.; at the same time, it's a historic district, a traffic circle, and a progressive neighborhood that's been home, since the mid-'70s, to the city's gay and lesbian community. In fact, every year, on the Tuesday before Halloween, they stage the "High Heel Race" during which two dozen or so drag queens, in outrageous regalia, dash around the circle. (And then have a party, of course!)

Named for Civil War naval hero Samuel Francis du Pont, the circle is placed exactly where Washington's famed architect Charles Pierre L'Enfant envisioned it, though construction didn't begin until 1871, long after L'Enfant's death. For its center, Congress commissioned a small bronze statue of the admiral, but the proud du Pont family would have none of it. Without asking permission, they commissioned the two men behind the Lincoln Memorial—sculptor Daniel Chester French and architect Henry Bacon—to create the fountain you see in front of you. It replaced the bronze statue in 1921; on its shaft are allegorical figures representing the elements a sea captain needs to navigate and propel the boat forward. See if you can figure out which is "the stars," which "the sea," and which "the wind."

Cross Massachusetts Avenue to New Hampshire Avenue until you come to Sunderland Place and see:

❷ The Brewmaster's Castle (the Christian Heurich House Museum, 1307 New Hampshire Ave. NW)

Known in less polite circles as "burp castle," this is the house beer built. Christian Heurich was a highly successful brewer, who was the largest landowner in Washington, D.C., after the Federal Government. He loved his work so much that he never retired, continuing to manage his brewery until his death at the age of 102 in 1945. That wasn't just a work ethic—the man had murals celebrating the joys of beer in his breakfast room and used as the slogan for his company, "Beer recommended for family use by Physicians in General." Yup, those were the days. You can see the interior on sporadic **tours** (Thurs–Fri at 11:30am and 1pm, Sat 11:30am, 1, 3pm; $5 requested donation; www.brewmasterscastle.com).

And if you can tour it, do so—the house is notable not just for the colorful history of its owner but also for its importance architecturally. Built between 1892 and 1894, it is likely the first domestic structure framed with steel and poured concrete, an effort to make it fireproof. (Another effort: the salamander symbol at the top of the tower. In ancient mythology, the salamander repelled fire.) Many consider this Romanesque-style, 31-room home to be one of the most intact late Victorian structures in the country. Take a moment to look for the gargoyles.

Walk toward 20th Street, turn right, and continue north two blocks to Massachusetts Avenue. Turn left and on the corner you'll find:

❸ Blaine Mansion (2000 Massachusetts Ave. NW)

The last standing mansion from the early days of Dupont Circle, this imposing brick and terra-cotta structure retains the name of its first owner: James G. Blaine. Had it not been for the Mugwumps—and don't you love it that we used to have political parties with such colorful names?—he might well have become president instead of Grover Cleveland. As it was, charges of corruption involving illicit dealings with the railroads, ahem, derailed his campaign. This, despite the fact that Blaine at that point had a longer and arguably more distinguished career than Cleveland, having served as secretary of state twice, Speaker of the House, and congressman and senator from Maine.

The vertical sweep of the house surely impresses as much as the man, though to be honest, he barely lived here. Once the home was built, he

Walking Tour: Dupont Circle/Embassy Row

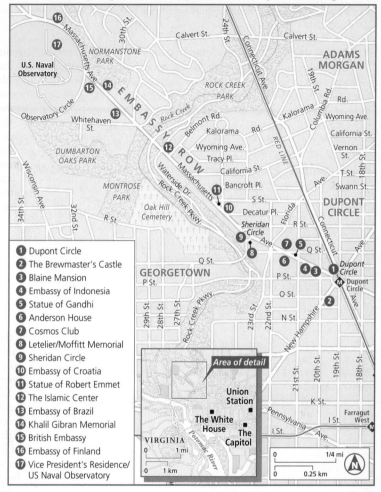

1 Dupont Circle
2 The Brewmaster's Castle
3 Blaine Mansion
4 Embassy of Indonesia
5 Statue of Gandhi
6 Anderson House
7 Cosmos Club
8 Letelier/Moffitt Memorial
9 Sheridan Circle
10 Embassy of Croatia
11 Statue of Robert Emmet
12 The Islamic Center
13 Embassy of Brazil
14 Khalil Gibran Memorial
15 British Embassy
16 Embassy of Finland
17 Vice President's Residence/ US Naval Observatory

decided it would be too costly to maintain and he leased it, first to Levi Leiter (an early co-owner of Marshall Field's) and then to George Westinghouse. Yes, that Westinghouse. The latter bought it in 1901 and lived here until his death in 1914. As we write this, it's under renovation. Hopefully the view-impairing scaffolding will be gone by the time you read this.

Continue in the same direction on Massachusetts Avenue to our first embassy, the:

4 **Embassy of Indonesia (2020 Massachusetts Ave.)**

The ornate structure occupied today by the Embassy of Indonesia is said to have cost $835,000 when it was built in 1903—the city's most expensive house at the time. Sadly, by the time the

Some Advice on the Route

This is a rather lengthy walk. It's worthwhile, we think, especially because you'll see nearly the whole world—or at least its embassies—on this route. (To see more, look for the national flags of other embassies located on side streets a few steps to the left or right.)

If you feel yourself tiring, you can catch the N2 **Metrobus** at a number of stops along this route and it will take you back to Dupont Circle. Some of the walk is uphill, which is why we're suggesting this precaution. You can do the walk in reverse, taking the bus to your starting point as well, though the more interesting Gilded Age sites are closer to Dupont Circle, and we want you to see those while you're still fresh.

Embassies are not normally open to visitors. Some do organize art shows and concerts featuring homeland artists. For example, the Embassy of Finland at 3301 Massachusetts Ave. NW schedules two art shows annually, advertising them in a banner stripped across the front of the building. The *City Paper,* a free tabloid newspaper, lists embassy shows in its Thursday Galleries column. Take advantage of these shows to step inside for a look at the embassy itself.

house was purchased by the Indonesians in 1951, the family fortune was so depleted, they let it go for a mere $350,000: a reminder that housing bubbles have been around for quite some time.

The man who commissioned its construction, Thomas Walsh, came to the United States from Ireland in 1869 at the age of 19. He headed west, and in the 1870s struck it rich not once but twice, finding what is widely thought to be the one of the richest veins of gold in the world. Suddenly a modern-day Midas, he moved his family to Washington, figuring a grand 60-room mansion was the way to make a splash in society. And remembering his roots, he's said to have embedded a nugget of gold ore in the porch. You'll notice that this neo-Baroque mansion is unusually curvaceous. That's because it's meant to evoke the look of an ocean liner. A grand staircase in the home itself is a direct copy of one on the *White Star* ocean liner.

The fortune depleter, daughter Evalyn Walsh McLean, was notable for the tragic turn her life took. Despite the jaunty title of her autobiography, *Father Struck It Rich!,* not much else went right in her life. Her son was killed at the age of 9 in a car crash and her daughter overdosed as a young woman. Husband Edward Beale McLean, an heir to the Post fortune, turned out to be an alcoholic and together they burned through some $100 million. A large chunk of it went to the purchase of the famed Hope Diamond. Those who believe the diamond is cursed claim that her misfortunes started with that purchase. She died nearly penniless at the age of 58. The diamond is now on display at the Smithsonian (p. 112).

Keep walking in the same direction to a small triangular park where you'll find the:

⑤ Statue of Mahatma Gandhi

Striding purposefully, the man who led India to freedom from British rule in 1947 seems to be headed (aptly) for the **Embassy of India** (#2107), just across the adjacent side street. His walking stick, simple bowl, dress, and age in the sculpture suggest that this is a portrait of him on the famed protest march to the Arabian Sea when he and hundreds of followers walked 200 miles to collect salt (and evade the British tax on that condiment). A turning point in the struggle for Indian independence, it's an apt subject for this striking portrait.

Keep walking in the same direction to:

⑥ Anderson House (2118 Massachusetts Ave.)

Larz Anderson, an American diplomat, and his wife Isabel Weld Perkins, author and Red Cross volunteer, took advantage of their immense Boston wealth and built not just a home but a palace. Their intent? To create a space large enough to serve as a headquarters of the Society of the Cincinnati, of which Larz was a member (they bequeathed the home upon their deaths). Guided tours to this museum of the Gilded Age and clubhouse are offered Tuesday through Saturday between 1 and 4pm (☎ 202/785-2040; www.societyofthecincinnati.org; donation requested). The membership of the society, founded in 1783, is composed of male descendants of officers in George Washington's Continental Army.

The building itself, sporting a cavernous two-story ballroom, a dining room seating 50, grand staircase, massive wall murals, acres of marble, and 23-karat gold trim, is more palatial than Hillwood, Washington's other

palace museum. But the Andersons couldn't match Marjorie Merriweather Post's astute and energetic collecting of European treasures. The Andersons bought lots of nice objects on their world travels, but they are of only slight interest. If you have time for only one palace, make it Hillwood (p. 136).

Head across the street to the:

⑦ Cosmos Club (2121 Massachusetts Ave.)

A prestigious private social club, it was founded in 1878 as a gathering place for scientists and public policy intellectuals. The National Geographic Society spun off from the Cosmos 10 years later. The Cosmos Club's first meeting was held in the home of John Wesley Powell, the soldier and explorer who first navigated the Colorado River through the Grand Canyon in a dory. Since then, three presidents, two vice presidents, a dozen Supreme Court justices, 32 Nobel Prize winners, 56 Pulitzer Prize winners, and 45 recipients of the Presidential Medal of Freedom have numbered among its ranks.

But none of them were women, until 1998, that is, when the Washington, D.C. Human Rights Commission ruled that the Club's "men only" policy was illegal and discriminatory.

The club is the latest occupant of a French-inspired chateau built in 1901 with the railroad wealth of Richard and Mary Scott Townsend. His fortune came from the Erie Line; hers from the Pennsylvania Railroad. They hired the famed New York architectural firm of Carrere & Hastings, which created the New York Public Library, to build a chateau built to resemble the Petit Trianon—the royal hideaway at Versailles. Highly superstitious, the couple had the structure built around an older one. Apparently, a gypsy had once predicted that Mrs. Townsend would die "under a new roof." Despite these precautions, Mrs. Townsend did eventually pass away.

As you head toward Sheridan Square, look for the Romanian Chancery and the **Embassy of Ireland** (#2234). In front of these two is the:

❽ Letelier/Moffitt Memorial

On September 21, 1976, Orlando Letelier, the former foreign minister of ousted President Salvador Allende, offered his colleague Ronni Karpen Moffitt a ride home. A car bomb at this spot killed them both; this small cylindrical monument honors their memory. Thousands showed up later that week for a hastily organized protest funeral march. Eventually, five men were prosecuted for the crime. One, who led police to the others, was given just 2 years of prison before being taken into the witness protection program. For years, rumors circulated that the American government was involved in the killings in some way.

Turn away from the Memorial and cross (carefully) to the center of:

❾ Sheridan Circle

The Civil War officer mounted on his muscular horse is General Philip H. Sheridan, commander of the Union cavalry and the Army of the Shenandoah. His horse Rienzi, who carried him through 85 battles and skirmishes, became almost as famous during the war, as "the steed that saved the day."

Sculpted by Gutzon Borglum, who carved the presidential faces on South Dakota's Mount Rushmore, the statue depicts Sheridan rallying his men at the Battle of Cedar Creek in Northern Virginia on October 19, 1864. Sheridan was 15 miles north in the town of Winchester when a Confederate force under General Jubal A. Early surprised and drove back his army. Racing to the battle site on stouthearted Rienzi, Sheridan led his men in a victorious counterattack.

Sheridan's wife is said to have chosen the site for the statue, which is flanked by two hidden pools. His son, Second Lieutenant Philip H. Sheridan, Jr., served as a model for the statue. He was present at the unveiling in 1908, as was President Theodore Roosevelt.

Carefully cross the Circle again, back to Massachusetts Avenue and continue going northwest to the:

❿ Embassy of Croatia (2343 Massachusetts Ave. NW)

Outside the building, the muscular figure of St. Jerome the Priest (A.D. 341–420) sits hunched over a book, his head in his hand. Jerome, the pedestal of the statue informs us, was "the greatest Doctor of the Church." This is a reference to his work in translating the Bible from Hebrew into Latin, a version called the Vulgate because it was in the language of the common people of the day. Historically, it is considered the most important vernacular edition of the Bible. At times in his younger years, Jerome's religious faith declined; he became involved in numerous theological disputes, and he spent several years in the desert leading an ascetical life while fighting temptations. We get the feeling this glum statue is commemorating those troubled times. The statue initially sat on the grounds of the Franciscan Abbey near Catholic University; it was moved here when the nation of Croatia was created at the breakup of Yugoslavia.

Embassy Row: Some Explanations

Today, about 75 embassies, chanceries, or ambassadorial residences are located on or near the 2-mile stretch of Massachusetts Avenue between Dupont Circle and Wisconsin Avenue NW. As a result, it was dubbed Embassy Row.

A word on those distinctions: An **embassy** is the official office or residence of the ambassador. Some ambassadors live and work in the embassy; others maintain separate residences, commuting to their jobs like the rest of us.

A **chancery** is the embassy's office; this is where you might apply for a visitor's visa. It could be located within the embassy or not.

Some countries also provide separate offices for special missions, such as the military attaché's office. In all, about 180 countries maintain a diplomatic presence in Washington.

Continue walking to the 2400 block of Massachusetts Avenue where, in a triangular park, you'll see the:

⑪ Statue of Robert Emmet

Though somewhat obscured by foliage, the Irish revolutionary stands in a pose that he reportedly struck in Dublin in 1803 when a British court sentenced him to death by hanging. He appears to be gazing toward the Embassy of Ireland 2 blocks away. Born in 1778, Emmet led a failed uprising in Dublin on July 23, 1803. The statue was presented to the Smithsonian Institution in 1917 as a gift to the American public from a group of American citizens of Irish ancestry. It was moved to its present site in 1966, marking the 50th anniversary of Irish independence.

Note the numerous embassies en route to the next stop. Two marble elephants guard the **India Supply Mission** (no. 2536). Above them, a strip of blue squares across the front of the building serves as a backdrop to a white water lily, symbolizing peace and tranquillity, and a wheel, which represents

the continuous cycle of life. Its neighbor is the **Embassy of Japan** (no. 2516). The structure set back behind the cobblestone courtyard dates to 1932. Georgian revival in style, it suggests the Far East with a subtle "rising sun" above the balcony over the door.

On the right is the new **Embassy of Turkey** (no. 2525). The statue in front is of Mustafa Kemel Ataturk, the founder of modern Turkey.

Just before the bridge, head to:

⑫ The Islamic Center (2551 Massachusetts Ave.)

The 160-foot tall white limestone minaret, soaring above Embassy Row, makes the Islamic Center impossible to miss. From it, a loudspeaker intones the call to prayer five times daily. Built in 1949, the center does not line up directly with the street; instead, it faces Mecca. On Friday afternoons, throngs of the faithful pour into the mosque for prayer services, many of them embassy employees attired in their native dress. At times, prayer rugs are spread in the courtyard or even on the sidewalk outside the iron railing fence. This is when Embassy Row takes on its most dramatic multicultural look.

Visitors are welcome inside (daily 10am–5pm), so don't be shy about stepping through the open gates. But be sure to remove your shoes before entering the mosque itself; leave them in one of the slots provided on the entrance wall. Men should dress neatly; no shorts. Women are not allowed to wear sleeveless clothes or short dresses and must cover their hair. The interior, filled with colorful Arabic art, is well worth these preliminaries. Persian rugs drape the floor, overlapping one another; 7,000 blue tiles cover the lower walls in mosaic patterns; eight ornate pillars soar overhead, ringing a huge copper chandelier. The carved pulpit is inlaid with ivory, and stained-glass windows add more color.

Exit the Islamic Center and cross the bridge. Take a look down: 75 feet below is Rock Creek Parkway as well as the 1,700-acre Rock Creek Park (chapter 7, p. 169). At the other end of the bridge, walk on and take time to look at the embassies you'll be passing until you get to the:

⑬ Embassy of Brazil (3000 Massachusetts Ave. NW)

This stately, palace-like building next to the big, black boxlike building (the chancery) is the ambassador's residence. The older building, derived from an Italian Renaissance palazzo, was designed in 1931 by John Russell Pope, a leader of the city's early-20th-century neoclassicist movement. The Jefferson Memorial, National Gallery of Art, and National Archives are among Pope's other local works.

Keep walking in the same direction and look to the right side to find the:

⑭ Kahlil Gibran Memorial

An elaborate 2-acre garden, eight-sided star fountain, circular walkway, shaded benches, and bronze bust celebrate the life and achievements of the Lebanese-American philosopher. Dedicated on May 24, 1991, it is a gift "to the people of the United States" from the Kahlil Gibran Centennial Foundation. Born in 1883 in a village near the Biblical Cedars of Lebanon, Gibran arrived in Boston as a child. Building a successful career as artist and author, he published widely quoted books in English and Arabic. He died in New York City in 1931. Excerpts from his writings are etched into the memorial's circular wall, among them: "We live only to discover beauty. All else is a form of waiting." If you need to rest your feet for a few moments, this lovely garden is the place.

Continue your stroll to the:

⑮ British Embassy (3100 Massachusetts Ave.)

Out in front and instantly recognizable in a familiar pose, **Sir Winston Churchill** stands in bronze. One foot rests on embassy property, thus British soil; the other is planted on American soil. Anglo-American unity is the symbolism, but the placement also reflects Churchill's heritage as the child of a British father and American mother. And, of course, his right hand is raised in the iconic familiar V for Victory sign he displayed in World War II. His other hand often sports a small bouquet of fresh flowers, left by admirers.

The English-Speaking Union of the United States commissioned the statue, which was erected in 1966. The statue stands on a granite plinth; beneath it are blended soils from Blenheim Palace, his birthplace; from the rose garden at Chartwell, his home; and from his mother's home in Brooklyn, New York.

The U-shaped, redbrick structure rising behind the World War II prime minister is the main chancery, built in 1931. Sir Edwin Lutyens, one of Great Britain's leading architects of the day, designed both it and the ambassador's residence, located out of sight behind the chancery. The American Institute of Architects describes the pair as a "triumph," noting that Lutyens rejected the prevailing passion for neoclassical structures and instead created a Colonial American design. Others suggest it looks like an 18th-century English country house. Whatever, it makes an impressive show. Too bad the concrete box on the right, an office building dedicated by Queen Elizabeth II in 1957, failed to match the architectural standard Lutyens set. The round glass structure, another unfortunately bland modern addition, is used for conferences.

On your right as you continue around Observatory Circle (a wide curve in Embassy Row) is a steep, heavily wooded slope that drops into a slender canyon. It is Rock Creek Trail, and if you wish, you can take a little nature detour. It's amazing how quickly, in just a moment really, you leave the hubbub of the city and find yourself in nature. Okay, enough greenery. Continue walking to the dramatic:

⑯ Embassy of Finland (3301 Massachusetts Ave.)

An abstract metal-and-glass front forms a green wall of climbing plants on a bronze, gridlike trellis. Within, huge windows in the rear look out onto a thickly forested slope, as if—to quote architectural historian William Morgan—"The Finns have brought a

bit of the woods to Washington." The architects, Mikko Heikkinen and Markku Komonen, are considered one of Finland's hottest architectural partnerships. Completed in 1994, the embassy was designed to display the life and culture of Finland. To see the interior, attend one of the two annual art shows displaying Finnish artworks. You can get a very limited glimpse by stepping into the all-glass reception—if only to pick up a tourist brochure for Finland. The embassy is open Monday through Friday from 8:30am to 4:45pm.

> ❝ An embassy in Washington, D.C., is different from embassies in most other capitals, where people visit them only if they have to; that is, to get a visa or to conduct official business. In Washington, D.C., embassies are expected to be much more. They need to be able to open windows on the life and culture of the countries they represent, not only for the select few, but for all Washingtonians and visitors to the capital who want to know. Many do, because Americans are curious by nature. ❞
>
> —Jukka Valtasaari, Finnish ambassador, 1988–96 and 2001–05

From the Finnish Embassy, look across the street to the green slope behind the tall iron fence. That white Victorian-style house atop the hill partially visible is the:

⑰ Vice President's Residence/U.S. Naval Observatory (Massachusetts Ave. at 34th St.)

Number One Observatory Circle is the official residence of the U.S. Vice

Tours of the Observatory

Public tours of the observatory (but not the Vice President's residence) are offered, but you have to make advance plans for this walkabout. Tours are scheduled on selected Monday evenings from 8:30 to 10pm. Visitors learn about the observatory's timekeeping responsibilities and (weather permitting) take a look at the night sky through the telescope. Make a request for free tickets at least 4 to 6 weeks in advance. Do so either online at **www.usno.navy.mil** or by fax to the Public Affairs Office at 202/762-1489. For more on what the Observatory does, see p. ### in chapter 6, "The 'Other' Washington."

President. As we write this, it is home for Vice President Joseph and Dr. Jill Biden. The wooded estate surrounding the residence is the site of the U.S. Naval Observatory; the large white dome holding its 12-inch refracting telescope is easily seen on the right.

Built in 1893, the Veep's house initially was assigned to the observatory's superintendent. But in 1923 the Chief of Naval Operations took a liking to it, booted out the superintendent, and made the house his home. In 1974, Congress evicted the Navy and transformed it into the Vice President's residence.

Up to that time, Vice Presidents occupied their own homes, as Supreme Court judges, cabinet members, and senators still do. But providing full security apparatus for the private homes of the Veep became expensive. Nelson Rockefeller, Vice President in the Gerald Ford administration, was the first potential resident, but he used the house only for entertaining. So Vice President Walter Mondale became the first official occupant, followed by the elder Bush, Dan Quayle, Al Gore, and Dick Cheney. The latter's penchant for secrecy forced Google maps to blur out

its live satellite pictures of the observatory, rumor has it. If you see a big tent on the front lawn, it usually means the Vice President is hosting a gala reception. Traffic along Massachusetts Avenue is brought to a halt many mornings and afternoons when the Vice President's motorcade races past, carrying him to or from his offices at the White House or U.S. Capitol.

The observatory moved from Foggy Bottom to its present location in 1910. At the time, the hilltop site was rural countryside. One of the oldest scientific agencies in the country, it was established in 1830. Its primary mission was to oversee the Navy's chronometers, charts, and other navigational equipment. Today it remains the preeminent authority on precise time. Scientists take observations of the sun, moon, planets, and selected stars; determine the precise time; and publish astronomical data needed for accurate navigation.

And with that, we'll allow you to navigate on to wherever else your travels may take you today in D.C. We hope you enjoyed this walking tour and the others.

9

Attention, D.C. Shoppers!

When you've seen enough of the city's museum treasures, take a look at the shopping goodies to carry home as souvenirs.

By Jim Yenckel

WHAT ARE THE BEST BUYS IN WASHINGTON, D.C.? THAT'S HARD TO SAY. The city doesn't make or grow much of anything except reports, studies, regulations, laws, and a lot of hot air. The most significant manufacturing plant is the Bureau of Engraving and Printing, which spits out U.S. paper currency by the millions. Buy as many dollar bills as you want, but there's no discount for bulk purchases.

If souvenir shopping is your hobby, however, Washington is the place for you. The city's shops boast quality souvenirs—White House snow globes! Reproductions of the Declaration of Independence! Obama T-shirts of every possible design—in abundance. Many will be found in the outstanding museum shops that dot the city and are filled with unique, not necessarily expensive items, perfect for a gift or keepsake. You're into politics? In the capital of American politics, check out a political memorabilia outlet. See badges, posters, and life-size cutouts of politicians you love or love to hate.

As an international capital, Washington has also seen a small boom of shops displaying ethnic clothing, crafts, and artworks—fun to see even if your budget says "No, don't do it."

For anything else, however, Washington is *not* much of a shopper's paradise, particularly if you're looking for budget fashions for the family or for something intrinsically "Washington." But whether souvenirs are your goal, or something else, at least some of you are going to want to shop, and I'm here to guide you to the best the city offers.

WHERE TO SPEND

Odd as it may seem, Washington does not have a major downtown shopping street. It disappeared (becoming office space) in the '60s and '70s when the population plummeted from a high of more than 800,000 to about 582,000 today. Most who left headed for the suburbs, and the big department stores either followed them to fancy malls or went bust. Downtown Washington supports one authentic department store: Macy's, where you can find clothing, cosmetics, appliances, and home furnishings. Someday, the recent surge in downtown condominium construction may create a new "Main Street," but not anytime soon.

So I'm going to take you to easy-to-reach neighborhood stores, where you will find offbeat items—hand-painted Italian pottery, chic hand-loomed garments

What Is the Best Washington Souvenir?

Even nonshoppers are tempted to take home a souvenir from a memorable trip. What should it be? You will find plenty of the standard tourist stuff: coffee mugs; miniature busts of Washington, Jefferson, and Lincoln; mini bronze replicas of the Washington Monument and the U.S. Capitol. But maybe you want something extra-special to remember your visit to the nation's capital—a souvenir with lasting value:

- Go to a book signing and get an **autographed copy** of a novel or non-fiction work by a local author whose work intrigues you.
- Buy a quality **photo book** of Washington that does justice to its monuments and memorials.
- Look in galleries for a small painting, piece of art glass, or other **artwork** created by a Washington artist.
- Choose a **poster** from a current museum show or sporting event you attended and when you get back home, have it framed.
- Take home a **biography** or history you will read from the Jefferson, Lincoln, or Roosevelt memorials or the National Archives or Supreme Court.
- And don't forget to pick up a **Washington T-shirt.** After $1 bills, they may be the city's second leading manufactured item. Nobody leaves the city without one.

from Asia, contemporary American crafts—while seeing hometown Washington beyond the ceremonial Mall. I'll also talk about the best shopping neighborhoods, really small villages within the city, all providing a choice of cafes, banks, drugstores, and other mini-"Main Street" outlets. With so much museum art, Washington also supports an artist's colony, and I'll show you where to find some of the top galleries.

My task is also to help you find bargains—and I'll show you some spiffy consignment shops with bargain-basement prices—but also we'll take a look at some high-end shops, many of which are playing "Let's Make a Deal" to stay afloat in the current recession. It's now possible to bargain hunt in stores that never discounted before. And one more affordable reason to visit these more fancy shops: Many of the showrooms, especially at the upscale end, are architectural delights. It's interesting to see how different designers turn the interiors of the city's slender old row houses into exciting spaces.

WASHINGTON'S TOP SHOPPING AREAS
CHAINS & BOUTIQUES: GEORGETOWN

Intriguing, high-fashion boutiques and large multinational chains cluster side by side in **Georgetown** (Wisconsin Ave. and M St. NW; K St. Circulator Bus or Metrobus: 30, 32, 34, 35, 36), making it the most efficient (and I'd say, fun) area to shop in Washington, D.C. Saturday is the big day, drawing throngs of Washingtonians checking out what's new. But most places are open daily, usually from about 10 or 11am to 9 or 10pm. On Sunday, noon to 6pm is fairly standard. If you are a savvy shopper, you're likely to find some bargains in the lineup of men's and women's clothing. Though Washington isn't noted for cutting-edge fashion, Georgetown is where you will find not only name designer wear but also the funkiest, hippest, and even most outrageous attire in the city. Need a proper belly-dancing costume? You'll find it here. Nearly 1 entire block is devoted to antiques shops; another is lined with chic furniture stores displaying the latest international styles.

The heart of Georgetown's shopping district is the intersection of Wisconsin Avenue and M Street. A shopping excursion might first take you about 4 blocks up Wisconsin (north) and then back, beginning and ending at M Street. When I say up, I mean it literally; you climb steady from the valley of the Potomac River. This is where younger shoppers with tighter budgets will find fashions more to their liking. A number of the shops are local branches of European chains; though generally expensive, they display items you might not see at home. The second phase of a shopping trip might tackle M Street—first east from Wisconsin 2 blocks and back and then west from Wisconsin 3 blocks and back. This is where you will find higher-end boutiques appealing to executives, lawyers, and diplomats of both sexes.

THE "NEW" DOWNTOWN: FRIENDSHIP HEIGHTS/CHEVY CHASE

Even though it is located on the northern edge of the city, and Maryland claims half of it, I think it's correct to dub this area D.C.'s new "Main Street." **Friendship Heights/Chevy Chase** (Metro: Friendship Heights) is what downtown used to look like—a stretch of 3 or 4 blocks on Wisconsin Avenue lined on each side with low-rise department stores, shops, cafes, banks, hair and skin salons, furniture stores, and other commercial outlets. Friendship Heights, the Washington end, offers more off-price shopping places—although Neiman Marcus, the purveyor of luxury, shares their company. Chevy Chase, the Maryland half, is totally upscale, and getting more so all the time (see box below).

OFFBEAT & FUNKY: PENN QUARTER/CHINATOWN

Though it's primarily an evening dining and entertainment strip, stretching for about 5 blocks, **Penn Quarter/Chinatown** (7th St. NW btw. D and I sts.; Metro: Gallery Place–Chinatown or National Archives–Navy Memorial/Penn Quarter) has attracted numerous offbeat shops and galleries that make for interesting shopping or browsing. Buy a deck for your skateboard, the proper garb for your martial arts class, artisanal cheeses and chocolates, or 18th-century Venetian glass trade beads. The neighborhood is one of the city's newest and hottest commercial hubs, spurred by the opening of the huge Verizon Center, a major sports arena. Even if you don't shop, 7th Street is worth a look for its lineup of gorgeous, rehabilitated 19th-century structures. Brick sidewalks, old-fashioned street lamps, shade trees, and hanging baskets of flowers add to the Victorian look.

AROUND THE WORLD: ADAMS MORGAN

This is the neighborhood for shopping ethnic—Egyptian candies, Ethiopian ceremonial wear, Moroccan pottery, South American CDs. In the hour or two it takes to poke into these small, inexpensive places, you will have made a virtual tour around the world. Because **Adams Morgan** (18th St. NW from P St. to Columbia Rd.; Metro: Dupont Circle) is a prime dining and entertainment area, you will find the shops mixed in among coffeehouses, pubs, dance clubs, and a large array of ethnic restaurants.

GALLERY CENTRAL: DUPONT CIRCLE

A city where lots of people have lots of money to spend can support a large and varied array of art galleries, which is the case in Washington. No single neighborhood dominates as the city's center for art, but **Dupont Circle** (Metro: Dupont Circle) comes close. More than a dozen galleries—painting, sculpture, photographs, prints—are clustered near the Circle, which not coincidentally is home to the Phillips Collection, one of the country's leading museums of modern art (chapter 5, p. 124). This is the neighborhood in which to go gallery hopping. Dupont Circle, a popular residential neighborhood for gays and lesbians, offers a well-stocked gay/lesbian bookstore.

THE VILLAGE: CAPITOL HILL

The people you see on the streets in Georgetown are likely to come from all over the Washington area. On the not-quite-so-thronged streets of **Capitol Hill** (Metro: Eastern Market), it's the Capitol Hill dwellers themselves who are out and about. On a Saturday—the best day to visit and to shop—the neighborhood takes on the look of a small town, a village as it were. Mixed in with the unusual shops (which include a hot sauce emporium, tribal art works from Tibet and Afghanistan, scented oils from Egypt) you will see the ordinary places—banks, hairdressers, pharmacies, dry cleaners—that serve the needs of residents. This is a fairly prosperous neighborhood of renovated row houses that is home to U.S. senators, representatives, their Capitol staff members, a Supreme Court justice, and lots of lobbyists. Work is just a short walk away.

ON THE EDGE: U STREET/14TH STREET NW

Up, down, and on its way up again—this is the history of **14th and U** (Metro: U Street–African-American Civil War Memorial–Cardozo), a neighborhood defined by the two intersecting streets. In the 1920s and 1930s, U Street was the "Black Broadway," the upbeat nightlife center for African Americans. By the '70s and '80s, it had become a derelict area of homeless street people, abandoned storefronts, and drugs. Now it's on the upswing, a lively entertainment, shopping, and upscale condominium residential area. Look here for funky women's fashions, specialty bookstores, high-styled housewares and furnishings, and a growing number of art galleries.

POTLUCK: DOWNTOWN

For me, downtown is roughly the rectangle formed by E to M streets and 9th to 22nd streets NW—the extended neighborhood edging the White House complex north, east, and west. Unfortunately, the shops are widely scattered. But this is

Shopping Hours & Sales Days

Local shops are generally open daily. Many begin the day at 10am, but others follow at 11am. A few, located in nightspot areas like Adams Morgan, delay opening until noon. Evening closings are similarly staggered. Almost everyone remains open until 6pm, but others continue on until 7, 8, 9, or even 10pm. There's no real pattern. On Sunday, noon to 6pm has become somewhat standard, but there are many exceptions. If you plan to window shop in the neighborhoods I describe in this chapter, don't get going until 11am to avoid too many closed doors.

Long weekend holidays—the Rev. Dr. Martin Luther King's Birthday in January, President's Day in February, Memorial Day in May, Labor Day in September, Columbus Day in October, as well as Veterans Day (Nov 11)—prompt local merchants to hold big sales. Most federal employees get these holidays off. Throughout the year, Lord & Taylor department store runs big sales ads in the *Washington Post* with clip-out, money-saving coupons. Before you shop, check the ads. January and September are the major sale months for almost every store.

where you find Macy's, Washington's only department store; a first-rate shop selling memorabilia from America's presidential election campaigns; a quaint little shop brimming with music boxes from around the world; and a pair of specialty bookshops marketing serious tomes on economics, science, medicine, and engineering.

MUSEUM SHOPS: FOR OFFBEAT GIFTS & SOUVENIRS

As a travel writer, I've plunged into literally hundreds of museums all over the world. Surely, I'm not the only patron who has concluded that in many of them, their shops are more interesting than their exhibits. But I'm not saying this is true in Washington. My point is that museum shops should not be overlooked. In a museum, you can only gaze at something that appeals to you. In a shop, you can pick it up, examine it, and maybe even take it home with you.

One piece of advice: Don't assume that if you see an item you like in one museum that it will pop up in another. The museum stores will reflect the subject matter they're covering and will often carry goods you can't find elsewhere in D.C. This holds true of the many Smithsonian shops as well; each is unique.

The location, hours, and nearest Metro stations for the museums below are detailed in chapter 5. All the museums have shelves of books, fiction and nonfiction, related to the museums' exhibits. And there's lots of kids' stuff, too. Most items are moderately priced, but crafts by name artisans tend to be expensive. Credit cards (AE, MC, V) are welcomed at all of them. You pay no sales tax at the Smithsonian shops, which are nonprofit.

Gifts of Americana

It seems out of character for the repository of the U.S. Constitution and Declaration of Independence. But the **National Archives** ✭ sports a sense of

---

T-Shirt Talk

Each museum markets T-shirts with its own logo. They range in price from $14 to $25 for an adult size (compared to the generic Washington, D.C., tees sold in sidewalk vendor stands at 3 for $10). My advice: Pay extra for a T-shirt touting your favorite museum. The money goes to supporting a very good cause. And talking fashion, the cheap sidewalk vendor tees look cheap; the museum tees are classic, and they will mean more to you in the long run.

---

humor. Along with copies of these basic documents, you also can buy a Benjamin Franklin finger puppet ($4.95). Its "We the People" T-shirts go for $18. For something more serious, take a look at a recent Archives picture book, *Eyewitness: American Originals from the National Archives* ($21). It presents 25 firsthand accounts of historic moments as reported in Archives documents. Example: Thomas Jefferson on diplomatic assignment in France gives his account of the start of the French Revolution in 1789.

Items related to the White House and its occupants, past and present, are offered at the **White House Visitor Center** ✮. We decorate our Christmas tree in part with official White House ornaments. Since 1981, there's been a different one every year—still sold at this shop, operated by the White House Historical Association. My favorite of the ornaments is 2004, depicting a horse-drawn sleigh passing in front of the White House ($16). Other finds: A 500-piece White House puzzle ($15); a delightful White House bookmark, depicting the Marine Band conductor in bright red jacket ($9.95); and a CD featuring presidential campaign songs from 1789 to 1996 ($17).

Fancy items with a historic America theme are displayed at the **Decatur House** ✮. The most appealing souvenirs are the reproductions of White House china. You can buy pieces from the administrations of Washington, Madison, Monroe, Pierce, Grant, and Polk, among others, festooned with flags, eagles, and shields. Cup and saucer go for $66, a bowl for $79, and a teapot for $123. If that's too rich for your blood, there are lovely reproduction prints for $23.

Gifts for Art Lovers

Though most visitors don't know it before they arrive, Washington boasts a huge number of art museums and with them, dozens of museum stores with artsy, often one-of-a-kind goods that are like catnip to art lovers. Some favorites among the many are:

- **Hirshhorn Museum** ✮. Look for books, calendars, greeting cards, note paper, and more featuring the top artists of the 20th century—Picasso, O'Keeffe, de Kooning, Miró, Hopper. Large posters of works in the museum make affordable substitutes for the real thing in your home ($18–$28).
- **National Gallery of Art** ✮✮ (East and West buildings). An extraordinarily rich variety of goods, from artistically designed ties and jewelry to smart toys

for children to hundreds of beautiful art books. And if you enjoy the works of Leonardo da Vinci, Rembrandt, van Gogh, or Degas, you are likely to find an example of their work plastered on every gift item imaginable: greeting cards, postcards, notecards, calendars, soaps, scarves, ties, mugs, and on and on. The best buys are the small (8×11-in.) framed prints of notable works in the museum ($35)—great for that odd wall in your home that needs a splash of color or culture.

◆ At **Phillips Collection** ✿, one of the world's most popular paintings, Renoir's *Luncheon of the Boating Party* has been imprinted on everything imaginable—puzzles, sticky notes, mouse pads, bookmarks, wrapping paper, and mugs. Renoir fans can indulge their *Boating Party* love affair with these souvenirs from where the painting itself hangs.

◆ **American Art Museum.** First, view the elegant striped paintings of Washington-based artist Gene Davis in the galleries (Davis was a leader in the local "Color Field" of painting), then consider purchasing a silk multi-color striped scarf in the museum shop based on his works, an apt souvenir ($45). Another option: Gene Davis notecards ($16). Expensive, but fun to see is the carved wood Civil War chess set with the 6-inch figures of Abraham Lincoln and Jefferson Davis serving as opposing kings and their wives as queens ($350).

Unique Gifts

At the Smithsonian's **National Museum of African Art** ✿, the shelves overflow with quality handmade crafts from throughout the continent. The items that first catch your eye as you enter the large display room are the stuffed, stand-up pink giraffes ($35–$50) from Madagascar. Check out the deep purple *titja* (dyed sisal) baskets from Swaziland ($15); beaded table utensils from South Africa ($25–$40); and colorful *Kisii* soapstone animal carvings from Kenya ($8.50). All make lovely gifts for people with a flair for the exotic.

Zen is the overriding aesthetic at the **Freer Gallery** ✿✿, where you'll find Japanese pottery and origami, picture books featuring Asian paintings, and CDs of traditional music performed by such groups as the Formosa Aboriginal Song & Dance Troupe. Men seeking a gift for a spouse or significant other should take a look at the jade bracelets ($66). The museum's T-shirt, displaying the gold pea-cocks of the museum's famed Peacock Room, rates as the city's most attractive souvenir tee ($20). Next door, the Smithsonian's **Arthur M. Sackler Gallery** ✿✿ displays more Asian art in its huge, contemporary-looking shop—but with more of an emphasis on the jewelry and textiles of India. Pauline bought her mother a beautiful umbrella imprinted with scenes from an ancient Indian painting here ($18) that was a big hit. Chess players might be tempted by the chess set from Syria, handmade in the souks of Damascus and sporting mosaic inlay work ($165).

The prices of the high-quality Native American artifacts displayed on the main floor of the Smithsonian's **National Museum of the American Indian** ✿✿✿ will take your breath away. Its Chesapeake Museum Store features the works of top artists—Navajo rugs, Hopi Kachina dolls, and Pueblo pottery at prices that climb from the low hundreds to as much as $8,500 (for a handmade pot from New Mexico's San Ildefonso pueblo). You can climb to the second floor to visit the more affordable Roanoke Museum Store. You will find handmade Navajo folk art, Zuni fetishes, and colorful Nicaraguan pottery bowls for under $80.

Only American crafts—carvings, glass, jewelry, textiles, pottery—are carried by the Smithsonian's **Renwick Gallery** ✪✪. These are handmade, one-of-a-kind items, often from affordable emerging artists. Sea glass jewelry pieces fashioned with silver wire go for $15 to $125; multicolored hand-blown glass salt and pepper shakers are $65. Along with original works by local artists are a collection of fabulous knockoffs sanctioned by Jacqueline Kennedy Onassis's estate that range in price from about $45 for a pair of earrings up to $250 for earring/necklace pairs. Pauline says if she had any balls coming up, this is where she'd come to accessorize.

Best for Toys

It takes three floors to display all the airplane and spaceship merchandise marketed by the Smithsonian's **National Air and Space Museum** ✪✪✪. Give yourself at least 30 minutes to see it all. On the main floor, the aspiring young pilot in your family might like the jaunty "Top Gun" jacket sporting lots of zippers and official-looking patches ($68). For the toddler, how about a teddy bear dressed in an orange astronaut spacesuit ($12)? Upstairs, find aviation literature; downstairs, toys, airplane models, and spacecraft food—freeze-dried ice cream, anyone ($5)?

Also popular with the young 'uns are the many shops at the Smithsonian's **National Museum of Natural History** ✪✪✪. Stuffed lions, monkeys, lemurs, zebras, giraffes, elephants, bison, cheetahs, hippos, and, of course, those cuddly black-and-white pandas—priced at $14 to $24—are just off the Mammals Gallery. On the mezzanine, the Minerals Museum Store sells lots of rocks—literally. You also can buy costume jewelry patterned on the famed Hope Diamond: a pin ($85), earrings ($62). And kids love the tiny vial of Colorado gold flakes floating in liquid ($8.50). On the museum's lower level, the **Family Store** is the place to buy dinosaur-related items, including a stuffed dino ($24). The **Gallery Store** features affordable crafts from around the world—African baskets, Central American pottery, and Japanese kimonos. More dinosaur items are sold in the **Tricera Shop.**

You'll find mostly kid stuff relating to deep-sea creatures at the **National Aquarium.** Though small and haphazardly organized, the shop does have some finds. Tots go for the stuffed seals and other aquatic animals ($13). I liked the Toobs ($8.95), plastic tubes filled with 10 toy creatures; one features 10 kinds of sharks, another frogs and turtles, a third focuses on the Galápagos Islands.

If I were young again, I'd demand that my parents buy me building blocks from the Smithsonian's **National Building Museum** ✪✪. In particular, I'd point to the Haba blocks (67 pieces, 18 shapes) that would allow me to construct my own personal U.S. Capitol ($55). But that's just the start of the finds here (the shop is often more interesting than the museum itself); it offers terrific educational toys of all sorts and in all price ranges (it's a personal fave for stocking stuffers). Books on architecture and home design are also well represented, as are some whiz-bang kitchen gadgets.

And you don't have to pay the admission fee to shop at the **Spy Museum** ✪✪. It's another irresistible stop for kids between the ages of 8 and 14, what with all the invisible ink pens, hidden cameras, and other spy gadgets. Pauline had to drag her kids bodily out of this store.

And More . . .

Other great bets for unique souvenirs from museums and monuments include:

* Books about Thomas Jefferson and the Founding Fathers at the **Jefferson Memorial**
* Books about Abraham Lincoln and the Civil War at the **Lincoln Memorial**
* Books about Franklin D. Roosevelt, the Depression, and World War II at the **Roosevelt Memorial**
* More books on World War II, with an emphasis on the Holocaust, at the **U.S. Holocaust Memorial Museum** ✿
* American art-related gifts at the **Corcoran Gallery**
* Gifts relating to women in the arts at the **National Museum of Women in the Arts**
* More Native American crafts at the **U.S. Department of the Interior's Indian Craft Shop**
* Music, theater, and dance items at the **Kennedy Center**
* Fine-arts gifts with a French and Russian theme at **Hillwood Museum**

OTHER SPECIALTY STORES

Beyond the museum emporiums and shopping areas, the following stores offer consistent value and are worth a special visit.

ANTIQUES

The most intriguing of Georgetown's numerous antiques shops is **Carling Nichols Chinese Antiques** (Georgetown, 1675 Wisconsin Ave. NW; ☎ 202-338-5600; www.carlingnichols.com; Tues–Sat noon–5pm; Metrobus: 30, 32, 34, 35, 36; AE, MC, V). The three owners have filled their elegant, museum-like boutique with 18th- and 19th-century antiques from Beijing, Shanghai, and Hong Kong. Objects include lacquered cabinets and Han Dynasty painted pottery. Even if you can't afford anything, it's a fun place to browse.

BOOKSTORES

As Pauline says in the nightlife chapter (p. 242), Washington has one of the most vibrant theater scenes in the nation. Serving that theatrical community is **Backstage Inc.** ✿ (Capitol Hill, 545 8th St. SE; ☎ 202-544-5744; http://backstagebooks.com; Mon–Sat 11am–7pm; Metro: Eastern Market; AE, MC, V), a performing arts store. Cramped and untidy, like any backstage, it offers theater books and scripts, as well as makeup, posters, costumes (for sale and rent), dance wear and shoes, wigs, and more.

For the striving economist, the bookstore with many of the answers is the **Info Shop/The World Bank** ✿✿ (Downtown, 18th and Pennsylvania Ave. NW; ☎ 202/458-4500; www.worldbank.org/infoshop; Mon–Fri 9am–5pm; Metro: Farragut West; AE, MC, V). Entire shelves are dedicated to such topics as social and cultural issues, poverty, development economics, environment and pollution prevention, labor, infrastructure, and governance. More shelves focus on individual countries, such as Mexico. They also stock guidebooks, world music CDs, and World Bank T-shirts, though don't wear this latter when the anti-bank demonstrators are in town.

A massive warehouse-size store, **Reiter's Scientific & Professional Books** ★ (Downtown, 2021 K St. NW; ☎ 202/223-3327; www.reiters.com; Mon–Fri 9am–8pm, Sat 10am–6pm, Sun noon–5pm; Metro: Farragut West; AE, MC, V) is for those of a more scientific bent. Every topic from radars and antennas to marine engineering to medicine is extensively covered here.

Basically a gay and lesbian bookstore, **Lambda Rising** ★ (Dupont Circle, 1625 Connecticut Ave. NW; ☎ 202/462-6969; www.lambdarising.com; Sun–Thurs 10am–10pm, Fri–Sat 10am–midnight; Metro: Dupont Circle; AE, MC, V) also offers DVDs, greeting cards, magazines, posters, and humorous gift items. The shelves are packed with quality fiction and learned nonfiction relating to gays and lesbians. But think twice about taking youngsters into this shop; many items displayed, including photo books and magazines, are sexually explicit.

Both **Barnes & Noble** ★★ kids (www.barnesandnoble.com) and **Borders** ★★ kids (www.borders.com) have multiple outlets through the city and serve not only as convenient places to purchase a wide variety of books but also as lecture halls, when authors known and unknown come by for book readings and signings several times a month. There are simply too many outlets to list here, but if you go to one of the above sites, you'll find the location of the store nearest you.

USED BOOKSTORES

An old-timer on Capitol Hill, **Capitol Hill Books** ★ (Capitol Hill, 657 C St. SE; ☎ 202/544-1621; www.capitolhillbooks-dc.com; Mon–Fri 11:30am–6pm, Sat–Sun 9am–6pm; Metro: Eastern Market; MC, V) occupies a three-story town house so stuffed with volumes (hardback and paperback) you wonder if you can manage to squeeze inside. A certain whimsy is apparent. Cookbooks, appropriately, are stacked in what used to be the kitchen; books about the government crowd the bathroom—as in, our leaders are flushing us down the toilet. Upstairs, visitors will find fiction while the main level is devoted to nonfiction. Most standard paperbacks sell for $3.50 or less; a quality paperback goes for $6.50.

Find the bestsellers and the fiction you're looking for in the well-stocked **Idle Time Books** (Adams Morgan, 2467 18th St. NW; ☎ 202/232-4774; daily 11am–11pm; Metro: Woodley Park-Zoo; AE, MC, V). An Adams Morgan institution, it's been around for more than a quarter-century. You'll find most books for less (sometimes a lot less) than half the original price.

A Dupont Circle hot spot, **Second Story Books** ★ (Dupont Circle, 2000 P St. NW; ☎ 202/659-8884; www.secondstorybooks.com; daily 10am–10pm; Metro: Dupont Circle; MC, V) claims to be one of the largest used and rare bookstores in the country. In 1973, owner Allan Stypeck started out with 5,000 books on the second floor of the building. He currently stocks more than 1 million titles in three Washington-area outlets. Stypeck, who has appeared on the PBS program *Antiques Roadshow* appraising rare books, is also co-host of a syndicated radio program called "The Book Guys." The shop's emphasis is on hardback nonfiction in good condition. It tends not to carry bestsellers, favoring less-common titles that are current.

CHILDREN'S APPAREL & TOYS

The **Fairy Godmother** ★★ (Capitol Hill; 319 7th St. SE; ☎ 202/547-5474; Mon–Fri 10am–6pm, Sat 10am–5pm; Metro: Eastern Market; MC, V) is a quirky little shop selling toys, books, and music for kids. Items are stocked based on their

Washington's Best Buys

Washington is an expensive city in which to shop. But you can find bargains. The best buys:

◆ **Consignment fashions:** Substantially marked-down fashion apparel and luxury household goods sold in consignment and other second-hand shops. In a city with an active calendar of charity balls and other high-society functions, the fashionable rotate items in and out of their closets quickly.

◆ **Exotic imports:** Inexpensive ethnic goods—carpets, household accessories, artworks from Asia, Africa, and Latin America. The shop owners often are immigrants marketing items from their native land.

◆ **Used books:** Washingtonians are serious readers, eagerly consuming bestsellers in fiction and nonfiction. The city's used bookstores, selling goods at half off the original price, or less, keep well stocked on the latest literary hits.

educational value and whether they inspire youngsters to be creative. You will find books, of course, and puppets, art supplies, and foreign-language books. Age range: From infants up to about age 16 for books.

Buy clothing for children who never, ever get dirty at **Piccolo Piggies** (Georgetown; 1533 Wisconsin Ave. NW; ☎ 202/333-0123; www.piccolo-piggies. com; Mon–Sat 10am–6pm, Sun 11am–5pm; Metrobus: 30, 32, 34, 35, 36; AE, MC, V). This is a shop for well-heeled moms and dads who are raising a prince or princess. Take a look out of curiosity or for apparel for a special occasion. For less-expensive kid's togs, see the section below on discount clothing stores.

Organic children's clothing for newborns to 8 years is the raison d'etre of **Yiro** ✫ (Georgetown; 3236 P St. NW; ☎ 202/333-0032; www.yirostores.com; Mon–Sat 10am–6pm, Sun 11am–5pm; Metrobus: 30, 32, 34, 35, 36; AE, MC, V). "Organic," according to the manufacturer, means the clothing is made and dyed without the use of harmful chemicals. Yiro is a reasonably priced European chain.

CLOTHING FOR MEN, WOMEN & (SOMETIMES) CHILDREN

I start this section with the lower-cost national chains, and move up (in price) from there.

Discount Stores

Squeezed into every inch of display space, the crowded array of men's, women's, and children's clothing at **T.J. Maxx** ✫✫ (Friendship Heights, 4350 Jenifer St. NW; ☎ 202/237-7616; www.tjmaxx.com; Mon–Sat 9:30am–9pm, Sun 11am–6pm; Metro: Friendship Heights; AE, MC, V) put your bargain-hunting skills to test. You're sure to find good deals. But if you want something specific, you will have to work to find it. This chain of 800 U.S. outlets buys designer overstocks—too many jeans, for example—at steep discounts and passes the savings on to its customers. It claims to have new fashions arriving weekly.

Just across the street, another national discount clothing chain, **Filene's Basement** ✪ (Friendship Heights; 5300 Wisconsin Ave. NW; ☎ 202/966-0208; www.filenesbasement.com; Mon–Sat 9:30am–9pm, Sun noon–6pm; Metro: Friendship Heights; AE, MC, V) offers more bargain-hunting challenges. There's definitely a downscale look to this outlet of the Boston-based chain, which also carries brand-name men's and women's clothing. Utility pipes stretch overhead, and clothing racks are so tightly packed it's a struggle to extract hanging items. But you should find deals. The store tends to be well stocked in men's shirts. I spotted a $75 Ralph Lauren Polo dress shirt for a respectable $45. You might even be lucky enough to show up just after a truck has unloaded racks of sharply discounted Dolce & Gabbana jackets for women. Filene's Basement also has two downtown outlets (529 14th St. NW at F St.; ☎ 202/638-4110; Mon–Sat 9:30am–8pm, Sun noon–5pm; Metro: Metro Center; AE, MC, V; and 1133 Connecticut Ave. NW at L St.; ☎ 202/872-8430; Mon–Sat 9:30am–8pm, Sun noon–5pm; Metro: Farragut North; AE, MC, V). Their drawback is that you don't have the same comparison-shopping options close by that you do at the Friendship Heights location. On the other hand, some dedicated shoppers think the Connecticut Avenue store gets the best stuff. In both downtown shops, as at Friendship Heights, the clothing racks crowd the aisles. But determined hunters will find bargains.

On the opposite side of the street from the Friendship Heights Filene's, compare off-price bargains in women's and men's clothing at **Loehmann's** ✪ (Friendship Heights, 5333 Wisconsin Ave. NW; ☎ 202/362-4733; www.loehmanns.com; Mon–Sat 10am–9:30pm, Sun 11am–7pm; Metro: Friendship Heights). I found a rack of Ralph Lauren long-sleeved Polo pullovers, normally priced at about $70, going for under $45 each in a range of sizes and colors. The men's offerings are limited; the store really seems to focus on hip designs for women at a discount. Loehmann's is noted for its Back Room, where designer fashions for women are advertised at 30% to 60% off department store prices. But like the other discounters, you have to hunt in crowded aisles. Fashions by Theory and Diane von Furstenberg are the best buys here. Women in the know also shop here for coats.

Check out more discount apparel for the whole family next door at **Stein Mart** (Friendship Heights, 5345 Wisconsin Ave. NW; ☎ 202/363-7075; www.steinmart.com; Mon–Sat 10am–9pm, Sun noon–6pm; Metro: Friendship Heights). A century-old chain, it promises prices 20% to 60% less than department stores and specialty boutiques. Its merchandise is a curious mix of table lamps and sweaters, picture frames, and blouses.

Funky (and moderately priced) Italian apparel—especially jeans and T-shirts for men, women, and kids—fills the crowded racks at **Lifestyles U.S.A.** ✪ (Penn Quarter, 410 7th St. NW; ☎ 202/637-2070; daily 10am–9pm; Metro: National Archives–Navy Memorial; AE, MC, V). The place looks like a discount house, but management seems unwilling to admit it. I spotted a fine men's wool suit by Ralph Lauren selling for $299; the original sales tag, crossed out, read "$900."

The Boutiques & Trendier Chains

A decade ago, high-society ladies traveled out of town for glamorous attire. No more. Trendy boutiques dot the city, offering clothes in a number of price ranges.

Cheapest of the bunch is **H&M** (Downtown, 11th and F sts. NW; ☎ 202/347/3306; www.hm.com; Mon–Sat 10am–8pm, Sun noon–6pm; Metro: Metro Center; AE, MC, V), the king of knockoff fashions for men, women, and children. It's a brand that's become well known in the so-called "Blue States," though oddly enough, there are still very few of these stores in the more conservative parts of the country. That may well be because cuts tend to be clingy and necklines low. It's best for teens and folks in their early 20s who have fewer bulges to hide, and who will put up with shoddy construction in the name of fashion (H&M's clothes often hold up for just one season). The store carries everything from evening wear to T-shirts and collaborates annually with high-end designers.

Similar in sizing—it's best for the slim—Spanish chain **Zara** ✪ (Georgetown, 1238 Wisconsin Ave. NW; ☎ 202/944-9797; www.zara.com; Mon–Sat 10am–9pm, Sun noon–6pm; Metrobus: 30, 32, 34, 35, 36; AE, MC, V) stocks a range of colorful, casual clothes for the young and fashion-conscious, as well as dressier ensembles for both men and women.

Classic, well-priced duds for the office for men and women (white shirts and blouses, trim khakis) are the draw at **Club Monaco** ✪✪ (Georgetown, 3235 M St. NW; ☎ 202/965-2118; www.clubmonaco.com; Mon–Thurs 10am–8pm, Fri–Sat 10am–8pm, Sun noon–7pm; Metrobus: 30, 32, 34, 35, 36; AE, MC, V). Not a discounter, the chain markets its label at reasonable prices. Its sale items rate high with savvy shoppers in this office-oriented city.

Jeans are the draw at **Up Against the Wall** ✪✪ (Georgetown; 3219 M St. NW; ☎ 202/337-9316; www.upagainstthewall.com; Mon–Thurs 10am–9pm, Fri–Sat 10am–10pm, Sun 11am–7pm; Metrobus: 30, 32, 34, 35, 36; AE, MC, V). The place is packed with "premium denim," a trio of helpful clerks informed me—priced at $20 to $200 a pair. Lots of decorative trim sets these jeans apart.

The under-21 crowd will appreciate the funky/grunge look of **Commander Salamander** (Georgetown, 1420 Wisconsin Ave. NW; ☎ 202/337-2265; Mon–Thurs 10am–9pm, Fri–Sat 10am–10pm, Sun 11am–7pm; Metrobus: 30, 32, 34, 35, 36; AE, MC, V). Want to look totally disheveled? Outfit yourself here.

Slacker clothing also makes an appearance at **Urban Outfitters** ✪ (Penn Quarter, 737 7th St. NW; ☎ 202/737-0259; www.urbanoutfitters.com; Mon–Sat 9am–10pm, Sun 11am–7pm; Metro: National Archives–Navy Memorial; AE, MC, V), alongside dressier outfits. The chain displays affordable copies of hip, high-fashion casual wear for the under-30 crowd headed out for a Saturday night on the town along with gift items such as mirrors, candles, pillows, and other knickknacks.

Comfortable Attire for Women

My wife's favorite clothing shop is **Pua Naturally** ✪✪✪ (Penn Quarter, 701 Pennsylvania Ave. NW; ☎ 202/347-4543; www.pua-naturally.com; Mon noon–6pm, Tues–Wed noon–7pm, Thurs–Fri noon–8pm, Sat 1–7pm, Sun 1–7:30pm; Metro: National Archives–Navy Memorial; AE, MC, V). Look for moderately priced women's textiles and designs from India, Nepal, and Afghanistan. Exotic in look, and comfortably loose fitting, every item is made from natural fabrics.

Something a little different is the marketing ideology that motivates **Art & Soul** ✫✫✫ (Capitol Hill, 225 Pennsylvania Ave. SE; ☎ 202/548-0105; www. artandsouldc.com; Mon–Wed and Fri–Sat 11am–6pm, Thurs 11am–7pm; Metro: Capitol South; AE, MC, V). Contemporary wearable art and jewelry for women and a few crafts are the boutique's mainstays. It sells only limited production work that is customarily found in crafts galleries, buying from individual designers from all over the country. Again, the clothing is generally loose fitting, unique, and a little funky. Not too expensive.

Consignment/Vintage Clothing Shops

Aimed at bargain hunters, **Annie Creamcheese Vintage Boutique** ✫✫ (Georgetown, 3279 M St. NW; ☎ 202/298-5555; www.anniecreamcheese.com; Mon–Wed 11am–7pm, Thurs–Sat 11am–8pm, Sun noon–6pm; Metrobus: 30, 32, 34, 35, 36; AE, MC, V) buys secondhand fashions for women (Gucci, Pucci, Dior) made from the 1940s to the 1980s, and sells them at sharply discounted rates. The really good stuff in the high-end department begins at about $100 and climbs into the thousands for a fur coat. The "mod" department—clothing from the '60s—offers items from $5 to $75. Given its Georgetown location, the store gets first-rate items, many barely worn. You may also want to browse **Christ Child Opportunity Shop** (p. 238), a consignment shop that specializes in homewares instead of clothing.

For contemporary bargains in women's fashions, don't miss the second-floor showroom of **Secondi** ✫ (Dupont Circle, 1702 Connecticut Ave. NW btw. R. St. and Florida Ave.; ☎ 202/667-1122; www.secondi.com; Mon–Tues and Sat 11am–6pm, Wed–Fri 11am–7pm, Sun 1–5pm; Metro: Dupont Circle; AE, MC, V). A consignment house, it receives "good as new" secondhand designer clothing. To be sold, items—often from the closets of society ladies—must be no more than 2 years old and in fashion.

Another excellent source for upscale women's wear at bargain-basement prices is the **Second Affair Consignment Shop** (Adams Morgan, 1904 18th St. NW; ☎ 202/265-1829; Tues–Fri 11:30am–6pm, Sat 10am–5pm; Metro: Dupont Circle; AE, MC, V). Lots of used (but still usable) designer clothing fills the racks of this small shop. You will have to hunt to find something you like in your size. But management notes that items that may have originally carried $3,000 price tags go for as little as $300. But you will find plenty under $100 too.

ETHNIC CRAFTS & CLOTHING
African/Middle Eastern

For Middle Eastern crafts and books on Middle Eastern affairs, take a look at **American Educational Trust/Palestinian Arts and Crafts Trust** (Adams Morgan, 1902 18th St. NW; ☎ 202/939-6050; www.amedtrust.org; Mon–Fri 9am–5:30pm; Metro: Dupont Circle; MC, V). The organization, which publishes a magazine called *The Washington Report on Middle East Affairs,* says its function is to "promote the cause of peace in Palestine." It also supports the work of Palestinian artisans in the West Bank, Gaza, and elsewhere in the Middle East. Along with issue-oriented literature, it sells hand-embroidered cloth from Palestinian refugee camps and colorful pottery from Jerusalem.

West African attire, jewelry, and accessories for men and women are the focus of **Kobos Afrikan Clothiers** ✰ (Adams Morgan, 2444 18th St. NW; ☎ 202/332-9580; www.kobosclothiers.com; Mon–Sat 11am–8pm; Metro: Woodley Park–Zoo; AE, MC, V). Beautifully colored and patterned, the mostly West African items are made in Ghana for everyday wear. Customers come from the local African community and from Africans living elsewhere in the United States. Peace Corps volunteers and State Department diplomats are known to drop in before flying off to their assigned post.

Lovely Ethiopian homeland attire and fabrics are the focus at **Yerus** (2204 18th St. NW; ☎ 202/483-7017; Mon–Sat 11am–8pm; Metro: Woodley Park–Zoo; AE, MC, V). The elegant little shop markets modern and traditional Ethiopian wear for men and women to the local Ethiopian community. Made in Ethiopia, the clothing is worn at church, weddings, and other important occasions.

Asian

Inspect one of the East Coast's largest collections of Buddha statuary at **Designer Art & Craft USA** ✰ (Dupont Circle, 1709 Connecticut Ave. NW; ☎ 202/462-5489; daily 10am–8pm; Metro: Dupont Circle; AE, MC, V). The shop looks small only from the outside; inside the showroom spills over into an adjacent building. The focus is on handicrafts—rugs, jewelry, furniture, chess sets, shawls—from 20 countries in Central and South Asia. Rugs are sorted by size, which is a convenience to customers. And the prices are quite reasonable.

For martial arts weapons, clothing, and other items, go to Chinatown's **Kung Fu Gift Shop** (Penn Quarter–Chinatown, 815 7th St. NW; ☎ 202/737-1919; daily 9:30am–8pm; Metro: National Archives–Navy Memorial; MC, V). The hole-in-the-wall shop is redolent of China. So is its neighbor, **Da Hsin Trading Co.** (Penn Quarter–Chinatown, 811 7th St. NW; ☎ 202/789-4020; www.dahsin.com; Mon–Sat 9:30am–7:30pm, Sun 10am–7:30pm; Metro: National Archives–Navy Memorial; MC, V). Two rooms are crammed full of Chinese pottery, jewelry, fans, furniture, foods, herbs, and other items. You will think you are in Asia.

All things Japanese fill the shelves of **Ginza** (Dupont Circle, 1721 Connecticut Ave. NW; ☎ 202/332-7000; Mon–Wed 11am–7pm, Thurs–Sat 11am–7:30pm, Sun noon–6pm; Metro: Dupont Circle; AE, MC, V). Look for teapots and cups, lacquerware, ceramics, jewelry, and a large selection of men's and women's kimonos. I've worn Japanese cotton kimonos for years, finding the wraparound style comfortable. I also appreciate their drape-to-the-floor length when I step outside on a winter morning to pick up the newspaper.

Peruvian Styles

Comfortable, festive, sophisticated and not at all "costumey" clothing is the lure at **Peruvian Connection** ✰✰✰ (950 F. St. NW; ☎ 202/737-4405; www.peruvianconnection.com; Mon–Wed and Fri–Sat 10am–6pm, Thurs 10am–7pm, Sun noon–5pm; Metro: Metro Center; AE, MC, V). Along with intricately embroidered jackets and skirts, often in beautiful jewel-tones or rich neutrals, are T-shirts and basics, with just a bit of extra character. In the basement are all the sale items and discounts can be steep. A wonderful shop for all sizes.

The museum-quality work of Peru's master artisans is displayed in the upscale gallery **Toro Mata** ✰✰ (Adams Morgan, 2410 18th St. NW; ☎ 202/232-3890;

www.toromata.com; Tues–Fri noon–10pm, Sat 9am–10pm, Sun noon–6pm; Metro: Woodley Park–Zoo; AE, MC, V). Browse folk art, furniture, decorating accessories, and pottery.

Other International Items

A shop with a conscience (no child labor; safe and healthy working conditions): Purchase international crafts and at the same time aid the artisans of a developing country at **Pangea Artisan Market & Café at the International Finance Corporation** ✪✪✪ (Downtown, 2121 Pennsylvania Ave. NW; ☎ 202/8PANGEA; www.pangeamarket.com; Mon–Fri 7am–7pm, Sat 11am–5pm; Metro: Farragut West or Foggy Bottom; AE, MC, V). The large, museum-like store sells items from 30 countries, providing the artisans a fair-priced market they couldn't develop on their own. This is the place to find unusual quality items at affordable prices: Metal figurines in native costume from Burkina Faso cost $15. Pottery tree ornaments from Bolivia are $13. Silk scarves from India start at $30. Stuffed children's fantasy animals from Kenya are $40.

You can't miss **Silk Road** ✪✪ (Capitol Hill, 311–315 7th St. SE; ☎ 202/543-1705; www.wovenhistory.com; Tues–Sun 10am–6pm; Metro: Eastern Market; MC, V). Oriental rugs, pottery, and other Asian goods spill out the front door and down to the street—as they might in the old country. For proprietor Mehmet Yalcin, that was Turkey. He claims to buy in places "nobody knows exist"—from Tibet, Afghan tribes, and from a dozen Asian countries—which allows him to beat his competitors in price.

For its sheer abundance of exotic Asian and African goods, no place is as much fun to explore as **Village Art & Craft** ✪✪ (Georgetown, 1353 Wisconsin Ave. NW; ☎ 202/333-1968; Mon–Sat 10am–7pm; Metrobus: 30, 32, 34, 35, 36; AE, MC, V). Tapestries, drums, fabrics, clothing, jewelry, Pashmina shawls, porcelains, and other goods from more than 32 countries are crammed into the slender store. Look here for belly-dance supplies (something you might not find at home). This is the place to find lots of home decorating objects at bargain prices.

International Foods

Curiosities await at **Cost Plus World Market** (Friendship Heights, 5335 Wisconsin Ave. NW; ☎ 202/244-8720; www.worldmarket.com; Mon–Sat 9am–9pm, Sun 10am–7pm; Metro: Friendship Heights). Find food products from around the world (Italian gnocchi, Australian ginger beer, Jamaican coffee) side by side with toys, rugs, glassware, and dining room furniture produced around the world. It's a good place to find offbeat, inexpensive gifts for friends and family back home.

Small and crowded, **Khartoum Grocery** (Adams Morgan, 2116 18th St. NW; ☎ 202/265-7100; Mon–Sat 10am–9pm, Sun 10am–7pm; Metro: Dupont Circle; MC, V) markets Middle Eastern and African goods. You probably won't want or need any of this stuff, but it's fun to look at the Egyptian candies, bags of rice from Pakistan, Turkish cheese, Shanghai tea, packages of dried figs from Turkey, and boxes of Egyptian corn flour. Incense atmosphere to the shop.

More scents of Africa greet you as you enter an exotic Ethiopian mart called **Addisu Gebeya** (Adams Morgan, 2202 18th St. NW; ☎ 202/986-6013; daily 9am–8pm; MC, V). Definitely a homespun kind of place, it displays barrels of ground wheat and barley (buy by the scoop); honey from Egypt; tapes, CDs, and

A Dupont Circle Gallery Walk

Art fanciers can get a glimpse of Washington's lively art scene on a short walk near Dupont Circle. Begin at Connecticut Avenue and R Street NW. This delightful, tree-shaded residential street is home to a cluster of galleries, all operating out of architecturally interesting town houses. Maybe the loveliest interior—lots of dark wood in the Victorian style—is the showcase for contemporary art and works by living artists at **Marsha Mateyka Gallery** (2012 R St. NW; ☎ 202/328-0088; www.marshamateyka gallery.com; Wed–Sat 11am–5pm; AE, MC, V). One of her artists is Sam Gilliam, a leader in the Washington Color Field school of art; her only exception to living artists is Gene Davis, another member of the Washington Color Field. For a brief description of the Color Field, see the Hirshhorn Museum, chapter 5, p. 115. On the next block, climb the steps to **Alex Gallery** (2106 R St. NW; ☎ 202/667-2599; www.alexgalleries. com; Tues–Sat 11am–5pm; AE, MC, V), which shows modern American and European painting, sculpture, and works on paper. Step down to **Gallery A**, a separate arm of Alex Gallery, which features emerging (read: less expensive) artists.

See the work of Washington-area artists (usually) at **Studio Gallery** (2108 R St. NW; ☎ 202/232-8734; www.studiogallerydc.com; Wed–Thurs 1–7pm, Fri–Sat 1–8pm, Sun 1–5pm; AE, MC, V). Artist-owned, the gallery features the work of 37 local, professional artists in solo and group exhibits. Don't miss the outdoor sculpture garden.

As much a museum as gallery, the **Washington Printmakers Gallery** (1732 Connecticut Ave. NW; ☎ 202/265-9235; www.washingtonprint makers.com; Tues–Sat 12:30–5:30pm; cash only) celebrates one medium: hand-pulled printmaking. Represented are a wide-range of well-respected contemporary artists.

Double back to 21st Street; turn right one block to Hillyer Place. Turn left on Hillyer to **Jane Haslem Gallery** (2025 Hillyer Place NW; ☎ 202/ 232-4644; www.janehaslemgallery.com; Wed–Sat noon–5pm; AE, MC, V). Haslem specializes in American art—paintings, prints, drawings—from the second half of the 20th century.

books from Ethiopia; and cellophane bags filled with what look to be small twigs; the label says GESHO. I had to ask. "Hops for homemade beer," the proprietor informed me.

Less exotic, but no less tasty treats await at **Cowgirl Creamery** (919 F St. NW; ☎ 202/393-6880; www.cowgirlcreamery.com; Mon–Fri 7:30am–7pm, Sat 11am–7pm; Metro: Gallery Place–Chinatown; AE, MC, V), an outpost of the famed California cheese store. Artisanal cheeses from just about every animal that has hooves and gives milk (even water buffalo!) will be on sale here, including many hard-to-find cheeses from Europe. You probably won't be able to take these home, but, boy, is this an awesome place to stop for a snack.

GALLERIES

Moderately priced paintings and prints, many of them by emerging Washington artists, are displayed at **Attitude Exact Gallery** (Capitol Hill, 739 8th St. SE; ☎ 202/546-7186; Tues–Sat 11am–7pm; Metro: Eastern Market; AE, MC, V). Many of the works are Africa- and African-American themed.

Wouldn't we all like to take travel photos like this? When you visit his tiny shop, **Claude Taylor Photography Gallery** (Dupont Circle, 1627 Connecticut Ave. NW; ☎ 202/518-4000; www.travelphotography.net; daily 9am–10pm; Metro: Dupont Circle; AE, MC, V), you're likely to find Taylor himself selling color prints of his travel photos. He has visited 20 countries and most major U.S. cities, all represented in his stock. Framed photos ($40–$120) hang on the wall; matted photos ($20–$60) fill easy-to-search baskets.

Climb a long flight of stairs to the city's largest cooperative art gallery, **Touchstone Gallery** (Penn Quarter, 406 7th St. NW; ☎ 202/347-2787; www. touchstonegallery.com; Wed–Fri 11am–5pm, Sat–Sun noon–5pm; Metro: National Archives–Navy Memorial; AE, MC, V). More than 30 artists are represented, displaying paintings, sculptures, textiles, and pottery. Prices soar into the thousands, but here and there you might find something affordable. On my last visit, I fell for an exquisitely shaped stoneware vase entitled "Rain Bottle," which cost $170.

GIFTS

My favorite Georgetown store, featuring high-quality handmade crafts from leading American artisans, is **Appalachian Spring** (Georgetown, 1415 Wisconsin Ave. NW; ☎ 202/337-5780; Mon–Sat 10am–6pm, Sun noon–6pm; Metrobus: 30, 32, 34, 35, 36; AE, MC, V). The crafts—wood, glass, metal, fabric, pottery—are beautifully displayed; the showroom resembles a classy museum. Despite the name, the crafts come from all over the country. Prices are high, but looking is free.

Washington's favorite novelty store for its goofy gadgets and whimsical gifts is the **Chocolate Moose** (Downtown, 1743 L St. NW; ☎ 202/463-0992; www. chocolatemoosedc.com; Mon–Sat 10am–6pm; Metro: Farragut North; AE, MC, V). Buy comical greeting cards, miniature windup toys, holiday-related items (masks at Halloween, chocolate turkeys at Thanksgiving, hula Santas at Christmas). I fill my wife's Christmas stocking with this kind of nonsense stuff. There's nothing expensive in this shop except the Leonidas chocolates from Belgium.

Step downstairs from the street to the shop for the **Human Rights Campaign** (Dupont Circle, 1629 Connecticut Ave. NW; ☎ 202/232-8621; www.hrc.org; Mon–Thurs 11am–9pm, Fri–Sat 11am–10pm, Sun 11am–7pm; Metro: Dupont Circle; AE, MC, V). The organization, which works for equal rights for lesbians, gays, bisexuals, and transgender individuals, operates this store. It sells T-shirts, sweatshirts, coffee mugs, and lots of other stuff carrying its equality logo—a gold equal sign against a blue background. A big seller is the Dupont Circle T-shirt. Proceeds help fund the organization's work.

Let's get, well, nostalgic at the **Music Box Center** ✪ (Downtown, 1920 I St. NW; ☎ 202/783-9399; Mon–Fri 10am–4:30pm, Sat 10am–3pm; Metro: Farragut West; MC, V). This is a delightful store, if somewhat old-fashioned, filled with about 1,500 music boxes—large and small, expensive and not, new and antique—most of them different. They come from around the world; feature figures of dancers, soldiers, angels, animals; play marches, operas, rock, pop, and more; and range in price from $17 to $6,000. Not to be sexist, moms and young daughters will love this shop. Personally, I like the whirling merry-go-rounds.

A self-proclaimed anti-tourist gift shop—"not the stuff you find where the tour buses pull up"—**Pulp** (1803 14th St. NW; ☎ 202/462-2857; www.pulpdc. com; Mon–Fri 11am–7pm, Sat 10am–7pm, Sun 10am–5pm; Metro: U Street–African-American Civil War Memorial; AE, MC, V) is a little naughty and politically incorrect. It stocks such items as small tins of mints reading, for example, "Every time you masturbate, God kills a kitten,"—and this is one of the less risqué ones. Residents of blue states (or foreign visitors) might go for the (now-on-sale) T-shirt proclaiming "Bush's Last Day 01-20-09." Pulp has a second store on Capitol Hill (303 Pennsylvania Ave. SE; ☎ 202/543-1924; www.pulpdc.com; Mon–Fri 9am–7pm, Sat 10am–7pm, Sun 10am–5pm; Metro: Capitol South; AE, MC, V), which has an especially large stock of unusual greeting cards. No Hallmark clichés in this card and gift shop; it seeks out small card companies with limited distribution, including GLBT-themed cards. Most gift items are under $20.

The name of this shop with two branches more than hints at the merchandise. It's the **Pleasure Place** (Dupont Circle, 1710 Connecticut Ave. NW; ☎ 202/483-3297; Metro: Dupont Circle and Georgetown; 1063 Wisconsin Ave. NW; ☎ 202/333-8570; www.pleasureplace.com; Mon–Tues 10am–10pm, Wed–Sat 10am–midnight, Sun noon–7pm; Metrobus: 30, 32, 34, 35, 36; AE, MC, V), an erotic boutique selling sexual toys, apparel, DVDs, books, and games—for straights and gay/lesbians. In business for a quarter-century, the shops are an indication that legislation isn't the only thing Washington thinks about.

FOR FIDO & FLUFFY

Who is your best friend? Well, remember him or her at **Doggie Style, Boutique & Pet Spa** (Adams Morgan, 1825 18th St. NW; ☎ 202/667-0595; www.doggie stylebakery.com; Mon–Wed and Fri–Sat 11am–7pm, Thurs 11am–8pm, Sun noon–6pm; Metro: Dupont Circle; MC, V). Pick up homemade, all-natural treats for the pooch you left with neighbors. No bargains here, but then would you really want to go cheap on a gift for your best friend?

Don't these pet stores come up with clever names? **Pawticulars** (Capitol Hill, 407-A 8th St. SE; ☎ 202/546-7387; www.pawticulars.com; Mon–Thurs noon–7pm, Fri 10am–7pm, Sat 9am–6pm, Sun noon–6pm; Metro: Eastern Market; AE, MC, V) is another pet boutique and bakery where you can also pick up a souvenir gift for the little friend you left at home. Brightly decorated cookies and other treats might tempt you to nibble. Despite the appearance—more to appeal to the pet owners than the pets themselves, I suspect—the frosted items are made of healthy, organic ingredients.

HOUSEHOLD GOODS/FURNISHINGS

Examine the handiwork of French and Italian artists at **A Mano** (Georgetown, 1677 Wisconsin Ave. NW; ☎ 202/298-7200; www.amano.bz; Mon–Sat 10am–6pm, Sun 10am–5pm; Metro: 30, 32, 34, 35, 36; AE, MC, V). Its well-stocked showroom and elegant courtyard garden overflow with bright, colorful ceramic tableware, textiles, and other decorative accessories. Every summer we fill a hanging pot from A Mano in our patio garden with marigolds, and it's always a tossup whether the pot or the blooms provide the best show.

Check out the cool furniture designs at **Apartment Zero** (Penn Quarter, 406 7th St. NW; ☎ 202/628-4067; www.apartmentzero.com; Wed–Sat 11am–6pm, Tues and Sun noon–5pm; Metro: National Archives–Navy Memorial; AE, MC, V). Colorful and hip, the shop strives to be the cutting edge of contemporary design. Initially it concentrated on the works of American and Canadian designers. But it has expanded to include Dutch, German, Italian, and Scandinavian furnishings. Penn Quarter has seen a boom in condo apartment construction since the opening of the Verizon Center. It's like stepping into a contemporary art museum.

Cutting-edge contemporary furniture is also the focus at **Skynear & Company** (Adams Morgan, 2122 18th St. NW; ☎ 202/797-7160; www.skynearonline.com; Mon–Fri 11am–7pm, Sat 11am–8pm, Sun noon–6pm; Metro: Dupont Circle; AE, VC, V). Lots of Italian and Danish pieces on three floors. Those icons on the stairway are all that remain from the store's debut 2 decades ago selling mostly goods from Egypt and the Middle East. Informed sources (not connected to the store) tell me that although the furniture isn't cheap, it's priced lower than many of its competitors in the city.

Real bargains for lucky shoppers are always a possibility at **Christ Child Opportunity Shop** ✪✪ (Georgetown, 1427 Wisconsin Ave. NW; ☎ 202/333-6635; Mon–Fri 10am–5pm, Sat noon–4pm; Metrobus: 30, 32, 34, 35, 36; cash only). Given its upscale Georgetown location, the consignment shop gets high-quality household items—silver, china, crystal, porcelain, decorative objects—and everything is at least 50% off its original price. Lots of unwanted, unused wedding gifts are left here to be sold, as are the first wife's furnishings when the new wife moves in. Proceeds benefit needy children.

Everything for the tabletop—colorful and mostly inexpensive—fills to overflowing in an odd but delightful little shop called **Go Mama Go!** (U St. Corridor, 1809 14th St. NW; ☎ 202/299-0850; www.gomamago.com; Mon noon–7pm, Tues–Sat 11am–7pm, Sun noon–5pm; Metro: U Street–African-American Civil War Memorial; MC, V). The interior looks like a flea market, with piles of tabletop items—attractive Japanese serving dishes, Austrian candles, painted glassware, pottery—all stacked high atop tables or in baskets.

On a street of new condos, there's got to be a kitchen store catering to apartment dwellers, and it's **Home Rule** ✪✪ (U St. Corridor, 1807 14th St. NW; ☎ 202/797-5544; www.homerule.com; Mon–Sat 11am–7pm, Sun noon–5:30pm; Metro: U Street–African-American Civil War Memorial; AE, MC, V). The name means a lot to longtime Washington residents. The U.S. Congress okayed the Home Rule Act of 1973, allowing residents to vote for a Mayor and City Council. Previously, an appointed commission governed. Look here for high-style kitchen appliances and utensils (Italian and other European designs) for chic urban dwellers. Items tend to be of moderate size, just right for small spaces. This is the store for apartment dwellers with limited kitchen storage space.

My favorite cooking wares shop, as much fun to browse as it is to buy, is **Sur La Table** ✪✪✪ (Friendship Heights, 5211 Wisconsin Ave. NW; ☎ 202/237-0375; www.surlatable.com; Mon–Wed and Sat 10am–6pm, Thurs–Fri 10am–8pm, Sun noon–6pm; Metro: Friendship Heights; AE, MC, V). Much larger than Home Rule, it carries all the gadgets you might buy if you have plenty of kitchen cabinet space to store them. If you need something for the kitchen or for your dining room table, you're likely to find it here: pots, pans, glassware, painted Italian bowls, appliances, and table linens. I often stuff my wife's Christmas stocking with handy, inexpensive gadgets, like an olive prong (to remove olives from a jar) or asparagus "tweezers" (to serve cooked stalks of asparagus). The store, part of a national Seattle-based chain, is packed full of the useful and the whimsical—a real treat for browsers. Catch the clearance sales in January and July for the best buys.

JEWELRY

The marquee of what once was the Georgetown Theater, a movie house, now announces the **National Jewel Center** (Georgetown, 1351 Wisconsin Ave. NW; ☎ 202/333-5555; Tues–Sat 11am–6pm, Sun 12:30–5:30pm; Metrobus: 30, 32, 34, 35, 36). Inside, 20 individual vendors operate stalls selling watches, rings, gold and silver chains, and similar adornments. This is Washington's modest equivalent of the diamond districts in Manhattan and downtown Los Angeles. Stall keepers assure me they sell at a discount. If you know jewelry you could find a bargain. Be sure of the quality of any gem before you spend big money.

Part museum, part shop, is the **Bead Museum Store** (Penn Quarter, 400 7th St. NW; ☎ 202/624-4500; www.beadmuseumdc.org; Wed–Sat 11am–4pm, Sun 1–4pm; Metro: National Archives–Navy Memorial; MC, V). The museum, opened in 1995, explores the history and the cultural aspects of bead-making and design from around the world. Its small shop sells beadwork of all kinds—including Native American and African—as well as publications dealing with beadwork. Pop in for a look.

To create a beaded necklace or bracelet for yourself, visit **Beadazzled** ✫ (Dupont Circle, 1507 Connecticut Ave. NW; ☎ 202/265-2323; www.beadazzled. net; Mon–Sat 10am–8pm, Sun 11am–6pm; Metro: Dupont Circle; AE, MC, V). It displays beads from around the world from 10¢ each for simple colored glass to $38 each for antique Venetian trade beads.

MUSIC STORES: CDS, RECORDS & INSTRUMENTS

Pop music fans will want to plunge into the used and new CD and LP stacks at **Crooked Beat Records** ✫✫ (Adams Morgan, 2318 18th St. NW; ☎ 202/483-BEAT; www.crookedbeat.com; Mon 2–9pm, Tues–Wed noon–9pm, Thurs–Sat noon–10pm; Sun noon–7pm; Metro: Woodley Park–Zoo; MC, V). This well-stocked, step-down hole-in-the-wall specializes in hard-to-find independent label music and obscure major label releases "outside the radar of the mainstream." As a souvenir, take home a CD featuring a Washington group. Ask the knowledgeable staff to help you choose a D.C. winner.

Look for other hard-to-find CDs at **Melody Record Shop** ✫ (Dupont Circle, 1623 Connecticut Ave. NW; ☎ 202/232-4002; www.melodyrecords.com; Sun–Thurs 10am–10pm, Fri–Sat 10am–11pm; Metro: Dupont Circle; AE, MC, V). Fans love the wide selection of everything, including a large stock of classical works, and a staff that also knows a lot about contemporary music. If you go for the classical CDs, check out the sales items at the store entrance, and then head for the rear where you find the bulk of the classics.

Capitol Hill's Historic Market

Capitol Hill's prime shopping attraction, a community institution and village center since 1873, is **Eastern Market** 55 (Capitol Hill, 7th St. and North Carolina Ave. SE.; www.easternmarketdc.com; Tues–Sat 7am–6pm, Sun 9am–4pm; Metro: Eastern Market). A slender, block-long brick structure with a high vaulted ceiling, its crowded interior is filled with vendors selling fresh meat, fish, poultry, fruits and vegetables, cheeses, and baked goods. On the outside, a cast-iron open-air shed shelters the Saturday and Sunday **Farmers Market**. In late summer, ripe aromatic local peaches are stacked high, and bouquets of fresh-cut flowers add a festive note. Lots of vendors set out plates of sliced fruit and vegetables so you can sample before buying. On Saturday, there's also a **Crafts Fair** from 10am to 5pm. Dozens of artisans tempt you with handmade (mostly) jewelry, pottery, clothing, prints, furniture, and toys. On Sunday, the crafts folks give way to a **Flea Market** from 10am to 5pm at which practically anything might be for sale, usually at a good price. Look for small furniture pieces, tableware, books, gardening tools, and assorted knickknacks. And just across 7th Street, a competing crafts fair and flea market, operating on the grounds of a public school, adds 50 or more vendors to be checked out.

As we went to press, the Market was scheduled to reopen in June 2009.

Ignore the ear-shattering beats pulsating from inside and dive into **Ritmo Latino** ✪✪ (Adams Morgan, 1775 Columbia Rd. NW; ☎ 202/299-0411; www.ritmo latino.com; daily 9:15am–10pm; Metro: Woodley Park–Zoo; AE, MC, V). A large, color-splashed shop in the heart of the city's Hispanic neighborhood, it stocks the latest pop CDs, videos, and other entertainment from Mexico and Central and South America. English-speaking staff members can help you choose from covers emblazoned with Spanish and Portuguese names. Every time I've ventured inside, the hip-swinging, finger-snapping customers caught up in the music seem to be creating a sort of mini-fiesta.

Students of the guitar, and anyone curious about guitars, must make a pilgrimage up the steep, worn steps to the venerable **Guitar Shop** ✪✪ (Dupont Circle, 1216 Connecticut Ave. NW; ☎ 202/331-7333; www.theguitarshop.com; Mon–Fri noon–7pm, Sat 11am–6pm; Metro: Dupont Circle; MC, V). More than 80 years old, it may be America's oldest shop designing, selling, repairing, and teaching guitars. In its incredibly cramped and cluttered second-floor space, it maintains a catalog of 2,000 guitars (not all of them within the shop), some dating back to the 1700s. They are priced from $200 to $200,000.

POLITICAL MEMORABILIA

Political junkies and students of American history won't want to miss **Political Americana** ✪✪✪ (Downtown, 1331 Pennsylvania Ave. NW; ☎ 202/737-7730; www.politicalamericana.com; Mon–Sat 9am–8pm, Sun 10am–6pm; Metro: Metro

Center; AE, MC, V), which overflows with presidential political memorabilia: campaign buttons, posters, bumper stickers, and more. Buttons for recent candidates (winners and losers) go for as little as five for $10. But the price increases as you delve back in history; a William Jennings Bryan campaign ribbon (he was a three-time loser in 1896, 1900, and 1908) is $75. You can also buy official presidential items, such as the White House cufflinks and tie clasps that presidents give as a thank-you to their aides and supporters (who in turn sell them to the shop) or playing cards with the Air Force One or Air Force Two logo. Cufflinks go for $195 to $1,200, depending on the president. Signed White House Christmas cards are another big seller. The shop claims to have items from most presidencies.

SPORTING GOODS & APPAREL

Find active sports attire at affordable prices at **City Sports** (Penn Quarter, 727 7th St. NW and 1111 19th St. NW btw. L and M sts.; ☎ 202/638-3115; www.citysports. com; Mon–Sat 10am–9:30pm, Sun 11am–8pm; National Archives–Navy Memorial; AE, MC, V). Items in this well-organized shop are displayed by sport: tennis, hiking, boxing, soccer, running, workout, and so on. As someone who buys this stuff, I find the layout a real convenience.

I buy my running shoes at **New Balance DC** (Friendship Heights, 5301 Wisconsin Ave. NW; ☎ 202/237-1840; www.newbalancedc.com; Mon–Sat 10am–8pm, Sun noon–5pm; Metro: Friendship Heights) because the staff seems to make a special effort to assure I get a proper fit.

STATIONERY

A small shop run by the owners, **Just Paper & Tea** ✦✦ (Georgetown, 3232 P St. NW; ☎ 202/333-9141; www.justpaperandtea.com; Tues–Sat 10am–5pm; Metrobus: 30, 32, 34, 35, 36; AE, MC, V) sells beautiful, and not-so-expensive, handmade paper from Italy and Japan. If you want to send a very special note, this is the place to buy paper and envelope. The packaging will so wow the recipient, your words will be superfluous. In addition to "Just Paper," you also can buy your choice of more than 30 loose teas from India, China, and Japan.

10 Washington After Dark

Whether you're a cultural maven or happening hipster, you've got plenty of choices in the nightlife department

By Pauline Frommer

WHEN PROHIBITION WAS REPEALED IN 1933, PRESIDENT FRANKLIN Delano Roosevelt decided he wanted to pen the new liquor laws for the District personally. Hoping to move away from the rowdy, even bawdy "old-time saloons" that had prompted the liquor ban in the first place, he drafted a set of rules meant to "civilize" the scene. No one was to be allowed to drink standing up. Beer could be served to those sitting on bar stools but to order anything with distilled liquor, the patron had to take a table and order from a waitress. And so on.

Much to his chagrin, his regulations did not become a model for the rest of the United States, as he'd intended. But they certainly did set a tone for the Capital's nightlife, one that outlasted Roosevelt's original regulations. Even today, I think you'll find the nightlife here to be just a hair more muted than it is in other cities of similar size. Oh, sure you can still find collegiate-style hijinks and even binge drinking in Adams Morgan; and there are dance clubs where partyers whip themselves into a lather. But for the most part, the scene in Washington, D.C., is more genteel than, say, New York, London, or other world cities. Yes, you can find a party (and I'll tell you how to do so below), but you might have to look a little harder, especially if you want to keep the good times going beyond happy hour.

Instead, much of the after-dark energy in D.C. is focused on the arts. Opera, dance, music, and most especially theater, thrive in our nation's capital. Every season, world premières are unveiled—usually contemporary, often controversial, and occasionally outrageous. Big-name entertainers appear regularly at the Verizon Center, Warner Theatre, and other stages. The Smithsonian and other Mall attractions schedule music, film, and additional cultural entertainment.

With this arts emphasis in mind, we'll start with what D.C. does best—theater—before moving along to the many other nightlife options.

LIVE THEATER, THE CITY'S TOP ENTERTAINMENT BUY

In *Pauline Frommer's New York City* I wrote that you couldn't say you'd "done" New York until you'd been to the theater. The same could be said of D.C. In both cities, the quality of the performances is so high, and the act of going to the theater so integral to the life of the city, that skipping this experience is like, well, refusing to look directly at the Capital Dome or avoiding the Smithsonian.

Theater has truly become a highlight of the Washington experience. So buy a ticket—you won't regret it.

As in New York, Washington has two main tiers of theater, which are the equivalent of Broadway and off-Broadway. The first takes place at the city's largest auditoriums—the **John F. Kennedy Center for the Performing Arts** (see box); the **Warner Theatre** (see below); and the **National Theatre** ✪ (1321 Pennsylvania Ave. NW; ☎ 202/628-6161; www.nationaltheatre.org; Metro: Metro Center), one of the oldest continually operating theaters in the country. All three host a number of different types of performances, but for the purposes of this discussion, you can think of them as the home to the city's theatrical extravaganzas. It's on these big stages that you'll see big-name actors in shows that are splashed across the national media. (Often these productions originate in New York City, or are on their way to the Big Apple, using D.C. as a "tryout" town). We're not going to spend too much time on this type of theater because this is a budget guidebook and let's be frank: Ticket prices for these shows cost a small fortune. As two examples, in early 2009, the national tour of *A Chorus Line* played the National Theatre and charged a top ticket price of $151; across town the national tour of *Legally Blonde* was packing the Kennedy Center with tickets in the same range.

Better for budgeters—and anyone who enjoys thought-provoking, cutting-edge theater, for that matter—are the shows that are nurtured at the city's smaller, local theaters (the off-Broadway equivalent). Ticket prices are lower (usually ranging from $35 to no more than $75), and there are almost always ways to get discounts (see box). Altogether there are about three dozen of these theaters in the metropolitan area, too many for most locals to keep up with, never mind visitors. So, I'll try to point you toward the surefire winners, the ones that put on the most consistently exciting work.

> ❝ *Washington is no doubt the boss town in the country for a man to live in who wants to get all the pleasure he can . . . But I wasn't built that way . . . My doctor told me that if I wanted my three score and 10, I must go to bed early, keep out of social excitements, and behave myself. You can't do that in Washington. Nobody does.* ❞
>
> —Mark Twain, quoted in the *St. Louis Post Dispatch*, May 19, 1889

◆ **Arena Stage** ✪✪✪ (1101 6th St. SW; ☎ 202/488-3300; www.arenastage. org; Metro: Waterfront–Southeastern University). The biggest of the city's smaller theaters, it's also the largest theater in North America to be wholly focused on American plays. Although it occasionally premières new works, its forte is reviving American classics—including musicals, such as *I Love a Piano* (a retrospective of the works of Irving Berlin) and such classics as *Guys and Dolls* and *Damn Yankees*. Of all the off-Broadway–style theaters, this is also the one most likely to get big-name talent; in 2008–09, Linda Lavin, Maureen McGovern, and Carrie Fisher trod the boards here. As we go to press, the Arena is in the midst of a multimillion-dollar, multiyear upgrade

Discounts at D.C.'s Theaters

You likely won't have to pay full price to see a great show in D.C. Here are some of the ways to save:

Visit the half-price ticket booth or website: To assure yourself of low-priced tickets for a variety of performing arts theaters and other events, including Kennedy Center productions, head for **Ticket Place** (407 7th St. NW, btw. D and E sts.; ☎ 202/TICKETS [842-5387]; www.ticketplace.org; AE, MC, V; Metro: National Archives–Navy Memorial–Penn Quarter; Tues–Fri 11am–6pm, Sat 10am–5pm). Tickets at the booth itself are sold at half-price but a fee amounting to 12% of the ticket's full price is added. Example: A $20 ticket is sold for $10. The 12% fee (from $20) is an additional $2.40, bringing the total to $12.40. You can also purchase tickets online; however, for that the fee is 17%. (So, a ticket originally priced at $20 would cost you $13.40 online). Half-price ticket events include theater, dance, opera, concerts, lecture series, films, and youth programs throughout the Washington metropolitan area. Usually, two dozen or more performances are listed—although some may be in the suburbs. At times, Ticket Place lists almost all the shows currently running in the area. With occasional exceptions, tickets are available the day of performance only. Tickets can be purchased online on the day of the show through 4pm.

Take advantage of last-minute pricing: A number of theater companies heavily discount last-minute seats. At **Woolly Mammoth** (below) unsold seats called "Stampede Seats" are sold 15 minutes prior to showtime for $10 each, on a first-come, first-served basis. Call ahead before you go to find out if stampede seats will be sold. At **Shakespeare Theater Company,** last-minute seats are available only to those with student ID ($10 during previews, 50% off the cost of the seat otherwise) 1 hour before curtain. If you're willing to stand, however, you can get into sold-out shows here also for $10, though you won't know if these standing places are available until an hour before the performance. The **Signature Theater** sells $30 "Rush Tickets" an hour before the show, if the show hasn't sold out (call in advance to find out).

of its facilities and so is using venues all across D.C. to present its season (see the website for details). **Ticket prices** are $27 to $66 Sunday, Tuesday, Wednesday, and Thursday evenings; $27 to $76 for Friday and Saturday performances. The most expensive tickets are for musicals.

◆ **Woolly Mammoth Theater Company** ✮✮✮ (641 D St. NW; ☎ 202/289-2443; www.woollymammoth.net; Metro: National Archives–Navy Memorial). If you think the name is out there, wait until you see their shows. For the 2008–09 season, these included a reworking of Shakespeare's *Macbeth* using

Discounts for seniors, students, young folks, people with disabilities, and military: Again, many of the theaters in town engage in these sorts of discounts, so if you don't see the one you're interested in listed here, by all means ask. At the **Shakespeare Theater Company,** seniors 60 and older get a 20% discount, and students can snag preview-week seats for 50% off. At **Woolly Mammoth** those under 25 can purchase tickets to any performance for $10 based on availability (unless the show's expected to sell out, there's usually availability). **GALA Hispanic Theater** shaves $12 off the ticket price for students, seniors, and those in the military. **Arena Stage** gives seniors over the age of 60 a 15% discount on all but Saturday night tickets; for young folks ages 5 to 25 about 10 to 20 $10 tickets are set aside for each performance (these can be purchased up to 90 min. in advance on the day of performance). Full-time students over the age of 25 can get 35% off the cost of a ticket with ID and pending availability. The **Kennedy Center** offers half-price tickets to seniors over the age of 65, enlisted military grades E-1 to E-4, and students, for the first performance of nearly every run. These can be purchased in advance; half-price tickets to non-sold-out shows are also sold to these groups of people. For matinees they become available at noon, for evening performances 6pm.

Pay-What-You-Can: This odd strategy is just what it sounds like and is offered by **Woolly Mammoth** for the first two performances of each production (tickets go on sale 90 min. before curtain, but often the line starts forming as early as 5:30pm). "Pay What You Can" tickets are also sometimes offered by **Shakespeare Theater** and at the **Arena Stage** (where they're called "Hot Tix" and the price is 50% off, rather than "what you can pay"). These Hot Tix go on sale 90 minutes before the performance; you may be asked why the regular price would be prohibitive for you.

characters from the hit cartoon show *The Simpsons (McHomer);* an evening of 30 miniature plays in 60 minutes; and a sex comedy revolving around the theory of evolution. Sounds weird, I know, but through the talent of those involved—especially their crack permanent acting company—somehow it all works brilliantly (and often hilariously; this company knows how to get laughs). About 70% of what you'll see here was developed just for this theater, though often the plays they commission go on to productive lives elsewhere (since their founding in 1978, plays developed by Mammoth have had

The Kennedy Center: Cultural Colossus

If any one thing boosted Washington's reputation as a city of the cultural arts, it was the 1971 debut of the **John F. Kennedy Center for the Performing Arts** (On the Potomac River at Virginia Ave., New Hampshire Ave., and 25th St. NW; ☎ 800/444-1324 and 202/467-4600; www.kennedy-center.org; Metro: Foggy Bottom–GWU, with 3-block walk south via New Hampshire Ave.; free tours; Mon–Sat 10am–9pm and Sun noon–9pm). Considered the nation's busiest arts venue, the center presents more than 3,000 performances annually to an audience of nearly two million. Major artists and groups from around the world appear in opera, dance, musicals, jazz, classical concerts, theater, and more. The National Symphony Orchestra and the Washington National Opera make their home at the Kennedy Center. In 2009 alone, the roster read like a Who's Who of the arts world from such famed dance companies as Paul Taylor and Alvin Ailey to the Bolshoi Ballet to the national tours of Broadway's *Spring Awakening* and music greats Andre Previn and Anne-Sophie Mutter. And of course this is the place where the Kennedy Center Honors are broadcast from, an event which celebrates legendary living artists. At the same time the center serves as a living memorial to President Kennedy, a patron of the performing arts.

Ideally, you should attend a performance to get the full Kennedy Center experience. On a budget, catch the nightly free performances, a series dubbed the **Millennium Stage,** presented in the Grand Foyer. They tend to feature up-and-coming artists in all categories from opera to Cajun and country. No reservations are necessary. Check out the next month's schedule on the center's website (see above).

Free escorted tours are engaging no matter your musical tastes. They're offered Monday through Friday 10am to 5pm and Saturday and Sunday 10am to 1pm on a walk-up basis—that is, no set times. (Call ☎ 202/416-8340 for information.) On the tours, visitors get a peek inside the center's three major theaters if no performance is scheduled.

Architectural critics generally slammed the center when it was built. It is, basically, a giant rectangular box of white marble. But its Potomac

productions in over 200 other theaters worldwide). In addition, the Mammoth brings in celebrated monologists like Mike Daisey, and noted new plays from New York, Chicago, and London. In 2005, Mammoth finally got its own specially designed 265-seat theater in the heart of the lively Penn Quarter neighborhood—there's not a bad seat in the house. **Ticket prices** are $38 and $48 on Wednesday, Thursday, and Sunday evenings; $45 to $55 for Friday and Saturday shows.

* **Studio Theatre** ✪✪✪ (1501 14th St. NW; ☎ 202/332-3300; www.studio theatre.org; Metro: Dupont Circle or McPherson Square and 6-block walk;

River setting is lovely. At night, theatergoers gather on the River Terrace at intermission to watch the gleaming lights of Georgetown just upriver. Inside, an aura of grandeur greets you. Most visitors enter first at the **Hall of States,** which is lined by flags representing all 50 states, five territories, and the District of Columbia. A second parallel entrance several yards south leads to the **Hall of Nations,** which flies the flags of all the countries with which the United States has diplomatic relations. Ticket booths, restroom access, information desks, and a gift shop are found in the halls.

Both halls lead on plush red carpets to the even more elegant **Grand Foyer,** which is the shared lobby for the Concert Hall, Opera House, and Eisenhower Theater. Its length of 630 feet makes it one of the largest rooms in the world. You could lay the Washington Monument on its side in the foyer and still have 75 feet to spare. Huge windows look out to the Potomac. In the hall is a massive bronze bust of Kennedy, a well-regarded work that captures the intelligence and wit that captivated so many people. Nearby interactive exhibits examine Kennedy's life and legacy.

If you get a look inside the **Concert Hall,** note the soaring pipes of the 4,144-pipe organ behind the stage. In the **Opera House,** the sparkling crystal chandelier, which looks like giant clusters of snowflakes, was a gift to the center from Austria. Canada gave the **Eisenhower Theater** its distinctive curtain of red and black hand-woven wool.

As well, the **Kennedy Center Theater Lab,** a 350-seat theater, rates special mention. Since 1987, it has been presenting *Shear Madness,* a comedy whodunit set in a hair-styling salon in present-day Georgetown. Frequent new dialogue additions touching on current events keep it fresh. At the end, the audience is invited to solve the crime. It's light and hokey but fun and easy to take after a day of heavy sightseeing. *Shear Madness* now ranks as the third longest-running play in the history of American theater. Numbers 1 and 2 are *Shear Madness* productions in Boston and Chicago. Tickets range from $38 to $50. But check out Ticket Place before you commit. Since the theater is so small, all seats are good.

—*Jim Yenckel*

half-price "student rush" tickets sometimes available, 30 min. prior to shows on every night but Sat). Almost as outrageous, the Studio Theater has made its mark primarily with innovative revivals of older plays and with its staging of contemporary plays that may have only recently debuted in New York (such as Tom Stoppard's *Rock and Roll* and Connor McPherson's *The Wayfarer,* which both performed in early 2009). A major player in the redevelopment of 14th Street, it operates three 200-seat theaters in what formerly were automobile showrooms. Blending with its regular-season productions is Studio's 2nd Stage, which features even more unconventional productions,

Washington by Moonlight: Night Tours

When the sun goes down, Washington takes on a different, almost magical look. Lighted at night, the white marble monuments and memorials seem to glow, looking their most beautiful. National Park rangers are on duty at most of the sites until midnight; they are quite safe to visit. But I would hesitate to walk between them after dark. A tour by trolley, tram, bus, Segway, or bike is a safer alternative. The tours visit the same sights, and the dialogue I've heard is pretty uniform, not varying much from company to company. So make your choice on the type of transportation you prefer or the price. For more information on seeing the city by guided tour, see chapter 5.

- **Old Town Trolley** (Union Station; ☎ 202/832-9800; Metro: Union Station; www.trolleytours.com; $35 adults, $18 children 4–12; spring–summer daily 7:30pm, winter–fall daily 6:30pm). The firm's "Monuments by Moonlight" trolley tour lasts about 2½ hours. Reservations by phone are required. Departure is from Union Station.

- **Tourmobile Sightseeing** (Union Station; ☎ 202/554-5100; Metro: Union Station; www.tourmobile.com; $30 adults, $15 children; 7pm mid-March through mid-Nov). Called "Washington by Night: Twilight Tour," the tour lasts about 3 hours. Generally it is offered daily March through December, but the schedule can vary. You might get more background information on the Old Town Trolley (above) and Martz Gold Line/Gray Line bus tour (below), but it's a lot easier to get on and off the trams than the trolley or the bus.

- **Martz Gold Line/Gray Line** (Union Station; ☎ 800/862-1400; Metro: Union Station; www.graylinedc.com; $47 adults, $25 children; daily 7:45pm). Dubbed "Tour L: Washington after Dark," it lasts 3 hours. This tour has the advantage of being air-conditioned, but you'll have to decide whether that's worth the hefty uptick in price.

- **Bike the Sites** (Old Post Office Pavilion, Rear Plaza, 12th St. and Pennsylvania Ave. NW; ☎ 202/842-2453; Metro: Federal Triangle; www.bikethesites.com; $45 adults, $35 children, Mon–Sat 7pm). Biking during the day in Washington can be hair-raising, thanks to heavy traffic and (sometimes) humidity. At night it's a delight and this 3-hour ride, called "Sites @ Night Tour," covers about 4 miles and includes the bike rental, helmet, water, and a snack.

- **City Segway Tours** (1455 Pennsylvania Ave. NW; ☎ 877/734-8687; Metro: Federal Triangle; www.citysegwaytours.com; $70; Apr 1–Nov 30 daily 6:30pm). Okay, it's pricey. But I can tell you from direct experience that learning to ride a Segway is buckets of fun (and not at all difficult). This 3-hour tour, which includes instruction time (so you don't crash!), travels much of the Mall. And riding one of these things, you become as much of a tourist site as the Lincoln Monument, so this isn't the tour for shy types.

such as Suzan-Lori Parks' meditation on abortion, *F***ing A*. **Ticket prices** are $34 to $42 Tuesday, Wednesday, and Sunday evenings; $40 to $53 the rest of the week. Add $10 for a musical. 2nd Stage tickets are $30.

◆ **Ford's Theatre** ✪✪ (511 10th St. NW; ☎ 202/347-4833; www.fords theatre.org; Metro: Metro Center). The assassination of Abraham Lincoln carved its name in American history. But since 1968, when it reopened after 103 years, the Ford has worked to attain recognition also as an important local stage—serving as a living tribute to a president who loved the performing arts. Like Arena Stage, it spotlights the works of modern American playwrights, often with a political or Washington theme—in 2009, the theater reopened after a major renovation with a play on Lincoln and the Emancipation Proclamation and followed it with a revival of the musical *The Civil War*. Though not American in origin, its version of *A Christmas Carol* is a yearly sellout. **Ticket prices** range from $20 to $46 for midweek performances; $39 and $52 Friday and Saturday evenings; $34 and $36 weekday matinees; and $49 to $52 on weekends. *Christmas Carol* seats are often a bit higher. I've detailed Ford's history on p. 126.

◆ **GALA Hispanic Theatre** ✪ (3333 14th St. NW; ☎ 202/234-7174; www. galatheatre.org; Metro: Columbia Heights). Arguably the leading Spanish-language theater in the United States, the GALA presents plays in their original language from across the Hispanic world. You're as likely to find classic plays from Spain, as recent hits from Argentina all performed in a jewel box of a theater—the Tivoli, a former movie palace. Don't skip a show here just because you can't speak the language: All are offered with simultaneous translations via subtitles on the theater's proscenium. **Tickets** are $32 Thursday and Sunday; $36 Friday and Saturday.

◆ **Shakespeare Theatre Company** ✪✪✪ (Penn Quarter, 450 7th St. NW; ☎ 202/547-1122; www.shakespearetheatre.org; Metro: National Archives–Navy Memorial–Penn Quarter). Yes, it does just what you'd expect it to: Shakespeare and the classics, but often with a twist that makes these much revived plays seem quite a bit fresher than usual. A production of *Romeo and Juliet* might have an all-male cast, or *Twelfth Night* a set that bursts with rosebuds, rose petals, and other floral motifs (the latter worked out to be quite lovely in the production I saw in Dec 2008). Now 2 decades old, Shakespeare Theater Company has been acclaimed as one of the world's greatest Shakespearean theaters and has a gorgeous state-of-the-art auditorium in Sidney Harman Hall, which opened in 2007. **Ticket prices** are $35 to $68 Tuesday, Wednesday, Thursday, and Sunday evenings and Wednesday matinees; $43 to $75 Friday evening and Saturday and Sunday matinees; and $48 to $80 for Saturday evening.

◆ The **Signature Theater Company** (4200 Campbell Ave., Arlington, Va.; ☎ 703/820-9771; www.sig-online.org; Metro: Pentagon City). Though not in D.C. proper, the Signature has become such a powerhouse in recent years that it draws audiences not only from the District, but also from Baltimore, Philadelphia, and even New York City. The Signature received the 2009 Tony Award for Regional Theatre. Artistic director Eric Schaeffer has made a name for himself and his company by audaciously reinventing recent works of musical theater, usually creating productions that are at once much more intimate (the theater's a small one) and more intense. In 2009, he gave "the treatment" to *Les Miserables;* past hits have included *Into the Woods, Merrily We Roll Along,* and the American première of a new musical based on *The Witches of Eastwick.* You'll need to take either a bus or a taxi from the Metro stop. **Ticket prices** are $44 to $52 during previews, $56 to $65 for regular weeknight shows and matinees, and $61 to $69 for Friday and Saturday night shows. Add about $5 to $10 if you're seeing a musical. Shows often run in repertory, so check the schedule closely.

MULTIUSE STAGES

The following theaters sometimes create their own productions. But more often they are the venues for visiting shows that are either en route to a Broadway opening, post-Broadway roadshow presentations, or one-night stands with name comedians or musicians. Many productions are first-rate, starring name casts. Others seem to have wearied from the road, and the cast looks tired and sloppy. This is seldom, if ever, a problem with the "small" theaters described above. Check out the critics' reviews beforehand if possible. Both the *Washington Post* (**www.washington post.com**) and the *City Paper* (**www.washingtoncitypaper.com**) keep reviews on their sites for the complete runs of these shows (and often longer).

A former movie theater, the **Atlas Performing Arts Center** (1333 H St. NE; ☎ 202/399-7993; www.atlasarts.org; Metrobus: X2 from near the McPherson Square, Metro Center, and Gallery Place–Chinatown) was a leader in the revitalization of H Street NE, part of which was badly damaged in the riots following the assassination of the Rev. Dr. Martin Luther King in 1968. It hosts some presentations of the Washington Savoyards, a light opera company, as well as other D.C.-based musical groups (choruses, orchestras, and the like).

Like the Atlas above, the **Lincoln Theatre** (1215 U St. NW; ☎ 202/397-7328 for tickets; www.thelincolntheatre.org; Metro: U Street–African-American Civil War Memorial–Cardozo) is another former movie theater transformed into a performing arts stage that is helping bring life back to a neighborhood with a rich heritage. Currently, it's serving as the temporary home to Arena Stage (see above) while it renovates its own theater. By the time you get this book, however, it may be back to its old eclectic ways, hosting an Asian dance group one night, a comedian the next. Ticket prices vary greatly by performance, from $15 to $60 and more. Check the website for schedule and ticket details.

Warner Theatre ★ (1299 Pennsylvania Ave. NW; ☎ 800/551-7328 and 202/397-7328; www.warnertheatre.com; Metro: Metro Center) is still another drop-dead gorgeous former movie palace; its offerings ranged from the Broadway tour of *Avenue Q* and *Rent* to concerts with jazz legend Diane Reeves and the Dave Brubeck Quartet in 2009. The Warner is also home to the National Ballet's very popular production of *The Nutcracker* each December.

CLASSICAL MUSIC OF ALL STRIPES

Washington supports an ever-growing opera company, an acclaimed orchestra, and an overflowing calendar of classical musical performances by local and touring artists, groups, and orchestras. And it does so without the government support for artists typical in many world capitals and without a strong base of business contributors. Obviously, classical music fans like what they are seeing and hearing and are willing to ante up for it. The prime performance venues are the stages of the

Kennedy Center, DAR Constitution Hall, and George Washington University's Lisner Auditorium. All are in the downtown area reached by the Metrorail Foggy Bottom station. While up-front orchestra seats tend to be expensive, if you don't mind the balcony (especially at the Kennedy Center) ticket prices drop into the affordable range. At the Concert Hall, where the National Symphony Orchestra performs, dress is fairly casual. At the Opera House, when an opera is on the bill, folks tend to spruce up more, and you're likely to spot a few tuxes and evening gowns.

OPERA

With famed tenor Plácido Domingo at its helm as general director, the **Washington National Opera** ✪✪✪ (Kennedy Center, 2700 F St. NW; ☎ 800/USOPERA [876-7372] or 202/295-2400; www.dc-opera.org; Metro: Foggy Bottom) is a powerhouse organization, best known for shining fresh light on works of the canonical composers. Every once in a while, it will commission a new piece but the current financial climate seems to have put a halt to that, for now; it's been keeping its choices a hair more conservative. The *Ring* cycle of Wagner was supposed to be the centerpiece of the 2008–09 season but that was shelved in favor of such perennial favorites as *Turandot* and *Carmen* as well as such little-performed, but worthy works as *The Pearl Fishers* by Bizet and Donizetti's *Lucrezia Borgia* starring Renee Fleming. A highlight (and a hallmark of the type of talent this organization attracts): Andrea Bocelli in a concert staging of Rossini's *Petite Messe Solennelle,* conducted by Domingo himself. Pretty heady stuff! I could tell you how I think the company rates on the world scene, but I'll let the experts do it. The British magazine *Opera Now* wrote: "Washington National Opera is carving out a new area of expertise . . . staging grand spectacles to exacting standards with precision and power not often seen at the world's top houses." For those operas sung in a foreign tongue, simultaneous subtitles—as you see in French or Italian movies—provide an English translation. Keep in mind that many performances sell out—season ticket holders get first crack at them—so you might want to book in advance. Ticket prices range from $45 (rear orchestra and second tier) to $300 (premier box). You have to act fast to get the cheap seats. And one drawback: The subtitles aren't visible from rear orchestra. They are visible from the second tier, so you might want to opt for the loftier seating.

DISCOUNTS: Unfortunately, the opera management is stingy with discounts. Occasionally **Ticket Place,** the half-price ticket outlet (see box earlier in this chapter), offers seats. In addition, the Kennedy Center maintains a specially priced tickets program for many performances, including some operas. If available, half-price tickets are sold on day of performance at the **Hall of States Box Office** (Mon–Sat 10am–9pm, Sun noon–9pm). To qualify, you must be a full-time student, senior 65 or older, enlisted military (E1–E4 grade), or have a permanent disability. Tickets are not available for Saturday evening performances. **Standing Room Tickets** at $25 each are sold at the Box Office or by phone (☎ 202/467-4600 or 800/444-1324) only for sold-out performances.

CLASSICAL MUSIC CONCERTS

Washington's concert calendar is headlined by the **National Symphony Orchestra** (Kennedy Center, 2700 F St. NW; ☎ 800/444-1324 or 202/467-4600; www.kennedy-center.org/nso; Metro: Foggy Bottom), an institution in Washington that

Where to Hear Music for Free

You don't have to pay big bucks to hear music in Washington. Free concerts, and quality ones at that, occur all the time. Here are just a few places to check:

◆ **National Gallery of Art** (On the Mall, 6th St. and Constitution Ave. NW; ☎ 202/842-6941; www.nga.gov; Metro: National Archives–Navy Memorial). From fall to spring it hosts free concerts primarily with Washington area–based artists and groups (soloists, trios, quartets, full choruses, you name it), though performers from abroad who come under the auspices of their country's embassy in Washington also show up occasionally. Most performances are scheduled at 6:30pm Sunday in the West Garden Court of the West Building. In summer, the concerts are moved outdoors and the groove swings to jazz, with the popular **Jazz in the Garden** series; picnicking is encouraged; concerts take place Fridays from 5 to 8:30pm in the sculpture garden. Admission for all these concerts first-come, first-served, beginning a half-hour before the performance.

◆ **Library of Congress** ✪✪ (Coolidge Auditorium, 1st St. and Independence Ave. SE; www.loc.gov/rr/perform/concert; Metro: Capitol South or Union Station). A smidge more prestigious—Dave Brubeck himself opened the season here several years ago—the concerts often revolve around the scores that are housed in the Library's vast collection. A specialty: chamber music (the *Washington Post* once wrote, "You can trace the popularity of chamber music in the United

has, in recent years, been roiled by gossip and controversy, leading to the exit of its famed conductor Leonard Slatkin. In his place, but only through 2010, is Hungarian conductor Ivan Fischer; Broadway composer Marvin Hamlisch has taken over baton duties at the Pops. It will be interesting to see how it plays out, but in the short run, it seems like the orchestra has been attracting fewer big-name soloists than in the past. Its season is a lengthy one, running from September to June. Performances in the Concert Hall are scheduled Thursday, Friday, and Saturday evenings with occasional Friday matinees. Tickets are $20 to $80, and the acoustics in the hall—including the back balcony—are excellent.

Visiting orchestras show up regularly, often under the auspices of the **Washington Performing Arts Society** ✪✪ (2000 L St. NW; ☎ 202/785-9727; www.wpas.org) and play the Kennedy Center, Constitution Hall, Lisner Auditorium, Warner Theatre, and elsewhere in the city. The types of performances are as varied as the choice of venues—classical, jazz, dance, gospel, vocal, world music, you name it. In 2008–09, its offerings included Broadway legend Barbara Cook, the London Philharmonic, violinist Joshua Bell, cellist YoYo Ma and the Silk Road Ensemble, Wynton Marsalis with his Jazz at Lincoln Center

States directly to the Library of Congress's Coolidge Auditorium.") Concerts are held at 8pm various nights of the week; tickets are distributed up to 6 weeks in advance by Ticketmaster (☎ 800/551-7328; www.ticketmaster.com), which adds on shipping and handling fees of $5. Free standby tickets, however, are handed out at the door beginning at 6:30pm the night of the concert, when available.

- **The Kennedy Center's Millennium Stage** (2700 F St. NW; www.kennedy-center.org/millennium; Metro: Foggy Bottom–GWU). The most prolific venue in town, it hosts hour-long concerts at 6pm every night of the year in the Grand Foyer. No tickets are required; just show up for seating or standing room. The performances are eclectic, featuring up-and-coming soloists, international troupes, and sometimes artists appearing in one of the shows on the Center's big stages. In a typical month, you might hear an American jazz quartet, native Quichuan singers from the Ecuadorian Andes, a French choir rendering Renaissance tunes, or young singers from the Washington National Opera.

- **Army, Navy, and Marine Corps bands** (www.usarmyband.com; www.navyband.navy.mil; www.marineband.usmc.mil; Metro: Union Station or Capital South). Patriotism at its best: In summer these three groups perform alternately Monday through Friday at 8pm on the west steps of the Capitol. No tickets needed.

Orchestra, and Ravi Shankar. Rates vary . . . greatly. So greatly that I'd suggest checking the website for prices; there's no average pricing on these performances.

MORE LIVE DIVERSIONS

DANCE

"Maverick" is a term that gets thrown around a bit too loosely in Washington (just look at the 2008 presidential race!) but it fits perfectly when discussing Septime Webre, the artistic director of the **Washington Ballet** ✪✪ (☎ 202/362-3606; www.washingtonballet.org). In just 10 years he has managed to transform what had been the capital's rather mediocre troupe into a standard bearer, tripling the budget and subscription list. His stamp is everywhere, from the Balanchine-esque training of the company to the exotic-for-ballet influences he brings to his choreography (his mother was from Cuba, and many of his works have a sensual, Latin sensibility, though Weber's work borrows from African dance as well). Weber has also been able to engineer some superb artistic collaborations in the past few years, most notably with famed illustrator Maurice Sendak and the musical group Sweet Honey in the Rock. Performances are held either in the Eisenhower Theater at the

Kennedy Center or at the Warner Theatre (see earlier in this chapter) from September through May. Tickets, alas, are expensive, often ranging from $65 to $115, though for *The Nutcracker* (a wonderfully D.C.-themed affair, with George Washington as the Nutcracker and George III as the Rat King) prices can drop to just $29 for the cheap seats.

The **Washington Performing Arts Society** and the **Kennedy Center** also bring major national and international dance companies to the city. (For schedule and tickets, check the websites above.)

COMEDY

Part of a national chain of comedy clubs, the **DC Improv** (Downtown, 1140 Connecticut Ave. NW btw. L and M sts.; ☎ 202/296-7008; www.dcimprov.com; Metro: Farragut North) is the city's only full-time comedy stage. Its lack of competition hasn't led it to rest on its laurels, though—the biggest names on the circuit play here from political satirist Will Durst to Chris Rock to "Cash Cab" host Ben Bailey. Heck, usually you'll laugh more here than you will at the antics on the House floor! Tickets are easy on the budget, generally $10 to $22, depending on who is appearing, but you must buy two additional items—defined as food, drink, coffee, or dessert. Admission is limited to age 18 and older. Showtimes are Tuesday through Thursday 8:30pm; Friday and Saturday 8 and 10:30pm; and Sunday 8pm. Weekend shows tend to be more expensive than weekday.

JAZZ

You'd think that New Orleans or perhaps Chicago would have the country's longest, continuously operated jazz supper club, but that honor goes to Washington. Opened in 1965 in an 18th-century redbrick carriage house, the **Blues Alley** ✪✪✪ (Georgetown, 1073 Wisconsin Ave. NW below M Street; ☎ 202/337-4141; www.bluesalley.com; 8 and 10pm nightly; Metrobus: 30, 32, 34, 35, 36; reservations recommended) remains one of the best places in the U.S. for a meal and a swinging tune. The look of the place harks back to the jazz clubs of the 1920s and 1930s; the menu is New Orleans Creole. Over the years Blues Alley has showcased such artists as Dizzy Gillespie, Sarah Vaughan, Charley Bird, and Nancy Wilson, and it continues to attract such top names as Ahmad Jamal, Les McCann, Marva Wright, and Rachelle Ferrell. The cover charge ranges from $20 to $60, depending on the artist or group appearing. Students get half off the cover charge for the 10pm shows Sunday through Thursday. Dinner entrees at the early show range from $17 to $23. But to cut costs, dine elsewhere and take in the late show when available; snacks are an easier $5 to $9.75.

Come by on the right night and you'll find a line snaking down the block, filled with jazz lovers of all ages, hoping to get within earshot of the music at **Bohemian Caverns** ✪✪ (2003 11th St. NW; ☎ 202/299-0800; www.bohemian caverns.com; Metro: U Street–African-American Civil Rights Memorial–Cardozo). If the name sounds familiar, it's because this club (and its earlier incarnations as Club Caverns and Crystal Caverns) served as one of the main launch pads for such greats as Washington son Duke Ellington, Cab Calloway, Sarah Vaughan, Dizzy Gillespie, and John Coltrane. Abandoned for some 30 years, it's risen phoenix-like from the ashes, and the new owners have given its performance space a fun, if somewhat hokey "1920s in a cave" look, with Art Deco furnishings and walls that are supposed to look like the rocks (the hokey stalactites unfortunately sometimes block sightlines). Among the musicians you might see today are David Ornette Cherry, Donald Harrison, and Ron Carter. General admission can range anywhere from $22 to $40 a person, depending on the night and performers.

You'll hear jazz in a less expensive (no cover) setting at **U-topia Bar and Grill** ★ (U St. Corridor, 1418 U St. NW at 14th St.; ☎ 202/483-7669; www. utopiaindc.com; Metro: U Street–African-American Civil Rights Memorial–Cardozo). It was one of the first of the recent crop of U Street nightspots when it opened a dozen years ago. Groups of mostly local performers alternate throughout the week in the narrow, brick-lined room with a vaulted ceiling and colorful contemporary artwork. Monday to Wednesday (from 9pm) and Sunday (9:30pm), settle in for mellow jazz and blues; on Thursday, it's Brazilian jazz (9:30pm); on Friday and Saturday (11pm), just jazz. If you go for dinner—a blend of Cajun, Creole, and Moroccan—the entrees go for between $13 and $21.

Where else but in Washington would jazz be paired with Ethiopian food? That's the fare at **Twins Jazz** ★ (1344 U St.; ☎ 202/234-0072; www. twinjazz.com; Metro: U Street–African-American Civil Rights Memorial–Cardozo), and it sets the tone for this offbeat, tiny, likably gritty, U Street mainstay. As with any club there are going to be some disappointments. Here it's the watered down quality of the pricey drinks and the weird lighting. But if you come for music, you'll be satisfied—the club hosts some of the best emerging artists around, folks who aren't afraid of the experimental side of jazz (it's a great place for bebop, too). The cost of a night here can be high with a $10 to $30 cover and two-drink minimum (those with college ID get half off the cover), but for the quality of the entertainment, most think the cost is justified.

For more than 25 years the Federal Jazz Company has been turning **Colonel Brooks' Tavern** (901 Monroe St. NE; ☎ 202/529-4002; Metro: Brookland–Catholic University of America; no cover charge) into one of the toe-tappingest places in the District. They play on Tuesday nights only, and their groove is Dixieland Jazz, so the audience tends to skew older. Still, if you like this type of music, you can't do better. Most of the players are retired federal employees; the clarinetist played for the U.S. Navy Band for 20 years. A night at the tavern is a slice of neighborhood life in Washington.

LIVE MUSIC CLUBS

Like most large cities, Washington is on the headliners' circuit. But it also generates plenty of good, up-and-coming local talent. You'll find loads of music venues in Washington, and of course part of your decision of where to go will be based on what musicians are playing where. But if you haven't heard of any of the acts, you can usually find something worth guzzling beer and possibly dancing to, at one of the following venues:

The city's top rock venue is the famed **9:30 Club** ★★★ (U St. Corridor, 815 V St. NW; www.930.com; Metro: U Street–African-American Civil War Memorial–Cardozo), a place that features a veritable genius as a talent booker (I don't know who he or she is, but I love his/her lineups). Other pluses: A cutting-edge sound system and that club rarity, darn good sightlines from pretty much everywhere (though I know many who claim that the view from the balcony is best). Without too much hyperbole, I can say that it's one of the best live

Be Cautious After Dark!

Unfortunately, no part of the city can be considered safe late at night, particularly such entertainment areas as Adams Morgan, the Atlas Theater/H Street District, and the U Street Corridor. Stay on lighted, well-populated streets. If you're clubbing or barhopping, try to go in a group and call it quits before closing time. Take the Metro in the early evening, but after 10pm take a taxi unless the nightspot is within a block or so of the Metro station. Street crime is an occasional thing, but it can be violent and even deadly.

music clubs in the U.S.; I've known music lovers to come from cities a good 2 to 3 hours away just to hear such acts as the Pretenders, Justin Timberlake, Joan Jett & the Blackhearts, and My Chemical Romance play here. *A historical note:* The alley behind the club, where musicians unload their instruments, is the same alley through which John Wilkes Booth fled after assassinating President Lincoln at nearby Ford's Theatre. The cover charge, $15 to $40, varies with the act and the venue periodically sells out, so plan in advance if you can. From Sunday to Thursday, doors open at 7:30pm, and the first act gets underway (maybe) at 8:30pm. On Friday and Saturday, the doors open at 9pm, and the first act goes on 45 minutes later. All ages admitted.

In early 1993, a group of musicians hoping to revive the tradition of independent music in Washington opened the **Black Cat** ✪✪ (U St. Corridor, 1811 14th St. NW btw. S and T sts.; ☎ 202/667-7960; www.blackcatdc.com; Metro: U Street–African-American Civil War Memorial–Cardozo), helping spark an explosion of indie rock in the past decade and a half. Accommodating nearly 1,000 people at the huge 7,000-square-foot Mainstage, it presents a nightly show with a mix of local, national, and international artists (Blur and Bloc Party among them), playing both indie rock and alternative music. The choice of artists is top-notch, the acoustics less so (if you're in a dead zone, push your way to another part of the room). On some Saturdays, instead of live music DJs spin Brit-pop for the very popular "Mousetrap" party (see the website for details). On the ground level, the **Backstage,** accommodating 150, features emerging indie rock artists in an intimate, cabaret-type setting. The cover charge, $5 to $20, varies with the show. Advance tickets for name groups are recommended as shows do sell out. Patrons of any age are admitted, though management requires that those under 18 get their parent's permission or come with a parent. No cover charge is imposed at a third room, the casual Red Room Bar, which features vegetarian snacks, pool tables, and a killer juke box.

The **Velvet Lounge** ✪ (915 U St.; ☎ 202/462-3213; www.velvetloungedc.com; Metro: U Street–African-American Civil War Memorial–Cardozo) has a rec room vibe for sure, a tiny, second-floor space perched above a gay bar, but it manages to ferret out some real up-and-comers in the world of punk and experimental rock. Yeah, your shoes will get sticky from all the spilled beer and on some nights simply getting money out of your wallet to pay the drink tab can become a yoga exercise—the crowd packs in that tight. But heck, everyone's friendly and you'll probably get to know the band. Sorry, 21-years-old and older only for most shows.

If blues and R&B are more your groove, **Madam's Organ Restaurant and Blues Bar** (Adams Morgan, 2461 18th St. NW at Columbia Rd.; ☎ 202/667-5370; www.madamsorgan.com; Metro: Woodley Park–Zoo/Adams Morgan and 10-min. walk), a rowdy bar and soul food restaurant, should be your pick. A different band plays every night, some on a rotating schedule that brings them back every week or so. Wednesday is bluegrass night. The cover charge, $2 to $10, varies with the entertainment. Shows begin at 9 or 10pm. For the curious: Madam's Organ is a play on Adams Morgan, the bar's neighborhood.

BARS & DANCE CLUBS

Where can you go for music, dance, and drinks? The busiest and best-known hot spots are Adams Morgan, Georgetown, Dupont Circle, and the U Street Corridor, though the downtown area has recently debuted a number of pulsing dance clubs. Georgetown tends to attract both upscale revelers and college kids on the prowl (Georgetown U is here, after all); Dupont Circle is popular with gay revelers and embassy workers; Adams Morgan buzzes with 20-somethings intent on getting rowdy; and the U Street Corridor is the area for edgy, up-and-coming nightspots. To find out what's happening on the live music scene for the week ahead, check the Friday Weekend section of the *Washington Post* or—actually the best source—the free *City Paper,* published every Thursday and distributed widely in the Washington area in street boxes outside Metrorail stations and at drugstores, bookstores, and in a wide variety of other shops. Gay and lesbian nightlife happenings are listed in *Metro Weekly,* a free magazine published each Thursday and also distributed widely in street boxes.

Adams Morgan

A long string of bars, each heaving with 20-somethings, lines 18th Street. For a slightly more civilized scene, I recommend **Tryst Coffeehouse and Bar** ★★ (2459 18th St. NW near Columbia Rd.; ☎ 202/232-5500; www.trystdc.com; Metro: Woodley Park–Zoo/Adams Morgan), which is just what it sounds like: a coffeehouse by day that plies its patrons with martinis come evening. But even after dark, it retains a sweetly laid-back vibe. Young people lounge on sofas and easy chairs, some playing board games, others debating the latest happenings at the World Bank. Live music might start, or people may gather in little clusters around the artworks for sale on the wall. It's all friendly, relaxing, and fun—a good place to hit if conversation is a key element of nightlife for you.

On the edge of the sometimes intimidating Adams Morgan hubbub, the **Adams Mill Bar and Grill** ★ (1813 Adams Mill Rd. NW; ☎ 202/332-9577; Metro: Woodley Park–Zoo/Adams Morgan) is another mellow option. In essence, it's a neighborhood bar for the neighbors. In warm weather, the big attraction is the huge outdoor patio, certainly the largest in Adams Morgan. You will find a good selection of beers on tap.

Capitol Hill

I'm guessing that more legislation has been written in the row of bars on Pennsylvania Avenue between 2nd and 4th streets SE than in the Cannon, Longworth, and Rayburn House office buildings combined. At happy hour especially, the possibilities for noteworthy eavesdropping are stupendous.

Where's the Beer?

Entering the **Brickskeller** (1523 22nd St. NW at P St.; ☎ 202/293-1885; www.lovethebeer.com; Metro: Dupont Circle) is like descending into a dim dungeon. Lights are low, the walls are windowless brick, the ceiling is painted black, and the dingy ruby red carpet doesn't look like it's been replaced since opening day. But Washington beer fans love it because this dive may well have the largest beer menu *in the world*. All in all it serves about a thousand varieties from around the world, so many that the beer menu is actually a thick, little pamphlet. They offer dozens of American beers, of course, but plenty of international brews too, including Keos ($5.50) from Cyprus, Saku ($4.95) from Estonia, and Carib Lagers ($3.75) from Trinidad. You get the picture; if it's brewed, the Brickskeller probably sells it, and the list keeps growing. None sell for under $3, and some go for more than $40.

There's not much difference between the downstairs and upstairs bars—both are claustrophobic when crowded. But upstairs does boast 14 taps for from-the-keg imbibing.

—Jim Yenckel

Each of the bars has a slightly different vibe: the **Pourhouse** (319 Pennsylvania Ave. SE; ☎ 202/546-0779; www.pourhouse-dc.com; Metro: Capitol South) is trying to be all things to all congressional staffers. Fifteen TVs, always tuned to sports, reel in those who have bets in the office pool. Downstairs, the basement area has a beer hall theme for those feeling, um, Germanic. And the top floor, now known as Top of the Hill, is going for a classier vibe, with a martini-heavy menu, plush leather couches, and a dress code.

Half-price pizzas, $4 bottles of happy hour beer, and 10¢ wings on Tuesday nights keep the **Capitol Lounge** (231 Pennsylvania Ave. SE; ☎ 547-2098; www. capitolloungedc.com; Metro: Capitol South) hopping. Beyond its affordability, this bar is the one with the most overtly political vibe, thanks to all the election memorabilia on the walls. Interestingly, the sport of choice here is soccer and you'll see an ever-growing collection of soccer scarves on the wall behind one of the bars. In the basement are billiard tables.

My final choice on this Strip is the divey **Tune In** (331½ Pennsylvania Ave. SE; ☎ 202/543-2725; Metro: Capitol South), the kind of place where a moose head watches you as you drink, and regulars pop behind the bar to grab an extra slice of lime, without anyone raising an eyebrow. It gets the most mixed crowd, young and old, cops and staffers, all races. A fun, unpretentious place to grab a brewski.

If you are a fan of piano bars, try the oh-so-tropical **Banana Café & Piano Bar** (Capitol Hill, 500 8th St. SE at Pennsylvania Ave.; ☎ 202/543-5906; www. bananacafedc.com; Metro: Eastern Market). Neon-colored walls and polished margaritas set the tone; jazz, show tunes, and oldies-but-goodies alternate depending on the pianist (Tues–Thurs 7:30–11pm, Fri–Sat 8:30–10:30pm, Sun 7–10pm). It's gay and lesbian friendly, but a mixed crowd mingles easily.

Downtown

A friendly and well-priced basement bar, the **Bottom Line** (Downtown, 1716 I St. NW at 17th St.; ☎ 202/298-8488; www.thebottomlinedc.com; Metro: Farragut West) gets a crowd so corporate you may assume that even their pajamas have ties. But if you're an older visitor, no longer on the prowl for a mate, you may find that it hits just the right notes.

Bottom Line's polar opposite in pretty much every way is the would-be biker bar **Tattoo** (1413 K St.; ☎ 202/408-9444; www.tattoobardc.com; Metro: McPherson Square). Here, corrugated metal covers the walls and is used in the benches, big posters of tattooed people glower down as you drink, and a thumping soundtrack of current pop and '80s hits accompanies music videos on a large screen. It's a place you come if you're trying to get lucky or want to dance in the thin corridor at the center of the room. Some will find it erotic, others a bit skanky, but it's one of the easiest clubs for straight guys to get into on a Saturday night in this nightlife corridor, when it morphs from bar to dance club.

Dupont Circle

I'm not usually a fan of hotel bars—too many businessmen trying to drown their boredom in beer—but **Urbana** ✪✪ (at the Palomar Hotel, 2121 P St. NW; ☎ 202/956-6650; www.urbanadc.com; Metro: Dupont Circle) is different. Part restaurant, part wine bar (its motto "give it a swirl"), Urbana seems to be as much a gathering place for neighborhood folks as it is for visitors. And is it any wonder? This is a chic and yes, urbane hang (with the kind of lighting that makes everyone look 10 years younger) that also discounts: During the aperitif hour (4–7pm) Italian beers go for $4 and wines for $5. Don't assume you won't like it if you're not a vino-phile; the expert and expertly gregarious bartenders mix up mean cocktails as well (they're also quite proud of their collection of unusual scotches).

Vodka, vodka, and more vodka (over 90 varieties on offer), in a bar where the native tongue is as likely to be Latvian, Lithuanian, or Russian as it is English, is the special allure of **Russia House Restaurant and Lounge** ✪✪ (1800 Connecticut Ave. NW; ☎ 202/234-9433; www.russiahouselounge.com; Metro: Dupont Circle). Really, you're going to feel like you've crossed the Atlantic here. A favorite of nearby embassy workers, it's set in a town house that's a fantasy of red velvet and chandeliers, a throwback to the days of the czars. I very much like this place, though be warned: All of that flowing vodka and eastern European tempers mean that sometimes it can get a bit dicey in the wee hours of the morning (I've witnessed several heavy scenes here).

Seedy in looks, **Lucky Bar** ✪ (1221 Connecticut Ave. NW at M St.; ☎ 202/331-3733; www.luckybardc.com; Metro: Dupont Circle) nevertheless has two perks that keep it one of the most popular watering holes in the city. On Thursday, the price of a can of Bud drops to just $2 all night long. And there's no better place in the city to watch soccer; it boasts 25 TVs, a large projection screen, and a clientele of rabid fans from the nearby embassies. Dress any way you care to; the bike messengers and other budget imbibers who flock to the place for cheap beer set the tone.

Georgetown

The first thing you'll see when you descend down the stairs to the **Tombs** (Georgetown, 1226 36th St. NW at Prospect St.; ☎ 202/337-6668; www.tombs. com; Metrobus: D2, D4, D6, D8) is a bar overhung (as opposed to hungover) with literally dozens of plastic pitchers. I think that says it all: This is a college bar (Georgetown U, to be precise), a place where groups of frat boys come to down beer en masse. The Bush twins were also regulars when they came home from college to see mom and pop in the White House; in the 1985 movie *St. Elmo's Fire*, the characters played by Rob Lowe and Demi Moore hung out at the Tombs. You get the picture. If you're into this kind of scene, and sure, it can be fun, you won't mind the rather ratty look of the brick or the low basement ceilings. If you're over 25 or not an alumnus of Georgetown . . . well, you might want to search out a more adult scene.

And that may be found at **Tony and Joe's** (Georgetown, 3050 K St. NW on the Potomac River; ☎ 202/944-4545; www.dcseafood.com/taj; Metrobus: 30, 32, 34, 35, 36), but only in the summer months. That's when this upscale seafood restaurant opens its outdoor patio for bar service. The river views, looking out to the Kennedy Center, are gorgeous and well worth a detour and some time nursing a chardonnay. Go here only when the bar patio is open.

Penn Quarter

Clyde's of Gallery Place (Penn Quarter, 707 7th St. NW at H St.; ☎ 202/349-3700; www.clydes.com; Metro: Gallery Place–Chinatown) is where the masses descend when they pour out of the Verizon Center next door. Brass fixtures and dark wood walls and furnishings give it an appropriately testosterone-charged ambiance for this sporty crowd. And the massive venue (its 23,000 sq. ft. house three different barrooms) can accommodate the hordes . . . just barely (even with all the space it can get elbow-to-elbow after a game). It's not my favorite, but I'll bow to local tastes: Clyde's is part of a Washington-area chain which keeps on growing and growing, and locals love the place.

Just next door, with a 50-foot bar and a dramatically lit interior that even pin-shy Barack Obama might find cool, are the **Lucky Strike Lanes** ✸ (701

Drinking by the Rules

Twenty-one is the minimum age permitted to buy alcoholic beverages in the District of Columbia. Some bars and clubs restrict admission to that age as well.

Bars close at 2am, except on Friday and Saturday nights, when they remain open until 3am.

The D.C. Metropolitan Police Department is fully aware of the city's drinking hours. So don't drive if you have been imbibing. They'll catch you, especially if you are on the street after midnight.

Metrorail shuts down at midnight Sunday to Thursday. It operates until 3am Friday and Saturday nights. Party any later, and you are going to have to flag down a taxi.

Nightspot Shuttle Link

Two of Washington's liveliest entertainment areas are linked by shuttle bus, the **98 Adams Morgan U Street Link,** which operates nightly. A ride costs 25¢. The bus runs about every 15 minutes between the Woodley Park–Zoo–Adams Morgan Metro station and the U Street–African-American Civil War Memorial–Cardozo Metro stop. Buses are scheduled from 6pm to midnight Sunday to Thursday, 6pm to 3am Friday, and 10am to 3am Saturday. From the Woodley Park Metro station, the bus crosses Duke Ellington Bridge on Calvert Street NW, turns right onto 18th Street to U Street, and turns left on U Street to the U Street Metro station. Complete schedule is at **www.wmata.com/bus/timetables/dc/98.pdf.**

Seventh Ave. NW; ☎ 202/347-1021; www.bowlluckystrike.com; Metro: Gallery Place–Verizon Center), where just as many people come to tipple as they do to throw strikes. It's a mighty entertaining place—along with bowling, there's a pool table, a menu of bad-for-you-but-tasty food, a blaring R&B soundtrack, and several TVs all tuned to whatever sport's in season.

U Street Corridor

The edgy allure of U Street is heightened at the **Gibson** ✪✪✪ (2009 14th St. NW at U St.; ☎ 202/232-2156; Metro: U Street–African-American Civil War Memorial–Cardozo), which is, quite simply, a modern-day speak-easy. No sign or even plate glass window signals its presence, only those on the list get in (call the number above for reservations; no standing is allowed, so if you don't reserve a table or place at the bar, you won't be drinking here), and the lighting, via Edison-esque filament bulbs and candles, seems designed to protect patrons' privacy. It's all very sexy and that extends to the artful cocktails, some of which are assembled tableside by the waitress (she might light an orange rind with a flourish before anointing the rim of your glass with it). Sounds pretentious, I know, but really, these are some of the most expertly concocted cocktails in the city and quite unusual, too (if it's on offer, try the merlot float, $12; or the Appleton Estate, $10, a spiced rum drink like you've never tasted before). In summer, a patio will open, increasing the number of guests the Gibson can accommodate (in the cold weather months, the cutoff number is 48).

Nearby and right next door to the long-standing anchor of this neighborhood, **Ben's Chili Bowl** (p. 71), is a new bar named, appropriately enough, **Next Door** ✪ (1211 U St.; ☎ 202/667-0909; Metro: U Street–African-American Civil War Memorial–Cardozo). It's owned by the folks who own Ben's and has been long in the planning. A waiter at Ben's told me, "People have been getting drunk and then coming to Ben's for a late-night chili dog for decades. So the owners thought we should be the ones serving the alcohol." You can get the famous chili dog as well as drinks at the bar, though its menu will be a bit more extensive. Rahman "Rock" Harper, winner of season three of the reality show *Hell's Kitchen,* has been hired to create a more refined bar menu, and his crab cakes are already drawing raves. As for the ambiance, it lies somewhere between sports bar (TVs are interspersed with black-and-white photos of Ben's through the ages) and a neighborhood social club, so get ready to overhear choice local gossip.

Named for aviator/author Antoine de Saint-Exupery, **Café Saint-Ex** ✪✪ (U St. Corridor, 1847 14th St. NW at S St.; ☎ 202/265-7839; www.saint-ex.com; Metro: U Street–African-American Civil War Memorial–Cardozo) has a groovy Gallic accent. Inside, the decor is all curvaceous Art Deco furnishings, with a charming aviation theme; in warm weather, the front of the cafe holds a flock of outdoor tables. Nightlife comes into the equation downstairs with Gate 54, a lounge where DJs spin mellow but toe-tapping tunes which can range from bossa nova to soul funk to electronica. The crowd is as cool as the music, a wonderfully sophisticated scene.

DANCE CLUBS

Fireflies on a summer night have a longer life span than most dance clubs. So though I'm listing what were the hottest clubs in town when we went to press, do some homework with the publications I listed at the top of this section before you slip on your boogie shoes.

That being said, **Park at 14th** ✪✪ (920 14th St. at K St.; ☎ 202/737-7275; www.theparkat14th.com; no cover charge most nights; Metro: McPherson Square) was wowing partyers in early 2009 and with good reason. Dale Chihuly–esque chandeliers set a festive but classy tone as did the swank leather-covered furniture. Floor-to-ceiling windows allow those on the street to peek in and see what a great time everyone's having (they're also an interesting innovation: Most dance clubs have a subterranean feel, but this one makes the most of Washington's lovely cityscape). To make things even more interesting, the club has four floors (one VIP/private party only), often with different types of music on each, which is a good thing as the crowd here may well be among the most diverse in the city. Black and white, young and middle aged, they all come to party here. You'll understand why after you've visited (by the way, this is a club/restaurant, meaning you can get some sustenance if all that dancing burns too many calories).

Occupying a former 19th-century bank building, **Platinum** ✪ (915 F St. NW at 9th St.; ☎ 202/393-3555; www.platinumclubdc.com; $15 cover most nights; Fri-Sun 10pm; Metro: Metro Center; age 18 and older) is another stylish place, this time with three dance floors. You enter via a grand staircase at the entrance to dance on polished marble floors below a high ceiling. And one bar occupies what was once a row of teller windows. The club caters to an international crowd, and a line forms early most nights. Dress to impress—no baggy jeans, no sneakers, no baseball caps—if you want to get in. Free entrance for women arriving before 11pm on Saturdays and Sundays, and up until midnight on Fridays. Occasionally, the club pays visiting celebs, like LL Cool J, to stop by and liven up the scene.

Bigger may be better, especially if you're looking to pick someone up. That's certainly why thousands head to D.C.'s largest dance club, **Love** ✪ (1350 Okie St. NE; ☎ 202/636-9030; www.lovetheclub.com; cover $10–$15; Metro: Rhode Island Ave.–Brentwood), which absolutely pulses with energy. A four-level club, each with its own design (the first floor looks a bit like a fancy hotel, the outdoor patio has a tropical island theme, the main dance floor features a huge stage for live

Atlas: A New Nightlife Edge

Until just 5 years ago, the so-called **Atlas District** (H St. NE btw. 12th and 15th sts.), named for the landmark performing arts center that sits at its heart, was a forlorn strip of boarded-up shop fronts that never recovered from the riots of the '60's. But then, a spate of young entrepreneurs started opening up restaurants, clubs, and bars, and the neighborhood started to revive. Today the area is still a bit sketchy, but for those who keep their wits about them, it offers some of the most unique and downright fun nightlife options in the city. My faves:

◆ **Rock n' Roll Hotel** (1353 H St. NE; ☎ 202/388-ROCK [7625]; www.rockandrollhoteldc.com). A former funeral home, now a quirky dance club. Talented DJs and live bands playing mostly rock music keep everyone on his or her feet in the main room. And for those who just want to hang, there are a number of Asian- and hotel-theme rooms, with colonial-style couches and chairs (very D.C.-looking) that are good for conversation. Drinks are cheap and sometimes free early in the evening, with the payment of a $6 cover charge.

◆ **Showbar Presents the Palace of Wonders** (1210 H St. NE; ☎ 202/398-7469; www.palaceofwonders.com). An oddball "performance bar" that hosts burlesque, vaudeville, and circus-style acts. On-site is an actual sideshow or "dime" museum with relics from the last century, including an embalmed turkey-headed chicken, and a tattooed mummy arm.

◆ **Red & the Black** (1212 H St. NE; ☎ 202/399-3201; www.redandblackbar.com). A New Orleans–themed bar that hosts a lot of singer-songwriters. The jambalaya's top-notch.

◆ **The H Street Martini Lounge** (1236 H St. NE; ☎ 202/397-3333). One of the pioneers on the block, this friendly bar serves 63 different types of martinis, including some that taste like candy and others that have lollipops stuck in them.

Now the bad news: The Atlas District is not easy to reach. From the Metro Center station, catch Metrobus X2 to get to H Street, and don't go alone. When the night is done, flag a taxi back to your hotel.

performances), it's best for those who like hip-hop, and has attracted a number of celebs in that genre to perform or just party. Saturday is "international" night and gets the most diverse crowd, mixing in electronica with all the hip-hop. As at Platinum, a dress code is enforced (see above for what that will be). The cover is sometimes waived for women; you can also find coupons for free entry sometimes on the website. ***One warning:*** The neighborhood is sketchy and the Metro a long walk away. Consider taking a cab to and from, just for safety.

GAY & LESBIAN NIGHTLIFE

Washington is home to a large gay and lesbian population, attracted by its diverse, generally tolerant, and enlightened residents. The Dupont Circle neighborhood is considered the center of GLBT nightlife, though bars, clubs, and cafes catering to gays and lesbians are located in other close-in neighborhoods, such as Capitol Hill and the U Street Corridor. *Metro Weekly*, the GLBT newspaper, is a great source for specific events and "nights" around town; you can also peruse their nightlife listings at **www.metroweekly.com**.

The city's only exclusively lesbian bar, so far, is **Phase One** ✿ (Capitol Hill, 525 8th St. SE at Pennsylvania Ave.; ☎ 202/544-6831; www.phase1dc.com; Metro: Eastern Market). It's also the nation's oldest lesbian bar. An informal hole-in-the-wall kind of place, it sports a pool table, big TV screens, and a small dance floor. But its notable amenity is the friendly, welcoming clientele and staff.

The newest gay club, at this writing, is the truly fabulous **Town Dance-boutique** ✿✿✿ (2009 8th St. NW just off U St.; ☎ 202/234-TOWN [8696]; www.towndanceboutique.com; $10 cover; Metro: U Street–African-American Civil War Memorial–Cardozo). A glitter-filled drag show starts things off every Friday and Saturday night, followed by dancing in a large round-ish room, over which a small balcony hangs (a great location for spotting your next conquest). The crowd is eclectic, the dancing can get frenzied, and the club is so popular it's been pulling patrons from the other bars in town. Though the show only takes place on Fridays and Saturdays, there are other events on other nights of the week and dancing every day of the year.

If two-stepping is more your style, you'll enjoy the sawdust, fence posts, and neon of **Remington's** (639 Pennsylvania Ave. SE; ☎ 202/543-3113; www.remingtonswdc.com; Metro: Eastern Market). Yup, they've got the *Brokeback Mountain* look down pat. Country dance lessons happen many nights of the week (see the website) and are a great way to meet new folks, as you change partners a lot.

Be Bar (Logan Circle, 1318 9th St. NW; ☎ 202/232-7450; www.bebardc.com; Metro: Mount Vernon Square–7th Street–Convention Center). Occupying a restored row house, it draws rave reviews for its cool decor, large martini menu, Top-40 DJ tunes that propel you onto the dance floor, and the comfy couch that runs the length of the room. Equally chic, **Halo** (1435 P St. NW; ☎ 202/797-9730; www.theartoflounge.com; Metro: Dupont Circle and 5-block walk) has a NYC vibe, thanks to its cool lighting and ultramodern leather furniture. Though it's not as white-hot as it was when it opened in 2004, it still gets a good crowd of pretty young thangs.

If you're looking for the gay equivalent of "Cheers," head for **JR's Bar & Grill** (1519 17th St. NW; ☎ 202/328-0090; www.jrswdc.com; Metro: Dupont Circle), a casual brick-walled den at Dupont Circle where many come to relax and hang out with old friends. Yeah, it's a bit divey, but that doesn't stop folks from showing up; on some nights, it's so packed that it can be difficult to walk from one end of the bar to the other. This is certainly the case for the Broadway show-tune singalongs on Monday nights at 9:30pm.

Get Out of Town

Four rewarding, easy-as-pie day trips

By Jim Yenckel

WASHINGTON SITS IN THE MIDST OF WHAT MIGHT BE CALLED AMERICA'S historyland. Within easy reach are important reminders of the country's Colonial, Revolutionary, and Civil War past.

George Washington's footprints stride the surrounding countryside in profusion, as do those of Thomas Jefferson, James Madison, and James Monroe. The Civil War raged for 4 years virtually in the city's front yard, and several of its blood-drenched battlefields are preserved as national historical parks. Despite its urban setting, Washington is not much more than an hour from scenic Shenandoah National Park, a near-wilderness where mist-draped ridges and hollows recount tales of early Appalachian pioneers. A huge outdoor playground, the park is a great big bonus for Washingtonians.

Each of the four destinations I describe—Shenandoah National Park in Virginia; Gettysburg National Military Park in Pennsylvania; Annapolis, Maryland's colonial capital; and George Washington's Mount Vernon Plantation in Virginia—can be visited in an unrushed day trip by rented car, provided you get a reasonably early start—let's say 9am. Gettysburg and Mount Vernon also can be reached by tour bus. Mount Vernon can also be reached by tour boat and by bicycle on the paved Mount Vernon Trail (see "On Wheels," chapter 7, p. 177) and by public transportation (see "How to Get There" later in this chapter).

The most distant, Shenandoah, is about a 90-minute drive from most downtown lodgings. Weekday rush-hour traffic could slow you somewhat, but going and returning you will be traveling in the opposite direction of the overwhelming majority of commuters. Expect to be back at your hotel by dinner, unless you choose to stay awhile longer. Each of the four is a major attraction—the mid-Atlantic region's most significant ones, I think, outside the nation's capital itself.

MOUNT VERNON

Called to lead his nation first in war and then in peace, George Washington still found time—even while absent so often—to micromanage his beloved Virginia home and farm, officially **George Washington's Mount Vernon Estate & Gardens** ★★★ kids (Northern Virginia, 16 miles; ☎ 703/780-2000; www. mountvernon.org; adults $15, seniors $14, ages 6–11 $7; daily 5am–5pm Apr–Aug, 9am–5pm Mar and Sept–Oct, 9am–4pm Nov–Feb). On a visit here, you'll meet the man and the farmer, getting an up-close and intimate look at the life of America's number-one national hero. By turns genial and even flirtatious, the Washington of Mount Vernon is nothing like the aloof icon so often portrayed in classroom history texts.

Day Trips from Washington

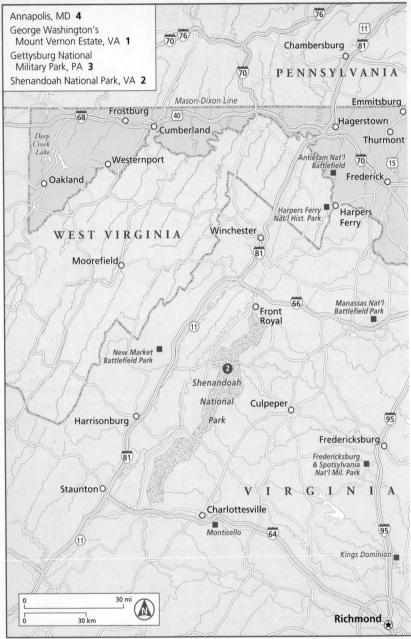

Annapolis, MD **4**

George Washington's
   Mount Vernon Estate, VA **1**

Gettysburg National
   Military Park, PA **3**

Shenandoah National Park, VA **2**

Mason-Dixon Line

PENNSYLVANIA

Chambersburg

Emmitsburg

Frostburg

Cumberland

Hagerstown

Thurmont

Antietam Nat'l Battlefield

Frederick

Deep Creek Lake

Westernport

Oakland

WEST VIRGINIA

Harpers Ferry Nat'l Hist. Park

Harpers Ferry

Winchester

Moorefield

Manassas Nat'l Battlefield Park

Front Royal

New Market Battlefield Park

❷

Shenandoah

National

Culpeper

Park

Harrisonburg

Fredericksburg

Fredericksburg & Spotsylvania Nat'l Mil. Park

Staunton

VIRGINIA

Charlottesville

Monticello

Kings Dominion

0   30 mi
0   30 km

N

Richmond

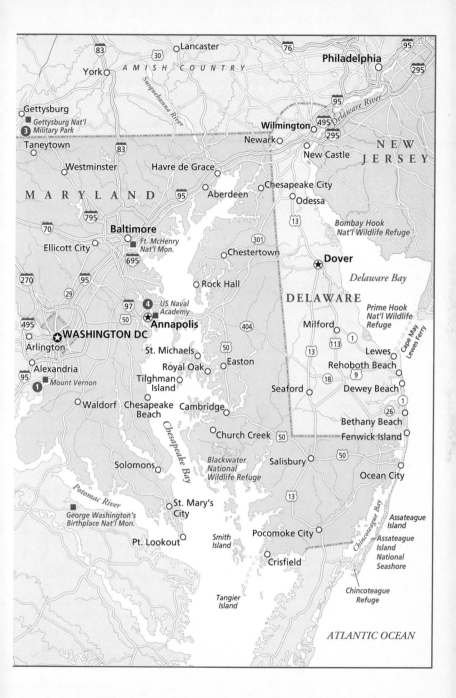

For 45 years, the greater part of Washington's life, Mount Vernon was his home—and a major ongoing improvement project. The origins of the mansion are not known exactly, although Washington's grandfather may have built a tenant house on the site. George acquired Mount Vernon, then a modest six-room house, at the death of his half-brother and soon began improving it and the grounds. Over the decades he more than tripled the size of the stately white, Palladian-style mansion (from 6 rooms to 21). He redesigned its grounds and outbuildings and acquired a total of 8,000 acres, which he farmed.

Today, the mansion and grounds look much as they did in his day, although the acreage has diminished to about 500. Even the grand view across the Potomac River, enjoyed from the columned piazza in front, remains much the same, preserved by national parkland. Thirteen trees from the landscape plan he designed still stand. Many personal objects are displayed, including the very bed in which he died on December 14, 1799, at the age of 67. He and his wife Martha are entombed on the estate.

Mount Vernon, which attracts about one million visitors a year, is owned and maintained by the Mount Vernon Ladies' Association. Founded in 1853, it is the oldest national historic preservation organization in the country. Its Board of Regents, as the name suggests, is comprised solely of women. The association purchased Mount Vernon from the Washington family in 1858 and opened it to the public 2 years later. Indoor and outdoor exhibits include 20 original structures, a reconstructed 16-sided treading barn, 50 acres of gardens duplicating those of 1799, and a 4-acre working farm.

The fall of 2006 saw the completion of two major buildings—an orientation center and an education center. Because both are located just inside the estate's main entrance, I'll begin a tour with them. The **Ford Orientation Center** (as in Ford Motor Company) is where you first meet George as a regular guy, not a marble statue, grappling with the nonstop challenges of Colonial life. This introduction is achieved by means of an 18-minute, Hollywood-style movie filmed primarily at Mount Vernon. It is shown in rotation in two adjacent theaters. "We have found in recent years that visitors are coming to Mount Vernon with only the most basic knowledge about George Washington," writes James C. Rees, Mount Vernon's executive director. The goal of the new facilities is "to show visitors specifically why George Washington, the most dynamic leader of his time, was chosen again and again by the Founding Fathers to lead this country."

The new center's other major attraction is **Mount Vernon in Miniature,** a one-twelfth scaled replica of the mansion. Its doorknobs turn; its windows open and close; the candles light, and the latches latch. The walls can be lowered and the roof removed to reveal detailed reproductions inside of furnishings, paintings, and books. A single whisker, plucked from a mouse, was the paint brush used to decorate mini porcelain pieces. The other new building is the **Donald W. Reynolds Museum and Education Center.** The Reynolds Foundation, one of the country's largest private foundations, donated $24 million. (Reynolds was a media entrepreneur who owned 70 businesses at his death in 1993.) The museum houses 500 objects related to George and Martha in six permanent galleries. These include decorative arts furnishings used at Mount Vernon and artifacts from Washington's career as soldier and statesman. The largest exhibit, **"At Home with the Washingtons,"** offers a peek at their everyday lives. The Education Center features high-tech interactive displays and nine videos produced by the History Channel. To me, the most intriguing exhibit displays three life-size models created by artists and forensic and computer experts that show Washington as a teenage surveyor, a 45-year-old general at Valley Forge, and a 57-year-old American president. No portraits of Washington under the age of 40 exist; so you will be getting a first glimpse at young George (at least as technology sees him). At the exhibit's Valley Forge, he sits astride his horse. Nearby, a typical cabin for troops is cooled to winter temperature to show what his army faced at that brutal encampment.

After this introduction to Washington, head for the mansion. In summer, the line often is long, and you may have to wait up to 30 minutes. Much like a tour of the White House, you will be funneled in one side, climb to the second floor, descend, and exit from the opposite end onto the piazza. This might take 8 minutes. (It's a hurried look, so keep your eyes open.) On the first floor, the **Large Dining Room,** so called because it is two stories high, was the final addition to the house. In 1776, though threatened by British forces in New York, Washington sent off detailed instructions to his manager about its construction. It remained unfinished until long after the war because he could not find a satisfactory craftsman to provide the ceiling and woodwork decoration that he desired. The room's light green color is based on his original choice, and the wallpaper border also duplicates original fragments. An obvious question: Where is the dining room table? None is mentioned in Washington's inventory. It is thought he liked to keep the room open, bringing in trestles and boards to serve as a temporary table when a crowd was expected for dinner.

The central hall, called the **Passage,** stretches the width of the house from the front door to the river-view piazza. In summer, it was the most comfortable place to be because of the cross breezes, and it's where George and Martha enjoyed much of their informal social life. Look for the key hanging on the wall between the bedroom and dining room. A gift of General Lafayette in 1790, it was a key to the French Bastille. "It is a tribute," Lafayette wrote, "which I owe as a son to my adoptive father—as an aide-de-camp to my general—as a missionary of liberty to its patriarch." The key presumably has hung in the same location since Washington had it placed there. The walls resemble mahogany, but the wood grain is simulated by paint, per Washington's instructions in 1797.

The **West Parlor,** painted in Prussian blue, is regarded as one of the finest surviving examples of a Colonial Virginia interior. Much of the family social life took place in this room; it's where the important family portraits hung. Five water colors to the left of the fireplace are originals. On the pediment above the mantel is a carved replica of Washington's coat of arms. An intense green in color, the **Small Dining Room** is furnished with a mahogany table, believed to be an original Mount Vernon piece. The **Downstairs Bedroom** was a customary feature of even large Virginia homes. Washington's extended family (including two secretaries) numbered eight, and they occupied the upper-floor bedrooms. Guests were accommodated downstairs.

Also downstairs is the **Study,** partially lined in pinewood painted to look more expensive than it was. Escaping his crowded household, Washington managed his farm from this room. It's the first place he went each morning; his dressing table, purchased during his presidency, rests between the windows.

On the second floor are five smaller bedrooms and the master bedroom, known officially as **General and Mrs. Washington's Bedchamber.** The bed, made in Philadelphia in 1794, is where he died. It may appear short because of its width and the height of the posts, but it is 6½ feet long. After all, Washington was a tall man. This is where Martha managed the busy household, sitting at a French desk presumed to have been purchased in 1791 from France's first minister to America.

After seeing the mansion, you can tour the estate at your own pace. Peek into the kitchen, the storehouse, the overseer's quarters, the coach house, and the stable. Washington delighted in fox hunting; Thomas Jefferson considered him the finest horseman of the age. And don't overlook the tomb.

If the youngsters are getting antsy, hustle them off to the **16-sided Threading Barn,** a reproduction of the design Washington invented to thresh wheat. Initially, plantation slaves spread the wheat out on the bare ground, and horses trampled it to break out the grain. To protect the wheat from foul weather and to keep it clean, Washington brought the operation inside under the roof of his new barn. Horses continued to tread the wheat underfoot, but the grain dropped through slits in the floor to a collecting area below. You can watch an actual demonstration, standing inside the barn while the horses parade around you as if on a carousel. The barn is part of a 4-acre working farm, stocked with rare breed farm animals—oxen, mules, sheep, roosters, and hens—that date from Washington's era.

The estate offers a number of daily events from spring to fall. They include "Slave Life at Mount Vernon," a 30-minute walking tour; "The National Treasure Tour," an hour-long tour introducing guests to where filming for that movie took place (with info on how George and Martha used those areas as well, of course); a 30-minute "Garden and Landscaping Tour;" and a daily public wreath-laying ceremony at the Washington tomb. Check the Calendar on Mount Vernon's website. Restrooms, a restaurant, snack shop, and gift shop are available.

In Washington's Footsteps

George Washington Memorial Parkway links Washington with Mount Vernon. One of the country's loveliest river drives, the 16-mile route traces the Potomac River south of Alexandria. It was opened in 1932 to mark the 200th anniversary of Washington's birth. At the time, it was dubbed "America's Most Modern Motorway." A landscaped, limited-access road, it is dotted with picnic areas, pleasure craft marinas, and bird sanctuaries. Paralleling it is the Mount Vernon Trail, a paved bicycle route. Washington reportedly considered Alexandria, the town nearest Mount Vernon, as his hometown. Its historic Old Town preserves numerous 18th- and 19th-century structures dating from its origins as a prosperous Colonial seaport. King Street, its main street, teems with shoppers and boutique browsers on weekends. At Washington Street (your driving route) and Cameron Street, consider stopping at redbrick Christ Church (1773). Washington's pew is Number 60.

HOW TO GET THERE

By Car

Drive west across the 14th Street (NW) Bridge over the Potomac River. At the far end of the bridge, take the exit to Reagan Washington National Airport and Alexandria. You will be heading south of George Washington Memorial Parkway. Continue on the parkway through Alexandria to Mount Vernon, where the parkway ends.

By Boat

Spirit Cruises (Pier 4, 6th St. and Water St. SW; ☎ 866/211-3811; Metro: Waterfront Station; www.spiritofwashington.com; $38 adults, $36 seniors, $31 children) runs Tuesday through Sunday cruises downriver to Mount Vernon, from March 31 until August 23, with Friday through Sunday sailings through the end of October (and occasionally in Nov and Mar—check the website). The boat picks up passengers at 8:30am, returning them by 3pm. Three hours of that time are spent exploring Mount Vernon. If you have a full day, this is definitely the most relaxing way to visit Washington's home.

By Bus

Martz Gold Line/Gray Line (Union Station; ☎ 800/862-1400; Metro: Union Station; www.graylinedc.com; daily except Thanksgiving, Dec 25, and Jan 1) offers several tours of Mount Vernon, often in combination with excursions to Alexandria, or the top sights in Washington, D.C., itself. Rates start at $47 and go up depending on the length of the tour (children pay about half the adult price). "Mount Vernon by Candlelight" is the most unusual offering and includes a visit to the third floor of the house where Martha lived after George's death (an area rarely open to visitors). Buses depart from Union Station.

> *I can truly say I had rather be at home at Mount Vernon with a friend or two about me, than to be attended at the seat of government by the officers of State and the representatives of every power in Europe.*
>
> —George Washington,
> June 15, 1790

SHENANDOAH NATIONAL PARK

Overdosed on museums and history lessons? Then take a day off and head for the hills along one of America's most scenic roads. The kids will love the chance to run a little wild. They may even spot a black bear, a flock of wild turkeys, or almost certainly, lots of deer. My choice, when I want to escape Washington's urban hubbub, is **Shenandoah National Park** ★★ (Northwestern Virginia, 70 miles; ☎ 540/999-3500; www.nps.gov/shen; $15 per car Mar–Nov and $10 Dec–Feb).

For motorists, the park's primary attraction is Skyline Drive, which traces the crest of the Blue Ridge Mountains for 105 miles, the entire length of the long, slender park. (The routing I suggest covers just over half the distance. Give yourself at least 5 hours for the whole trip.) Built over the course of 9 years, it was designed to provide the best views. From north to south, nearly 80 overlooks tempt you to enjoy them. Pick a half-dozen at random; you won't miss anything by skipping more.

The drive begins in the town of Front Royal at Shenandoah's northern gateway, flowing south like a stream among the rocky peaks of the Blue Ridge. On either side of the road, forested slopes drop away steeply, forming a rumpled landscape of shady hollows and dark canyons. On the east, far below, lies Virginia's Piedmont, a land of rolling hills where green pastures and golden fields form a patchwork-quilt landscape. On the west, you see the state's famed Shenandoah Valley, where the placid Shenandoah River carves glistening loops.

Unlike most national parks, Shenandoah was created from settled land. To make way for it, the residents had to move, giving up homes that had been in families for generations. In the early 19th century, as good farmland became scarce in the Piedmont and Shenandoah Valley, Shenandoah's first settlers, forbearers of the families who had to leave, moved up onto the Blue Ridge slopes. Eventually numbering about 5,000, they cleared small, hardscrabble plots in streams and valleys called hollows. They fished, farmed, and logged until the land wore out and the timber was gone. Some moved away. In the mid-1920s along came the National Park Service looking for Appalachian Mountain park sites near the East Coast's big cities. Officials chose what would eventually become Shenandoah and Great Smoky Mountains National Park in Tennessee. At this point, about 450 families remained within the park's proposed boundaries. Many sold out; others were forcibly evicted. Descendants still live in nearby communities. The Civilian Conservation Corps, a military-like job-creation program organized during the Depression, built campgrounds and other facilities, and President Franklin D. Roosevelt dedicated Shenandoah on July 3, 1936. Today a thick blanket of trees again drapes the mountains, and the returning wildlife is almost too abundant.

The story of the Appalachian people who once lived along the Blue Ridge is told at the **Dickey Ridge Visitor Center** (Mile 4.6 from the northern entrance). From here the **Fox Hollow Trail,** a gentle 1-mile loop, leads to the former home site of the Fox family. A free trail guide notes that beginning in 1837 four generations of Foxes farmed a 450-acre plot on the east side of the ridge. You will pass the family cemetery; just beyond, the farm's spring still bubbles from the ground.

One of Skyline Drive's most spectacular stops is **Range View Overlook** (Mile 17.1). Instead of focusing on the flatlands far below, it directs your gaze to the peaks of the Blue Ridge, lined up like soldiers in a formation that stretches south as far as the eye can see. If you didn't pack a picnic, stop for picnic supplies or a snack bar lunch at the park's **Elkwallow Wayside** (Mile 24.1; ☎ 800/778-2851; www.visitshenandoah.com; Apr 9–Nov 8 Sun–Thurs 9am–7pm, Fri–Sat 8am–7pm). For a shortened trip, exit the park at Thornton Gap (Mile 31.5; U.S. Rte. 211; see below) to return to Washington, or continue south. I recommend continuing on. In countless twists and turns, Skyline gradually climbs to an elevation of 3,680 feet. You are almost that high at **Stony Man Mountain Overlook** (Mile 38.6), so named because of the facelike shape of the peak.

The **Appalachian Trail,** en route from Georgia to Maine, parallels Skyline Drive the full length of the park, crossing the drive 28 times. To claim you have hiked part of this famous route, pull over at any of the well-marked trail heads and amble north or south for a few steps or a few miles, and then double back. Keeping to the ridge top, the trail is mostly level.

Motel and cabin lodgings and a restaurant with sweeping views and hearty country fare are available at **Skyland Lodge** (Mile 41.7; ☎ 800/778-2851; www. visitshenandoah.com; cabins, $68–$123 for two; lodge rooms, $89–$138; late Mar–Nov). On a day trip, you aren't going to want to rent a room. But the cliffside setting at the drive's highest elevation is gorgeous; a gift shop sells typical national park souvenirs and sweatshirts; the food is good; and, at the very least, the restrooms are clean. Just beyond, **Limberlost Trail** (Mile 43) is a 1.3-mile woodland circuit built for wheelchair access. It leads to a grove of massive hemlock trees, up to 3 feet in diameter and 350 to 400 years old. If you're up to a challenge, tackle **Dark Hollow Falls Trail** (Mile 50.7), a round-trip hike of about 1.5 miles. It drops sharply from Skyline Drive alongside Hog Camp Branch, a cascading stream that forms several scenic pools before plunging 70 feet down a series of rocky steps. It's the closest of the park's waterfalls to the drive. Going down is easy; climbing back up can be a struggle. **Big Meadows** (Mile 51; ☎ 800/778-2851; www.visitshenandoah.com; lodge rooms, $74–$139; cabins $96–$109; mid-May to early Nov) is the appropriately named location of another park and visitor center. Stop here to view the visitor center exhibits, which focus on the park's history. If you skipped lunch at Skyland Lodge, the restaurant serves all-American fare. Continue south and exit Shenandoah at Swift Run Gap.

HOW TO GET THERE

Take I-66 west from downtown Washington (23rd St. and Constitution Ave. NW) to the town of Front Royal. Follow the road signs to the park gate just south of town. Continue south on Skyline Drive through the park to Swift Run Gap (Mile 65). Exit the park east on U.S. 33, connecting to U.S. 29 north to I-66 east into Washington. The total distance is about 260 miles. To cut the distance to about 200 miles, exit the park on U.S. 211 at Thornton Gap (Mile 32), connecting to U.S. 29 north to I-66 east. Ask for a free park map at the entrance gate. Check the website (above) for regularly scheduled ranger-led programs.

GETTYSBURG

Stand on Cemetery Ridge at Gettysburg and picture an army of 12,000 racing your way, well armed and determined to kill you. Scary? You know it. Then put yourself in the ranks of the charging troops. Across the slender valley ahead awaits the enemy, equally well armed and also well protected by stone walls and other barriers. Even scarier, don't you think? At a Civil War battlefield park such as Gettysburg, you can put yourself into the actual footsteps of the combatants. You become an imaginary participant in the infamous Pickett's Charge, the horrendous turning point of the Civil War.

If you visit only one Civil War battlefield in your life, make it **Gettysburg National Military Park** ✰✰ (kids) (Southeastern Pennsylvania, 80 miles; ☎ 717/334-1124; www.nps.gov/gett; admission to the park itself is free, it opens at 6am; visitor center hours are Nov–Mar daily 8am–5pm, Apr 1–May 31 and Sept 1–Oct 31 8am–6pm, June–Aug 8am–7pm; admission, including a film, *The New Birth of Freedom* and cyclorama: $7.50 adults; $6.50 seniors and active military; $5.50 for ages 6–18; children 5 and under free). America was shaped by the series of bloody battles that raged on the outskirts of a crossroads village called Gettysburg from

July 1 to July 3 in 1863. Until these 3 fateful days, the Confederate army under General Robert E. Lee had been victorious, and the South's goal of separating from the Union seemed a possibility. But Gettysburg changed this outlook. After Lee's disastrous loss here—Pickett's Charge was a costly failure—the Union gained the upper hand. In the months ahead, General Ulysses S. Grant would take command of Union forces, ultimately forcing Lee's surrender and ending the war at Appomattox Court House in Virginia on April 9, 1865. At Gettysburg, you trace the major events of the 3-day conflict—the bloodiest ever fought on American soil. But you and the youngsters also take home a good grasp of what preceded Gettysburg and what followed. This overview will serve you well when touring other Civil War battlefields.

Gettysburg is well on its way to becoming the Civil War's most authentic battlefield. Under an ongoing program fostering historical integrity, the battlefield landscape is being returned to the way it looked when the fighting broke out. A famous peach orchard and wheat field, both of which played an important role, are being replanted. Fences and farm roads are being rebuilt along their original routes. You can see the terrain as the soldiers experienced it.

In September 2008, a brand new, $103-million museum, visitor center, and parking lot were opened, allowing removal of the current outdated facilities, which for decades have occupied part of Cemetery Hill. The new center has information to orient visitors to the park and Gettysburg, hosts a museum on the Civil War from beginning to dramatic end featuring items from the massive museum collection of Civil War and Gettysburg artifacts, and houses the fully restored famed **Gettysburg Cyclorama,** a colossal circular painting of Pickett's Charge. Using sound and light, the 20-minute cyclorama program seems to put you in the fury and chaos of the fighting. More than 10,000 figures are represented on the canvas—about half the number that actually fought on this day—and countless horses, cannons, and wagons.

As you enter the new visitor center, you will find a rotunda, leading to 12 galleries, 11 of which are inspired by phrases from Lincoln's Gettysburg Address, each depicting moments from the battle and the Civil War, with illustrations, displays, and memorabilia.

The **National Cemetery,** which President Abraham Lincoln dedicated with his Gettysburg Address on November 19, 1863, is located just outside the old Visitor Center. In it are buried 3,555 Union soldiers killed at Gettysburg, their bodies removed from the battlefield over a period of months. Confederate dead remained buried on the battlefield until their bodies were removed to Southern cemeteries.

Now you are ready to take the park's **18-Mile Auto Tour.** You can drive the route on your own with a free detailed park map; hike partway; rent a bicycle in the town of Gettysburg and pedal the route; hire a licensed battlefield guide who rides in your car; or take a scheduled bus tour, offered two to six times daily from late March through August. Though it's expensive, I recommend signing up for a **private guide** at the Visitor Center; you can reserve up to 10 days in advance (☎ 877/438-8929). An informative 2-hour tour for one to six passengers is $45 per car and takes in the battle's major landmarks. For information about guided bus tours departing from the Visitor Center, call ☎ 717/334-6296. They cost $25 per person, $14 for children 6 to 12.

The Northern and Southern armies clashed in separate engagements on the first 3 days of July in 1863. In those 3 days, the two armies experienced a total of more than 50,000 casualties—10,000 killed, 30,000 wounded, and 10,000 missing or captured. The South bore the brunt of the losses. If you are a summer visitor, you can suffer the same hot, sticky climate they endured.

The tour is laid out chronologically with 16 stops and takes you through the town of Gettysburg, which had a population of about 2,400 in 1860 (7,000 today). Plaques on houses indicate the 160 still-standing structures that date back to the battle. The bullet-nicked **Jennie Wade House** was the home (now a museum) of the only Gettysburg civilian killed in battle. The historic downtown area retains its 19th-century character, in contrast to the modern-day tourist strip (restaurants, fast-food outlets, T-shirt shops, lodgings) adjacent to the battlefield.

On Oak Ridge (Stop 2), the **Eternal Light Memorial** is one of the battlefield's most prominent memorials. President and Mrs. Kennedy visited it shortly before the president was assassinated. It is thought that this is where Mrs. Kennedy got the idea for a similar eternal flame at Kennedy's gravesite in Arlington National Cemetery.

Most of the monuments honor Union soldiers, but increasingly Southerners are being remembered. At **Seminary Ridge** (near Stop 6), General James Longstreet, Lee's second in command, is shown in bronze reining in his charging horse. Note the lack of a pedestal; horse and rider appear as if they just emerged from the surrounding woods.

Little Round Top (Stop 8), a rocky hill at the southern end of the Union line, recalls a crucial second-day battle. A Maine regiment successfully defended the hill, ultimately attacking the charging enemy with bayonets when they ran out of ammunition. The story is told beautifully in Michael Shaara's *The Killer Angels,* a Pulitzer Prize–winning novel.

The **Copse of Trees** (Stop 15) on Cemetery Ridge was the focal point of Pickett's Charge. Flags flying, his battle line of 12,000 troops stretching a mile long, he advanced across open fields toward the Union line on Cemetery Ridge, where 7,000 soldiers awaited. In 1 hour, the Confederates suffered 5,000 casualties. The next day, Lee retreated to Virginia. The Civil War would last 2 more years, but ultimate Union victory was virtually assured.

HOW TO GET THERE
By Car
Gettysburg is about 80 miles north of Washington. Take I-270 north from the Capital Beltway (reached via Wisconsin Ave. north from Georgetown) to Frederick, Maryland. Connect to U.S. 15 north. A few miles into Pennsylvania, a large road sign will indicate the exit on Business U.S. 15 (Steinwehr Ave.) to Gettysburg. The military park will be on the right.

By Bus
Martz Gold Line/Gray Line (Union Station; ☎ 800/862-1400; Metro: Union Station; www.graylinedc.com; Mon, Wed, Fri, and Sat Mar 17–Nov 1; $92 adult, $82 child) operates 47- and 55-passenger motor coaches on 10½-hour tours to Gettysburg. Reservations by 3pm the day before required.

Ike & Mamie's Farm

What did Ike and Mamie Eisenhower do when they retired from the White House to their Gettysburg farm? Often they welcomed distinguished visitors. But when they were alone, they set up TV trays on the sun porch for dinner and watched *I Love Lucy*. This is one of the many personal glimpses of the Eisenhowers that make a tour of the **Eisenhower National Historic Site** (☎ 717/338-9114; www. nps.gov/eise; $6.50 adults, $4 ages 6-12; daily 9am–4pm except Thanksgiving, Dec 25, and Jan 1) rewarding fun. The 189-acre Eisenhower retirement home and farm is a 7-minute shuttle bus ride (the only access) from the Gettysburg Battlefield Visitor Center. Departures are every half-hour during busy summer months; as few as twice a day in midwinter (see website for details).

ANNAPOLIS: DOWN COLONIAL LANES

In Maryland's capital, stroll down narrow, angled streets lined with what is believed to be the greatest concentration of 18th-century buildings in the United States. They are a historical and architectural treasure. About 50 structures built before the Revolutionary War still stand, many beautifully restored. Before 1776, the Chesapeake Bay seaport of **Annapolis** ✪✪ (Eastern Maryland, 35 miles from Washington; ☎ 888/302-2852; www.visit-annapolis.org) became celebrated throughout the colonies for the elegance of its architecture and the spirit of its political, intellectual, and social life. The evident prosperity reflected the city's status as Maryland's premier port. George Washington, Thomas Jefferson, and other Founding Fathers joined wealthy tobacco planters for the gala winter season of horse racing, dancing, and entertainment in the style of London society. If they returned now, they could with good reason think that not all that much has changed.

Annapolis thrives today as perhaps the region's most charming and most romantic weekend getaway destination. My wife and I lived on the edge of the historic district for 5 years when a work assignment took her to the city. I fell in love with the place then, and we visit frequently. Elegantly restored mansions, beautiful gardens, superb water views, sailing races, and the U.S. Naval Academy along with excellent seafood, lively pubs, and off-beat shops conspire to attract visitors.

When Annapolis was laid out in 1695, its master plan featured the French-influenced baroque style, considered the most sophisticated of its day. Like those in Washington, the streets radiate from circles. A visitor can get lost for a moment wandering the odd twists. But the feel is one of intimacy, as if you are moving from one small courtyard to another.

To explore, park your car at the **Visitor Center** (24 West St.) at Church Circle and amble down the old streets, as the Colonial residents did. To reach the Visitor Center, follow the VISITOR CENTER signs after you turn onto Rowe Boulevard, the city's principal gateway. Join an escorted walking tour, trolley tour, or (my preference) tour on your own with the city's free walking tour guide. The historic district is compact, and distances are short.

Perched atop a modest hill on nearby State Circle is the **Maryland State House** ✪, the oldest state capitol (begun in 1772) in continuous legislative use in the United States. When Annapolis briefly served as the new nation's capital (Nov 1783–Aug 1784), George Washington appeared before the U.S. Congress, then meeting in the State House, to resign as commander-in-chief of the Continental Army on December 23, 1783. The Treaty of Paris, officially ending the Revolutionary War, was ratified here on January 14, 1784. The **Old Senate Chamber** where these events occurred has been preserved as it was then. A life-size statue of Washington stands among numerous pieces of original furniture. The two-story redbrick capitol, Georgian in style, supports an octagonal dome made of cypress beams. It is the largest wooden dome in the country. Not a nail was used in its construction, because they were scarce during the war. Instead, pegs hold the beams together.

Streets radiating from the State House slope down to the harbor. Two of the city's great 18th-century Georgian mansions, located within steps of each other and the State House, invite visitors inside. If you have time to visit only one, make it the **William Paca House and Garden** ✪ (186 Prince George St.; ☎ 410/267-7619; www.annapolis.org; $8 adults, $7 seniors, $5 ages 6–17; from the last week in Mar to Dec, except Dec 24–25, Mon–Sat 10am–5pm, Sun noon–5pm, and from Feb to late Mar Fri–Sun 10am–5pm), which dates to 1765. Paca, a signer of the Declaration of Independence, served as Maryland's governor during the Revolution. He built his grand 37-room home in a five-part Georgian style. From the large central building, two passageways (called "hyphens") extend to smaller wings on each side. It is a graceful design, though Paca forgot to build a back stairway. It had to be added later, so (if for no other reason) servants did not have to whisk the chamber pots down the grand staircase. In the past century, it served as a boardinghouse and hotel. A move to demolish it sparked creation of the Historic Annapolis Foundation, which restored the house and its 2-acre formal garden to its Colonial grandeur and went on to spur the city's historical revitalization.

Is it the most beautiful doorway in America? That's what the brochure claims. Certainly this Palladian-style door is lovely, but you'll have to decide for yourself when you visit the **Hammond-Harwood House** (19 Maryland Ave.; ☎ 410/263-4683; www.hammondharwoodhouse.org; $5 adults, $3 children; Apr–Oct Tues–Sun noon–5pm). Step inside the five-part house built in 1774 for a 40-minute escorted tour. It displays one of the best collections anywhere of Maryland's furniture and paintings from the 18th and early 19th centuries. Regarded by the experts as one of the finest Colonial houses in America because of its carved woodwork and plaster ornamentation, it also tells a sad story. Mathias Hammond, a plantation owner and lawyer, reportedly wanted to build one of the finest houses he could for his bride-to-be. But he became so obsessed with the work that he all but abandoned his young lady. She decamped, and he never lived in the house. William Harwood, a teacher, later purchased it, and in 1940, it was acquired by the organization that maintains it as a house museum.

Head now for the **Naval Academy** ✪✪ (Main Gate, King George and Randall sts.; ☎ 410/263-6933; www.usna.edu/visit.htm; daily 9am–5pm; free admission) for a glimpse of the uncommon life of the 4,000 midshipmen who reside on the 338-acre waterside campus. Visitors 16 and older will need a photo ID to enter; on foot only. The Armel-Leftwich Visitor Center is located a block inside the gate.

A 12-minute movie, *To Lead and To Serve,* is so upbeat about life at the academy you may well want to apply for admission then and there. The second-floor museum details the daily routine and explains many traditions. The campus is called "the Yard" because a dockyard preceded the academy at this location.

You can tour on your own, but I recommend taking a **guided tour** ($8.50 adults, $7.50 seniors, $6.50 students grades 1–12; Apr–June and Sept–Nov Mon–Fri 10am–3pm, Sat 9:30am–3pm and Sun 12:30–3pm, July–Aug Mon–Sat 9:30am–3pm, Sun 12:30–3pm, Dec–Mar Mon–Sat 10am–2:30pm and Sun 12:30–2:30pm). Your guide will fill you in on the traditions that have evolved since the academy was founded in 1845. In **Lejeune Hall**'s swimming pool, you see where students jump fully clothed from a three-story diving tower in an abandon-ship drill. Step inside **Bancroft Hall,** the massive dorm, to see a sample midshipman's room. Space is cramped, but everything is neatly stored, as the academy requires. The **Chapel** is where many a graduate has married in a crossed sword ceremony. In the ornate crypt below, the remains of naval hero **John Paul Jones** lie in honor. The guide will leave you here. On your own, visit the Naval Academy Museum's **Gallery of Ships,** just across the street. It's one of the world's finest collections of warship models from centuries past, many of them hand-carved.

These are Annapolis's historical highlights. Now stroll the residential side streets, where colored markers note Colonial and other historic houses. The 19th-century, Queen Anne–style home at 138 Conduit St. is a standout. A white-shingled wedding cake of fanciful turrets and gables, known as the **Zimmerman House,** it was built in 1887 as the home of the Naval Academy bandmaster who wrote "Anchors Aweigh." After your historic stroll, browse the shops on Main Street. Chat with the yachting crowd, sunning on their vessels tied up at City Dock. And of course, don't forget to try a famous Chesapeake Bay crab cake sandwich at a waterside restaurant.

HOW TO GET THERE
By Car
Take New York Avenue northeast out of Washington, connecting to U.S. 50 east to Annapolis. From U.S. 50, take the Rowe Street, Historic District exit into Annapolis. At press time, no tours from Washington to Annapolis were offered, and there was no regular public bus service.

12 The Essentials of Planning

By Jim Yenckel & Pauline Frommer

THE HIGHLIGHTS OF A VISIT TO WASHINGTON, D.C.—THE TOP SIGHTS and activities, the hotels, restaurants, shops, and tours that best serve your needs—have filled the bulk of this book. But almost as important is the miscellany that doesn't fit into broader categories. Those nitty-gritty details—from trip-planning essentials to perks to tips for travelers with special interests and needs—are what you'll find in this chapter.

The good news is that Washington, D.C., is undeniably a visitor-friendly city and has, in its tourist office **Destination DC** (☎ 800/422-8644 or 202/789-7001; www.washington.org) one of the best resources in the U.S. for travelers. It's a well-run, efficient organization staffed by real experts who love their jobs; and its website offers a wealth of information and discounts for the traveler.

In addition, for neighborhood history, a daily schedule of lectures and arts events, and additional walking tours, check the website for **Cultural Tourism DC** (www.culturaltourismdc.org).

Information about federal attractions and events on or near the National Mall is at three National Park websites: **National Capital Parks–Central** (www.nps.gov/nacc); **National Capital Parks–East** (www.nps.gov/nace); and the **National Register of Historic Places** (www.cr.nps.gov/nr/travel/wash/sitelist.htm).

Anything that you can't find in this book—and hopefully that won't be much—you should be able to find through these tourist offices.

WHEN TO VISIT

"Whenever you're ready," is our answer, which is our way of saying Washington never shuts down. Sure, members of Congress take one of their too-many breaks in August—so you can't see them in action. But museums, monuments, and memorials are open year-round (except for Dec 25), and those who live here see to it that cultural events and nightlife activity rarely slack off in any season.

If money is no object, the best times to visit, weather-wise, are **spring** and **fall.** In spring, nearly all of Washington becomes a flowering garden as a procession of bulbs (daffodils, tulips, irises), azalea bushes, and flowering trees (Japanese cherries, magnolias, dogwoods) fill parklands and neighborhood yards with vibrant colors. Fall brings more color in a surprisingly dramatic foliage display up and down our avenues (best in Oct). Perhaps it's not as glorious a show as New England's, but it's a dazzler nonetheless. In both seasons, the weather is mild, ideal for sightseeing. The drawback, of course—you could see this coming—is that they are both high-occupancy seasons at city hotels. You will pay peak rates, except at bed-and-breakfast inns and small guesthouses that charge the same fee year-round (see chapter 3 for more details).

Cherry Blossoms: The Lowdown

Nature is unpredictable, and the Tidal Basin cherry blossoms do not always bloom on schedule. Often the 2-week festival, scheduled months in advance, takes place before the blossoms come into full bloom or after a freak windstorm has whipped the fragile blossoms away. Planning a cherry blossom trip too far in advance is an expensive gamble. Check the official website, www.nationalcherryblossomfestival.org, for predictions on peak blooming days.

For generally lower hotel rates—your major expense on a Washington trip—plan to visit in summer, particularly mid-July through August, and in winter from Thanksgiving (late Nov) to mid-February. Unlike New York City, Washington doesn't get an influx of pre-holiday shoppers. Instead, business travel tapers off substantially—few big conventions are scheduled between Thanksgiving and New Year's Day—and hotel rates drop.

Weather-wise, neither summer nor winter is extreme, although both seasons can get uncomfortable for days at a stretch. July and August can get hot and sticky, and brief afternoon thunderstorms roar through, dousing the unprepared. Our advice for summer visitors: Do the outdoor stuff (Lincoln, Jefferson memorials) in the morning, then duck into the air-conditioned museums in the afternoon. In winter, the city sometimes gets a heavy snowfall or two, but more often any flakes that fall are merely a light dusting. A few days may see bitter cold temperatures in the low teens, but it's unusual. A ski jacket, wool hat (that covers your ears), and gloves will keep you plenty warm. So our advice for winter travelers is the reverse: Head for the indoor attractions in the morning; save the outdoor memorials and monuments for the afternoon when the sun has warmed the day up a bit.

Washington's cultural scene never goes dark. Prime time is from fall into spring, when the National Symphony Orchestra and the Washington National Opera schedule performances. But so many visiting musical groups and entertainers pass through in the summer, nobody feels deprived. Anyway, summer is the time for lots of free entertainment on the Mall and elsewhere: Military band concerts on the Capitol steps; daily noon concerts (ranging from rock to country) at Woodrow Wilson Plaza (behind the Ronald Reagan Bldg., 14th St. and Constitution Ave. NW; Thurs noon pop concerts at Farragut Square).

A Temperate Climate

Monthly high and low average temperatures are as follows (Fahrenheit/Celsius):

	Jan	Feb	Mar	Apr	May	June	July	Aug	Sept	Oct	Nov	Dec
Temp °F (Max & Min)	44/30	46/29	54/36	66/46	76/56	83/65	87/69	85/68	79/61	68/50	57/39	46/32
Temp °C (Max & Min)	5/-1	8/-1	12/2	19/8	25/14	29/19	31/20	30/20	26/16	20/10	14/4	8/0

WASHINGTON'S MAJOR ANNUAL EVENTS

The Washington event known around the world is the National Cherry Blossom Festival in late March and early April. But other major events fill the calendar throughout the year—as if your sightseeing agenda wasn't busy enough. And many of these events draw us locals to the Mall. It's your chance to see real Washingtonians rather than hordes of other fellow tourists. The Cherry Blossom Festival is the only event (other than the presidential inauguration, held every 4 years on Jan 20) that is such a big attraction that hotel prices shoot sky high, with hotels and guesthouses selling out.

Check the list that follows to see if you want your trip to coincide with a major annual event. Current dates and prices are provided on the website of **Destination DC** (www.washington.org). A schedule of the upcoming week's current events—a dizzying array of lectures, poetry readings, gallery openings, neighborhood street parties, gala soirees, free stuff, kids' stuff, and more—is published every Thursday in the *City Paper,* an alternative tabloid distributed free in street boxes throughout the downtown area. The *Washington Post* prints its own weekend-ahead list on Friday in the Weekend Section, a tabloid insert. It's sold in newspaper boxes all over town. On the Web, check the sites of the **Smithsonian Institution** (www.si.edu) for more upcoming events. The **White House Visitor Center** (www.nps.gov/whho) distributes a brochure describing current National Park ranger tours on the Mall.

Washington Special Events

February

Washington, D.C., Restaurant Week. Making the best of post-holiday slack time, dozens of local restaurants—including some of the ritziest—offer three-course, prix-fixe lunch and dinner menus (soup/salad, entree, dessert) at just $20 for lunch, $35 for dinner. A list of participating eateries can be found at www.washington.org/restaurantwk.

Washington Auto Show. America's love affair with cars, and maybe everyone else's, is made manifest at this huge display of automotive design and technical wizardry held at the D.C. Convention Center, Pennsylvania Avenue NW at 9th Street. Thousands throng the aisles to view new auto models and manufacturers. The entrance fee is $10 weekday, $12 weekend for adults, $8 to $10 seniors, $5 children 6 to 12, 5 and under free. For specific dates, go to www.washingtonautoshow.com.

George Washington's Birthday Celebration. The city itself is quiet on the first president's birthday, February 22. But Mount Vernon Estate, Washington's beautifully preserved home and gardens in the Virginia suburbs, celebrates it with appropriate pomp and ceremony. Anyone sharing a birthday with Washington (Jim happens to qualify) is admitted free. Others pay a fee. Read more about Mount Vernon in chapter 11 (p. 265). For information about the birthday program, contact ☎ 703/780-2000 or www.mountvernon.org.

March

St. Patrick's Day Parade. No, it doesn't rival New York's tribute to Ireland. But now, more than 35 years after its debut, the parade does take advantage of its Washington home to proclaim itself "The Nation's St. Patrick's Day Parade." Scheduled from noon to 3pm down Constitution Avenue NW between 7th and

17th streets (adjacent to the Mall), it features traditional parade hoopla: marching bands, pipe bands, military units, firefighters, floats, novelty groups, and a whole lot of Irish or Irish-wannabes bedecked in every shade of green imaginable. Get full details at www.dcstpats parade.com.

March–April

National Cherry Blossom Festival. The 2-week festival, now more than 95 years old, commemorates the gift of 3,000 cherry trees given to the United States by the Mayor of Tokyo, Yukio Ozaki, in 1912. It draws more than one million visitors annually, filling the city's hotels and restaurants. A wide variety of cultural, sporting, and culinary events take place during the festival. But for residents and visitors alike, the big deal is circling the Tidal Basin on foot (3¼ miles) beneath a canopy of fragile pink blooms. Daily cultural performances are scheduled at noon at the Tidal Basin. A gala parade—huge floats, giant helium balloons, marching bands—begins on 10am on one Saturday along Constitution Avenue NW, adjacent to the Mall. Following at 11am is the Sakura Matsuri Japanese Street Festival, an all-day celebration of Japanese performances, events, crafts, and food—held downtown on Pennsylvania Avenue NW between 11th and 14th streets. And more: a rather photogenic kite-flying festival on the Mall; sushi and saki tasting; rugby, soccer, and lacrosse tournaments on the Mall; crew races on the Potomac River from Thompson's Boat Center, near the Kennedy Center; the 10-mile Cherry Blossom Run on the Mall. Most events are free to spectators. The festival's website, www.national cherryblossomfestival.org, maintains a "blossom watch" to inform you when the trees are at their peak beauty.

April

Filmfest DC—Washington International Film Festival. A 12-day festival, 2 decades old, it features more than 100 international movies, documentaries, short films, and special programs. For a schedule of performances, check www. filmfestdc.org.

Smithsonian Craft Show. The 4-day show, a quarter-century old, is considered the nation's most prestigious juried exhibition of contemporary crafts. On display are the works of 120 master craftsmen and women as well as those of emerging artists. Occupying the massive National Building Museum, it gathers a dazzling array of basketry, ceramics, decorative fiber, furniture, glass, jewelry, leather, metal, paper, wearable art, and wool, all of which are for sale. For more details, go to www.smithsoniancraftshow.org.

White House Easter Egg Roll. An annual tradition for more than 130 years (Rutherford B. Hayes initiated it), the giddy celebration draws thousands of youngsters and their parents from 8am to 2pm on Easter Monday. Held on the South Lawn of the White House, it's a lot more than colored eggs. Often the president and first lady attend, for a little while anyway, to watch (and maybe take part in) face painting, the reading corners, art activities, magic shows, music, and, oh yes, egg coloring. Tickets (free) are required, and because of heavy demand, snagging them for you and your children is complicated. For information, refer to www.whitehouse.gov/easter/eggroll.

May

National Memorial Day Parade. For 60 years until 2005, the city, filled as it is with military monuments and memorials, did not hold a commemorative parade. To remedy this failure, the World War II Veterans Committee put together a parade featuring 40 bands and 150 other units. The parade route begins at the foot of the U.S. Capitol and proceeds down Constitution Avenue to the White House. The website is www.nationalmemorial dayparade.com.

June–July

Safeway's National Capital Barbecue Battle. Who said bureaucrats can't have fun? Tens of thousands of barbecue fanciers (after all, Washington is just across the Potomac River from the South) turn out to watch barbecue whizzes from around the country and the world compete for prize money. Plenty of free samples means nobody goes hungry. Check the website at www.barbecuebattle.com for information.

Smithsonian Folklife Festival. Since 1967, the Smithsonian Institution has brought an annual array of artists, musicians, crafts workers, dancers, and other talented folks from around the country and around the world to the grassy expanse of the Mall. So far, 60 foreign countries have been represented. In 2008, the country of Bhutan, the NASA space program, and the state of Texas were highlighted. For several days leading up to the Fourth of July, you can take in music, dance, crafts and cooking demonstrations, storytelling, and more. It all takes place in a sprawling village of tents and is free. For 2009's program, take a look at www.folklife.si.edu.

June

DC Caribbean Carnival. The city's Caribbean residents show their stuff in a colorful Extravaganza Parade of 21 masquerader bands and 5,000 costumed participants dancing and singing to the infectious tunes of the islands. It concludes at Bannecker Recreation Park, which is transformed into an international marketplace. For 2 days, the music throbs, dancers gyrate, and you can sniff the scent of island foods. Expect a crowd that numbers a half-million. Check the website at www.dccaribbeancarnival.org for the dates.

Capital Pride Festival. A multiday festival, it is the fourth largest gay pride event in the United States. Primary events include a parade and street festival centered around Dupont Circle and nearby Pennsylvania Avenue NW. Other programs focus on diversity, cultural achievement, and civil rights issues involving gays, lesbians, bisexuals, transgender individuals, and their families and friends. Events are free. For a program schedule, visit the website at www.capitalpride.org.

July

Independence Day Celebration. Washington's massive show, as it should be, is televised nationally. Always on July 4, a 60-unit parade struts down Constitution Avenue NW (alongside the Mall) from 7th to 17th streets beginning at noon. In the late afternoon, popular music groups entertain on the Mall. At 8pm, big name entertainers headline a patriotic program leading up to a stupendous fireworks display. One of the country's great fireworks demonstrations, it draws half a million spectators, many of whom show up early in the day for a good view. Be prepared for massive crowds and a hot, sticky evening.

August

Washington, D.C. Restaurant Week. A repeat of the February prix-fixe menus stirs up business when Congress and high-spending lobbyists take their vacations. See February for details.

Legg Mason Tennis Classic. A men's tennis tournament that attracts such champions as Andy Roddick and Juan Martin del Potro. In all, 48 singles players and 16 doubles teams compete. Find details at www.leggmasontennisclassic.com.

September

Black Family Reunion Celebration. Recognized as America's largest family event, the 2-day gathering celebrating African-American families draws a half-million attendees. Pavilions erected on the Mall focus on such themes as Health; Sports and Fitness; Education; Children; Fathers, Sons, and Brothers: Spirituality; and Family Values. On the lighter side, the program includes music, ethnic foods, and an arts and crafts marketplace. More details are provided on the website of the National Council of Negro Women, www.ncnw.org/events/reunion.htm.

National Book Festival. A 1-day salute to the joy of reading, the Library of Congress–sponsored festival invites about 80 authors, illustrators, and poets to read and discuss their work—and maybe sign and sell a few copies of it. Personal note: Pauline and Arthur Frommer appeared here together in 2008. Other attending authors that year included Salman Rushdie, Phillippa Gregory, and Jan Brett. Check the latest roster of participants at www.loc.gov/bookfest.

Reel Affirmations Film Festival. Though attendance is listed at about 30,000, this multiday event ranks as one of the largest gay and lesbian film festivals anywhere. Now more than 15 years old, it showcases some 60 films from around the world. A schedule and ticket charges are found at www.reelaffirmations.org.

Marine Corps Marathon. Run for more than 30 years, this legendary race threads a 26.2-mile course that begins near Arlington National Cemetery, navigates 19th-century Georgetown, tackles a portion of shady Rock Creek Park, circles the Mall past the Capitol and the Smithsonian museums, and concludes at the Iwo Jima Memorial. No wonder it's been nicknamed "the Marathon of the Monuments." It's limited to 30,000 participants, and it always gets far more applications than that! Oprah herself completed the course in 1994. Jim's editors at the *Washington Post* dispatched him to run with her partway. Even if you don't run, it's a great show. Jim goes out most years to cheer the stragglers; they appreciate the encouragement. Race details are available at www.marinemarathon.com.

November–December

Washington Craft Show. Just in time for holiday shopping, the 3-day crafts fair presents the work of 185 contemporary American craftsmen and women and emerging artists. The place is the Washington Convention Center; the fee, $14. For more details, check www.crafts americashows.com.

December

National Christmas Tree Lighting and Pageant of Peace. The president traditionally flips a switch to light the tree, and it twinkles throughout December in the Ellipse behind the White House. Each state, district, and territory is represented by a smaller tree standing side by side in a giant loop. Nightly concerts serenade, and a giant bonfire adds more seasonal glow. For more information, check the website at www.pageantofpeace.org.

ENTRY REQUIREMENTS FOR NON-AMERICAN CITIZENS

Be sure to check with the U.S. embassy or consulate for the very latest in entry requirements, as these continue to shift since 9/11. Full information can be found at the U.S. State Department's website, **www.travel.state.gov**.

VISAS

As of this writing, citizens of western and central Europe, Australia, New Zealand, and Singapore need only a valid passport and a round-trip air ticket or cruise ticket to enter the U.S. Canadian citizens can also enter without a visa; you simply need to show proof of residence.

Citizens of all other countries will need to obtain a tourist visa from the U.S. consulate; depending on your country of origin, there may or may not be a charge attached (and you may or may not have to apply in person). To get the visa, along with a passport valid to at least 6 months from the end of your scheduled U.S. visit, you'll need to complete an application and submit a 1½-inch square photo. It's usually possible to obtain a visa within 24 hours, except during holiday periods or the summer rush.

For info about U.S. visas, go to **http://travel.state.gov** and click on "Visas."

PASSPORTS

To enter the United States, international visitors must have a valid passport that expires at least 6 months later than the scheduled end of your visit.

For Residents of Australia: You can pick up an application from your local post office or any branch of Passports Australia, but you must schedule an interview at the passport office to present your application materials. Call the Australian Passport Information Service at ☎ 131-232, or visit the government website at **www.passports.gov.au**.

For Residents of Canada: Passport applications are available at travel agencies throughout Canada or from the central Passport Office, Dept. of Foreign Affairs and International Trade, Ottawa, ON K1A 0G3 (☎ 800/567-6868; **www.ppt. gc.ca**). *Note:* Canadian children who travel must have their own passports. To obtain a passport for a child under 16, you can find the required information and application form at **www.ppt.gc.ca/cdn/16-.aspx**.

For Residents of Ireland: You can apply for a 10-year passport at the Passport Office, Setanta Centre, Molesworth Street, Dublin 2 (☎ 01/671-1633; **www.irl gov.ie/iveagh**). Those under age 18 and over 65 must apply for a 123€ 1-year passport. You can also apply at 1A South Mall, Cork (☎ 021/272-525) or at most main post offices.

For Residents of New Zealand: You can pick up a passport application at any New Zealand Passports Office or download it from the website. Contact the Passports Office at ☎ 0800/225-050 in New Zealand or 04/474-8100, or log on to **www.passports.govt.nz**.

For Residents of the United Kingdom: To pick up an application for a standard 10-year passport (5-year passport for children under 16), visit your nearest passport office, major post office, or travel agency, or contact the United Kingdom Passport Service at ☎ 0870/521-0410. Or search its website at **www.ukpa. gov.uk**.

MEDICAL REQUIREMENTS

No inoculations or vaccinations are required to enter the United States, unless you're arriving from an area that is suffering from an epidemic (cholera or yellow fever, in particular). A valid, signed prescription is required for those travelers in need of **syringe-administered medications** or medical treatment that involves **narcotics.** It is extremely important to obtain the correct documentation in these cases, as your medications could be confiscated, and if you are found to be carrying an illegal substance, you could be subject to significant penalties. Those who are **HIV-positive** may also require a special waiver in order to enter the country (as you will be asked on your visa application whether you're a carrier of any communicable diseases). The best thing to do is contact **AIDSinfo** (☎ 800/448-0440 or 301/519-6616; www.aidsinfonih.gov) for up-to-date information.

CUSTOMS REGULATIONS
FOR INTERNATIONAL VISITORS

Strict regulations govern what can and can't be brought into the United States—and what you can take back home with you.

WHAT YOU CAN BRING INTO THE U.S.

Every visitor more than 21 years of age may bring in, free of duty, the following: (1) 1 liter of wine or hard liquor; (2) 200 cigarettes, 100 cigars (but not from Cuba), or 3 pounds of smoking tobacco; and (3) $100 worth of gifts. These exemptions are offered to travelers who spend at least 72 hours in the United States and who have not claimed them within the preceding 6 months. It is altogether forbidden to bring into the country foodstuffs (particularly fruit, cooked meats, and canned goods) and plants (vegetables, seeds, tropical plants, and the like). Foreign tourists may carry in or out up to $10,000 in U.S. or foreign currency with no formalities; larger sums must be declared to U.S. Customs on entering or leaving, which includes filing form CM 4790. For details regarding U.S. Customs and Border Protection, consult your nearest U.S. embassy or consulate, or U.S. Customs (☎ 202/927-1770; www.customs.ustreas.gov).

WHAT YOU CAN TAKE HOME FROM THE U.S.

For a clear summary of Canadian rules, write for the booklet "I Declare," issued by the **Canada Border Services Agency** (☎ 800/461-9999 in Canada, or 204/983-3500; www.cbsa-asfc.gc.ca).

For information, U.K. citizens contact **HM Customs & Excise** (☎ 0845/010-9000, from outside the U.K. at 44-2920-501-261); www.hmce.gov.uk.

A helpful brochure for Australians, available from Australian consulates or Customs offices, is "Know Before You Go." For more information, call the **Australian Customs Service** (☎ 1300/363-263, or log on to www.customs.gov.au).

Most questions regarding New Zealand rules are answered in a free pamphlet available at New Zealand consulates and Customs offices: "New Zealand Customs Guide for Travellers, Notice no. 4." For more information, contact **New Zealand Customs** (The Customhouse, 17–21 Whitmore St., Box 2218, Wellington ☎ 04/473-6099 or 0800/428-786; www.customs.govt.nz).

FINDING A GOOD AIRFARE
TO WASHINGTON, D.C.

Washington is served by three airports, all of which host one or more low-fare carriers. All three are busy airports, offering a wide choice of arrival and departure times. Using the tactics we describe below, you should be able to snag an affordable fare—maybe even a bargain.

Important note: A major item to factor into your calculations when trying to find the cheapest fare is the cost of getting from the airport to downtown Washington, where you will presumably be staying.

The city's closest airport, handling only domestic flights and no wide-body planes, is **Ronald Reagan Washington National Airport (DCA).** Metrorail can get you into town from here in 10 to 15 minutes for a fare of $1.65 per person. Washington's two other airports are more distant, so many take taxis to and from them (adding a hefty $55 or so to your transportation costs). That's because while both are served by public transportation, the trip from both is time-consuming. **Washington Dulles International Airport (IAD)** is located about an hour west of downtown in Virginia. **Baltimore–Washington International Thurgood Marshall Airport (BWI)** is 45 minutes north of downtown in Maryland. SuperShuttle van service is $37 for the first person, and $12 for each extra person in the same party age 3 and up (under is free). You'll see full information on getting to and from the airport below (p. 291).

Keeping transportation costs in mind, **your strategy for getting a reasonable fare** should include these steps:

♦ **Do a smart search:** Such websites as **www.kayak.com**, **www.momondo.com**, **www.sidestep.com**, and **www.farecompare.com** allow users to search both the sites of the Web discounters and the airlines themselves, quickly and efficiently. You'll be surprised at how greatly prices can vary, even for flights on the same carrier and at the same time of day.

♦ **Fly when others don't, and take an itinerary business travelers don't want.** Take a midday, midweek flight and stay overnight on a Saturday. Or fly overnight on a "red-eye." On these less popular flights, fares drop to attract more passengers.

♦ **Book at the right time.** With the wilting economy, airlines are trying to get as much revenue as they can from each ticket. Those who book too far in advance, therefore, often end up paying top dollar. But when seats don't sell, they slash rates dramatically. What that means is that we're seeing more **last-minute sales** than we used to. Usually these pop about 90 days before the date of your departure. Start looking then, but don't tarry too long: **about 21 days before departure, airfares often rise dramatically.** Also, **try to book midweek** to take advantage of sale fares. Because most consumers book on the weekends when they have more time airfares tend to rise when booked then. Keep an eye on **Frommers.com** and **SmarterTravel.com,** which also feature fare sales.

♦ **Forget about air/hotel/car packages:** First, you don't need a car. Second, if you take the time to find a good air fare and book one of the budget or moderately priced hotels described in this guide (see chapter 3), you're usually going to beat a hotel package. And third, booking independently, you can choose an alternative and (often) less expensive lodging, such as a bed-and-breakfast inn or rental apartment, rather than the tourist hotels that generally come as part of a package deal. On the other hand, if you don't have time to shop around, an air/hotel package may be a time- and money-saver for you if you plan to stay in a tourist hotel or motel anyway. But be sure to know where your accommodations are located before you purchase the package. Some of the least expensive packages we've seen feature lodgings miles from the city.

♦ **From abroad, try a consolidator fare:** Often called "bucket shops," consolidators or discount brokers buy tickets in bulk and pass the savings to their customers. If you are flying to Washington from outside the United States, a consolidator might be able to give you the best deal. In Europe, one way to find a consolidator that serves your area is to go to the website www.CheapFlights.co.uk. It acts as a clearinghouse for a variety of bucket shops, large and small. You also will see them advertised in metropolitan newspapers. But be aware of potentially outrageous fees if you want to change your ticket. Within the United States, consolidators can't match the fares of low-cost carriers. To quickly search standard airfares from abroad, www.mobissimo.com generally is the best search engine.

♦ **Don't forget to calculate all fees:** Nowadays, many airlines charge extra for luggage and for more comfortable, though still economy-class, seats on the plane. These costs can add up, so be sure to crunch all the numbers before booking a ticket. An airline that at first glance looked costlier might end up being the more cost-effective choice.

TRAVELING BEYOND WASHINGTON TO OTHER AMERICAN DESTINATIONS

AIR TRAVEL: Washington's three airports are served by all major airlines, linking you to every commercial airport in the country—that is, with a connection or two to its more remote corners. For info on saving money on air tickets, see p. 286.

RAIL TRAVEL: Trains to and from NYC are on the pricey side with one-segment tickets, between New York City and Washington, D.C., for example, often scraping the $80-to-$100 mark (though Amtrak's high-speed Acela train can get you up and down the Northeast Corridor, from downtown to downtown, faster than some shuttle flights, when you factor in the time to get to the airport). The Acela is expensive, and more of an option for business rather than budget travelers, unless there's a sale or special on.

For those planning on making a number of rail journeys, the **USA Rail Pass**, offered by **Amtrak** (www.amtrak.com), is akin to Europe's Eurailpass and as of 2008, is now available not only to those living outside the United States but also to U.S. residents. The passes are sold for 5-day, 15-day, and 30-day journeys and only make sense if you plan to do *a lot* of traveling by rail. The cheapest ($389) allows for 8 rail journeys over the course of 15 days. This might work out if you were planning to travel to and from Kansas City, but for most travelers it won't pay off. The most expensive ($789) provides 18 rail segments over the course of 45 days. Keep in mind that the United States operates a bare-bones rail network; delays are common and trains can be overcrowded.

BUS TRAVEL: Thanks to the so-called **Chinatown shuttles**, busing to and from D.C. has become the single most cost-effective way to get into town, at least from other cities on the Eastern seaboard. These bus services, originally created by Chinese-Americans as a means of getting between New York City and the cities of Boston, Philadelphia, and Washington, D.C., are open to everyone and offer rock-bottom prices. To Philadelphia, the average ride is just $12; for the other two cities you won't pay more than $20, but there are times when specials reduce the fares to just $1. There are now nearly a dozen smaller bus companies operating along these routes, and fare information plus bookings can be made on one well-designed agency site called **BusJunction** (www.busjunction.com).

If you'd prefer to contact one of the cushier, non-Chinatown companies (their prices match those of the Chinatown buses, but their buses are newer, often offer Wi-Fi, and their drivers are more likely to speak English) look at:

- **Megabus** (☎ 877/G2MEGA [426-342]; www.megabus.com)
- **Boltbus** (no phone; www.boltbus.com)
- **Vamoose** (☎ 877/393-2828; www.vamoose.com)
- **DC2NY** (☎ 202/332-2691; www.dc2ny.com)

Greyhound/Trailways (www.greyhound.com) also serves D.C. Their routes tend to be more far-reaching than the companies listed above (which serve a narrow slice of the East Coast). Do *not* use them if you're traveling to or from Boston, New York City, or Philadelphia, unless you enjoy overpaying. The Chinatown and specialty bus companies listed above have undercut the Dog's prices by so much, and the likes of Bolt and Megabus offer so much more in amenities, that they are a much better value than Greyhound.

RENTAL CARS: As we mentioned in chapter 2, unless you absolutely have to, don't drive in Washington, D.C. Save your wheels (and your patience) for making day trips from Washington. The interstate system is relatively easy to navigate, and destinations are usually well marked. If you need to rent a car while you're in the city, wait until you're going to be making day trips, and consider planning them near your date of departure.

Some of the national car-rental companies with offices in the Washington area include **Alamo** (☎ 800/462-5266; www.alamo.com), **Avis** (☎ 800/230-4898; www.avis.com), **Budget** (☎ 800/527-0700; www.budget.com), **Dollar** (☎ 800/800-3665; www.dollar.com), **Hertz** (☎ 800/654-3131; www.hertz.com), and **National** (☎ 800/227-7368; www.nationalcar.com).

To save money on rental cars, try the following strategies:

- **Bid for your car:** Companies such as **Priceline** (www.priceline.com) and **Hotwire** (www.hotwire.com) work only with the major car-rental chains. So, bidding on a rental is really no more risky than going to a rental company direct, though you might get a Pontiac Grand Prix rather than a Chevrolet Monte Carlo. Be sure to research the current pricing before you book. To quickly survey the rental options, do a search on one of the following "aggregator" sites: BNM.com, Sidestep.com, or Mobissimo.com. Be aware, though, that reservations made through Priceline and Hotwire are **not cancelable.** You'll be asked to pay upfront, and you will lose your money if, for some reason, you end up not being able to use the car.
- **Use your VIP status:** If you're a member of AAA or AARP, make that known . . . after you get your quote. (Do it before and you might not get as good a deal.) If you work for a large corporation or are a member of a labor union, see if it has arranged benefits at the car-rental counter. If you're going to be using a credit card, go to the site of the rental company you've picked first and see whether there are printable coupons there for credit card discounts. (Sorry, just using the credit card won't usually get you the discount;

you have to hand in the darn coupon!) And if you shop at Sam's Club, Costco, or BJ's Wholesale, see whether they have any rental car coupons at their travel counters—often they do, and these can save you between 5% and 30%.

◆ **Check, check, and recheck:** If you book a car rental directly from a company, revisit its site before you get to the airport. Sometimes the prices drop. Simply rebook yourself at the lower rate (Pauline has saved $60 this way), and bring a copy of your confirmation letter so that the counter folks are clear on the cost.

SHOULD YOU BUY TRAVEL INSURANCE?

We recommend trip cancellation insurance only when you make a big, non-refundable deposit for a trip—for a cruise, an escorted tour, a safari, or a week at an all-inclusive resort. This is money you don't want to lose if you are forced to cancel a trip—perhaps because of a last-minute accident or illness involving you or a family member or close friend. You don't need travel insurance for deposits you generally can recover—such as an airline ticket—or for refundable hotel deposits (provided you cancel prior to your scheduled arrival).

Consider **trip-cancellation insurance** if your airline does not allow a schedule change or (for whatever reason) you are not going to book an alternative flight within the next year. You'll also need insurance if you end up renting an apartment as those deposits are usually non-refundable. You could **insure against the loss of valuables,** but why would you bring them along on vacation? Leave the dazzling diamond tiara at home. However, your baggage may be covered by your homeowner's insurance; check before buying additional insurance.

Americans with health insurance generally do not need additional coverage for a trip to Washington. A few HMOs may be an exception, so check in advance of your trip. International visitors are urged to buy **medical insurance**—if they are not already covered for travel abroad. Unlike much of Europe, the United States does not provide any form of national healthcare. Doctor and hospital visits can be extremely expensive for the uninsured, and in nonemergency situations you will be expected to pay in advance or provide a credit card. In an emergency, you won't be turned away, but you are apt to get a stiff bill at check-out.

If you decide to buy insurance, compare policies and coverage using the website **InsureMyTrip.com.** Or contact a travel agent or one of the following reputable companies:

◆ **Access America** (☎ 800/729-6021; www.accessamerica.com).
◆ **Travel Guard International** (☎ 800/826-4919; www.travelguard.com).
◆ **CSA Travel Protection** (☎ 800/873-9855; www.csatravelprotection.com).

GETTING FROM THE AIRPORT

As noted above, Washington's close-in airport is Ronald Reagan Washington National—henceforth referred to (as all Washingtonians do) as National—a breeze, however you do it. The other two are a bit trickier. Here's our advice:

IF YOU LAND AT NATIONAL

Your best option is to take the train. The airport has its own **Metrorail** stop for the Blue and Yellow lines, both taking you into the heart of downtown. The one-way fare is a mere $1.65. (See chapter 2, p. 10, for details on using the Metro system.) You can connect easily to a line that serves your hotel, although you may have to pay a bit more if the hotel is outside the city center. The Yellow Line, which makes fewer stops, will get you into Washington a few minutes quicker than the Blue Line. Figure on a 10- to 15-minute ride.

A few hotels listed in chapter 3 are located on a **Metrobus** route. You'll need to pay an additional fee to take the bus (transfers are available only to those who buy weekly and monthly passes). Savvy travelers know that using public transportation is more convenient if you pack lightly. The ride into town by taxi—lined up at the airport exit—costs about $20 to $25, plus a 15% to 20% tip. Except in morning rush hour, the trip from airport to hotel, a 5-mile ride, should take about 20 minutes.

IF YOU LAND AT WASHINGTON DULLES INTERNATIONAL

Dulles is 30 miles west of Washington. So expect to pay about $55 for a taxi and $75 for a private car service, plus a 15% to 20% tip. Ouch! On the plus side, the first dozen miles of the ride into Washington is on the Dulles Access Road. It is a four-lane divided freeway for airport traffic only. It feeds into I-66, an Interstate freeway that carries you swiftly into town. Travel time: About 30 to 35 minutes, except during the morning rush hour.

On a budget, you're going to want to use a cheaper way into town. A shared van service provided by **SuperShuttle** (☎ 800/258-3826; www.supershuttle.com) charges $37 between the airport and Washington hotels. The fare for each additional person in your party is $12. The trip will take longer if the van delivers other passengers to their hotels first.

The least convenient, but cheapest, way into town is via a combination of bus and Metrorail. At Dulles, board a bus operated by **Washington Flyer** (☎ 888-WASHFLY; www.washfly.com). Departures are every 30 minutes from 7:45am to 10:40pm. The bus takes you to the West Falls Church (Virginia) Metrorail station, a non-stop ride of about 20 minutes. The one-way cost is $10; round-trip is $18. There you catch the Orange Line into Washington, another 15 minutes. The Metrorail fare is an additional $1.85.

IF YOU LAND AT BALTIMORE–WASHINGTON INTERNATIONAL THURGOOD MARSHALL

This final airport is 31 miles north of Washington. So expect to pay about $60 for a taxi to your hotel, plus a 15% to 20% tip. **SuperShuttle** (☎ 800/258-3826; www.supershuttle.com) has not established a set fee, as at Dulles, but charges according to which ZIP code you are headed to. Expect to pay about $38 for a shared van and $12 for each additional person in your party. The ride will take at least 45 minutes, maybe more, thanks to the congested roads.

BWI is 1 mile from Amtrak's New York to Washington rail line; a free shuttle links it with the airport. Fares on the frequent **Amtrak trains** from the station into Washington's Union Station range from $12 to $39. On weekdays, the station is also served by the **MARC Penn Line,** a commuter line into Union Station. The fare is $8. Between the two lines, trains depart for Washington about once every hour daily, more often during rush hour periods.

As at Dulles, the least convenient but cheapest way into town is via a combination of bus and Metrorail. At BWI, board the **Greenbelt–BWI Airport Express Line** B30 (☎ 202/637-7000; www.wmata.com/bustimetables/md/b30.pdf). It will take you nonstop to the Metrorail's Green Line station at Greenbelt, Maryland. The bus fare is $3; the Metrorail fare into Washington is another $2.35. Buses operate about every 40 minutes from 7am to 10:45pm, with slightly fewer trips on Saturdays and Sundays. Check the schedule on the website above. Count on an hour to make the trip.

WHAT TO WEAR

When Pauline was researching this book, she ended up walking so many miles in a day, she had to buy her first pair of orthopedic shoes. Her feet hurt *that* much. Many tourists encounter the same problem, simply because there are literally miles of hard, marble floors to pace and countless stairways to climb if you want to see the city's great monuments and museums. So make sure to bring a sturdy pair of walking shoes—water resistant, if possible, for rain and snow. If you are in the city for pleasure, pack casual wear. No restaurant recommended in this book demands coats and ties of men. If you're planning on clubbing, however, do pack for the occasion; doormen will not let would-be partyers in if they look too sloppy.

But you don't want to dress down too much—particularly if you hope to mix and mingle with the city's young professionals. Washington is populated by folks who came to the city to get ahead. They dress for it. If you want to fit in, so should you. Instead of cut-off shorts and tank tops, think, instead, in terms of casual chic, especially after business hours.

In summer, sandals, shorts, and tees are the accepted costume for sightseeing on the Mall; wear anything heavier, and you will melt into a puddle of sticky perspiration. An exception would be if you have a private White House tour or a staff tour of the U.S. Capitol; dress a little spiffier, or you may feel embarrassed seeing all the neatly attired suits zipping by you in the corridors. In spring and fall, tote along a jacket and a warm sweater. In winter, pack a heavy coat, a hat, warm gloves, and a scarf. And don't forget an umbrella; you could need it any day of the year.

MONEY MATTERS

Nowadays the best way to get spending money is from an **automated teller machine (ATM).** In downtown Washington, there's a bank with an ATM on nearly every other corner. Foreign visitors should note that ATMs give much better conversion rates, even when fees are charged, than you'll find at banks and other facilities that change money. You'll also find ATMs in drugstores, grocery stores, and entertainment venues, but their transaction fees are generally higher than those in banks. For hotel bills, dining, barhopping, theater and concert tickets, and other major purchases, use a **credit card.** American Express, Discover, MasterCard, and Visa are widely accepted.

Traveler's checks are still sold and accepted in the United States. But expect to be asked for identification and sometimes a look of confusion, as traveler's checks are no longer widely used. If you don't have an ATM card, then bring traveler's checks or better yet, a traveler's check card, which can be easily replaced if

What Will Your Vacation Cost?

To Americans from elsewhere in the country, Washington is one of the country's most expensive cities for goods and services. On the other hand, if you arrive from Moscow or Tokyo (recently ranked as the first and second most expensive cities in the world) you may think it's a bargain. To give you an idea of what to expect, we've made a list of items you might purchase. If the prices seem high to you, bring what you can from home. If they seem low, stock up after you arrive.

Metro (subway) or bus ride	$1.65 minimum peak/ $4.50 maximum peak
Taxi ride, downtown	$6.50 for one, $8.00 for two
Tube of toothpaste (4.2 oz.)	$2.70
Box of tampons (pack 20)	$4.70
Package of diapers (package of 40)	$15
Contact lens solution ($\frac{1}{2}$ oz.)	$5.30
Bran muffin	$1.50
Cup of coffee	$1.50 (more for lattes and the like)
Cup of tea	$1.35
Sandwich in a deli	$3–$6.50
Hot dog on the Mall	$1.20–$4.75
Sit-down lunch on the Mall	$6–$15
Restaurant dinner (moderate)	$8–$15 per person (budget); $16–$30
Draft beer in a neighborhood bar	$3.50–$7
Cocktail in a neighborhood bar	$6–$14
Bottle of water (20 oz.)	$1.50
Museum entrance fee	Free for most; $5–$10 for others
Movie ticket	$13
Walking tour	$15
Souvenir T-shirt	$4–$10 from street vendors; $14–$18 in museum shops

lost; it allows you to put a set amount down for your vacation and is used just like a credit card. You can exchange traveler's checks and cash for U.S. dollars at **Travelex Currency Services** (www.travelex.com), a reputable firm that has offices in each of Washington's airports, at Union Station (Amtrak), and at three other downtown locations. You will pay for this service, and expect to show your passport. The three downtown offices are located at 1800 K St. NW; 825 14th St. NW; and 701 15th St. NW. Exchange fees are generally higher at airports; use these services only for convenience.

TIPPING & TAXES

When budgeting for your trip, don't forget to factor in **Washington's taxes.** Total hotel tax including the sales tax is 14.5%. The tax on all prepared food and beverages is 10%. No tax is imposed on edible groceries. The sales tax on goods and services is 5.75%.

But the city's suburban neighbors charge different rates. In **Maryland,** the hotel tax varies by county, averaging 5% to 8%. The sales tax is 5%. Keep this in mind if you are shopping at Friendship Heights in Northwest Washington, a major complex of department stores and boutiques. Western Avenue, the D.C.-Maryland state line, slices through its heart. The tax situation changes when you cross Western from a Washington shop to a store in Maryland.

In **Virginia,** just across the Potomac River bridges, the hotel tax varies according to the jurisdiction, averaging 9.5% to 10%. The sales tax is 5%.

Tips are expected everywhere in the United States and really, they're mandatory (people's livelihoods depend on them in no small measure; waiters, in particular, are taxed on their tips, whether or not they get them). Give waiters 15% to 20% of the cost of the meal, depending on the quality of service. Bellhops should get $1 per bag. Leave $1 to $2 a day for hotel housekeepers. Our practice is to leave the tip daily on the pillow so that we know the housekeeper who is servicing the room gets it. Tip taxi drivers 15% to 20%.

IS IT SAFE?

Explore the attractions outlined in this guide during daylight hours with an easy mind. Dine out, attend the theater, take in a sporting event, and ride the Metro in the evening similarly at ease—but use common sense. The nightlife areas generally are thronged until midnight or so, so stick to the busy well-lighted streets. (There's safety in numbers.) If your hotel is a long, dark walk from a Metro station, take a taxi back when you're out late. Although the Metro is generally considered safe, get into a car that has other riders. Infrequent Metro incidents typically occur late at night at outlying stations.

Generally, it's prudent to avoid neighborhoods across the Anacostia River in northeast and southeast Washington, especially at night. Trouble also erupts with some frequency in such prime nightlife areas as Adams Morgan (18th St. and Columbia Rd. NW) and the U Street Corridor (14th and U sts. NW). Georgetown is normally quite safe. Nearly every incident there occurs after the bars empty out. Don't walk alone between the monuments and memorials on the Mall; nighttime muggings have been known to occur there. And be cautious after dark on the side streets of Capitol Hill.

After all this, keep in mind that Washington is a large city with all types of people. Be vigilant. Though we're unaware of a pickpocket ring operating in the city, never carry large amounts of money with you. Don't stow your wallet in a back pocket where it can be filched. Keep your passport and other valuables in the hotel safe. (If you are traveling with a passport, make a copy of it so that you have the essential information needed for a replacement.) Women should keep purses in sight at all times, or better yet, not carry a purse. (They can be an inconvenience at museum security checks.)

You will probably be approached by panhandlers soliciting money. Some are regulars at certain street corners. These unfortunate street people pose no danger. Give them a coin or two if you feel generous, but remember that public and private agencies do provide free food; your money may feed a drug or alcohol habit.

WHAT IF I GET SICK?

If you think you need a doctor or dentist while in Washington, check with the desk staff at your hotel. They may have an arrangement with a medical practitioner to see guests on an emergency basis. Doctors almost never make "house" calls. Office hours vary, but weekdays from 9am to 5pm are fairly standard. Another option, especially if you are in pain and can't wait for an appointment, is to go to a hospital emergency room. Your hotel can direct you to the one nearest your hotel. In an emergency, dial ☎ 911 for an ambulance. You can use this number anywhere in the United States to reach the police, fire department, and ambulance dispatcher.

If you bring prescription medications into the country, make sure you pack them in their original containers in your carry-on bag. Bring a copy of the prescription in case you run out of or somehow lose your medication. **CVS Pharmacy** operates three branches with 24-hour pharmacies at 6 Dupont Circle NW, near 20th and P sts. (☎ 202/785-1466; Metro: Dupont Circle); 2240 M St. NW, at 22nd and M sts. (☎ 202/296-9876; Metro: Foggy Bottom); and 4555 Wisconsin Ave. NW at Albemarle St. (☎ 202/537-1587; Metro: Tenleytown).

STAYING WIRED WHILE YOU'RE AWAY

Most (but not all) of the lodgings listed in chapter 3 provide a free link to the Internet, usually wireless. At smaller properties, especially those listed under the "Alternative" heading, access may be at a terminal in the lobby only and not in individual rooms. Ask in advance if this is important to you. Some of the larger hotels will charge a fee, usually $9.95/day, for Internet access.

Branches of the Washington Public Library are scattered throughout the city, and all offer free Internet service. Each branch has at least one computer and most have four. The main branch, the **Martin Luther King Memorial Library** (Penn Quarter; 901 G St. NW; ☎ 202/727-1111; www.dclibrary.org; Mon–Thurs 9:30am–9pm; Fri–Sat 9:30am–5:30pm; Metro: Gallery Place–Chinatown), has 40. Check the website for location of other branches.

Dupont Circle is a free wireless hot spot—grab a park bench. Numerous coffee shops and cafes also provide free wireless Internet (Wi-Fi) points in Washington. Current lists are provided at www.auscillate.com/wireless/Washington and www.wififreespot.com/dc.html. Tryst Coffeehouse and Bar (p. 257) in Adams Morgan is a cozy place to catch up on e-mail. The **Smithsonian Castle** (p. 110) also provides free Wi-Fi, as do the many **Cosi** (www.cosi.com) sandwich shops that are dotted around the city. Starbucks coffee outlets also provide Internet access, but for a fee.

TRAVELERS WITH SPECIAL NEEDS
FAMILY TRAVELERS

Washington is a family-friendly city with lots of special activities designed just for family groups and youngsters. We detail many of these programs on p. 144.

Although the city's downtown area, including the Mall, is lacking in playground equipment, there are plenty of parks and other open spaces for the kids to work off excess energy when museumgoing palls. A good, well-equipped playground is located in Georgetown in **Rose Park** at 27th and N streets NW. (It's on the Georgetown Walkabout, outlined in Chapter 8, p. 197). The **Carousel on the Mall** (near the Castle) is always a big hit with young visitors.

Most restaurants listed in this guide (see chapter 4, p. 145) cater to families, but if you need a highchair or want a kid's menu, then call ahead. Those places that don't provide them probably prefer that you bring only older children.

With younger kids especially, it's wise to stay in a downtown hotel close to the Mall, so you can easily take a refresher break when the toddler is ready for a nap. Most hotels allow a family of four to share a room at no extra cost; some set an age limit. But a free stay for the young is not generally the case at guesthouses and bed-and-breakfast inns, many of which discourage young children.

Ask your hotel (before you arrive; reservations are needed) if babysitters are available; they're expensive, but you may want a night on your own. Typically, larger hotels maintain a list of on-call babysitters, but you may have to sign a waiver exempting the hotel from liability if a problem occurs.

Children age 4 and under ride free on the Metrorail, Metrobus system, and in taxis. But this freebie is limited to only two children per parent.

TRAVELERS WITH DISABILITIES

Washington's tourism promoters claim that Washington is one of the world's most accessible cities for travelers with disabilities, in part perhaps because this is the city where Congress created the Americans with Disabilities Act. We'd say they're on the mark: All of the city's major tourist attractions are fully accessible, as are most transportation options, restaurants, and hotels.

The premier source for disability-related information in the Metropolitan area is the **Washington, DC Access Guide.** It provides first-hand accessibility reviews of hotels, restaurants, movies, attractions, shopping malls, recreational facilities, and more. You can order a free copy at ☎ 301/528-8664 or www.disabilityguide. org or read the reviews online.

Hotels: Accessibility varies in the lodgings described in chapter 3. Be aware that small guesthouses, bed-and-breakfast inns, and some budget hotels may not have elevators. Some have entrance stairways with no ramp. Be sure to ask about facilities before booking rooms. Larger and newer hotels—that is, the more expensive ones unfortunately—are accessible. The website www.disability.org lists Washington's most accessible lodgings.

Restaurants: Can vary widely in accessibility. Many are too small for wheelchairs. Some have upstairs or downstairs seating, and the restrooms may be on a different floor. If you are a wheelchair user or have mobility impairments, call in advance to make sure the restaurant can accommodate you. The website www. disability.org lists Washington's most accessible places to eat.

Transportation: Public transportation in Washington is fully accessible. All buses are equipped with either low floor ramps or lifts for wheelchairs, and there are designated areas on board for wheelchairs. As buses are retired, new ones are equipped with audio devices that announce each upcoming stop for the sight impaired. All Metrorail stations are equipped with elevators, and audio devices announce the next stop. Extra-wide fare gates for wheelchairs are located in every station. Rubber bumps along the rail platform warn the blind or seeing impaired that they are near the platform's edge. To learn more, order a free copy of the **Metro System Guide** for seniors and people with physical disabilities at ☎ 202/637-7000 or www.wmata.com. Taxis will pick up wheelchair passengers who can maneuver into a taxi seat; the collapsed wheelchair goes in the trunk. Passengers with disabilities are entitled to a half-price fare discount on Metrorail and Metrobus. Check chapter 2, "Getting Around in the City," for details.

Those wishing to rent their own set of wheels are advised to contact **Avis Rent a Car** to take advantage of its "Avis Access" program (☎ 888/879-4273), which offers customized cars and vans with such features as swivel seats, spinner knobs, hand controls, and accessible bus service.

Theaters: The city's major theaters are accessible. Three theaters—the **John F. Kennedy Center for the Performing Arts** (p. 246), the **Arena Stage** (p. 243), and the **National Theatre** (p. 243)—are particularly so, offering free headphones to the hearing impaired, TTY phones, Braille programs, special performances with sign language interpreters, and more. The National offers half-price tickets on a limited basis to persons with disabilities. For full information on any of these theaters, go to their individual websites. Accessibility varies at the small theaters, so check ahead before you book.

Museums: The city's museums are also generally very accessible. The **Smithsonian Access Brochure** is a free guide that provides an overview of accessibility features at the Smithsonian Institution's museums. It is available on audiocassette, in Braille, or on compact disc. For a free copy, call ☎ 202/357-2700 (voice) or 202/357-1729 (TTY). The website is www.si.edu. Copies also can be picked up at museum information desks. The monuments and memorials on the Mall are all accessible. The situation at historic house museums varies.

GAY & LESBIAN TRAVELERS

You will find plenty of company in Washington, which is gay- and lesbian-friendly territory with a large and politically active population. Traditionally, the GLBT community has been centered around Dupont Circle. That's where you will find a wide choice of gay bars and clubs. But the U Street Corridor is a developing area. Two free weekly publications distributed widely in downtown Washington highlight bars, clubs, restaurants, and events catering to the gay community. *Metro Weekly* is a news and entertainment magazine; the *Washington Blade* is a tabloid newspaper.

SENIORS

As a senior (usually over 60–65), you are entitled to numerous discounts, so ask. At hotels, belonging to **AARP** (601 E St. NW, Washington, DC 24009; ☎ 888/687-2277; www.aarp.org) can save you 10% on your bill. Most museums that charge a fee offer a senior rate. All movie theaters and most live performance theaters discount tickets of at least a buck or two (these discounts are detailed on p. 244). Seniors are entitled to a half-price fare on Metrorail and Metrobus. (See p. 10 for more on that.) Many downtown restaurants offer pretheater menus at a reduced price, available to all patrons, no matter what age. Otherwise, you won't find early-bird specials. But remember, portions can be big. Pauline's father Arthur notes that seniors, like himself, often have smaller appetites. His advice to seniors: Share food. One appetizer and one entree is what Arthur and his wife order when they dine out, and he says they leave perfectly satisfied.

WASHINGTON BOOKS FOR THE WELL-PREPARED VISITOR

The books we've selected tell you not so much about Washington—we've covered that territory in this guide—but how the nation's capital works. Behind those imposing marble facades that house the government, wheeling and dealing—the game of politics—keep the ship of state on a more or less steady course. These books reveal how it's done.

- *Advise and Consent,* the 1959 novel by journalist Allen Drury, depicts the U.S. Senate in action, warts and all. Some political observers regard it as the best novel ever written about the workings of the U.S. government.
- *Master of the Senate,* Robert A. Caro's Pulitzer Prize–winning biography (2002) of Lyndon B. Johnson, is an insider's guide to how the U.S. Senate—and political Washington—work. It is a masterful book, daunting in size but full of revelations, both significant and gossipy.
- *All the President's Men* by *Washington Post* reporters Carl Bernstein and Bob Woodward is the quintessential story of investigative journalism and its role in the fall of Richard Nixon. Jim was an editor at the *Post* when the team's Watergate stories were a must-read around the world. The book that followed re-creates those exciting, troubled days.
- *Lincoln,* the Pulitzer Prize–winning biography by David Herbert Donald (1995), is a captivating account of how the president guided the Union through the Civil War. As such, it focuses on Washington during the crisis. Consider it also a primer to Washington place names. Much of the city's statuary, and many of its circles and squares, are named for Civil War military figures.
- **Any of the 14 mystery novels** by George Pelecanos, set in the city's crime-troubled eastern precincts. They illuminate the hidden corners of the capital.
- *Lost in the City* by Edward P. Jones, the Pulitzer Prize–winning author's collection of stories set in Washington's predominantly African-American neighborhoods. They provide a sympathetic look at how the city's black residents live ordinary lives in a hurtful world.
- *Washington Goes to War* by David Brinkley. With colorful anecdotes and telling statistics, journalist Brinkley explores how the war effort during World War II fundamentally altered life in the capital.
- *AIA Guide to the Architecture of Washington, D.C.,* by Christopher Weeks, is an informative—and highly opinionated—architectural assessment of the city's major buildings and a short architectural history of the city.
- *The Outdoor Sculpture of Washington: A Comprehensive Historical Guide* by James M. Goode is a fascinating look at the stories behind the city's wealth of commemorative and decorative statuary.

Washington's ABCs

Area Code Washington has one area code, 202. If you are calling the city from anywhere outside the District of Columbia you have to begin with this number. In the United States, all long-distance calls begin with the prefix 1. Calls that begin with 800, 877, and 888 are free, no matter where you are calling. Of course, they must be preceded by 1 also.

Business Hours Most offices are open Monday through Friday 9am to 5pm. Many banks are open Monday through Friday 9am to 3pm. But increasingly they are staying open until 5pm and keeping 9am-to-noon hours on Saturday and Sunday. Shops generally open at 10am, and those located in large malls may remain open until 9pm. Some grocery stores open as early as 6am and don't close until 9pm.

Closings Banks, federal offices, and post offices close on the following holidays: January 1 (New Year's Day); the third Monday in January (Martin Luther King Day); the third Monday in February (Presidents Day); the last Monday in May (Memorial Day); July 4 (Independence Day); the first Monday in September (Labor Day); the second Monday in October (Columbus Day); November 10 (Veterans Day); the fourth Thursday in November (Thanksgiving Day); and December 25 (Christmas). Most museums, including the Smithsonian, remain open except for December 25 and January 1. The monuments and memorials on the Mall never close.

Drinking Laws The legal age for the purchase and consumption of any sort of alcohol is 21, and proof of age is likely to be requested at liquor stores, bars, clubs, and restaurants. Be sure to carry identification; carding is more rigorous here than in other cities. Pauline hasn't been carded in years in New York, but had to show ID in D.C. whenever she ordered a drink. It is illegal to carry open containers of alcohol in any public area where alcohol is

not specifically permitted. You can be ticketed. Bars close at 2am except Friday and Saturday nights, when you can keep downing those drinks until 3am.

Electricity The United States uses 110–120 volts AC (60 cycles), compared to 220–240 volts AC (50 cycles), the standard in Europe, Australia, and New Zealand. Adaptors to use with appliances from these nations are difficult to find in the United States and should be brought with you when arriving from outside the United States.

Emergencies Telephone ☎ 911 for police, fire, or ambulance. If you have a medical emergency that does not require an ambulance, you should be able to get to the nearest hospital emergency room on your own.

Hospitals The following Washington hospitals are well regarded and maintain emergency rooms that are open 24 hours. All are located in upscale neighborhoods where the clientele is apt to demand, and get, prompt, top-notch medical care.

Georgetown University Hospital (3800 Reservoir Rd. NW; ☎ 202/444-2000).

George Washington University Hospital (900 23rd St. NW; ☎ 202/715-4000). Located at Washington Circle, GWU Hospital is the most convenient to downtown hotels, but the emergency room may also be the busiest.

Sibley Memorial Hospital (5255 Loughboro Rd. NW; ☎ 202/537-4000). Because of its semisuburban location, its emergency room may be less harried and so able to get to you sooner.

Libraries Branches of the Washington Public Library are scattered throughout the city and all offer free Internet service. The Martin Luther King Memorial Library, the main branch, is located downtown at 901 G St. NW. The library building was designed in 1972 by famed architect Mies van der Rohe. As was his style, it is a glass box—his only work in Washington. The library (☎ 202/727-1111; www.dc library.org) is open Monday to Thursday from 9:30am to 9pm and Friday and Saturday 9:30am to 5:30pm. It is closed Sunday. Check the website for location of other branches.

Newspapers & Magazines Washington has one major daily newspaper, the *Washington Post,* and two lagging challengers, the *Washington Times* and the *D.C. Examiner.* The *Post* and the *Times,* a publication of the Rev. Moon organization, are full-size daily newspapers for which you must pay. The *Post* is considered liberal in its editorial opinions; the *Times* is the conservative one. The *D.C. Examiner,* a tabloid, is distributed for free downtown on weekdays in boxes near Metro exits. The *Post* also distributes a free newspaper weekdays called the *Express.* You can do nicely with the free papers; no need to spend your money for one. The *Express,* condensing items from the illustrious *Post,* is the thoughtful tabloid. It is thicker and livelier and more fun to read. The *City Paper,* a weekly tabloid distributed widely throughout the city on Thursday, covers the nitty-gritty of Washington and is a good source of information for arts and entertainment information.

Pharmacies See p. 295 for a listing of 24-hour pharmacies.

Restrooms Every Smithsonian museum on the Mall has one or more restrooms as

do all of the other museums in town, all of the historic houses, and many of the larger memorials. Look for them also in coffee shops, such as Starbucks; in the lobby of large convention hotels; in food courts; at Union Station; in cabinet-level office buildings (yes, you can enter); and in big chain bookstores.

Smoking As of January 1, 2007, District of Columbia law bans smoking in most indoor public spaces, including offices, apartment building lobbies, restaurants, taverns, nightclubs, and bars. Exemptions include outdoor areas of bars and restaurants, cigar bars, and hotel rooms. Many hotels in the accommodations list ban smoking on the premises.

Taxes See the "Money Matters" section, p. 292.

Time The continental United States is divided into four time zones: Eastern Standard Time (EST), Central Standard Time (CST), Mountain Standard Time (MST), and Pacific Standard Time (PST). Washington is on Eastern Standard Time, which is the earliest of the time zones. When it's noon in Washington, it's 11am in Chicago (CST), 10am in Denver (MST), and 9am in Los Angeles (PST). Beginning in 2007, the period during which daylight saving time is in effect has been extended. In most (but not all) parts of the country, clocks are set forward 1 hour from the second Sunday in March to the first Sunday in November.

Tipping See p. 294.

Index

See also Accommodations and Restaurant indexes, below.